R. Gupta's®

Popular Master Guide

NATIONAL TESTING AGENCY (NTA)

CUET-UG

Common University Entrance Test for UG Programmes

Mass Media / Mass Communication

SECTION-II
DOMAIN SPECIFIC SUBJECT

SUBJECT CODE: 318

Anant Srivastava
&
RPH Editorial Board

2026-27
EDITION

RAMESH PUBLISHING HOUSE, NEW DELHI

Published by
O.P. Gupta *for* Ramesh Publishing House

Admin. Office
12-H, New Daryaganj Road, Opp. Officers' Mess,
New Delhi-110002 ✆ 23275224, 23245124

E-mail: info@rameshpublishinghouse.com
For Online Shopping: www.rameshpublishinghouse.com

Showroom
- Balaji Market, Nai Sarak, Delhi-6 ✆ 23282525 📱 9354373464
- 4457, Nai Sarak, Delhi-6, ✆ 23918938

Book Code: R-2829

ISBN: 978-93-5477-818-6

Price: ₹ 240

Printed at: Deepak Offset, Delhi

CONTENTS

SECTION-II: DOMAIN SPECIFIC SUBJECT

MASS MEDIA / MASS COMMUNICATION

★★★★★

Previous Years' Paper

Common University Entrance Test for UG Programmes

CUET (UG) Mass Media / Mass Communication

Entrance Exam, 2025

(Exam held on 21-05-2025)

1. Who is the author of the book, "Public Opinion"?

1. James Currian 2. Orson Welles
3. Walter Benjamin 4. Walter Lippmann

2. Early human beings expressed their feelings and experiences using:

1. Words
2. Language
3. Mail
4. Their body parts and expressions

3. Which of the following statements are correct?

A. Phiroj Shah founded the Bombay Chronicle
B. The Searchlight newspaper was first started in Bihar
C. The National Herald was first started in Lucknow
D. The Pioneer newspaper was first published under the editorship of K.M. Panikar

Choose the ***correct*** answer from the options given below:

1. A and B only 2. B, C and D only
3. A, B and C only 4. B and D only

4. In which year did Printing come to India?

1. In 1856 2. In 1656
3. In 1556 4. In 1756

5. "Many Voices One World" is an UNESCO report on ______?

1. Flaws in the political system
2. Flaws in the flow of news
3. Flaws in the economic system
4. Flaws in the health sector

6. Identify the criterion which is not considered as a news value?

1. Timeliness 2. Colourfulness
3. Impact 4. Proximity

7. Which among the following is a news agency?

1. CPI 2. BCCI
3. UPI 4. RTI

8. Arrange the following newspapers in correct sequence according to their year of launch, beginning from the first.

A. The Tribune
B. Harijan
C. National Herald
D. Young India

Choose the ***correct*** answer from the options given below:

1. B, A, D, C 2. A, D, B, C
3. C, A, B, D 4. D, C, B, A

9. Which of the following is not a feature of "Yellow journalism"?

1. Sensationalism
2. Rumours and gossip
3. Bold and screaming headlines with large photographs
4. Serious news

10. 'Freedom of speech and expression' comes under which article of the constitution of India?

1. Article 15 2. Article 16
3. Article 17 4. Article 19

1. 4	**2.** 4	**3.** 3	**4.** 3	**5.** 2	**6.** 2	**7.** 3	**8.** 2	**9.** 4	**10.** 4

11. Match List-I with List-II.

List-I (Concepts)	List-II (Scholars)
A. Manufacturing Consent	I. Aristotle
B. Encoding and Decoding	II. Noam Chomsky
C. Culture Industry	III. Stuart Hall
D. Catharsis	IV. Max Horkheimer

Choose the ***correct*** answer from the options given below:

1. A-II, B-III, C-IV, D-I
2. A-III, B-II, C-I, D-IV
3. A-I, B-II, C-III, D-IV
4. A-II, B-I, C-IV, D-III

12. "Making tomorrow brighter" is the slogan of:

1. ONGC (Oil and Natural Gas Corporation)
2. Indian Oil
3. Sarva Shiksha Abhiyan
4. SAIL (Steel Authority of India Ltd.)

13. The pre-shooting stage does not consist of ____?

1. Writing
2. Editing for sound
3. Budgeting the project
4. Casting

14. The post-shooting stage in film-making consists of:

1. Finalizing the technical and production team
2. Editing
3. Script-writing
4. Acquiring finance

15. 'Proxemics' is the study of _____.

1. Body movements
2. Eye movements
3. The kind of zones (distance) people maintain while interacting
4. Touch

16. Which of the following is not a characteristic of a radio script?

1. Active voice
2. Conversational language
3. Simple sentences
4. Technical jargons

17. The ability of the audience to resist being persuaded by a commercial or a news program if they are warned beforehand about an attempt to persuade them, is about to occur is called _____?

1. Cultivation effect
2. Inoculation effect
3. Limited effect
4. Personal Influence effect

18. When episodes of the same syndicated series are scheduled Monday through Friday at the same time, it is called _____?

1. Bridging
2. Stacking
3. Theming
4. Stripping

19. Which of the following provides all the support that is required for the functioning of a radio station?

1. Administration Wing
2. Transmission Studio
3. Engineering Wing
4. Programme Wing

20. Which was the first television soap opera to be telecast on Doordarshan?

1. Tamas
2. Buniyaad
3. Karamchand
4. Hum Log

21. The ability to sift through and analyse media messages that inform, entertain and sell to us every day is called _____?

1. Media effects
2. Media literacy
3. Media entertainment
4. Media Culture

22. Identify the film based on the suicide of cotton farmers in Vidarbha.

1. Framework of Famine
2. To Live
3. The Damned Rain
4. Ardh Satya

23. The issue of "embedding journalists with the military" first emerged as a turning point in Journalism in _____?

1. Kargil War
2. Persian Gulf War I
3. Gulf War 2003
4. Vietnam War

24. Identify the scholar associated with the concept of "Public Sphere"?

1. Jurgen Habermas
2. George Ritzer
3. Manuel Castells
4. James Curran

25. Who is the author of the book "Digital democracy"?

1. Noam Chomsky
2. Marjorie Ferguson
3. Jan Dijk
4. Basil Bernstein

26. The systematic study of texts on the basis of their language and how people interpret texts is known as _____?

1. Chronemics
2. Cybernetics
3. Optics
4. Hermeneutics

11. 1	**12.** 1	**13.** 2	**14.** 2	**15.** 3	**16.** 4	**17.** 2	**18.** 4
19. 1	**20.** 4	**21.** 2	**22.** 3	**23.** 3	**24.** 1	**25.** 3	**26.** 4

27. Which of the following films is an example of a story in a linear form?

1. Pather Panchali 2. Sholay
3. Dil Chahta Hai 4. Kora Kagaz

28. What do you understand about information overload?

1. Web journalism
2. New journalism
3. Exposure to too much information
4. Difficulty in using information

29. What is the correct order of the process of mass communication?

A. Communicator B. Message
C. Channel D. Receiver

Choose the *correct* answer from the options given below:

1. A, B, C, D 2. A, C, B, D
3. B, A, C, D 4. C, A, B, D

30. Arrange the following movies chronologically, according to their release year beginning from the first:

A. Taare Zameen Par B. Swadesh
C. Gadar D. Border

Choose the *correct* answer from the options given below:

1. A, B, C, D 2. A, C, B, D
3. B, A, D, C 4. D, C, B, A

31. Arrange the following sites chronologically, according to their launching year, starting from the first:

A. Facebook B. YouTube
C. Snapchat D. Twitter (now X)

Choose the *correct* answer from the options given below:

1. A, B, C, D 2. A, B, D, C
3. B, A, D, C 4. C, B, D, A

32. Arrange the following technological developments according to their launch beginning from the first.

A. Google Chrome B. Yahoo
C. Mozilla Firefox D. Internet Explorer

Choose the *correct* answer from the options given below:

1. A, B, C, D 2. B, D, C, A
3. B, A, D, C 4. C, B, D, A

33. A good news report should have the following qualities:

A. Ambiguity B. Objectivity
C. Subjectivity D. Credibility

Choose the *correct* answer from the options given below:

1. A, B and D only 2. A, B and C only
3. B and D only 4. B, C and D only

34. Which of the following is not an ethical practice?

A. Sensationalism B. Plagiarism
C. Paid news D. Fake news

Choose the *correct* answer from the options given below:

1. A, B and D only 2. A, B and C only
3. A, B, C and D 4. B, C and D only

35. Advertising is a paid form of communication to inform and persuade people to buy:

A. An idea B. A product
C. A service D. A fantasy

Choose the *correct* answer from the options given below:

1. A, B and D only 2. A, B and C only
3. A, B, C and D 4. B, C and D only

36. Identify the option which has all journalistic terms listed together.

A. Byline, Headline, Dateline, Beat
B. Cub, Sub editor, Editor, Reporter
C. Undermine, Byline, Headline, Masthead
D. Masthead, Beat, Stringer, Sub Editor

Choose the *correct* answer from the options given below:

1. A, B and D only 2. A, C and D only
3. B and C only 4. B, C and D only

37. Match List-I with List-II.

List-I (Author/thinker)	List-II (Newspapers)
A. Raja Rammohan Roy	I. Mooknayak
B. Mahatma Gandhi	II. Kesari
C. Dr. B.R. Ambedkar	III. Mirat-ul-Akhbar
D. Bal Gangadhar Tilak	IV. Navjeevan

Choose the *correct* answer from the options given below:

1. A-I, B-II, C-III, D-IV
2. A-I, B-III, C-II, D-IV
3. A-I, B-II, C-IV, D-III
4. A-III, B-IV, C-I, D-II

27. 1	**28.** 3	**29.** 1	**30.** 4	**31.** 2	**32.** 2
33. 3	**34.** 3	**35.** 2	**36.** 1	**37.** 4	

38. Match List-I with List-II.

List-I (Ancient civilizations)	List-II (Form of advertising that was used)
A. Emperor Ashoka	I. Used signs to sell arts and crafts
B. Harappa and Mohenjodaro	II. Stones or pillars for making public announcements
C. Rome	III. Sales messages and wall posters on papyrus
D. Egypt	IV. Acta Diurna - a wall newspaper

Choose the ***correct*** answer from the options given below:

1. A-I, B-II, C-III, D-IV
2. A-I, B-III, C-II, D-IV
3. A-II, B-I, C-IV, D-III
4. A-III, B-IV, C-I, D-II

39. Match List-I with List-II.

List-I (Films)	List-II (Made by)
A. Charulata	I. K. Asif
B. Mughal-E-Azam	II. Dada Saheb Phalke
C. Yuva	III. Satyajit Ray
D. Raja Harishchandra	IV. Mani Ratnam

Choose the ***correct*** answer from the options given below:

1. A-I, B-II, C-III, D-IV
2. A-I, B-III, C-II, D-IV
3. A-III, B-I, C-IV, D-II
4. A-III, B-IV, C-I, D-II

40. Match List-I with List-II.

List-I (Concepts)	List-II (Explanation)
A. Netiquettes	I. Online frauds
B. Cyber crime	II. Cyber activism
C. Online deliberation of issues in a democracy	III. Rapid circulation of information/opinion on local and global scale
D. Social media	IV. Respect other's privacy

Choose the ***correct*** answer from the options given below:

1. A-I, B-II, C-III, D-IV
2. A-IV, B-I, C-II, D-III
3. A-IV, B-II, C-III, D-I
4. A-II, B-I, C-IV, D-III

Directions (Qs. No. 41-45): *Read the passage and answer the questions that follow/s:*

Social impact of social media

The social impact of social media is by far the biggest, as social media work through the formation of social networks by users in a virtual world. Its most significant impact is the formation of networks which span space and time and leads to the free-flowing of cultures and formation of new cultures which impacts the world. It has impacted how people consume information, how the consumption of media has gone from public to private and personal. However, on the flip side, social media work on algorithms. The information a user gets through social media is determined by the user preferences, which is self-declared by the user and detected by the algorithm. Hence, if one is an environmentalist, then one will get news and user-generated content on environmental activism. This selective exposure of information is harmful to the user as the user is not able to get alternate perspectives, for example, the trade-off between development and the environment. In politics, this can lead to things like political polarization, being associated with a political party or ideology which is detrimental to democracy. This is also what is called the "echo chamber" effect. Meanwhile, research has also shown evidence that social media use leads to the persuasion of political beliefs, i.e., individuals who use social media were more likely to have their political beliefs persuaded than those who did not.

41. According to the passage, selective exposure of information leads to ____?

1. Diverse information
2. Alternate perspective
3. Echo chamber effect
4. Development

42. Social media functions on:

1. Perspectives
2. Polarisation
3. Algorithms
4. Equations

43. Who determines the information which a user gets through social media?

1. Private players
2. Media houses
3. Corporates
4. Social media user preferences

44. Social media works through:

1. Free flowing of cultures
2. Formation of new cultures
3. Social organization
4. Virtual social network

38. 3 **39.** 3 **40.** 2 **41.** 3 **42.** 3 **43.** 4 **44.** 4

45. What is the most significant impact of social media?

1. Formation of political organization
2. Formation of environmental activists
3. Formation of networks
4. Formation of economic chambers

Directions (Qs. No. 46-50): *Read the passage and answer the questions that follow/s:*

Community Engagement on the Internet for Social Change

The arena of community media has become much broader with the addition of the Internet. The medium is a great source to increase outreach through converging technology and transforming the content into a 'multimedia' format. We find fine instances of civil society and non-governmental organizations leading community-based newspapers and participatory video practices going for their online editions. For example, the newspaper Khabar Lahariya is published by the rural communities of Bundelkhand. This newspaper is also published on a portal in a multimedia format, including YouTube videos. This is being widely appreciated for being an 'alternative voice,' sensitizing, and mainstreaming the people. All of Khabar Lahariya's reporters are women who draw from their own experiences to share stories often ignored by the mainstream media. Similarly, with the local engagement of children in the age group of 15-18 years from marginalized tribal communities of northern Chhattisgarh, a UNICEF initiative - Sangwari Khabariya uses the medium of participatory videos to bring about social change in society. These children run their YouTube channel to post short news stories.

46. Which of the following is not associated with 'Khabar Lahariya'?

1. Local engagement of children
2. Alternative voice
3. Bundelkhand
4. Sensitising the people

47. Which of the following is incorrect about 'Sanwari Khabariya?

1. Newspaper
2. UNICEF initiative
3. Participatory videos
4. Tribal communities of Chhattisgarh

48. According to the passage, which of the following has all women reporters?

1. Khabar Khabariya
2. Sangwari Lahariya
3. Khabar Lahariya
4. Sangwari Khabariya

49. The newspaper 'Khabar Lahariya' is published by:

1. Government organization
2. UNICEF
3. Rural communities
4. Urban communities

50. Which of the following has helped the community media to become much broader?

1. Newspaper
2. TV
3. Radio
4. Internet

EXPLANATORY ANSWERS

1. (4): Walter Lippmann wrote Public Opinion in 1922. The book explores how media and stereotypes shape public perceptions and democratic decision-making. He introduced the idea of people forming opinions based on media-created images, making it a foundational work in communication studies.

2. (4): Before language developed, early humans used gestures, facial expressions, and body movements to communicate. These non-verbal cues helped them share emotions and coordinate actions for survival, like warning others of danger or expressing needs.

3. (3): A. Phiroj Shah Mehta did indeed found the *Bombay Chronicle*, a nationalist English-language newspaper.

B. *Searchlight* was first published in Bihar and became a significant voice in Indian journalism.

C. The *National Herald* was launched in Lucknow by Jawaharlal Nehru in 1938.

D. However, *The Pioneer* was not first published under K.M. Panikkar's editorship; it was much older, originally founded in 1865.

Thus, only A, B, and C are correct.

4. (3): Printing came to India in 1556 through the Portuguese in Goa. The first press was set up by Jesuit missionaries, making it the starting point of printing and publishing in Indian languages.

5. (2): Many Voices, One World is a 1980 UNESCO report on media imbalance. It highlighted how news flow was dominated by developed countries and called for fairer global information sharing.

6. (2): "Colourfulness" is not considered a standard news value. Core news values include timeliness (how recent the event is), impact (effect on the audience), and proximity (closeness to the audience). Colourfulness refers more to style or presentation, not to the intrinsic worth of a news item.

45. 3	**46.** 1	**47.** 1	**48.** 3	**49.** 3	**50.** 4

7. (3): UPI (United Press International) is a global news agency that provides news reports, photographs, and analysis to media outlets worldwide. It has been a significant player in international journalism since its founding in 1907. The others listed are not news agencies.

8. (2): The correct chronological order is:

A. The Tribune (1881),

D. Young India (1919),

B. Harijan (1933),

C. National Herald (1938).

Thus, option 2 reflects the correct sequence from earliest to latest publication.

9. (4): Yellow journalism is known for sensationalism, gossip, and eye-catching headlines rather than objective or serious reporting. It prioritizes attracting attention over factual accuracy or in-depth journalism, so serious news is not a feature of yellow journalism.

10. (4): Article 19(1)(a) of the Indian Constitution guarantees the right to freedom of speech and expression. This right allows individuals to express opinions freely through speech, writing, or other means, subject to reasonable restrictions for public order, morality, and national security.

11. (1): A. Manufacturing Consent – (II) Noam Chomsky exposed media's role in serving elite interests.

B. Encoding/Decoding – (III) Stuart Hall introduced this model in cultural studies to explain how audiences interpret media messages.

C. Culture Industry – (IV) Coined by Max Horkheimer and Theodor Adorno to critique mass-produced culture.

D. Catharsis – (I) Aristotle proposed it as the emotional release viewers experience through dramatic art.

12. (1): "Making tomorrow brighter" is the official slogan of ONGC. It emphasizes the company's role in securing India's energy future through innovation, sustainable practices, and exploration of oil and gas. The slogan reflects a vision of progress, responsibility, and national development.

13. (2): Editing for sound is part of post-production, not the pre-shooting stage. Pre-shooting involves all planning activities like writing the script, casting actors, creating a budget, and organizing logistics. Sound editing only begins once the footage has been shot and needs to be synchronized and enhanced.

14. (2): Editing is a post-shooting process where filmed content is trimmed, arranged, and combined with sound, music, and effects to produce the final version. It ensures continuity, rhythm, and storytelling flow in the finished film. Without editing, raw footage cannot be shaped into a coherent narrative.

15. (3): Proxemics is the study of how space and distance influence communication. It identifies zones like intimate, personal, social, and public distances, which vary by culture and context. Understanding proxemics helps in interpreting non-verbal cues and social behaviour more accurately.

16. (4): Radio scripts are designed for easy listening and wide comprehension, so they avoid technical jargon. Instead, they use active voice, simple sentences, and conversational language to ensure clarity and engagement for a diverse audience with varying education levels.

17. (2): The inoculation effect refers to the psychological concept where people become resistant to persuasion if they are warned beforehand. Just as vaccines work by exposing the body to a weak form of a virus, this effect works by exposing people to weak arguments so they can better resist stronger ones later.

18. (4): Stripping is the practice of scheduling the same television program at the same time slot every weekday (Monday to Friday). This format helps build habitual viewing, making it easier for audiences to remember and follow the series regularly.

19. (1): The Administration Wing provides all the support required for the overall functioning of a radio station. It manages coordination between departments, handles staff, budgeting, planning, legal matters, and ensures smooth day-to-day operations. While the Engineering Wing handles technical support, it is the Administration Wing that oversees and enables the entire station's functioning effectively.

20. (4): Hum Log, telecast in 1984, was India's first television soap opera on Doordarshan. It depicted the everyday struggles of a middle-class Indian family and blended entertainment with social messages, pioneering the "edutainment" format in Indian television history.

21. (2): Media literacy is the ability to critically access, analyze, evaluate, and create media in various forms. It empowers audiences to understand how media messages are constructed and their influence, helping individuals make informed decisions amidst the constant flow of content.

22. (3): The Damned Rain (Marathi: *Gabhricha Paus*) is a critically acclaimed film that portrays the tragic reality of farmer suicides in the Vidarbha region of Maharashtra. It sensitively explores the economic hardship, despair, and psychological toll faced by cotton farmers.

23. (3): The embedding of journalists with military units became a major practice during the 2003 Iraq War (Gulf War 2003). Journalists were allowed to travel and report from within combat units, giving them frontline access but also raising questions about objectivity and military influence on reporting.

24. (1): Jurgen Habermas is the German philosopher who developed the concept of the "Public Sphere," a space where individuals come together to freely discuss and influence political action. His theory emphasized the role of rational-critical debate in democratic societies.

25. **(3):** Jan van Dijk is the author of Digital Democracy and a leading scholar in communication and digital media studies. His work explores how digital technologies transform democratic participation, information access, and the structure of public communication in modern societies.

26. **(4):** Hermeneutics is the systematic study of interpretation, especially of texts, language, and symbolic communication. It examines how meaning is derived and understood, particularly in literary, religious, and philosophical contexts, focusing on readers' interpretations and cultural contexts.

27. **(1):** Satyajit Ray's Pather Panchali follows a straightforward, chronological (linear) narrative of a rural boy's life. The story progresses in a cause-and-effect sequence without flashbacks or disruptions, making it a classic example of linear storytelling.

28. **(3):** Information overload occurs when an individual is exposed to more data than they can process effectively. It can lead to confusion, stress, and difficulty in decision-making, especially in the digital age with constant updates from media and the internet.

29. **(1):** The correct order in the process of mass communication begins with the (A) Communicator (sender), who creates and sends a (B) Message. The message is transmitted through a (C) Channel (such as TV, radio, or internet), and finally reaches the (D) Receiver (audience). This linear model highlights how information flows from source to audience, and forms the foundation of many traditional communication theories.

30. **(4):** The correct chronological order of the movies is:

D. Border (1997) – A war drama based on the Battle of Longewala during the Indo-Pak 1971 war.

C. Gadar (2001) – A partition-era love story set during the India-Pakistan divide.

B. Swades (2004) – A story of an NRI returning to India to bring change in a rural village.

A. Taare Zameen Par (2007) – A touching tale of a dyslexic child and his teacher's efforts to help him thrive.

Each film was released progressively later, reflecting social and national themes over a decade.

31. **(2):** The correct chronological order based on official launch dates is:

A. Facebook (2004) – Initially launched for Harvard students, later expanded globally.

B. YouTube (2005) – Created as a platform for uploading and sharing videos.

D. Twitter (2006) – Introduced microblogging with short 140-character posts.

C. Snapchat (2011) – Known for disappearing messages and visual sharing.

This order reflects how social media evolved from networking to content sharing and real-time communication.

32. **(2):** The correct chronological order of technological launches is:

B. Yahoo (1994) – One of the first major web directories and internet portals.

D. Internet Explorer (1995) – Microsoft's first web browser, dominant during the late 1990s and early 2000s.

C. Mozilla Firefox (2002) – Launched as Phoenix, later became Firefox in 2004; it offered a free, open-source alternative to Internet Explorer.

A. Google Chrome (2008) – A fast and minimal browser by Google, which eventually became the most widely used browser worldwide.

This sequence shows the evolution of browsers and internet tools that shaped web usage.

33. **(3):** A good news report should have objectivity and credibility, ensuring accuracy and trustworthiness. Ambiguity and subjectivity undermine journalistic integrity and clarity, making them undesirable traits in news writing.

34. **(3):** All listed practices — Sensationalism, Plagiarism, Paid news, and Fake news — are unethical. They distort facts, mislead audiences, and violate core principles of responsible journalism and media ethics.

35. **(2):** Advertising aims to inform and persuade people to buy an idea, a product, or a service. While it may use fantasy as a creative tool, selling "a fantasy" is not its primary or direct purpose, making option D incorrect.

36. **(1):** These options include proper journalistic terms:

A. Byline (author's name), Headline (title of the news), Dateline (place and date), Beat (reporter's regular area).

B. Cub (trainee reporter), Sub editor, Editor, Reporter – all journalism roles.

D. Masthead (newspaper title), Beat, Stringer (freelance reporter), Sub Editor.

(C) includes "Undermine," which is not a journalistic term, making it incorrect.

37. **(4):** A. Raja Rammohan Roy – (III) Mirat-ul-Akhbar: A Persian journal advocating reform.

B. Mahatma Gandhi – (IV) Navjeevan: A Gujarati newspaper for socio-political awareness.

C. Dr. B.R. Ambedkar – (I) Mooknayak: Voice of the Dalit community.

D. Bal Gangadhar Tilak – (II) Kesari: A Marathi newspaper promoting nationalism.

38. **(3):** A. Emperor Ashoka – (II) Stones/Pillars: Used edicts carved on rocks for public messaging.

B. Harappa and Mohenjodaro – (I) Signs: Used seals and symbols for trade and craft identification.

C. Rome – (IV) Acta Diurna: Early public notices or daily acts posted in public places.

D. Egypt – (III) Papyrus scrolls: Used for messages, announcements, and advertising.

39. **(3):** A. Charulata – (III) Satyajit Ray: A Bengali film based on Tagore's work.

B. Mughal-E-Azam – (I) K. Asif: An epic historical romance released in 1960.

C. Yuva – (IV) Mani Ratnam: A political drama centered on youth activism.

D. Raja Harishchandra – (II) Dadasaheb Phalke: India's first full-length feature film (1913).

40. (2): A. Netiquettes – (IV) Respect other's privacy: Online manners and ethical behavior.

B. Cyber crime – (I) Online frauds: Includes hacking, phishing, identity theft, etc.

C. Online deliberation – (II) Cyber activism: Involves discussion and mobilization around civic issues.

D. Social media – (III) Rapid info/opinion flow: Platforms like Twitter and Facebook accelerate communication globally.

41. (3): The passage explains that selective exposure—where users only receive information aligned with their existing views—limits alternative perspectives. This leads to the "echo chamber" effect, where users are surrounded by similar opinions, reinforcing existing beliefs.

42. (3): Social media platforms function based on algorithms, which curate and show content based on user preferences and behaviour. These algorithms play a key role in what type of content a user sees.

43. (4): The content shown to users is determined by their own preferences—either self-declared or tracked by algorithms. These preferences shape what kind of information and news users are exposed to.

44. (4): Social media operates through the formation of virtual social networks, connecting users across space and time. These virtual interactions form the basis of how social media functions and spreads content.

45. (3): The most significant impact of social media, according to the passage, is the formation of networks that transcend geographic boundaries, facilitating the flow and creation of new cultures.

46. (1): Khabar Lahariya is run by rural women from Bundelkhand and is recognized for being an alternative voice that helps in sensitizing and mainstreaming local issues. The local engagement of children is not associated with Khabar Lahariya but with Sangwari Khabariya, a different initiative.

47. (1): Sangwari Khabariya is not a newspaper; it's a UNICEF-supported initiative involving tribal children in Chhattisgarh who use participatory videos to tell local stories and highlight social issues via platforms like YouTube. Hence, calling it a newspaper is incorrect.

48. (3): Khabar Lahariya is notable for being entirely reported and managed by women journalists from rural communities. These women draw from their personal experiences to cover issues often ignored by mainstream media, offering a unique grassroots perspective.

49. (3): The newspaper Khabar Lahariya is published by rural communities in Bundelkhand. It is a form of community journalism where local people—especially women—are involved in content creation, ensuring representation of rural voices.

50. (4): The Internet has significantly expanded the scope of community media by enabling the use of multimedia formats such as video, audio, and digital storytelling. This allows community initiatives like Khabar Lahariya and Sangwari Khabariya to reach broader audiences and have greater social impact.

Previous Years' Paper

Common University Entrance Test for UG Programmes

CUET (UG) Mass Media / Mass Communication Entrance Exam, 2024

(Exam held on 19-07-2024)

1. An advertisement, message, or public communication regarding economic, political, or social issue is called _____.

1. comparative advertising
2. advocacy
3. informational advertising
4. competitive advertising

2. Which of these statements characterise media literacy:

A. It is the ability to evaluate news sources

B. It builds essential skills of inquiry and self-expression

C. It helps in understanding the role of media in society

D. It is the proficiency in various film editing software's

Choose the correct answer from the options given below:

1. A, B and C only　　2. B, C and D only
3. A, C and D only　　4. A, B and D only

3. Identify the right order of the process of communication:

A. Feedback　　B. Message
C. Sender　　D. Receiver

Choose the correct answer from the options given below:

1. A, B, C, D　　2. A, C, B, D
3. B, A, D, C　　4. C, B, D, A

4. Who is the CEO of the AI start-up, OpenAI?

1. Arvind Srinivas　　2. Elon Musk
3. Sam Altman　　4. Sundar Pichai

5. Who among these is known as the 'Father of advertising'?

1. Walter Cronkite　　2. Paul Samuelson
3. David Ogilvy　　4. Edward Debono

6. Match List-I with List-II:

List-I (Television Channel)	List-II (Type)
A. Doordarshan	(I) International
B. Aaj Tak	(II) Conglomerate
C. BBC	(III) Government
D. Sony	(IV) Private

Choose the correct answer from the options given below:

1. A-(II), B-(I), C-(IV), D-(III)
2. A-(I), B-(III), C-(II), D-(IV)
3. A-(I), B-(II), C-(IV), D-(III)
4. A-(III), B-(IV), C-(I), D-(II)

7. Match List-I with List-II:

List-I (Publications)	List-II (Editors)
A. Bengal Gazette	(I) James Augustus Hicky
B. Mirat-ul-Akhbar	(II) Raja Ram Mohan Roy
C. Rast Goftar	(III) Dadabhai Naoroji
D. Young India	(IV) M.K Gandhi

Choose the correct answer from the options given below:

1. A-(I), B-(II), C-(III), D-(IV)
2. A-(I), B-(III), C-(II), D-(IV)
3. A-(I), B-(II), C-(IV), D-(III)
4. A-(III), B-(IV), C-(I), D-(II)

1. 2	2. 1	3. 4	4. 3	5. 3	6. 4	7. 1

8. Who among these was the director of the film, 'Do Beegha Zameen'?

1. Mrinal Sen
2. Ritvik Ghatak
3. Bimal Roy
4. P. C. Barua

9. When is the communication process considered complete?

1. When the sender transmits the message
2. When the message enters the channel
3. When the message leaves the channel
4. When the receiver understands the message

10. Who among these is the editor of 'The Indian Express' newspaper?

1. Jaideep Bose
2. Shekhar Gupta
3. Raj Kamal Jha
4. Sanjay Gupta

11. A 'stereotype' is _____.

1. a printing technique
2. a type of a mass media
3. forming beliefs about a certain group
4. to insult someone

12. Who directed the movie *Manthan*?

1. Satyajit Ray
2. Shyam Benegal
3. K. Asif
4. Govind Nihalani

13. USP stands for _____.

1. Unique Sales Product
2. Unique Sell Product
3. Unique Selling Point
4. Unique Sales Promotion

14. Which of these is also known as 'Speciality advertising'?

1. Covert Advertising
2. Merchandise
3. Celebrity Endorsement
4. Institutional Advertising

15. Match List-I with List-II:

List-I (Contribution)	List-II (Personality)
A. Filmmaker	(I) V.S. Naipaul
B. Author	(II) Amartya Sen
C. Invented Phonograph	(III) Majid Majidi
D. Economist	(IV) Thomas Edison

Choose the correct answer from the options given below:

1. A-(IV), B-(II), C-(III), D-(I)
2. A-(I), B-(III), C-(IV), D-(II)
3. A-(III), B-(II), C-(I), D-(IV)
4. A-(III), B-(I), C-(IV), D-(II)

16. Arrange these steps of pre-shooting stage in correct order:

A. Casting actors
B. Acquiring finance
C. Writing a script
D. Planning a time schedule

Choose the correct answer from the options given below:

1. A, B, C, D
2. C, B, A, D
3. B, A, D, C
4. B, C, D, A

17. Match List-I with List-II:

List-I (Social Media Platform)	List-II (Features)
A. X (Twitter)	(I) Professional networking
B. Snapchat	(II) Reels
C. Linkedln	(III) Microblogging
D. Instagram	(IV) Pictures sharing

Choose the correct answer from the options given below:

1. A-(I), B-(II), C-(III), D-(IV)
2. A-(I), B-(III), C-(II), D-(IV)
3. A-(I), B-(II), C-(IV), D-(III)
4. A-(III), B-(IV), C-(I), D-(II)

18. Arrange these movies chronologically, according to their release year:

A. Neecha Nagar
B. Alam Ara
C. Ardh Satya
D. Bandit Queen

Choose the correct answer from the options given below:

1. A, B, C, D
2. A, C, B, D
3. B, A, C, D
4. C, B, D, A

19. Communication with oneself is called :

1. Intrapersonal Communication
2. Interpersonal Communication
3. Group Communication
4. Mass Communication

20. Identify the correct order of pages in a daily newspaper:

A. Sports Page
B. Op-ed Page
C. City Page
D. Editorial Page

Choose the correct answer from the options given below:

1. A, B, C, D
2. A, C, B, D
3. B, A, D, C
4. C, D, B, A

8. 3	**9.** 4	**10.** 3	**11.** 3	**12.** 2	**13.** 3
14. 2	**15.** 4	**16.** 2	**17.** 4	**18.** 3	**19.** 1

21. Which of the following media is non-linear?
1. Print media
2. Radio
3. Television
4. Social media

22. Which of the following shot is suitable to capture emotions and facial expressions in detail?
1. Close-up shot
2. Long shot
3. Wide shot
4. Mid shot

23. Advertisement of a Tour and Travel agency, whose target audience is young adults, shall use which form of media to catch maximum eyeballs ?
1. Newspaper
2. Radio
3. Periodicals
4. Social media

24. What is Cooperative Advertising?

A. Establishing a relationship between a product and its potential consumers

B. Generating and transmitting short and precise messages regarding a cause or a problem

C. A system that allows two parties to share advertising costs

D. Advertising that compares one brand directly or indirectly with one or more competing brands

Which of the options given below is correct:
1. A and D only
2. B and C only
3. C only
4. C and D only

25. While writing a radio script, what should be kept in mind?

A. Write simple sentences

B Understand the subject and primary audience

C Know the intended duration

D Use literary words

Which of the options given below is correct:
1. A, B and C only
2. A, B and D only
3. B, C and D only
4. A, C and D only

26. Which of the following is not considered an ethical journalism practice?
1. Sting Operations
2. Investigative Journalism
3. Political Journalism
4. Fashion Journalism

27. What does the cyber security protect?
1. Traffic Violations
2. Intellectual Property Rights
3. Internet connected systems
4. Verbal altercation

28. Which of the following is NOT a 'netiquette'?
1. Identification of oneself
2. Stalking
3. Appropriate language
4. Taking care of other's privacy

29. Match List-I with List-II :

List-I (Content)	List-II (Genre)
A. Gender sensitisation programmes	(I) Sensational news
B. Cookery shows	(II) Informative
C. Comedy shows	(III) Entertaining
D. Sting operation	(IV) Educational

Choose the correct answer from the options given below:
1. A-(I), B-(III), C-(II), D-(IV)
2. A-(IV), B-(II), C-(III), D-(I)
3. A-(III), B-(II), C-(I), D-(IV)
4. A-(II), B-(IV), C-(I), D-(III)

30. Identify the correct sequence of following stages in an advertising campaign:

A. Brief to the client
B. Promotion
C. Media Planning
D. Research

1. A, B, D, C
2. D, A, C, B
3. B, A, D, C
4. C, B, D, A

31. What do you understand by the term TRP?
1. Television Rating Points
2. Traffic Rating Points
3. Television Ranking Points
4. Television Reference Purpose

32. Which among these is not a film genre?
1. Eastern
2. Action
3. Western
4. Drama

33. Which of these characteristic(s) define journalism ?
1. Entertaining the audience
2. Collecting, analysing, verifying, and presenting information
3. Public service announcements
4. Advocacy for business concerns

34. A radio presenter should avoid the use of _____.
1. active voice
2. jargons
3. simple sentences
4. conversational language

35. Identify the brand associated with this tagline:

'JUST DO IT'
1. Adidas
2. Reebok
3. Nike
4. Puma

20. 4	**21.** 4	**22.** 1	**23.** 4	**24.** 3	**25.** 1
26. 1	**27.** 3	**28.** 2	**29.** 2	**30.** 2	**31.** 1

36. Radio broadcasting first started in which of the two cities of India ?
1. Delhi and Bombay
2. Bombay and Calcutta
3. Delhi and Calcutta
4. Calcutta and Chennai

37. A series of rough sketches which helps in visualising and organising camera treatment is called:
1. Rough cut
2. Call sheet
3. Story board
4. Recce

38. What does the term "public media" refer to?
1. Privately owned
2. Serving masses
3. Individual expression
4. Inaccessible

39. Which of these is an Indian News Agency?
1. Reuters
2. PTI
3. AFP
4. AP

40. Which among these is a news writing format ?
1. Inverted glass
2. Cylindrical
3. Inverted Pyramid
4. Pyramid

Directions (Q.No. 41-45): *Read the passage and answer the questions that follow/s:*

ADVERTISING TRENDS

Like most areas of marketing, advertising is changing rapidly. New forms of media available are blurring the distinction between different avenues. Convergence of different media is giving rise to an advertising convergence. The convergence of television and internet opens many potential opportunities for marketers to target customers in ways not available with traditional television advertising. Even the print is merging into web. However, these new media forms have limited reach as they are technology intensive and not affordable for everyone. The Internet has become new hub for the ICE age [information, Communication, Entertainment]. Podcasting Audio-Podcasting Video-RSS Feeds-Networked Gaming-may offer themselves as major outlets for advertising in the near future. The game of old plus new goes on and the marketers must stay informed of new developments and understand how their customers are using these in ways that may offer advertising opportunities.

41. What limitation is associated with using New Media?
1. Limited reach
2. Low production costs
3. Less brand associations
4. Low visual impact

42. What advertising trend is mentioned in the passage regarding digital convergence?
1. Traditional media dominance
2. Decreased reliance on the internet
3. Convergence of television and internet
4. RSS feeds

43. How does the passage describe the convergence of television and the Internet in advertising?
1. Decreased costs
2. More reach
3. Market opportunities
4. Traditional advertising dominance

44. What does the passage predict as potential outlets for advertising in the future?
1. Traditional media only
2. Print and television
3. Networked gaming
4. OOH

45. What is the Internet referred to as about Information, Communication and Entertainment?
1. Conventional media
2. Hub for the ICE age
3. Outdated medium
4. Print media

Directions (Q.No. 46-50): *Read the passage and answer the questions that follow/s:*

Public broadcasting has gone through multiple changes in India since the age of its inception. Radio broadcasting began here in early 1920's. Later, in 1936, the All India Radio started its operation. Lionel Fielden was instrumental in developing the radio programming on AIR. Television broadcasting started in the late 1950's. Earlier, television was a part of AIR but by 1970, television centres were opened in the various parts of the country other than Delhi. In 1976, Doordarshan which was working under All India Radio became an independent and separate department. Between August 1975 and July 1976, an experiment called the Satellite Instructional Television Experiment (SITE) was conducted. Under this programme Indian government used the American satellite ATS-6 to broadcast educational programmes to several villages of six states in India. Community TV sets were distributed and educational programmes were broadcast. Entertainment was also a part of these programmes in the form of dance, music, drama, folk songs etc. In the 1990's, television and radio were braught together under the Prasar Bharati.

32. 1	**33.** 2	**34.** 2	**35.** 3	**36.** 2	**37.** 3	**38.** 2
39. 2	**40.** 3	**41.** 1	**42.** 3	**43.** 3	**44.** 3	**45.** 2

46. When did the television centres open in the various parts of the country?

1. 1960
2. 1970
3. 1975
4. 1979

47. SITE stands for:

1. Satellite Instructional Television Experiment
2. Satellite Informational Television Experiment
3. Satellite Instructional Television Exposure
4. Satellite Instructional Television Examination

48. Doordarshan became an independent and separate department in which year?

1. 1974
2. 1972
3. 1976
4. 1978

49. Which programmes were aired on community TV sets?

1. Educational
2. Horror
3. Religious
4. Comedy

50. Dance and drama were broadcast under which category?

1. Informative
2. Educational
3. Entertainment
4. Lifestyle

EXPLANATORY ANSWERS

1. (2): An advertisement, message, or public communication regarding economic, political, or social issues is known as advocacy advertising. This type of communication aims to influence public opinion or policy decisions by promoting a specific cause, idea, or point of view rather than a product or service. Advocacy advertising is often used by non-profits, political organizations, and social movements to raise awareness and support.

2. (1): Media literacy is fundamentally about being able to analyze and judge the reliability of news sources, which is essential in the age of information overload and fake news. It also involves developing critical thinking and communication abilities, empowering individuals to question media content and express their views clearly. Additionally, it fosters an understanding of how media functions within society, including its impact on culture, politics, and behaviour. Simply knowing how to use editing software does not reflect media literacy—it is more about understanding media's purpose and influence.

Hence, correct options are A, B and C only.

3. (4): The correct order in the communication process is:

- **Sender:** the originator of the message.
- **Message:** the information or content being communicated.
- **Receiver:** the person or audience who receives the message.
- **Feedback:** the response or reaction of the receiver that is sent back to the sender.

This sequence represents the fundamental model of communication as outlined in various communication theories.

Hence, correct sequence is C, B, D, A.

4. (3): Sam Altman is the CEO of OpenAI, the AI start-up known for developing ChatGPT and other artificial intelligence tools. He co-founded OpenAI and has played a pivotal role in advancing the company's mission to ensure that artificial general intelligence (AGI) benefits all of humanity. Prior to OpenAI, Altman was the president of Y Combinator, a leading startup accelerator.

5. (3): David Ogilvy is widely recognized as the 'Father of Advertising' due to his influential role in shaping modern advertising. He founded Ogilvy & Mather and emphasized research, consumer behavior, and clear messaging. His classic campaigns and principles, like focusing on the "big idea" and making the product the hero, have left a lasting legacy on the advertising industry.

6. (4): Correct matching is:

- **Doordarshan — Government:** Doordarshan is India's official public service broadcaster, owned and operated by the Government of India.
- **Aaj Tak — (IV) Private:** Aaj Tak is a private Hindi news channel run by the India Today Group, a commercial media house.
- **BBC — International:** BBC (British Broadcasting Corporation) is a globally known public broadcaster based in the UK, serving international audiences.
- **Sony — Conglomerate:** Sony is part of the Sony Corporation, a global media and electronics conglomerate that owns multiple entertainment and media properties.

Hence, correct matching is: A-(III), B-(IV), C-(I), D-(II)

7. (1): Correct matching is:

- **Bengal Gazette — James Augustus Hicky:** Bengal Gazette, India's first newspaper (1780), was founded and edited by James Augustus Hicky.
- **Mirat-ul-Akhbar — Raja Ram Mohan Roy:** Raja Ram Mohan Roy launched this Persian journal to support social reforms and the freedom of press.
- **Rast Goftar — Dadabhai Naoroji:** Rast Goftar was a Parsi reformist publication led by Dadabhai Naoroji to advocate for social and national awareness.
- **Young India — M.K. Gandhi:** Mahatma Gandhi used Young India to spread his political philosophy and promote non-violent resistance during the independence movement.

Hence, correct matching is: A-(I), B-(II), C-(III), D-(IV)

46. 2	**47.** 1	**48.** 3	**49.** 1	**50.** 3

8. **(3):** The 1953 film *Do Beegha Zameen* was directed by Bimal Roy, a pioneer of realistic cinema in India. The film is a landmark in Indian neorealism, depicting the struggle of a poor farmer against socio-economic injustices. It was critically acclaimed and won several international awards, including at the Cannes Film Festival, establishing Roy's legacy in parallel cinema.

9. **(4):** The communication process is not truly complete until the receiver comprehends the message intended by the sender. This understanding is essential for effective communication because without it, the purpose of the message is lost, even if it is transmitted and received. Only with understanding can feedback be meaningful and the communication loop be fully closed.

10. **(3):** Raj Kamal Jha is the current Editor-in-Chief of The Indian Express, a prominent English-language daily known for investigative journalism and critical commentary. A journalist and novelist, Jha is known for his editorial leadership and deep commitment to ethical journalism. Under his direction, the newspaper has won several awards for exposing key national issues.

11. **(3):** A stereotype is a widely held but oversimplified and fixed idea or image about a particular group of people, often based on race, gender, religion, profession, or nationality. Stereotyping generalizes traits to all members of a group, ignoring individual differences. For example, saying "all engineers are introverted" is a stereotype. It can lead to prejudice and discrimination in society.

12. **(2):** The film *Manthan* (1976) was directed by Shyam Benegal, one of the pioneers of parallel cinema in India. It was based on the White Revolution and the cooperative milk movement in Gujarat. Remarkably, the film was crowdfunded by 500,000 farmers of the Gujarat Milk Marketing Federation, making it one of the earliest examples of people-funded cinema in India. It starred Naseeruddin Shah and Smita Patil.

13. **(3):** USP stands for Unique Selling Point or Unique Selling Proposition, a marketing concept that defines what makes a product or brand stand out from its competitors. It is the distinct benefit or value that convinces consumers to choose one product over another. For example, FedEx's USP was "When it absolutely, positively has to be there overnight."

14. **(2):** Merchandise in advertising refers to branded promotional products used to advertise a company, logo, or slogan and is also known as specialty advertising. Items like mugs, pens, t-shirts, and keychains with a brand name or logo fall under this category. They are designed to create brand recall and customer loyalty through repeated visual contact.

15. **(4):** Correct matching is:

- **Filmmaker — Majid Majidi:** Majid Majidi is an acclaimed Iranian filmmaker, internationally known for movies like Children of Heaven and The Color of Paradise.
- **Author — V.S. Naipaul:** V.S. Naipaul was a Nobel Prize-winning author recognized for novels such as A House for Mr. Biswas and In a Free State.
- **Invented Phonograph — Thomas Edison:** Thomas Edison invented the phonograph in 1877, the first device to record and reproduce sound.
- **Economist — Amartya Sen:** Amartya Sen is a distinguished Indian economist and Nobel laureate, noted for his work on welfare economics and development.

Hence, correct matching is: A-(III), B-(I), C-(IV), D-(II)

16. **(2):** Correct order are: C, B, A, D

- **Writing a script:** The very first step in filmmaking is creating the script, which serves as the blueprint for the entire production.
- **Acquiring finance:** Once the script is finalized, the producer seeks to secure funding based on the project details.
- **Casting actors:** With finances in place, the production team moves to casting actors suited for the roles in the script.
- **Planning a time schedule:** After casting, the production house then creates a shooting schedule, deciding when and where filming will take place.

Hence, correct order are C, B, A, D.

17. **(4):** Correct matching is:

- **X (Twitter) — Microblogging:** Twitter, now rebranded as X, is widely known for microblogging, allowing users to post short messages or "tweets."
- **Snapchat — Pictures sharing:** Snapchat is known for sharing disappearing photos and videos, with features like filters and stories focused on visual content.
- **LinkedIn — Professional networking:** LinkedIn is a dedicated platform for professional networking, job searches, and business-related content.
- **Instagram — Reels:** Instagram, owned by Meta, emphasizes Reels, a short-form video feature introduced to compete with TikTok.

Hence, correct matching is A-(III), B-(IV), C-(I), D-(II).

18. **(3):** Correct chronological order is:

- **Alam Ara (1931):** First Indian talkie film, marking the beginning of sound cinema in India.
- **Neecha Nagar (1946):** India's first film to win at Cannes, and a landmark of social realism in Indian cinema.
- **Ardh Satya (1983):** A key film in India's parallel cinema movement, dealing with police brutality and morality.
- **Bandit Queen (1994):** A biographical film based on Phoolan Devi, focusing on caste and gender-based violence.

Hence, correct chronological order is B, A, C, D.

19. **(1):** Intrapersonal communication refers to the communication that occurs within an individual. It includes thoughts, self-reflection, and internal dialogue. It plays a key role in decision-making, self-awareness, and emotional regulation. Unlike interpersonal or group communication, it doesn't involve another person directly.

20. (4): Correct order is: C, D, B, A

- **City Page:** Usually appears early in the paper with local or regional news most relevant to city readers.
- **Editorial Page:** Contains editorials written by the newspaper's editors, expressing the paper's official stance.
- **Op-ed Page:** Follows editorials, offering opinions and commentaries from guest writers or experts.
- **Sports Page:** Typically placed at the end section, covering sports news, fixtures, and analysis.

Hence, correct order is C, D, B, A.

21. (4): Social media is a non-linear medium because it allows users to interact with content in any order they choose—through likes, comments, shares, hyperlinks, and multimedia posts. Unlike print, radio, or television, where information is presented in a fixed, sequential format, social media is dynamic and user-driven, allowing content to be consumed, created, or responded to at any point without a fixed start or end.

22. (1): A close-up shot is best suited to capture emotions and facial expressions in detail because it frames the subject tightly, usually from the shoulders up. This shot magnifies subtle expressions—such as eye movement, tears, or a twitch—making it ideal for portraying emotional depth or reaction. It is frequently used in emotional or dramatic scenes in cinema and television.

23. (4): For a Tour and Travel agency targeting young adults, social media is the most effective platform due to high engagement levels among youth on apps like Instagram, YouTube, and Snapchat. These platforms support visually rich content like travel reels, stories, and influencer partnerships, which attract immediate attention and offer interactive features that traditional media like newspapers or radio lack.

24. (3): Cooperative advertising refers to a marketing strategy where two parties share advertising costs, typically a manufacturer and a retailer or distributor. For example, a national brand may pay part of the cost for a local dealer to run an ad featuring their product. This helps both parties reduce costs while boosting visibility. The other options describe different types of advertising (not cooperative).

25. (1): Writing a radio script should be kept in mind:
Writing a radio script effectively requires simple sentences because the listener cannot go back and re-read like in print. Understanding the subject and the target audience is essential for tailoring the message. Also, knowing the intended duration ensures the script fits within the time slot. Using literary words is not advised, as radio demands clarity and conversational language for easy comprehension.
Hence, correct option is A, B and C only.

26. (1): While sting operations can expose corruption or wrong doing, they often involve deception, hidden cameras, and intrusion into privacy, which raises serious ethical concerns in journalism. Unlike investigative or political journalism that follows transparency and fairness, sting operations risk violating consent, objectivity, and can manipulate facts. Hence, they are not widely accepted as ethical journalistic practice.

27. (3): Cyber security focuses on protecting internet-connected systems including computers, networks, servers, mobile devices, and data from cyberattacks, theft, or unauthorized access. It involves practices like encryption, firewalls, and antivirus software to safeguard both hardware and sensitive digital information. It does not relate to traffic violations, verbal disputes, or IPR directly, though it may help secure IPR online.

28. (2): Stalking is a clear violation of privacy and safety and is not a part of netiquette (network etiquette). Netiquette promotes respectful, responsible, and courteous behavior in digital communication. It includes practices like identifying oneself, using polite language, and respecting others' privacy and boundaries online. Stalking is unethical and illegal, completely contrary to netiquette principles.

29. (2): Correct match is:

- **Gender sensitisation programmes — Educational:** These are intended to educate people about gender equality, biases, and respectful behavior.
- **Cookery shows — Informative:** These programs share recipes and cooking techniques, offering viewers useful information.
- **Comedy shows — Entertaining:** Their primary purpose is to amuse the audience, fitting the entertainment genre.
- **Sting operation — Sensational news:** These are often high-impact, dramatic exposures aimed at grabbing public attention, thus categorized under sensational news.

Hence, correct match is A-(IV), B-(II), C-(III), D-(I).

30. (2): Correct sequence is:

- **Research:** First, research is conducted to understand the market, audience, and product insights.
- **Brief to the client:** Based on research, a detailed brief is shared with the client to define objectives and creative direction.
- **Media Planning:** After client approval, media planning is done to decide when and where the ads will appear for maximum reach.
- **Promotion:** Finally, the campaign is launched and promoted across selected media platforms to reach the target audience.

Hence, correct sequence is D, A, C, B.

31. (1): TRP (Television Rating Points) is a metric used to measure the popularity and viewership of a television program. It indicates how many viewers are watching a particular show, helping advertisers and broadcasters determine the show's reach and value. Higher TRP means more viewers, which attracts more advertising revenue. It is calculated using data from devices like people meters installed in sample households.

32. (1): Eastern is not recognized as a formal film genre in mainstream cinema classification. Common film genres include Action, Western, Drama, Comedy, Romance, etc. While "Western" is a genre typically set in the American frontier, there is no standard "Eastern" genre—though the term may loosely refer to Asian cinema styles, it's not used as a genre in the strict cinematic sense.

33. **(2): Collecting, analysing, verifying, and presenting information:** This defines the core function of journalism—to gather news, verify facts, analyze data, and present information to the public in a truthful, balanced, and responsible way. Journalism aims to inform society and support democratic discourse. Unlike advertising or entertainment, journalism emphasizes factual reporting and accountability.

34. **(2):** A radio presenter should avoid using jargons because complex or technical terms can confuse listeners. Radio communication must be clear, concise, and accessible to a general audience. Using simple language, active voice, and a conversational tone ensures better listener engagement and comprehension.

35. **(3):** The tagline "JUST DO IT" is famously associated with the brand Nike, introduced in 1988. It is one of the most iconic and successful slogans in advertising history, designed to inspire confidence, determination, and athletic spirit. Nike uses this tagline across global marketing campaigns to appeal to both professional athletes and general consumers.

36. **(2):** The first radio broadcasting in India began in 1927 through two privately operated stations: one in Bombay (now Mumbai) and the other in Calcutta (now Kolkata). These were run by the Indian Broadcasting Company (IBC). Bombay started on June 23, 1927, and Calcutta followed on August 26, 1927. Later, in 1936, these services were reorganized under the government and became All India Radio (AIR).

37. **(3):** A storyboard is a sequence of rough, hand-drawn or digital sketches that represent the planned shots in a film or video. It helps the director and crew visualize scenes, camera angles, and transitions before shooting begins. Storyboards are essential in pre-production as they organize how the narrative will visually unfold, saving time and resources during filming.

38. **(2):** Public media refers to media organizations that are funded and run for the public good, often by the government or through public funding. Their primary objective is to serve the interests of the masses, providing educational, cultural, and informative content rather than operating for commercial profit. In India, Doordarshan and All India Radio are examples of public media.

39. **(2):** Press Trust of India (PTI) is India's largest indigenous news agency, established in 1947. It supplies news to various newspapers, TV channels, and digital platforms across the country. Unlike Reuters (UK), AFP (France), or AP (USA), PTI is Indian-owned and operated, and plays a key role in news dissemination within India.

40. **(3):** The Inverted Pyramid is a common structure in news writing where the most important information comes first, followed by supporting details and background information. This format ensures that even if the reader stops midway, they still grasp the essential facts. It is favored for news stories to prioritize clarity and immediacy.

41. **(1):** The passage clearly mentions that "these new media forms have limited reach as they are technology intensive and not affordable for everyone." This limitation arises because not all consumers have access to or can afford the technology required for accessing digital platforms like podcasting, RSS feeds, or networked gaming. Hence, limited reach is a key drawback of new media.

42. **(3):** The passage specifically highlights "the convergence of television and internet opens many potential opportunities for marketers". This indicates a trend in digital advertising where previously separate media forms are now merging, offering integrated platforms for targeted marketing. It contrasts with the era when television and internet were used separately for advertising.

43. **(3):** According to the passage, the convergence of television and internet "opens many potential opportunities for marketers to target customers", which suggests that this integration creates new advertising possibilities and market opportunities. It doesn't mention reduced costs or dominance of traditional methods in this context.

44. **(3):** The passage lists "Podcasting Audio—Podcasting Video—RSS Feeds—Networked Gaming" as potential future outlets for advertising. Among the given options, networked gaming is the correct one explicitly mentioned in the context of emerging platforms that advertisers might explore.

45. **(2):** The passage refers to the Internet as the new hub for the ICE age, where ICE stands for Information, Communication, and Entertainment. This highlights the central role of the internet in delivering all three functions, making it a key platform for both users and marketers.

46. **(2):** The passage states: "by 1970, television centres were opened in the various parts of the country other than Delhi."

This clearly points to the year 1970 as the time when television broadcasting expanded beyond Delhi into other parts of India.

47. **(1):** SITE stands for Satellite Instructional Television Experiment, as mentioned directly in the passage: "an experiment called the Satellite Instructional Television Experiment (SITE) was conducted."

This was a collaborative educational project between the Indian government and NASA using the American satellite ATS-6.

48. **(3):** According to the passage: "In 1976, Doordarshan which was working under All India Radio became an independent and separate department."

This confirms that 1976 was the year when Doordarshan became independent from AIR.

49. **(1):** The passage says: "broadcast educational programmes to several villages..." and "Community TV sets were distributed..."

This shows that educational programmes were aired specifically through these community TV sets, under the SITE initiative.

50. **(3):** It is mentioned: "Entertainment was also a part of these programmes in the form of dance, music, drama, folk songs etc."

Hence, elements like dance and drama were categorized under entertainment, complementing the educational content of the SITE broadcasts.

MASS MEDIA / MASS COMMUNICATION

CHAPTER-1

COMMUNICATION

COMMUNICATION

Communication can broadly be defined as exchange of ideas, messages and information between two or more persons, through a medium, in a manner that the sender and the receiver understand the message in the common sense that is, they develop common understanding of the message.

The word communication is derived from the Latin word 'communis', which means to share, impart, participate, exchange, transmit or to make common. It emphasizes on sharing common information, ideas and messages. It is not merely issuing orders and instructions.

Communication is an ever continuing process and an integral part of the world of all living things. The need for communication is as basic as the hunger for food and drink, perhaps even more so. It is an individual as well as a social need.

The Encyclopedia Britannica defines communication as ***'the exchange of meaning between individuals or groups through a common system of symbols or language'.***

Dreaming, talking with someone, arguing in a discussion, speaking in public, reading a newspaper, watching a TV programme etc. are all different kinds of communication in every day life. It means that we are constantly exchanging our thoughts, ideas, and motions with someone or other either to satisfy our physical, emotional or other needs or to get work done. It is obvious that communication is an integral part of one's life. In fact, society cannot survive in the absence of communication.

NATURE OF COMMUNICATION

1. **Two-way process:** Mostly communication is a two-way interaction with at least two people – sender and receiver. However, during intrapersonal communication, the individual speaks with himself.
2. **Continuous Process:** Communication is a continuous process. It is present at all levels of organizations and they cannot exist without it. It is like the circulation of blood in organizations, as they need to exchange ideas, facts, information, etc.
3. **Objective driven:** Communications are also driven by their goals or objectives. When the receiver and sender know the objectives they expect to accomplish while communicating with each other; it ensures maximum functional utility.
4. **Consistency:** The communication process advances comprehension, proper understanding, and sharing of information applicable for making decisions.
5. **Verbal and non-verbal:** From written and verbal words to gestures, postures, signs, body language and other non-verbal cues, all are associated with the nature of communication.
6. **Dynamic process:** Communication takes various mediums and forms relying on their needs, audiences, and goals. It follows a dynamic process that continues to change in various circumstances.
7. **Mutual understanding:** For the communication to be effective, it is important that both sender and the receiver have a mutual understanding and identical minds. The receiver must understand the message the way sender wants him to understand.

OBJECTIVES OF COMMUNICATION

Communication objectives are the reasons that a business or an individual may choose to interact, or communicate, with customers, employees, coworkers or other businesses and what the business hopes to gain from the exchange. This communication may come in the form of conversations, written statements, marketing campaigns or any other strategy that conveys information.

Following are few of the main objectives of the Communication:

1. Providing Information
2. Motivating People
3. Creating Interest
4. Providing Instructions and training
5. Entertaining the audience
6. Building relationships
7. Facilitating change
8. Problem Solving

PROCESS OF COMMUNICATION

Communication is a dynamic process involving a series of actions and reactions with a view to achieve a goal. Communication is a two way process, that is, the ability to receive is as important as the ability to send. For successful communication, feedback is crucial because it tells how your messages are being interpreted. It can make or break the communication process. A complete act of communication is shown in the following Figure.

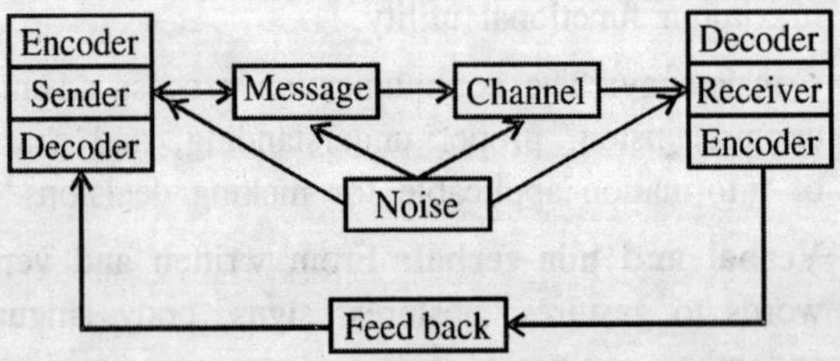

Fig.: *A Complete Act of Communication*

Here the communicator is the encoder, the message is symbol (verbal or non-verbal), the channel is one of the transmission medium, the receiver is the decoder, feedback is the response to the message, and noise is any interruption that breaks down the communication.

These, in fact, are the essential elements or ingredients which facilitate the communication process. Let us examine what role each element plays in the entire communication process and how all of them are important in making communication effective.

Communicator (Sender)

Communicator (sender or encoder) is the one who initiates the communication process. He may be an editor, a reporter, a film maker, a teacher, a writer, a speaker, a leader or anybody who takes the initiative to start a dialogue. Before one speaks or writes, the message is conceptualised first and then encoded. An effective communication depends on the communication skill, knowledge level, and attitude of the communicator and how he desires to affect his receiver (David K. Berlo). An ability to think, to organise thoughts quickly, and express himself effectively are some of the attributes of a good communicator.

Encoding

Encoding is the formulation of messages in the communicator's mind, that is, the communicator not only translates his purpose (ideas, thoughts or information) into a message but also decides on the medium to, communicate his planned message. He must choose the media (speaking, writing, signaling or gesturing) that the receiver can comprehend well. For instance, an illiterate receiver will fail to understand a written message, but can understand it well if told orally.

Message

A message is what a communicator actually produces for transmission using spoken or written words, photographs, paintings, films, posters, etc. A great deal of skill and effort is required to formulate a message, the meaning of which should be understandable to the receiver. Actually the purpose of communication is to influence the receiver and get favourable responses so that appropriate decisions can be taken. The success of communication, therefore, depends on **what we say** and **how we say it**.

Channel (Medium)

A channel is the vehicle through which a message is carried from the communicator to the receiver. The channels of communication are many-written, spoken, verbal, non-verbal, mass media like TV, radio, newspapers, books etc. Success and failure of communication depends on the selection of the right channel.

Receiver

The receiver, at the other end of the communication, is the recipient of the message and must possess the same orientation as the communicator. If the receiver does not have the ability to listen, to read, to think, he will not be able to receive and decode the messages in the manner the communicator wants him to. For effective communication, the receiver is the most important link in the communication process.

Decoding

Decoding is the interpretation of the message by the receiver. Actually, the receiver looks for the meaning in the message which is common to both the receiver and the communicator.

Feedback

Feedback is the response or acknowledgement of receiver to the communicator's message. The exchange is possible only if the receiver responds. Even through fluttering eyelids, raising an eyebrow, making a face, organising a point and asking for explanation, the message is shaped and reshaped by the communicator and the receiver until the meaning becomes clear. In this way both participants in communication interact and constantly exchange roles. In face-to-face communication the receiver responds naturally, directly and immediately. This provides the communicator an opportunity to improve and make his communication effective. Feedback, thus, provides an opportunity to evaluate what is right or wrong about a particular communication. It helps to regulate the conversation among two or more individuals and also stimulates and reinforces an idea that is desired to be communicated.

Noise

Noise is an interruption that can creep in at any point of the communication process and make it ineffective. Environment is one major cause that interferes, with message reception; like noises from the roadside, constant chattering of individuals outside the communication act, blaring loudspeaker, faulty transmission etc. Noise can occur in other forms also; poor handwriting, heavy accent or soft speech, communication in a poorly lit room etc. In fact, theses are barriers to effective communication. For smooth and effective communication, it is necessary to eliminate or reduce noise as far as possible.

BARRIERS TO EFFECTIVE COMMUNICATION

Message can be delayed or wrongly conveyed due to the barriers in effective communication and purpose of the message being transferred, which may result in failure of the communication process or an effect that is adverse.

The Barriers to effective communication could be of many types like linguistic, psychological, emotional, physical, and cultural etc.

- **Physical Barriers:** Physical barriers to communication are those that arise due to certain factors like faulty equipment, noise, closed doors and cabins that cause the information sent from sender to receiver to become distorted, which results in improper communication.
- **Semantic Barriers (Language Barriers):** These barriers are caused due to improper communication between the sender and the receiver. Words play a very important role in effective communication. Words sounding same can create a doubt in understanding the message. Inappropriate use of jargons, local slangs etc can cause confusion.
- **Psychological Barriers:** There are three important elements associated with psychological and social barriers: fields of experience, filtering and psychological distance.
- **Physiological Barriers:** Physiological barriers arise when a sender or the receiver of the communication is not in a position to express or receive the message with clarity due to some physiological issues like dyslexia, or nerve disorders that interfere with speech or hearing.
- **Cultural Barriers:** Cultural barriers are those that arise due to lack of similarities among the different cultures across the world. A term that can be harmless in one culture can be regarded as slang in another culture. Moreover, various beliefs can differ from one culture to another.

TYPES OF COMMUNICATION

Communication can be broadly classified into two types:

1. Verbal Communication
2. Non-Verbal Communication

Verbal Communication

Verbal communication describes the process where exchange of information takes place using words.

There are two types of Verbal Communication

(*a*) Oral Communication

(*b*) Written Communication

Oral Communication

Oral Communication mainly describes face to face conversations, speech, telephonic conversation, video conferencing, voice chat over internet. In this kind of communication, major elements are pitch, volume, speed, and clarity in speaking.

Written Communication

In this process, communication is mainly done through written signs and symbols. The message can be in printed and hand written manner. In written communication, ideas and information can be interchanged via email, letter, report, memo etc. In this type, the message is influenced by vocabulary and grammar, style, format, precision and clarity of thought and language used. Here are some forms of written communication:

- Letters
- Circulars
- Orders
- Reports
- Forms and questionnaires
- Newsletters
- Newspapers
- Manuals
- Magazines
- Handbills
- Posters
- Books
- Bulletin boards

Non-Verbal Communication

Non-verbal communication is the transmission of messages or signals through a non-verbal platform such as eye contact, facial expressions, gestures, posture, and body language. It includes the use of social cues, kinesics, distance and physical environments/appearance, of voice and of touch.

Verbal exchanges account for only a fraction of the messages people send and receive. Research has shown that between 70 and 90 percent of the entire communication spectrum is non-verbal.

Types of Non-verbal Communication

Vocalics (Para Language)

Vocalics is the study of paralanguage, which includes the vocal qualities that go along with verbal messages, such as pitch, volume, rate, vocal quality, and verbal fillers. E.g. Yawning indicates tiredness and boredom, belching after food or drinks shows one has eaten to his fill.

Pitch helps convey meaning, regulate conversational flow, and communicate the intensity of a message.

Vocal cues include

- **Pitch**: The highness or lowness of your voice
- **Rate**: How rapidly or slowly one is speaking
- **Volume:** The loudness or softness of your voice
- **Non-word sounds**: 'hmm', 'huh', 'ahh', 'sssh' and the pauses or the absence of sound used for the effect in speaking
- **Pronunciation:** The way in which a word is said
- **Enunciation:** Whether or not you combine pronunciation and articulation to produce a word with clarity so that it can be understood.
- **Articulation:** The formation of clear and distinct sounds in speech
- **Silence**: The lack of sound.

Kinesics (Body Language)

Kinesics is the interpretation of body motion communication such as facial expressions and gestures, nonverbal behavior related to movement of any part of the body or the body as a whole.

Oculesics (Eye Language)

Oculesics, a subcategory of kinesics, is the study of eye movement, behavior, gaze, and eye-related non-verbal communication.

Haptics (Touch)

Haptic communication refers to the ways in which people and animals communicate and interact via the sense of touch. Touch is the most sophisticated and intimate of the five senses.

Touch can come in many different forms; some can promote physical and psychological well-being. A warm, loving touch can lead to positive outcomes while a violent touch can ultimately lead to a negative outcome. The sense of touch allows one to experience different sensations such as: pleasure, pain, heat, or cold.

Proxemics (space)

Distance plays an important role in communication. Proxemics is the term used by Edward Hall (1969) to indicate our use of space and specifically the distancing behavior we employ. Hall studied the distancing behavior of Americans and proposed they have four personal space zones.

(*a*) **Intimate Zone (0-1.5 ft)**: Hall suggested this is the distance of making love, wrestling, offering, comfort and protection.

(*b*) **Personal Zone (1.5ft -4 ft)**: This is a friendship distance, usually not available to strangers or passing acquaintances. Touch is not usual, but the distance is close enough to enable conversation to be carried out in a quiet voice.

(*c*) **Social Zone (4ft -12 ft)**: In this zone, we carry out much of our casual conversations or business of an impersonal nature.

(*d*) **Public Zone (above 12ft)**: At this distance, we no longer communicate on a conversational level. This is appropriate distance for a public address or speaking.

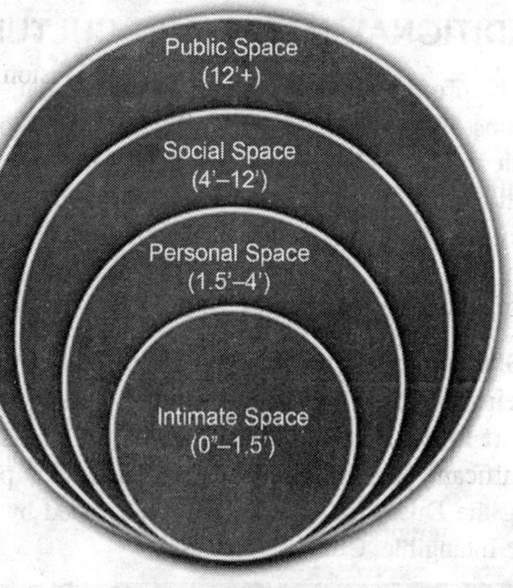

Fig. *Various space zones given by Edward Hall*

Chronemics (Time)

The way one uses his/her time shows or gives intentional or unintentional message about the importance and valuation of an individual.

FORMAL COMMUNICATION

Formal communication typically refers to an official exchange of information between people within the same organization who are often at different levels within the organizational hierarchy.

It's a controlled means of communication that follows predefined channels and adheres to predetermined rules, standards, processes and regulations set by the company.

Formal communication follows the organization's chain of command, with a top-down structure, meaning that higher-ranking employees often use it to send various messages and instructions to lower-level individuals.

Organizational Communication

Organizational communication is a type of formal communication. Communication within an organization performs the functions like planning, organizing, staffing, directing, and controlling. In an organization, there are four ways in which communication takes place:

- **Downward Communication:** This is the most common type of formal communication and represents the flow of information from the company's management to its subordinates. It usually consists of various instructions and orders that are passed down in written or oral form, through reports, memos, emails, manuals and others.
- **Upward Communication:** This is the opposite of downward communication and therefore represents the messages passed from subordinates to management. It can take various forms, such as requests, reports, complaints and suggestions.
- **Horizontal Communication:** It is also known as Lateral communication. This type of formal communication takes place between coworkers who have different roles but are on the same hierarchical level within the organization. Communication between managers of different departments within the same organization is typically the most common example of horizontal communication.
- **Diagonal communication:** Also known as Crosswise communication, diagonal communication is when employees who work for different departments within the same organization and are also on different hierarchical levels formally communicate with each other. It usually consists of various employees communicating with managers of different departments, such as HR, marketing or finance.

INFORMAL COMMUNICATION

Informal communication is multi-dimensional in nature. It flows freely in the organization without any restraint of predefined channels or routes. It is comparatively very quick and relational as people interact with each other freely and can talk about a diverse range of topics, often extending outside of their work duties.

- **Grapevine Communication:** Grapevine communication is a type of informal communication in a workplace. This type of communication focuses on how professionals share information. It is based on rumors and gossips and mostly prevalent at the lower levels of the organizational hierarchy.

CROSS-CULTURE COMMUNICATION

Cross cultural communication refers to the communication between people who have differences in any one of the following: styles of working, age, nationality, ethnicity, race, gender, sexual orientation, etc.

Cross cultural communication can also refer to the attempts that are made to exchange, negotiate and mediate cultural differences by means of language, gestures and body language. It is how people belonging to different cultures communicate with each other.

CULTURE

Culture can be defined as set of shared beliefs, values, traditions, social norms, and behaviors of a group of people who share the same living environment in a specific region of the world. It is a broad and a complex concept that includes many aspects of human lives.

Culture varies with region and religion. It encompasses key aspects of a society, including language, education, religion, folklore, lifestyles, attitudes, government, and the identity and personality of the people who are part of that culture. Culture shapes individuals and societies, fostering unity through shared values and traditions.

UNESCO defines culture as the distinct spiritual, material, intellectual, and emotional features characterizing a society. It encompasses arts, lifestyle, human rights, value systems, traditions, and beliefs.

CULTURE AND COMMUNICATION

Social interactions develop culture. All social units while communicating with each other exchange and share their values, traditions, ideas, taste, rituals that create a culture specific within those units. Even in two-person relationships, a culture develops over time. In friendship and romantic relationships, for example, partners develop their own history, shared experiences, language patterns, rituals, habits, and customs that give that relationship a special character—a character that differentiates it in various ways from other relationships.

Groups develop their culture. Work Organizations develop their own culture and it becomes possible due to communication. Without communication and communication media, it would be impossible to preserve and pass along cultural characteristics from one place and time to another. Culture can also be understood as the residue of social communication.

CULTURE AND MASS MEDIA

Culture is an ever-evolving entity. New beliefs, values, customs, traditions, and practices continually replace older ones. The process of cultural change is faster for societies that are open to outside influences and mass media act as a dominant influencer in this change.

Mass media significantly shapes culture by disseminating information, influencing values, and impacting behaviors, while culture also influences media content, creating a complex and an intertwined relationship.

The relationship between Culture and mass media is very dynamic. Each affecting and influencing each other. A potent cultural force like Bollywood that retains India's traditional culture in its creative expression through art, music and even advertisement, simultaneously facilitates new cultural expressions in the society.

TRADITIONAL MEDIA AND CULTURE

Long before the advent of radio and television, traditional mediums of amusement and folklore were dominant in societies. They were influential in cultural dissemination. Traditional media, also known as folk media, in India has been a dominant influencer for the people. They embodied Indian traditions, tales, values in form of street plays, dances, literature, paintings, etc.

Glimpses of different cultures and religion can be seen in their respective art and literature. 'Ramleela' is one such art form. It is traditional play of the Ramayana epic, a significant part of Hindu culture in India, particularly during the Dussehra festival, and recognized by UNESCO as an Intangible Cultural Heritage.

Ramleela
Image Source: Adarsh Upadhyay - Flickr

There are variety of folk forms in India, which includes Bhavai of Gujarat, Baul and Jatra of Bengal, Burrakatha of Andhra Pradesh, Yakshagana of Karnataka, Nautanki of the North India, Villupattu of Kerala, Ankhia nata of Assam, Chhau in Bengal, Odisha and Jharkhand and many more forms are there. Folk media tells real stories. It arouses interest among people and reflects their hope, strength, aspiration and perception in a simple way.

Governments have used traditional media as an influential tool to counter social evils and sensitize people. There were many practices that were deeply rooted in Indian culture but were hinderance to our societal growth. Indian governments have used such art forms to reduce gender bias, promote equality, and communal harmony.

REPRESENTATION AND STEREOTYPING IN MASS MEDIA

Mass media significantly shapes public perceptions through representation, and can perpetuate harmful stereotypes, influencing attitudes and reinforcing societal inequalities. Media portrayals of cultures, communities and identities greatly impact how people perceive about them. These stereotypes have far-reaching consequences that affect various aspects of society.

Stereotyping impacts identity formation, particularly among marginalized communities. When individuals are consistently exposed to stereotypical portrayals, they may internalize these representations, leading to self-stigmatization and a distorted sense of identity. Biased portrayals perpetuate discriminatory attitudes and contribute to social hierarchies, while the underrepresentation or misrepresentation of certain groups marginalizes their experiences and reinforces systemic inequalities.

Some examples of stereotyping in Indian media are:

- Fairness creams stereotype that all women must be fair skinned to look beautiful and confident.
- Automobile industry specifically features men in their advertisements, implying cars are only for men.
- Home appliances' ads like that of fridge, washing machine, oven, etc. specifically feature women, stereotyping household works to women.
- Men are usually shown working in offices whereas women are shown doing household chores in films and shows, stereotyping gender specific roles.
- Marginalized class are often overlooked and are only shown narrowly in stereotyped roles.
- Dalits are usually shown in dark skinned, devoid of basic facilities and doing menial jobs.

MEDIA AS A VEHICLE OF CULTURAL TRANSMISSION

Use of media is pivotal to cultural transmission. Cultures are common beliefs and ideas usually confined to a particular group of people. Media through its long and pervasive reach transfuses different cultures within people from the outside world.

Media has evolved over the years and has become faster and wider. Leaps from the print media to television and now to new media have made the world a unified place. Practices that were once limited in traditional media reached to wider audience when electronic media took over it. And now in the times of digital media, they can reach the world in no time. Earlier, plays or movies in South Indian languages were only known to the audience of the South India. But when television happened, their translated depictions also took it to the audience of North India.

Now, media content is available across internet in multiple languages, creating a wider audience base. American shows are viewed enormously in India, that introduce Indians to their culture.

Likewise, travel vlogging and food vlogging has introduced the outside world to the Indian culture. Festivals like Holi and Diwali are no longer limited to just India but are celebrated widely across the globe. Dance trends on Instagram and tik tok are widely followed. Campaigns and social causes draw support from across the geographical boundaries with a simple use of hashtag on Twitter (now X).

Technological advancements have made cultural exchanges rampant. World is now a unified place where different cultures are sharing ideas and values from each other. It is instrumental in influencing public opinions, behaviors, and cultural trends. For instance, social media popularizes fashion, language, and lifestyle choices.

COMMUNICATION AND SOCIAL CHANGE

Communication plays a crucial role in driving social change by enabling dialogue, raising awareness, mobilizing collective action, and fostering empowerment.

Social change refers to significant alterations in social structures, cultural patterns, and behaviours over time. It can be intentional (e.g., social movements) or unintentional (e.g., technological advancements).

Key Areas of Social Change can broadly be classified into:

- Social Justice (e.g., human rights, gender equality)
- Political Change (e.g., political movements)
- Cultural Shifts (e.g., changes in social norms)
- Environmental Advocacy (e.g., climate action plan)

Communication Sustains Social Change by

1. Raising Awareness – Sharing stories and facts to inform the public.
2. Building Communities – Connecting like-minded people to advocate collectively.

3. Challenging Power – Questioning dominant narratives and pushing for policy reform.
4. Changing Attitudes – Shifting societal perceptions through consistent messaging.

FORMS OF COMMUNICATION IN SOCIAL CHANGE

1. **Mass Communication:** Mass mediums like television, radio, newspapers, and digital media reach large audiences and influence public discourse.

   Example: The **Civil Rights Movement** in the U.S. gained national attention through media coverage of protests like the 1963 March on Washington.

2. **Interpersonal Communication:** The direct, face-to-face dialogue fosters deeper understanding and community building.

   Example: **Grassroots campaigns** use door-to-door conversations to mobilize local communities for social causes (e.g., Pulse Polio program).

3. **Digital Communication:** Social media and online platforms rapidly spread messages globally and foster virtual activism.

   Example: The **#MeToo** movement spread through social media, raising global awareness about sexual harassment and influencing policy changes.

4. **Strategic Communication:** Planned messaging and advocacy campaigns shape perceptions and motivate action.

   Example: **Public health campaigns** like **#StayHome** during the COVID-19 pandemic encouraged social distancing to curb virus spread.

SOME POPULAR EXAMPLES OF COMMUNICATION DRIVING SOCIAL CHANGE

1. **Arab Spring (2010-2012)**

   Communication Tool: Social media (Facebook, Twitter)

   Impact: Mobilized protests against authoritarian regimes across the Middle East, leading to leadership changes in countries like Tunisia and Egypt.

2. **Black Lives Matter (BLM)**

   Communication Tool: Hashtags, viral videos, protests

   Impact: Increased awareness of racial injustice and police violence, leading to police reforms and global discussions on racism.

3. **Greta Thunberg and Climate Action**

   Communication Tool: Public speeches, social media (#FridaysForFuture)

   Impact: Inspired a global youth-led climate movement, pressuring governments to act on climate policies.

4. **LGBTQ+ Rights Movement**

   Communication Tool: Film, literature, pride parades, and social media.

   Impact: Improved visibility and legal changes (e.g., marriage equality laws in multiple countries).

MULTIPLE CHOICE QUESTIONS

1. The word 'communication' is derived from the Latin word 'communis', which means-
   A. to write B. to speak
   C. to share D. None of these

2. When does the communication process end?
   A. when the message is sent
   B. when the recipient receives the message
   C. when the receiver decodes the message
   D. when the receiver has understood the message

3. Communication appearance is dependent on
   A. social interaction B. political activities
   C. economic activities D. All the above

4. "Communication is expressed in symbolic form through special kind of patterning." This definition is given by-
   A. Ordway Tead
   B. Theo Haimann
   C. MT Myers and GE Myers
   D. Alien Louis

5. What can be the medium of communication?
   A. Written B. Spoken
   C. Signs D. All the above

6. Communication instances are omnipresent which means-
   A. it is present at the first level of management
   B. it is present at the middle level of management
   C. it is present at the third level of management
   D. It is present at all the levels of management

7. Owing to evolution of technology, what was the medium introduced for long distance communication?

A. telephone B. letters
C. telegraph D. courier

8. .... is minimum in mass communication and is generally delayed.
A. audiences B. feedback
C. source D. None of these

9. Which one of the following is not included in mass media?
A. print media B. photography
C. films D. television

10. Who was the first one to develop the concept of wireless communication?
A. Samuel Morse
B. Robert Fulton
C. Alexander Graham Bell
D. Eli Whitney

11. Which one of the following is included in the functions of mass communication?
A. stimulation B. counseling
C. persuading D. All the above

12. Who called the study of communication 'rhetoric'?
A. Harold D Laswell B. Shannon Weaver
C. Gerbner D. Aristotle

13. There was a barrier to communication in Shannon Weaver's model of communication, that was-
A. psychological B. personal
C. noise D. language

14. Communication is:
A. unrepeatable B. inevitable
C. irreversible D. All the above

15. Which is an incorrect statement?
A. Guttenberg press made printing and written communication possible.
B. Fluent flow of communication first took place in Greece.
C. Communicating parties share an area of communicative commonality.
D. None of these

16. Sender and receiver should be available in the process of communication through a:
A. medium B. channel
C. middle management D. All the above

17. Verbal communication is:
A. continuous B. discontinuous
C. partial D. untimely

18. Signs or symbols of communication include:
A. lip movement B. nodding of head
C. hand movements D. All the above

19. Ambiguous message may lead to
A. misunderstanding B. miscommunication
C. Both 'A' and 'B' D. None of these

20. Which one is ***not*** the part of traditional media?
A. tamasha B. street theatre
C. nautanki D. mythological movies

21. Match the following:

(a) Language barriers	1. To share
(b) Speech	2. Verbal Communication
(c) Communis	3. Problem in effective communication
(d) Communication is	4. Omnipresent

A. (a)-2, (b)-3, (c)-1, (d)-4
B. (a)-3, (b)-2, (c)-1, (d)-4
C. (a)-4, (b)-3, (c)-1, (d)-2
D. (a)-3, (b)-2, (c)-4, (d)-1

22. Match the following:

(a) Ancestors	1. used body language for communication
(b) Comprehensive communication	2. face to face interaction between two people
(c) Sedition	3. Emergency
(d) Radio was limited by	4. Transmission

A. (a)-2, (b)-3, (c)-1, (d)-4
B. (a)-3, (b)-2, (c)-1, (d)-4
C. (a)-4, (b)-3, (c)-1, (d)-2
D. (a)-1, (b)-2, (c)-3, (d)-4

23. Match the following:

(a) Dialogue	1. Dynamic
(b) Nature of communication	2. Unwritten communication
(c) System design	3. Problems with the structure
(d) Attitudinal barriers	4. Problem with staff

A. (a)-2, (b)-3, (c)-1, (d)-4
B. (a)-2, (b)-1, (c)-3, (d)-4
C. (a)-4, (b)-3, (c)-1, (d)-2
D. (a)-1, (b)-2, (c)-3, (d)-4

24. Match the following:

(a) Accessibility factor	1. Disturbance in the communication process
(b) Guttenberg Press	2. E-mail
(c) Cyrus	3. Written communication
(d) Noise	4. Persia

A. (a)-2, (b)-3, (c)-4, (d)-1
B. (a)-2, (b)-1, (c)-3, (d)-4
C. (a)-4, (b)-1, (c)-2, (d)-3
D. (a)-1, (b)-2, (c)-3, (d)-4

25. Which among the following is ***not*** a true statement for the nature of communication?
(a) Communication is two-way process.
(b) Communication is a perpetual process.
(c) Communication is present only at the top level of management.
A. only (a) B. only (b)
C. only (c) D. All the above

26. The first ombudsman for any newspaper in the world was appointed in
A. Sweden B. Japan
C. Austria D. Great Britain

27. Layer by layer development communication is identified as
A. developmental convergence
B. developmental onion
C. developmental roll
D. developmental scape

28. Which among the following is ***not*** the physical barriers of communication?
A. competing stimulus
B. subjective stress
C. personal expectation
D. ignorance of medium

29. An acronym, 'KISS' which means keep it short and simple is very important in
A. verbal communication
B. non-verbal Communication
C. gestures
D. All the above

30. Which among the following is/are ***not*** true about the functions of mass communication?
(a) Mass-communication performs the function of persuasion.
(b) Mass-Communication helps in promoting culture from one generation to another.
(c) It cannot be used for the purpose of entertainment.
A. Only (a) B. Only (b)
C. Only (c) D. Both (a) and (b)

31. Verbal mode of communication may have barrier in delivering the proper message such as
A. thoughts B. perceptions
C. emotions D. All the above

32. .... is a type of verbal communication.
A. oral communication B. written communication
C. body language D. Both 'A' and 'B'

33. What is/are the major elements of oral communication?
A. pitch B. volume
C. clarity D. All the above

34. Auditory communication is dependent on
A. gestures B. hearing
C. ideas D. None of these

35. Which of the following are forms of traditional media of communication?
(a) Street demonstrations
(b) Yakshagana
(c) Puppetry
(d) Hari Katha
(e) Filmy dances
Choose the correct answer from the options given below:
A. (a), (b), (c) Only B. (b), (c), (d) Only
C. (c), (d), (e) Only D. (a), (d), (e) Only

36. Participatory communication can be ensured, through the use of following:
I. Community Radio II. Participatory Video
III. Street Theatre IV. Public Speeches
A. I, II, III and IV are correct.
B. I, II and III are correct.
C. I, II and IV are correct.
D. I and II are correct.

37. Which of the following is ***not*** a form of traditional media?
A. Radio advertising B. Print advertising
C. Door to door sales D. E-mail marketing

38. Orthoepy in communication means
A. discussion B. conversation
C. pronunciation D. expression

39. The major strategy of 'Participatory Communication' is:
A. Government Scheme
B. Top-down approach
C. Information dissemination
D. Dialogue

40. A word or phrase that is used to express a particular situation is termed as
A. discussion B. monologue
C. locution D. dictation

41. Idiolect is a type of
A. sign language

B. oral communication
C. written communication
D. None of these

42. Oral communication allows instantaneous exchange of
A. opinions B. attitudes
C. feelings D. All the above

43. In oral communication speaker must be confident enough for the
A. contents B. audience
C. adaptation D. All the above

44. Written communication include:
A. printed and hand written matter
B. speech
C. monologue
D. signs and symbols

45. The .... theory suggests that the intended message is directly received and wholly accepted by the receiver.
A. Reception theory
B. Two-step flow
C. The Hypodermic needle
D. All the above

46. Which of the following theories stress that mass media in a society is controlled by the state power?
A. Normative B. Authoritarian
C. Libertarian D. Social Responsibility

47. According to Denis McQuail, media is significant because
A. they are a power source
B. they are ticket to fame
C. they create benchmarks
D. All the above

48. Vocabulary, grammar, style and format are the major elements of
A. oral B. written
C. verbal D. None of these

49. Which of the following theories focuses on freedom of speech and expression?
A. Libertarian Theory
B. Democratic Participant Theory
C. Development Media Theory
D. None of these

50. .... acts in a dual manner between government and people.
A. executives B. judiciary
C. media D. All the above

51. Media prioritizes stories and issues that are important enough to receive public attention and which are not as it acts as a ....__.
A. watchdog B. gatekeeper
C. entertainers D. All the above

52. Which one of the following is the source of revenue for media?
A. selling ad spaces B. campaigning
C. Both A and B D. None of these

53. In the question given below are two statements labeled as Assertion (A) and Reason (R). In the context of the two statements which one of the following is correct?

Assertion (A): Prior consent is necessary from participants in a research project to film, tape or record in any form.

Reason (R): Research is always confidential and secretive and hence, any revelation will harm the objective of research.

A. Both A and R are true
B. Both A and R are true, but R is not the correct explanation of A
C. A is true, but R is false
D. A is false, but R is true

54. Identify the correct sequence of mass media as per the order of their introduction to society.
A. print media, traditional media, electronic media, wireless communication
B. wireless communication, electronic media, print media, traditional media
C. traditional media, wireless communication, electronic media, print media
D. traditional media, print media, electronic media, wireless communication

55. What can be the format for internal communication in the organization?
A. memo writing B. report writing
C. bulletins D. All the above

56. A set of rules or principles or laws can be termed as
A. correspondence B. black and white
C. codification D. All the above

57. Non-verbal communication include:
A. tone of voice B. body language
C. posture D. All the above

58. According to experts, almost **80%** communication is
A. verbal B. non-verbal
C. written D. None of these

59. Media serves in the society with the purpose of
A. education B. awareness
C. entertainment D. All the above

60. Vocalics can be termed as
A. body language B. tone
C. para language D. All the above

61. Feelings of a communication are labeled as
A. relational information
B. psychological information
C. personal information
D. social information

62. The verbal code for communication is:
A. visual cue B. picture
C. color D. language

63. Use of language in mediated communication imposes a grid on:
A. artificiality B. textuality
C. reality D. conformity

64. Which of the following is *not* included in vocalics?
A. pronunciation B. proxemics
C. articulation D. enunciation

65. S Sadanand is well known for ....
A. Free Press of India
B. Freedom of Speech and Expression
C. Right to Education
D. None of these

66. Emblems are the type of
A. illustrators B. touch
C. body language D. eye language

67. Messages conveyed through eyes by blinks, eye movement etc. is termed as
A. chronemics B. haptics
C. oculesics D. None of these

68. Haptics came from .... word.
A. Latin B. Greek
C. French D. Spanish

69. What does haptikos mean?
A. a sense of touch B. able to communicate
C. able to understand D. None of these

70. Why does media act as a mirror to the society?
A. it covers political agendas
B. it creates awareness
C. it reflects the incidents in the society
D. all of these

71. Who used the word proxemics for 'space'?
A. Edward T. Hall B. Erving Goffman
C. Ray Birdwhistell D. Clyde Kluckhohn

72. Which is the space zone given by Edward T Hall for people in proxemics?
A. intimate B. personal
C. public D. All the above

73. Which is not included in the 7Cs of effective communication?
A. Concreteness B. Courtesy
C. Chronemics D. Correctness

74. Parroting is the type of
A. speech B. feedback
C. conversation D. discussion

75. What is the basis for intra-personal communication?
A. expectation B. perception
C. self-concept D. None of these

76. .... communication is practiced in the participatory approach.
A. Intra personal B. Non-verbal
C. Inter-personal D. None of these

77. Day dreaming is a type of .... communication.
A. inter-personal B. intra-personal
C. group D. mass

78. Identify the order of distance zones in relation to body language.
A. Personal zone, Intimate zone, Public zone, Social zone
B. Social zone, Personal zone, Public zone, Intimate zone
C. Intimate zone, Personal zone, Social zone, Public zone
D. Public zone, Personal zone, Intimate zone, Social zone

79. Usually, a large number of people are involved in message production in
A. intrapersonal communication
B. interpersonal communication
C. group communication
D. mass communication

80. Direct face to face communication between the sender and the receiver of a message can be termed as ....communication.
A. organizational B. cross-culture
C. inter-personal D. intra-personal

81. What does dyadic communication relate to?
A. group discussion B. lecture in university
C. two friends talking D. All the above

82. The most popular form of primitive communication were the cave paintings.
A. True B. False

83. Match the following:

(a)	Advertisements	1.	Objectification of women
(b)	Social Onus	2.	Marathi
(c)	Bombay Darpan	3.	DAVP
(d)	Publicity	4.	Moral responsibility

A. (a)-1, (b)-4, (c)-2, (d)-3
B. (a)-4, (b)-2, (c)-3, (d)-1
C. (a)-2, (b)-1, (c)-3, (d)-4
D. (a)-4, (b)-1, (c)-3, (d)-2

84. The ability of the mass-media to cover the vast boundaries of space is termed as global village by
A. Marshal Mc Luhan B. Harold Innis
C. Nell Postman D. None of these

85. .... was the father of Green Revolution in India.
A. M.S Swaminathan B. Dr. Norman Borlaug
C. Verghese Kurien D. None of these

86. Through the correlation function, mass media help shape:
A. traditions B. environment
C. public opinion D. customs

87. Gerbner identifies a true information pointed beyond the normal elements of process. What is the point?
A. Destination B. Event
C. Message D. Context

88. Communication based on rumors and takes the form of informal communication is termed as .... communication.
A. diagonal B. grapevine
C. horizontal D. upward

89. 'Gobbledygook' is a term related to
A. channel B. language
C. culture D. None of these

90. What is included in the processing of data?
A. semantic B. syntactic
C. pragmatic D. All the above

91. Match the following:

(a)	Sounds	1.	facial expressions
(b)	Writing of a letter	2.	formal communication
(c)	Mannerisms	3.	speech rate
(d)	Office meetings	4.	written communication

A. (a)-2, (b)-3, (c)-1, (d)-4
B. (a)-3, (b)-4, (c)-1, (d)-2
C. (a)-4, (b)-3, (c)-1, (d)-2
D. (a)-3, (b)-2, (c)-4, (d)-1

92. Match the following:

(a)	Ratan Tata	1.	We the people
(b)	Arun Shourie	2.	Editor of Indian Express
(c)	Barkha Dutt	3.	Grapevine
(d)	Keith Davis	4.	Industrialist

A. (a)-2, (b)-3, (c)-1, (d)-4
B. (a)-3, (b)-2, (c)-1, (d)-4
C. (a)-4, (b)-3, (c)-1, (d)-2
D. (a)-4, (b)-2, (c)-1, (d)-3

93. Match the following:

(a)	Pictures	1.	high order skills
(b)	High skills	2.	visual communication
(c)	Hums	3.	speech art
(d)	Long distances	4.	public telephone networks

A. (a)-2, (b)-3, (c)-1, (d)-4
B. (a)-3, (b)-2, (c)-1, (d)-4
C. (a)-2, (b)-1, (c)-3, (d)-4
D. (a)-4, (b)-2, (c)-1, (d)-3

94. In the questions given below are two statements labeled as Assertion (A) and Reason (R). In the context of two which one of the following is correct?
Assertion (A): Media serves as a watchdog.
Reason (R): It protects the Society.
A. Both A and R are true, R is the correct explanation of A
B. Both A and R are true, R is not the correct explanation of A
C. A is true, R is false
D. A is false, R is true

95. **Assertion (A):** Misrepresentation of women is the disastrous attributes of media.
Reason (R): Media has turned completely unethical in modern times.
A. Both A and R are true, R is the correct explanation of A
B. Both A and R are true, R is not the correct explanation of A
C. A is true, R is false
D. A is false, R is true

96. **Assertion (A):** Media is expected to present accurate information in the society.
Reason (R): It is a moral obligation upon the media.
A. Both A and R are true, R is the correct explanation of A
B. Both A and R are true, R is not the correct explanation of A
C. A is true, R is false
D. A is false, R is true

97. The term mass communication must imply at least five things i.e. large audience, form of message reproduction, undifferentiated audience composition, rapid distribution and delivery and low unit costs to customers was suggested by ....

A. Sydney Head B. Barker
C. Mehta D. Dominick

98. Match the following:

A. Teleconferencing	1. First para of news
B. Angle	2. A website where you can add, remove or edit the content.
C. Lead	3. group of persons
D. Wikipedia	4. focus of the story

A. (a)-3, (b)-4, (c)-1, (d)-2
B. (a)-3, (b)-2, (c)-1, (d)-4
C. (a)-2, (b)-1, (c)-3, (d)-4
D. (a)-4, (b)-2, (c)-1, (d)-3

99. In the questions below there are two statements labeled as Assertion (A) and Reason (R). Which one of the following is correct?

Assertion (A): Downward communication flows from superior to downward.

Reason (R): Downward communication helps in resolving conflicts.

A. Both A and R are true, R is the correct explanation of A
B. Both A and R are true, R is not the correct explanation of A
C. A is true, R is false
D. A is false, R is true

100. In the questions below there are two statements labeled as Assertion (A) and Reason (R). Which one of the following is correct?

Assertion (A): Two-way communication is not possible in mass-media.

Reason (R): The message is conveyed, but the feedback is not immediate.

A. Both A and R are true, R is the correct explanation of A
B. Both A and R are true, R is not the correct explanation of A
C. A is true, R is false
D. A is false, R is true

101. In the questions below there are two statements labeled as Assertion (A) and Reason (R). Which one of the following is correct?

Assertion (A): Non-verbal communication is related to expression of feelings, emotions in a wordless manner.

Reason (R): Body language is very much helpful in creating an understanding of any matter or feelings.

A. Both A and R are true, R is the correct explanation of A
B. Both A and R are true, R is not the correct explanation of A
C. A is true, R is false
D. A is false, R is true

102. Which among the following is ***not*** true about the types of oral communication?

(a) Auditory communication is dependent on hearing.
(b) Idiolect is a language of an individual at a particular period in life.
(c) Monologue is a long utterance by many people simultaneously.

A. only (a) B. only (b)
C. only (c) D. None of these

103. Which among the following is ***not*** a true statement about an oral communication?

(a) Oral communication provides immediate feedback.
(b) Oral communication is more authentic than written communication.
(c) Oral communication is not frequently used in legal records.

A. both (a) and (b) B. both (a) and (c)
C. both (b) and (c) D. None of these

104. Which of the following best defines culture?

A. Biological traits inherited from parents
B. The total way of life of a group of people, including their customs, beliefs, and artifacts
C. Political systems of a nation
D. Individual preferences

105. Which of the following is ***not*** true about mass-media?

(a) Media do not create benchmarks.
(b) They are a ticket to fame.
(c) They act as source.

A. Only (a) B. Only (b)
C. Both (a) and (b) D. Both (b) and (c)

106. When was the first printing press established?

A. 1772 B. 1779
C. 1440 D. 1677

107. Culture is primarily:

A. Learned B. Instinctive
C. Genetic D. Immutable

108. Who is considered as the Father of Indian Press?
A. Warren Hastings B. James Augustus Hicky
C. James Buckingham D. None of these

109. Identify the correct sequences of phase of communication process.
A. Level of acceptance, understanding, reception, transmission of cognitive data
B. Understanding, level of acceptance, transmission of cognitive data, reception
C. Reception, understanding, level of acceptance, transmission of cognitive data
D. Transmission of cognitive data, reception, understanding, level of acceptance

110. The first book that was printed after the development of printing press was of .... genre.
A. Religious B. Humanist
C. Feminist D. None of these

111. "The term media effects not only refer to the consequences or impacts of media use on individuals, society and culture; it effects are rather well-defined area of scholarly inquiry that examines the impact of media". This definition was given by ....
A. Mc Quail B. Black et al
C. Jay Blumler D. George Gerbner

112. Which of the following is NOT a characteristic of culture?
A. Culture is shared
B. Culture is static
C. Culture is dynamic
D. Culture influences behavior

113. In communication, critical readings are
A. irrational B. probabilistic
C. contradictory D. cognitive

114. Semantic Noise is concerned with the understandability of
A. the medium B. the transmission
C. the encoder D. the message

115. Media effect can be assessed at .... level.
A. Societal group B. Family
C. Community group D. All the above

116. Material culture includes:
A. Beliefs and values
B. Languages and customs
C. Physical objects and technology
D. Social institutions

117. Media acts as a .... mirror to the society.
A. selective B. discriminating
C. limited D. None of these

118. .... carried out the research on the limited effects of media.
A. Elihu Katz B. Paul Lazarsfeld
C. Marie Jahoda D. None of these

119. Walter Lippmann establishes the principal connection between world, ... and events in the public mind.
A. news B. visuals
C. images D. None of these

120. Dominant ideology describes the set of cultural beliefs and practices that help to maintain .... interests.
A. social B. economic
C. political D. All the above

121. Non-material culture includes:
A. Art and architecture
B. Tools and technology
C. Beliefs, values, and traditions
D. Clothing and food

122. Which among the following is ***not*** true about Spiral of Silence Theory?
(a) There is a double opinion climate.
(b) There is an absence of silent majority.
(c) There is a snob-effect.
A. Only (a) B. Only (b)
C. Only (c) D. all of these

123. Where have Media studies taken inspiration from?
A. communication studies
B. social sciences
C. humanities
D. Both 'B' and 'C'

124. Which concept refers to judging other cultures based on one's own cultural standards?
A. Cultural relativism B. Ethnocentrism
C. Cultural diffusion D. Acculturation

125. The idea that cultures should be understood on their own terms is known as:
A. Ethnocentrism B. Cultural relativism
C. Cultural assimilation D. Cultural hegemony

126. The process of adopting the cultural traits of another group is called:
A. Enculturation B. Socialization
C. Acculturation D. Assimilation

127. Which of the following is an example of cultural transmission?
A. Genetic inheritance
B. Learning a language from one's parents

C. Developing personal habits
D. Instinctive behavior

128. Culture influences communication by:
A. Determining universal communication styles
B. Shaping norms and expectations for communication
C. Eliminating misunderstandings
D. Making all communication the same across groups

129. Mass media's role in culture is primarily:
A. To preserve culture unchanged
B. To solely reflect pre-existing culture
C. To both reflect and shape culture
D. To have no influence on culture

130. How does mass media reflect culture?
A. By ignoring cultural values
B. By showcasing current trends, values, and beliefs
C. By creating entirely new cultures
D. By focusing only on historical events

131. How does mass media shape culture?
A. By having no influence on cultural change
B. By promoting new ideas, behaviors, and lifestyles
C. By only reinforcing traditional values
D. By limiting cultural expression

132. Which of the following is a way mass media transmits culture?
A. By restricting access to information
B. Through storytelling and representation
C. By avoiding diverse perspectives
D. By only focusing on elite culture

133. What is a potential negative impact of mass media on culture?
A. Cultural preservation
B. Cultural exchange
C. Cultural homogenization
D. Cultural celebration

134. Cultural homogenization refers to:
A. The increasing similarity of cultures due to globalization and media influence
B. The celebration of cultural diversity
C. The preservation of unique cultural traditions
D. The resistance to cultural change

135. Mass media can contribute to cultural change by:
A. Reinforcing existing power structures
B. Challenging social norms and values
C. Ignoring social issues
D. Promoting cultural isolation

136. The global spread of American movies and music is an example of:
A. Cultural preservation
B. Cultural relativism
C. Cultural imperialism
D. Cultural exchange

137. Cultural imperialism refers to:
A. The equal exchange of cultural ideas between nations
B. The dominance of one culture over others through media and other forms
C. The preservation of indigenous cultures
D. The celebration of multiculturalism

138. Mass media can promote cultural understanding by:
A. Focusing only on differences between cultures
B. Presenting diverse cultural perspectives
C. Ignoring cultural traditions
D. Reinforcing stereotypes

139. The concept of stereotypes was advocated in mass media by
A. Michael Foucault B. Walter Lippman
C. William Raymonds D. Robert Herman

140. Cultural context in communication refers to:
A. The physical setting of communication
B. The shared understandings, values, and beliefs that influence communication
C. The technology used for communication
D. The clarity of language used

141. High-context cultures are characterized by:
A. Explicit communication and directness
B. Implicit communication and reliance on non-verbal cues
C. Emphasis on individual expression
D. Low tolerance for ambiguity

142. Which of the following is an example of a high-context culture?
A. The United States B. Germany
C. Japan D. Canada

143. Low-context cultures are characterized by:
A. Emphasis on non-verbal communication
B. Direct and explicit communication
C. Strong group orientation
D. Reliance on shared history

144. Which of the following is an example of a low-context culture?
A. China B. Mexico
C. France D. The United Kingdom

145. In communication, cultural noise refers to:
A. Loud sounds that disrupt communication

B. Cultural differences that interfere with effective communication
C. The use of slang and jargon
D. Technical difficulties in media

146. Cultural competence is:
A. The ability to speak multiple languages
B. The ability to understand and effectively communicate across cultures
C. The knowledge of world history
D. The ability to conform to any cultural norm

147. Which of the following is a key component of intercultural communication competence?
A. Ethnocentrism B. Stereotyping
C. Empathy D. Cultural ignorance

148. Cultural values influence communication by:
A. Having no impact on communication styles
B. Shaping what is considered appropriate and inappropriate communication
C. Making all cultures communicate the same way
D. Eliminating misunderstandings

149. Non-verbal communication:
A. Is the same across all cultures
B. Varies significantly across cultures
C. Is less important than verbal communication
D. Does not convey meaning

150. Mass media acts as a vehicle of cultural transmission by:
A. Limiting cultural exchange
B. Passing on cultural values, beliefs, and behaviors from one generation to the next
C. Creating entirely new cultures
D. Ignoring cultural heritage

151. Storytelling in media is a powerful tool for:
A. Promoting cultural uniformity
B. Transmitting cultural narratives and values
C. Avoiding cultural reflection
D. Restricting cultural expression

152. Which of the following is an example of media transmitting cultural traditions?
A. News reports on global events
B. Documentaries about cultural practices
C. Advertisements for consumer products
D. Science fiction movies

153. Media can contribute to the preservation of cultural heritage by:
A. Focusing only on modern trends
B. Documenting and showcasing traditional arts, music, and dance
C. Ignoring historical events
D. Promoting cultural amnesia

154. How can media influence cultural identity?
A. By having no impact on how people see themselves
B. By reinforcing or challenging cultural norms and values
C. By creating a single, global identity
D. By promoting cultural isolation

155. Media can transmit cultural values through:
A. The portrayal of role models and social expectations
B. Avoiding any value judgments
C. Focusing only on negative cultural aspects
D. Ignoring cultural diversity

156. The way media portrays family structures is an example of:
A. Cultural innovation B. Cultural transmission
C. Cultural relativism D. Cultural imperialism

157. Media can shape cultural attitudes towards:
A. Fashion trends B. Gender roles
C. Political ideologies D. All the above

158. The impact of media on cultural transmission is:
A. Always positive
B. Always negative
C. Complex and can be both positive and negative
D. Non-existent

159. Media literacy is important for:
A. Blindly accepting all media messages
B. Critically analyzing and understanding how media shapes culture
C. Avoiding media consumption entirely
D. Learning how to produce media content

160. Representation in media refers to:
A. The absence of certain groups in media
B. The way social groups are portrayed in media
C. The diversity of media ownership
D. The use of accurate historical accounts

161. Stereotyping in media involves:
A. Presenting complex and nuanced portrayals of individuals
B. Oversimplified and generalized portrayals of social groups
C. Celebrating diversity
D. Promoting cultural understanding

162. Which of the following is a common stereotype in media?
A. The portrayal of older adults as wise and active
B. The portrayal of women primarily as emotional
C. The portrayal of different ethnic groups in diverse roles
D. The portrayal of people with disabilities as capable

163. Negative stereotypes in media can lead to:
A. Increased empathy and understanding
B. Social prejudice and discrimination
C. Cultural harmony
D. Positive self-esteem

164. Underrepresentation in media means:
A. Certain groups are portrayed too frequently
B. Certain groups are not seen or heard enough in media
C. Media accurately reflects the diversity of society
D. All groups have equal representation

165. The lack of diverse representation in media can result in:
A. A more inclusive society
B. A limited understanding of different cultures and experiences
C. Increased cultural sensitivity
D. Greater empathy

166. Positive representation in media can:
A. Reinforce stereotypes
B. Challenge stereotypes and promote inclusion
C. Have no impact on social attitudes
D. Lead to cultural homogenization

167. Media literacy helps individuals to:
A. Create their own stereotypes
B. Critically analyze media representations and identify stereotypes
C. Avoid all media consumption
D. Accept all media portrayals as accurate

168. What is the potential impact of stereotyping on marginalized groups?
A. Enhanced self-esteem
B. Increased social opportunities
C. Internalized oppression and limited life chances
D. Greater cultural pride

169. The responsibility for addressing issues of representation and stereotyping lies with:
A. Media producers B. Consumers
C. Educators D. All the above

170. Social change refers to:
A. Individual changes in behavior
B. Transformations in social structures, institutions, and cultural practices over time
C. Changes in the natural environment
D. Technological advancements

171. Which of the following is NOT a characteristic of social change?
A. Social change is constant
B. Social change is always progressive
C. Social change is often contested
D. Social change can be intentional or unintentional

172. Which of the following can be a source of social change?
A. Technological innovation
B. Social movements
C. Economic factors
D. All the above

173. Social change can affect:
A. Family structures B. Political systems
C. Cultural values D. All the above

174. The pace of social change is:
A. Always slow and gradual
B. Always rapid and revolutionary
C. Variable and can be slow or rapid
D. Unpredictable

175. Which of the following is an example of social change?
A. The changing role of women in society
B. The development of personal habits
C. The cycle of seasons
D. The growth of an individual

176. Social change is often influenced by:
A. Isolation from other societies
B. Interaction between different cultures
C. A static economy
D. The absence of new ideas

177. Resistance to social change can arise from:
A. A desire to maintain traditional values
B. Fear of the unknown
C. Vested interests
D. All the above

178. Social change can be measured by:
A. Changes in laws and policies
B. Shifts in public opinion
C. Changes in social behavior
D. All the above

179. The study of social change is important for:
A. Understanding the past
B. Analyzing the present
C. Anticipating the future
D. All the above

180. Media can act as a catalyst for social change by:
A. Reinforcing the status quo
B. Raising awareness about social issues
C. Ignoring marginalized groups
D. Promoting apathy

181. Which of the following is NOT a characteristic of social change?
A. It can happen rapidly or slowly.
B. It is always planned and intentional.
C. It can be influenced by various factors.
D. It involves changes in social relationships

182. Which of these factors can contribute to social change?
A. Geographic stability
B. Technological innovations
C. Social isolation
D. Cultural stagnation

183. Social change is best described as a:
A. Static process
B. Dynamic process
C. Cyclical process
D. Linear process always leading to progress

184. Which of the following is an example of social change?
A. The daily routine of going to work.
B. The increasing acceptance of same-sex marriage.
C. The unchanging traditions of a small village.
D. The biological process of aging.

185. Social change can occur at which of the following levels?
A. Micro-level (individual interactions)
B. Meso-level (organizations and communities)
C. Macro-level (society as a whole)
D. All the above

186. Which statement best describes the pace of social change?
A. It is always gradual.
B. It is always revolutionary.
C. It can vary from gradual to revolutionary.
D. It is predictable and uniform across societies.

187. Which of the following is a potential consequence of rapid social change?
A. Increased social stability.
B. Social disruption and instability.
C. Decreased cultural diversity.
D. Enhanced social cohesion.

188. Social change is influenced primarily by:
A. Biological factors alone.
B. Environmental factors alone.
C. A complex interplay of cultural, economic, political, and technological factors.
D. Supernatural forces.

189. A "catalyst" for social change means that media:
A. Prevents social change from occurring.
B. Slows down the process of social change.
C. Accelerates or instigates social change.
D. Has no effect on social change.

190. Which of the following is a way media can challenge existing power structures?
A. By only representing the views of the elite.
B. By providing a platform for dissenting voices.
C. By censoring critical perspectives.
D. By avoiding controversial topics.

191. Media plays a role in social movements by:
A. Suppressing mobilization efforts.
B. Facilitating communication among organizations and activists.
C. Discouraging public participation.
D. Remaining neutral on social issues.

192. What is "agenda-setting" theory, and how does it relate to social change?
A. A theory that media has no influence on what people think is important.
B. A theory that media can influence the public's perception of the importance of certain issues, thus potentially driving social change.
C. A theory that only governments set the agenda for social change.
D. A theory about advertising techniques.

193. How can media contribute to changing attitudes and behaviors?
A. By only showing traditional roles and behaviors.
B. By presenting diverse perspectives and challenging stereotypes.
C. By promoting apathy and indifference.
D. By avoiding discussions of sensitive topics.

194. Which of the following is a potential drawback of media's role in social change?
A. Enhancing global awareness.
B. Promoting critical thinking.
C. The spread of misinformation and propaganda.
D. Empowering marginalized communities.

195. "Framing" in media refers to:
A. The technical aspects of media production.
B. The way media presents a story, which can influence how it is perceived.

C. The legal regulations governing media content.
D. The physical structure of a newspaper.

196. Media can empower marginalized groups by:
A. Giving them a voice and platform to share their experiences.
B. Ignoring their concerns and issues.
C. Perpetuating stereotypes about them.
D. Silencing their dissent.

197. The rise of the internet and social media has:
A. Reduced the potential for social change.
B. Increased the speed and reach of communication related to social change.
C. Made it easier to control information flow.
D. Decreased citizen participation in social movements.

198. The Civil Rights Movement in the United States primarily fought for:
A. Environmental protection.
B. Racial equality.
C. Women's suffrage.
D. Economic reform.

199. The Women's Suffrage Movement aimed to achieve:
A. Equal pay for women.
B. The right for women to vote.
C. Improved working conditions for women.
D. All the above.

200. The anti-apartheid movement in South Africa utilized media to:
A. Promote segregation.
B. Raise international awareness of the injustices of apartheid.
C. Suppress dissent within South Africa.
D. Support the apartheid regime.

201. How did music play a role in the anti-apartheid movement?
A. It had no role.
B. It became a form of protest and resistance.
C. It supported the government's policies.
D. It distracted people from the political issues.

202. What role do documentaries play in the environmental movement?
A. They have no role.
B. They can educate the public about environmental issues and inspire action.
C. They often spread misinformation.
D. They are only for scientific audiences.

203. The LGBTQ+ rights movement has used media to:
A. Promote discrimination.
B. Increase visibility and challenge stereotypes.
C. Maintain social exclusion.
D. Reinforce prejudices.

204. "Digital activism" refers to:
A. Activism that takes place only in virtual reality.
B. The use of digital technologies for social and political change.
C. The decline of traditional forms of activism.
D. Government surveillance of online activity.

205. Which of the following is an example of digital activism?
A. Organizing protests through social media.
B. Signing online petitions.
C. Raising funds for a cause through crowdfunding platforms.
D. All the above

206. Social media platforms can be used to:
A. Spread awareness about human rights abuses.
B. Coordinate relief efforts during disasters.
C. Monitor and censor activists.
D. Both A and B

207. What is "hashtag activism"?
A. Activism that involves defacing public property.
B. Using hashtags on social media to raise awareness about an issue.
C. A form of physical protest.
D. Activism that only occurs on Twitter.

208. "Slacktivism" refers to:
A. Effective online activism that leads to significant change.
B. Activism that is lazy or ineffective, often involving only minimal online participation.
C. Activism that focuses on environmental issues.
D. Activism that is violent and disruptive.

209. How can digital activism promote civic engagement?
A. By discouraging offline participation.
B. By making it easier for people to get involved in social and political issues.
C. By only appealing to young people.
D. By limiting access to information.

210. What is "cyber-disobedience"?
A. Obeying all laws online.
B. Using technology to engage in acts of civil disobedience.
C. Government control of the internet.
D. Following online etiquette.

211. Digital activism has been crucial for movements related to:

A. Political reform
B. Human rights
C. Environmental protection
D. All the above

212. While media can be a catalyst for positive change, it can also:
A. Always promote equality.
B. Reinforce existing inequalities.
C. Have no impact on social structures.
D. Only be used for good.

213. How can media ownership influence social change?
A. It has no influence.
B. Owners can control the narratives presented and limit diverse perspectives.
C. It always promotes progressive causes.
D. It guarantees unbiased reporting.

214. The concept of "hegemony" in media studies refers to:
A. The equal distribution of power in media.
B. The dominance of certain ideas and values, often those of the ruling class.
C. The complete absence of bias in reporting.
D. The diversity of voices in media.

215. Media representations can:
A. Always reflect reality accurately.
B. Shape our understanding of social issues and groups.
C. Have no impact on our beliefs.
D. Only influence people who are easily manipulated.

216. Which of the following is an example of stereotyping?
A. Showing different personalities
B. Portraying all teenagers as rebellious
C. A documentary on education
D. Showing historical accuracy

217. Which group is commonly stereotyped in action movies as villains?
A. European characters
B. Middle Eastern characters
C. Australian characters
D. Scandinavian characters

218. What is a common stereotype about women in advertisements?
A. They are mainly shown as homemakers or models
B. They are business executives
C. They are politicians
D. They are scientists

219. How are men often stereotypically portrayed in media?
A. Emotional and caring
B. Strong and emotionally detached
C. Weak and dependent
D. Absent from stories

220. Which of the following is a positive stereotype?
A. Asians are good at math
B. Teenagers are violent
C. Women are bad drivers
D. Elderly are forgetful

221. What is a major consequence of media stereotyping?
A. Better ratings
B. Better storylines
C. Reinforcement of societal prejudices
D. Higher production value

222. Underrepresentation in media can lead to:
A. Marginalization of certain groups
B. Diversity
C. Overexposure
D. Popularity

223. A stereotypical portrayal of elderly people in media often shows them as:
A. Adventurous
B. Frail and forgetful
C. Athletic
D. Trendy

224. What is the potential danger of "echo chambers" in online media?
A. They promote diverse viewpoints.
B. They can reinforce existing biases and limit exposure to different perspectives.
C. They have no impact on political polarization.
D. They encourage critical thinking.

225. "Fake news" can hinder social change by:
A. Promoting accurate information.
B. Undermining trust in credible sources and spreading misinformation.
C. Encouraging critical media literacy.
D. Fostering healthy debate.

226. How can media literacy help individuals navigate media's influence on social change?
A. By encouraging passive consumption of media.
B. By teaching people to critically analyze and evaluate media messages.
C. By promoting cynicism and distrust of all media.
D. By suggesting that media has no impact on society.

227. Ethical considerations in media are crucial for social change because:
A. Ethics are irrelevant to media's impact.
B. Unethical practices can distort information and manipulate public opinion.
C. Only profits matter.
D. There are no consequences to biased reporting.

228. Ultimately, the relationship between media and social change is:
A. Simple and straightforward.
B. Complex and multifaceted, with both positive and negative potential.
C. Entirely controlled by media organizations.
D. Unimportant for understanding social dynamics.

229. Which of these is an example of racial stereotyping in films?
A. Black characters often playing criminals
B. Balanced casting
C. Historical documentaries
D. Positive role models

230. What is meant by gender representation?
A. Number of actors
B. How genders are shown or portrayed in media
C. Role length
D. Audience type

231. One way media can reduce stereotyping is by:
A. Adding more ads
B. Avoiding real stories
C. Showing diverse characters in complex roles
D. Using animation only

232. Which group is often stereotyped as terrorists in Hollywood films?
A. Americans B. Europeans
C. Canadians D. Arabs

233. Which of the following statements is NOT true about folk media?
A. Folk media are indigenous equivalents of mass media
B. Folk media include plays, dances and songs
C. Folk media are used purely for entertainment
D. Folk media are used during fairs and festivals

234. Which film genre often reinforces gender roles?
A. Horror B. Romantic comedies
C. Documentaries D. Action

235. LGBTQ+ individuals in older films were often portrayed as:
A. Leaders
B. Heroes
C. Comic relief or villains
D. Teachers

236. Which is a harmful result of repeated stereotypes in media?
A. Viewers accept them as normal or true
B. Diverse opinions
C. Breaking biases
D. Audience growth

237. Which of the following is NOT a stereotype?
A. Women are shopaholics
B. Showcasing multiple perspectives in a character
C. Men hate housework
D. Teenagers are lazy

238. What does "tokenism" mean in media?
A. Paying for roles
B. Typecasting
C. Having multiple roles
D. Including one minority character to appear diverse

239. What is a stereotype about people with disabilities in media?
A. They are always inspirational or pitiful
B. They are always leaders
C. They are invisible
D. They are powerful

240. When media shows only one type of representation of a group, it is called:
A. Diversity B. Narrowcasting
C. Globalization D. Multiplexing

241. Which media format is known for reinforcing stereotypes?
A. Advertisements B. News reports
C. Biographies D. Documentaries

242. A stereotypical portrayal of rural people is:
A. Rich and modern
B. Uneducated and simple-minded
C. Smart and elite
D. Creative and artistic

243. How can documentaries challenge stereotypes?
A. By repeating generalizations
B. Using only famous people
C. By presenting real stories and experiences
D. Avoiding facts

244. Children's cartoons have been criticized for:
A. Gender and racial stereotyping
B. Educational value
C. Lack of color
D. Too much dialogue

245. What role does media literacy play in understanding stereotypes?
A. Makes media fun
B. Avoids technology

C. Helps audiences critically analyze portrayals
D. Teaches coding

246. Which industry plays a large role in shaping stereotypes?
A. Agriculture B. Film and television
C. Automobile D. Construction

247. Which of the following helps in promoting inclusive representation?
A. Repeating stereotypes
B. Using only white actors
C. Casting actors from diverse backgrounds
D. Avoiding social issues

248. A common stereotype in crime shows is:
A. Minorities are often shown as suspects
B. Justice is always served
C. Police are always right
D. All characters are neutral

249. Examples of traditional educational folk media in India are
(a) Jatra (b) Burra Katha
(c) Bhangra (d) Garba
(e) Bidesia
A. (a), (b) and (c) only
B. (b), (c) and (d) only
C. (c), (d) and (e) only
D. (a), (b) and (e) only

250. Given below are two statements:
Statement I: The power of the 'Press' to bring about social, political or economic development is limited.
Statement II: In capitalist societies, the press is primarily like any other business or industry.
In the light of the above statements, choose the most appropriate answer from the options given below:
A. Both Statement I and Statement II are correct.
B. Both Statement I and Statement II are incorrect.
C. Statement I is correct but Statement II is incorrect
D. Statement I is incorrect but Statement II is correct

251. Indian Broadcasting services is called as:
A. Big FM B. Club FM
C. Vividh Bharti D. AIR

252. Yakshagana is primarily popular in which Indian state?
A. Tamil Nadu B. Karnataka
C. Kerala D. Madhya Pradesh

253. 'Bhand Pather' is the traditional folk theatre of which state?
A. Assam B. Uttarakhand
C. Jammu and Kashmir D. Gujarat

254. Jatra is a traditional theatre form of:
A. West Bengal B. Andhra Pradesh
C. Maharashtra D. Bihar

255. Which of the following is a traditional theatre form of Haryana?
A. Swang B. Tamasha
C. Dashavatar D. Nautanki

256. What is the name of the famous folk drama of Bhils?
A. Swang B. Gavari
C. Rammat D. Tamasha

257. 'Madhubani' painting is related to which state?
A. Uttar Pradesh B. Bihar
C. Kerala D. Tamil Nadu

258. Which Indian state is known for its unique 'Warli' paintings?
A. Maharashtra B. Madhya Pradesh
C. Odisha D. Rajasthan

259. 'Pulikkali' is a recreational folk-art form from which of the following states of India?
A. Kerala B. Sikkim
C. Karnataka D. Punjab

260. Which among the following media group initiated "Save our Tigers" campaign?
A. NDTV B. IndiaTV
C. Times Now D. IBN 7

261. Which among the following is true about Narmada Bachao Andolan?
(a) Medha Patkar was the active reformer of the movement.
(b) It was started in 1985.
(c) It was against the large dams built across the Narmada River.
A. Only (a) B. Only (b)
C. Only (c) D. All the above

262. Which of the following best describes the term "Patachitras" in the context of art and culture in India?
A. Folk music B. Folk dance
C. Folk paintings D. Folk tradition

263. Which of the following pairs is INCORRECT with reference to paintings in India?

A. Phad Paintings – Rajasthan
B. Saura Paintings – Odisha
C. Bagh Paintings – Madhya Pradesh
D. Guler Paintings – Karnataka

264. The composition that belongs to Mewar style of painting is –
A. Bani-thani B. Geet Govind
C. Jyotish Ratnakar D. Vilaval Ragini

265. Tamasha form of folk theatre belongs to which place?
A. Maharashtra B. Kolkata
C. Delhi D. Ahmedabad

266. Jatra is folk theatre of
A. Bengal B. Odisha
C. Chennai D. Both (A) and (B)

267. Ram Lila is based on which epic?
A. Ramayan B. Mahabharata
C. Budh Charitra D. None of these

268. Why was Chipko Movement started?
A. pollution control
B. planting trees
C. deforestation
D. emission of carbon dioxide

269. Which folk theatre is from Gujarat?
A. Keertana B. Yakshagana
C. Bhavai D. Pawala

270. Dashavataar is a
A. movie B. dance
C. theatre D. None of these

271. .... brought in the concept of Global Village.
A. Marshall McLuhan B. Harold Innis
C. Neil Postman D. None of these

272. Which among the following is true about nautanki?
A. It is taken from Ramayan
B. It is taken from Mahabharat
C. It consists of vulgar and disrespectful stories.
D. All the above

273. Khayal is the form of drama performed mainly in ....
A. Gujarat B. Rajasthan
C. Uttar Pradesh D. Madhya Pradesh

274. Which of the following forms of traditional communication are used to motivate the audience so that they take fast action on several issues?
A. puppetry B. tamasha
C. street theaters D. story telling

275. Beautiful patterns and designs that are made on the entrance of the house as a mark of some spiritual symbol are termed as ....
A. pithora paintings B. mandana paintings
C. motifs D. None of these

276. .... is known for his contributions to the evolutionary theory.
A. Charles Robert Darwin
B. Herbert Spencer
C. Leonard Trelawny Hobhouse
D. None of these

277. Which of the following is true about mass media campaigns?
A. availability of required services and products
B. availability of community-based programs
C. policies that support behavior changes
D. all of these

278. Which among the following is *not* the objective of mass-media campaign?
A. to attract people
B. to demotivate the consumers to purchase
C. to give reminder about the availability of products
D. to communicate about the products and services

279. According to M.E. Jones, ... is a term used to describe the variations and modifications of, any aspects of the social processes, patterns or social organization.
A. Development B. Society
C. Social Change D. None of these

280. Which among the following is *not* included in the initiative by Government of India to control tobacco?
A. NTCP B. NEAC
C. NCTP D. None of these

281. When did the Tobacco Control Act came into being?
A. 2001 B. 2002
C. 2003 D. 2004

282. The display board on the sale of tobacco products cannot have promotional ....
A. message B. picture
C. both A and B D. None of these

283. Which among the following is a contrary effect of media campaign?
A. Message may not reach the target audience.
B. Message may be wrongly understood.
C. Both A and B
D. None of these

284. Social changes take place under two main categories – economic and political.

A. True B. False

285. Which among the following is/are a characteristic of social change?

A. It is universal.
B. It is a community change.
C. It may be short or long term.
D. All the above

286. Which among the following statements is/are correct?

(a) Social change is not uniform.
(b) Social change may create a chain reaction.
(c) Social change is continuous.
(d) Social change lacks definite prediction.

A. Only (b) B. Both (a) and (c)
C. (a), (c) (d) D. (a), (b), (c), (d)

287. Which among the following is/are the patterns of social change?

A. Linear change B. Cyclical change
C. Fluctuating change D. All the above

288. Social change is affected by the endogenous and exogenous factors.

A. True B. False

289. Which among the following is/are a factor that affect the social change.

(a) Demographic (b) Cultural
(c) Technological (d) Political

A. Only (a) B. (a), (b) and (d)
C. Only (c) D. (a), (b), (c) and (d)

290. According to the statistics of Audit Bureau of Circulation, 2024, which newspaper has the highest figure of circulation.

A. Dainik Bhaskar B. Dainik Jagran
C. Times of India D. Hindustan Times

291. NBA stands for ....

A. The National Broadcasters Association
B. The News Broadcasting Agency
C. The News Broadcasting Association
D. The News Broadcasters Association

292. TRAI stands for Television Regulatory Authority of India.

A. True B. False

293. .... is the earliest piece of legislation in India.

A. Indian Telegraph Act
B. Prasar Bharati Act
C. Cinematograph Act
D. None of these

294. Match the following:

(a) Prasar Bharati	1. 1995
(b) Indian Telegraph Act	2. 1990
(c) Cinematograph Act	3. 1885
(d) Cable, TV regulation Act	4. 1952

A. (a)-3, (b)-4, (c)-1, (d)-2
B. (a)-2, (b)-3, (c)-4, (d)-1
C. (a)-4, (b)-2, (c)-1, (d)-3
D. (a)-2, (b)-1, (c)-4, (d)-3

295. .... provides for the grant of autonomy to Doordarshan and AIR.

A. Cable, Television Regulation Act
B. Prasar Bharati Act
C. Electronic Media Act
D. Audio-visual Media Services Act

296. NWICO stands for ....

A. The New World Information and Communication Order
B. The Nation-Wide Information and Communication Order
C. The New World Information and Communication Organization
D. None of these

297. The Macbride Commission report was published under the report named ....

A. One World, Many Voice
B. Many Voices, One World
C. One voice, One World
D. None of these

298. Which movement became globally recognized with help from social media platforms like Twitter and Facebook?

A. Civil Rights Movement
B. Green Revolution
C. Arab Spring
D. Industrial Revolution

299. What form of media played a major role in the Civil Rights Movement in the U.S.?

A. Podcasts B. Television news
C. Radio dramas D. Comic books

300. Which social campaign in India heavily used media to protest against corruption?

A. Narmada Bachao Andolan
B. Save the Tiger Campaign
C. India Against Corruption
D. Quit India Movement

301. Which hashtag movement gained global attention on sexual harassment and assault?

A. #BlackLivesMatter B. #FridaysForFuture
C. #MeToo D. #OccupyWallStreet

302. What traditional medium helped spread the Quit India Movement message?
A. Podcasts B. Newspaper publications
C. YouTube videos D. Satellite radio

303. What is one primary reason media is effective in driving social change?
A. It restricts discussions
B. It educates, informs, and connects people
C. It only entertains
D. It creates more barriers

304. The "Black Lives Matter" movement gained momentum through:
A. Silent gatherings only
B. Live TV debates
C. Social media activism
D. Posters in small towns

305. Why is visual media powerful in promoting social change?
A. It is difficult to understand
B. It uses complex jargon
C. It creates emotional impact
D. It is restricted to academics

306. Two-step flow of communication argues that
A. people are not isolates
B. people live without communication
C. people-mass media nexus
D. people are not the subjects in communication

307. Public access broadcasting is a part of
A. deliberative democracy
B. numerical democracy
C. mediated democracy
D. fragmented democracy

308. In what way did radio influence the Indian freedom struggle?
A. Broadcasting only British rules
B. Spreading nationalist messages
C. Restricting information
D. Broadcasting foreign films

309. What made the Arab Spring protests different in terms of media use?
A. Television debates
B. Printed flyers
C. Use of social media for real-time updates
D. Door-to-door campaigning

310. The Chipko Movement in India used which type of media most effectively?
A. Social media
B. Traditional media like newspapers and documentaries
C. Billboard advertising
D. Mobile applications

311. How did mass media help during the Anti-Apartheid Movement in South Africa?
A. Hiding the issue
B. Globalizing the injustice
C. Suppressing protests
D. Spreading false information

312. Which youth movement addressing climate change grew with media support?
A. Silent Spring
B. Fridays for Future
C. Earth Hour
D. Greenhouse Alliance

ANSWERS

1	2	3	4	5	6	7	8	9	10
C	D	D	C	D	D	C	B	B	A
11	**12**	**13**	**14**	**15**	**16**	**17**	**18**	**19**	**20**
D	D	C	D	B	B	B	D	C	D
21	**22**	**23**	**24**	**25**	**26**	**27**	**28**	**29**	**30**
B	D	B	A	C	B	B	C	A	D
31	**32**	**33**	**34**	**35**	**36**	**37**	**38**	**39**	**40**
D	D	D	B	B	B	D	C	D	C
41	**42**	**43**	**44**	**45**	**46**	**47**	**48**	**49**	**50**
B	D	D	A	C	B	D	B	A	C
51	**52**	**53**	**54**	**55**	**56**	**57**	**58**	**59**	**60**
B	C	C	D	D	C	D	B	D	C

61	**62**	**63**	**64**	**65**	**66**	**67**	**68**	**69**	**70**
A	D	C	B	A	C	C	B	A	C
71	**72**	**73**	**74**	**75**	**76**	**77**	**78**	**79**	**80**
A	D	C	B	C	C	B	C	D	C
81	**82**	**83**	**84**	**85**	**86**	**87**	**88**	**89**	**90**
C	A	A	A	A	C	B	B	B	D
91	**92**	**93**	**94**	**95**	**96**	**97**	**98**	**99**	**100**
B	D	C	A	C	A	A	A	B	A
101	**102**	**103**	**104**	**105**	**106**	**107**	**108**	**109**	**110**
C	C	B	B	A	C	A	B	D	A
111	**112**	**113**	**114**	**115**	**116**	**117**	**118**	**119**	**120**
B	B	D	D	D	C	A	C	C	D
121	**122**	**123**	**124**	**125**	**126**	**127**	**128**	**129**	**130**
C	B	D	C	C	C	B	B	C	B
131	**132**	**133**	**134**	**135**	**136**	**137**	**138**	**139**	**140**
B	B	C	A	B	C	B	B	B	B
141	**142**	**143**	**144**	**145**	**146**	**147**	**148**	**149**	**150**
B	C	B	D	B	B	C	B	B	B
151	**152**	**153**	**154**	**155**	**156**	**157**	**158**	**159**	**160**
B	B	B	B	A	B	D	C	B	B
161	**162**	**163**	**164**	**165**	**166**	**167**	**168**	**169**	**170**
B	B	B	B	B	B	B	C	D	B
171	**172**	**173**	**174**	**175**	**176**	**177**	**178**	**189**	**180**
B	D	D	C	A	B	D	D	D	B
181	**182**	**183**	**184**	**185**	**186**	**187**	**188**	**189**	**190**
B	B	B	B	D	C	B	C	C	B
191	**192**	**193**	**194**	**195**	**196**	**197**	**198**	**199**	**200**
B	B	B	C	B	A	B	B	D	B
201	**202**	**203**	**204**	**205**	**206**	**207**	**208**	**209**	**210**
B	B	B	B	D	D	B	B	B	B
211	**212**	**213**	**214**	**215**	**216**	**217**	**218**	**219**	**220**
D	B	B	B	B	B	B	A	B	A
221	**222**	**223**	**224**	**225**	**226**	**227**	**228**	**229**	**230**
C	A	B	B	B	B	B	B	A	B
231	**232**	**233**	**234**	**235**	**236**	**237**	**238**	**239**	**240**
C	D	C	B	C	A	B	D	A	B
241	**242**	**243**	**244**	**245**	**246**	**247**	**248**	**249**	**250**
A	B	C	A	C	B	C	A	D	A
251	**252**	**253**	**254**	**255**	**256**	**257**	**258**	**259**	**260**
D	B	B	A	A	B	B	A	A	A
261	**262**	**263**	**264**	**265**	**266**	**267**	**268**	**269**	**270**
D	C	D	B	A	D	A	B	C	C
271	**272**	**273**	**274**	**275**	**276**	**277**	**278**	**279**	**280**
A	C	B	C	C	A	D	B	C	A
281	**282**	**283**	**284**	**285**	**286**	**287**	**288**	**289**	**290**
C	C	C	B	D	D	D	A	D	A
291	**292**	**293**	**294**	**295**	**296**	**297**	**298**	**299**	**300**
D	B	A	B	B	A	B	B	B	C
301	**302**	**303**	**304**	**305**	**306**	**307**	**308**	**309**	**310**
C	B	B	C	C	A	A	B	C	B
311	**312**								
B	B								

EXPLANATORY ANSWERS

4. (C): According to MT Myers and GE Myers, there are two requirements for the communication to take place. First is the symbolic form (same language, jargons or dialects) and the second is association between the symbols and their referents.

12. (D): Aristotle called the study of communication as rhetoric as it involves three elements- a speaker, a message and a listener.

26. (B): Japan was the first one to appoint news ombudsman. In 1922 The Asahi Shimbun in Tokyo formed a committee to address and investigate readers complaints.

60. (C): Vocalics is the other name for para language that deals with extra-linguistic or the non-word aspects of communication. Eg- yawning, belching etc.

71. (A): Proxemics in communication is the study of how people use space to communicate, including the physical distance they maintain during interactions. It's a key aspect of non-verbal communication, alongside kinesics (body language) and haptics (touch). Proxemics can convey messages about relationships, status, and cultural norms.

73. (D): Edward T. Hall's Proxemic Chart

Zone	Distance	Used for
Intimate Sapce	0 to 18 Inches (0-45 cm)	Close relations (e.g., family, partners)
Personal Space	18 inches to 4 feet (45 cm - 1.2 m)	Friends and informal conversations
Social Space	4 to 12 feet (1.2 -3.6 m)	Formal interactions (e.g., workplace, strangers)
Public Space	12 feet and beyond (3.6 m+)	Public speaking, lectures, large audiences

73. (C): 7Cs of effective communication include completeness, conciseness, consideration, clarity, concreteness, courtesy, and correctness.

74. (B): Parroting is repeating word to word of the speaker. It confirms the speaker that the message transferred is received exactly the same.

77. (B): Intra-personal communication is the process of communicating with oneself, also known as self-talk or inner dialogue. It involves the internal thoughts, feelings, and evaluations an individual has about themselves and the world around them.

80. (C): Inter-personal communication involves direct conversation between two people to serve the purposes such as to influence, help and discover, to share and to play together.

87. (B): In Gerbner's Cultivation theory there is an event that happens in the real life and the event content or message is received by man or a machine. When that event is received by the man it will not be exactly the same event because any man or machine can't remember the whole event rather, they remember only the part of the event.

88. (B): Grapevine communication refers to the informal and unofficial way employees share information within an organization, outside of formal communication channels. It operates through social interactions and personal connections, often spreading rumors and unverified news. While it can provide valuable insights and build social bonds, it can also lead to misinformation and negative impacts.

89. (B): Gobbledygook is a term coined by Maury Maverick for a language that is the part of informal communication in our day-to-day life. Gobbledygook literally mean meaningless language.

106. (C): Johann Gutenberg developed the first-known printing press in the 1440 at Strasbourg, Germany.

263. (D): Guler Painting is associated with Himachal Pradesh.

264. (B): The Geet Govinda (Song of Govinda) is a work composed by the **12**th-century Hindu poet, Jayadeva. It describes the relationship between Krishna and the gopis of Vrindavana, and in particular one gopi named Radha.

272. (C): Nautanki is the form mostly found in Northern India that make use of vulgar and disrespectful stories to entertain their audiences. They even include dancing, singing and use of drumbeats in their performances. Their themes are not based on the Indian religious epics.

280. (A): The Government of India launched an initiative program NTCP (National Tobacco Control Program) to monitor that all Anti-tobacco laws are implemented as well as they try to get control on all the stakeholders.

284. (B): Social changes take place under three main categories – economic, political and cultural. A society is mostly dependent on the economic factors and the industrial sectors. Political influences also shape the lives of the people living in the society. Culture includes behavior and beliefs that are common to the people who are living in a society.

288. (A): The factors that affect the social change can be categorized into two groups – endogenous and exogenous. Endogenous factors are the internal factors like the infrastructural facilities and their distribution among various people of the society. Exogenous factors are the external factors which are beyond the control of the human beings like the natural disasters etc.

290. (A): The highest circulated newspaper in India based on ABC data in 2024 is Dainik Bhaskar. It is a multi-edition Hindi newspaper with 34,47,264 copies circulated daily. The second largest is The Times of India. The largest circulated English daily is Hindustan Times with 5,13,521 copies.

292. (B): TRAI stands for Telecom Regulatory Authority of India. It was formed on 20 February, 1997. The aim of TRAI is to create and manage the growth of telecommunications in India.

293. (A): The Indian Telegraph Act 1885 intends to control the wireless broadcasting in India.

296. (A): The New World Information and Communication Order was coined by UNESCO in late 1970s. It grew out of the New International Economic Order in 1974. A lot of issues were discussed as a part of NWICO. Concerns regarding mass media arouse with the meeting of non-aligned nations in Algiers in 1973.

297. (B): The Macbride Commission published its report in 1980 under the title "Many Voices, One World". The aim of the report was to analyze the communication problems of the modern society. Few problems stated were the commercialization of media and unequal access of information. The report was written by the International Commission for the Study of Communication Problems.

CHAPTER-2

JOURNALISM

JOURNALISM

Journalism can be defined as the act of gathering, assessing, compiling and presenting news and information via mass media. It's essentially a form of sharing of information and facts, often from an objective perspective, with a commitment to accuracy and education.

The definition and role of journalism in any given society may vary depending on the various systems of government around the world and each country's regard for a free press.

Knowledge is power and journalism keeps the society informed of the events happening in the world, that draws attention to the matters we need to be aware of, and inspires us to action and navigate our lives.

QUALITIES OF A GOOD JOURNALIST

Journalism is a demanding profession that requires a unique combination of intellectual curiosity, linguistic skill, and a deep understanding of the world. Effective journalism is not just about presenting facts – it is about crafting narratives that engage, inform, and sometimes even challenge audiences. To achieve this, a journalist must inculcate certain qualities:

- **Curiosity:** A journalist needs to be curious to seek out truth and explore stories that may otherwise remain untold. This inquisitiveness drives them to ask questions, probe deeper, and investigate angles that others might overlook.
- **Accuracy and Attention to detail:** A journalist must be meticulous in verifying information before publication. Even a small factual error can erode credibility and damage reputations. Ensuring accuracy requires diligent note-taking, fact-checking, and cross-referencing sources.
- **Nose for News:** Nose for News can be defined as journalist's ability to identify and develop story that is newsworthy. A good journalist knows how to sift through vast amounts of information to identify the most important elements that will capture the interest of the audience.
- **Investigative Skills:** A good journalist should rely on facts and evidence, not on emotions while working on a story. An ideal journalist should be observant and possess strong analytical skills to assess a situation if there is something more to it. Whether it is about confirming the credibility of sources or assessing an incident, a journalist should know how to weight a situation critically.
- **Effective Language and Communication Skills:** A journalist must have a strong hold over his/ her language and communication. The ability to produce clear, concise and compelling narratives is fundamental for effective journalism.
- **Trustworthiness:** Journalism would not be effective if it can't be trusted. Trustworthiness in any news is paramount for developmental journalism. Missing an interview, failing to meet a deadline, or submitting inaccurate information can have serious consequences.
- **Empathy:** In present times, due to fast paced environments and competition, journalism has turned into business. In haste to match the requirements, sometime basic tenets of humanity like sensitivity, respect and compassion get overlooked. Great

journalists recognize that there are real people with their struggles, joys, and aspirations behind every headline, statistic, or political event and approach their work by cultivating empathy.

TYPES OF REPORTING

1. Objective Reporting

The term "objective reporting" refers to the straightforward presentation of facts as they occurred. Contextualizing, backgrounding, analyzing, and opining are not part of objective reporting.

The concept of objective reporting can be summarized as follows:

- Fairness and balance in presenting opposing viewpoints on a topic.
- Reporting accuracy and realism.
- Outlining all of the most important points.
- Distinguishing facts from opinions while still considering the latter to be relevant.
- Keeping the writer's own opinions, attitudes, and involvement to a minimum.
- Staying away from slant, malicious, or devious motives.

2. Interpretative Reporting

Facts and interpretation are combined in interpretative reporting. Many times, the reporter must interpret certain events for the benefit of the audience. It entails providing background information on a specific incident or event. Aside from the acts gathered on the ground, the reporter may need to provide background information so that the readers can better perceive and comprehend the news. As a result, the reporter investigates the causes and implications of a particular event and provides information as well as an interpretation of its significance.

It's possible that the entire event will not take place in a single day. It's a never-ending cycle, with one event often leading to the next. To comprehend the occurrence of an event, we must first comprehend the preceding one, or the sequence of events that led to the most recent one. And it is the reporter who interprets the event by informing the readers about the event's past history or the actions that led to its occurrence. This provides more contexts for events, and the reporter must keep track of all past, present, and future events, as well as forecast the future at times. As a result, interpretative reporting elucidates an event's hidden significance and distinguishes fact from fiction.

3. Investigative Reporting

Investigative reporting is when a news reporter has to dig deeper than what is stated in the hard news to find out the exact facts of an event, or, in other words, investigates beyond what is visible to the naked eye. Investigative reporting entails looking into any event. Investigative journalism is in-depth and involves extensive research and reporting over a long period of time. It reveals information that isn't widely known and that others want to keep hidden.

Investigations are usually conducted in the event of a major event, when a larger public concern is involved, or when public figures or celebrities are involved. In any type of reporting, the reporter conducts some sort of research to unearth information that would otherwise be unavailable. A sound copy or report cannot be produced without preliminary investigation. However, in some cases, particularly those involving scams or misappropriation of public funds, the reporter must conduct thorough research to obtain the necessary information in order to produce a good copy. Furthermore, in such cases, information is scarce, and the reporter must devote both time and effort to unearthing facts.

The importance of investigative journalism in today's world is undeniable. Long-held lies can be exposed, deceptive leaders can be exposed, and a corrupt government can be shaken to its core by the discovery of a dramatic set of new facts. Investigative journalism, when done correctly, poses a significant threat to powerful elites attempting to manipulate a population. Despite its flaws, modern journalism is widely regarded as the most effective monitor and defender of democratic values. And investigative reporting is without a doubt the most effective tool for carrying out this duty. Investigative reporting emphasizes the media's role as a watchdog and the accountability of institutions and individual in position of power.

KEY FUNCTIONS OF JOURNALISM

The key concepts of Journalism are:—

1. **Providing information that the public needs to know:** Many publications are devoted solely to information that the public wants to know; fashion and celebrity gossip magazines are good examples of this. Ideally, however, journalists strive to write less sensational stories because they are important for readers to know about.
2. **Giving a fair and truthful account of news:** There is a great deal of talk about bias in the media. Many journalists believe that if a publication is

being criticized for being too liberal by some and too conservative by others, it is doing a good job. On its Web site, the Associated Press defines fair and truthful as "reliability and objectivity with reports that are accurate, balanced and informed."

3. **Emphasizing the importance of free speech:** Journalists define freedom of speech and of the press in very broad terms. Many journalists have an absolutist approach while discussing free speech, meaning that they believe no limits whatsoever on speech should be imposed. Free speech and a free press are essential for journalism to exist the way it does in this country, able to criticize the government and conduct investigations.
4. **Spurring people to action:** Journalism is a service-oriented profession because journalism "isn't just about providing raw information. It's telling them how to use it to improve their lives and inspiring them to want to."
5. **Having courage:** According to Ugland, true objectivity requires the courage to go beyond two-sided, pro-con approaches and tell all sides of a story—even if it make angry those in power.

ROLE AND RESPONSIBILITIES OF JOURNALISTS

Principles of Journalism

A former correspondent of the Associated Press of America, Wes Gallgher, has laid down the following principle: "Journalism requires a discipline of mind. It requires a sympathetic understanding of mankind, and also a cold objective analysis of how mankind meets the problem of this age". Facts must not be tampered with. News must be reported with complete objectivity, without any distortion. A journalist should not mix news and views. He must be careful enough to clearly distinguish between the two. Maintenance of high professional standards is certainly a major responsibility of the publisher and the editor. On the one hand journalists ought to be vigilant to safeguard the freedom of the press and on the other they must see that this freedom is used and never misused, that they always act with a great sense of responsibility.

Role of Journalists

Generally, the primary duty of a journalist is to act as an interpreter of the world around him. He observes the events, transmits facts about the events and acts as an interpreter of these events. According to Prof. John Hohenberg, a journalist should stick to the following four ideals:

1. He should imbibe a never-ending search for the truth;
2. He should be able to meet needs of the changing times, instead of waiting to be overtaken by them;
3. He should be able to perform services of some consequence and significance to mankind;
4. He Should maintain a steadfast independence.

A journalist is an important unit of the democratic system in our country. He is supposed to gather facts, organise them and disseminate them to the masses. He also explains the significance of the facts and offers opinions on contemporary issues. He is expected to comment on matters of public interest in a fair, accurate, unbiased, sober, decent and responsible manner.

He should avoid distortion in the news story in an effort to attain striking effect.

"Attribution" or the "name of the source" is another thing which should not be overlooked. The best attribution is the name of the precise source. The next best is the name of the organization, office or group, represented by the source as a spokesman. The least satisfactory, but sometimes the most necessary, is some variation of the phrase, "informed source", if the origin of the news must be held in confidence.

Responsibilities of Journalists

The press is no doubt an industry, a business, but with a difference. What is published in newspapers and magazines, conditions the minds of readers: men and women, children, adolescents and adults. Journalists, therefore, have some social obligations. They must act with a profound sense of responsibility towards the society.

His primary duty is to serve his readers through fair, positive and timely information in a palatable, digestible and entertaining format. He must give special attention to the deprived and the weaker sections of society and try to involve them in the country's process of development. He must act as a harbinger of social change. Here, we discuss the journalist's responsibilities under three heads: Social, Professional and Legal.

Social

The social responsibility of journalists is of paramount importance. It is now well recognized that "journalism is the mirror of society". The journalist acts as a spokesman of mankind. He must therefore, provide a truthful, comprehensive, and intelligent account of the events in a context that gives meaning. Facts and opinions must be clearly differentiated by that effective sieve called "objectivity".

Legal

Publication of baseless, graceless and manipulated material should be avoided at all costs in order to safeguard yourself and your organization from the legal clutches. "Libel" or "defamation" is always a "live wire" on which a sensible journalist dreads to tread. He must be well aware of the various laws relating to the press such as Official Secret's Act, Copyright Act; he must always act within the limits of the law and never infringe them.

Professional

Besides social and legal obligations, journalists have certain professional obligations to honour. The basic responsibility of a journalist is to disseminate information in all circumstances, sometimes normal and sometimes otherwise. The information provided helps the readers to make up their minds on vital issues; this may also have a role in shaping their attitudes. In unusual times, a journalist has to think fast and act fast and he must not lose his composure and his sense of objectivity.

He must strictly adhere to the accepted professional norms. He must keep his biases at bay and should endeavour to be fair and balanced in the projection of news and views.

On contentious and sensitive issues, the professional responsibility of a good scribe is to pursue the event and report comprehensively but judiciously.

One of the most important responsibility of a professional journalist is to ensure that in hurry and haste, accuracy in the language is not sacrificed.

PROFESSIONAL CONDUCT OF JOURNALISTS

Respecting Human Rights

Journalists should respect individual's right to privacy. However, when the public interest of find the information arises, and the concerned individual is not disclosing the information, Journalists can go an extra mile to extract information.

Gathering information

The journalist shall use only fair methods to obtain information, images, documents and data and he/she will always report his/her status as a journalist and will refrain from using hidden recordings of images and sounds, except where it is impossible for him/her to collect information that is overwhelmingly in the public interest. It is suggested that when the information is published, journalist has to mention the use of special investigation techniques.

Ensuring the rules of Editing

The notion of urgency or immediacy in the dissemination of information shall not take precedence over the verification of facts, sources and/or the offer of a reply. The journalist shall do the utmost to rectify any errors or published information which is found to be inaccurate in a timely, explicit, complete and transparent manner.

Protection of Sources

The journalist shall observe professional secrecy regarding the source of information obtained in confidence. An extension of freedom of press gives journalists a legal provision to keep the identity of source private, even when demanded by police or prosecutors.

Refrain from Abuse of Status

The journalist shall not use the freedom of press to serve any other interest and shall refrain from receiving any unfair advantage or personal gain because of the dissemination or non-dissemination of information. He/she will avoid - or put an end to - any situation that could lead him/her to a conflict of interest in the exercise of his/her profession.

ETHICAL ISSUES IN JOURNALISM

Journalists, like professionals in other fields, adhere to a code of ethics that outlines moral principles, guidelines, and rules governing their conduct and interactions with the public. Ethical challenges are pervasive in journalism and require journalists to navigate complex decision making. Some of them are:

- **Sensationalism:** Sensationalism in journalism means focusing on unimportant stories and making them seem like they have a big impact on society. It can also mean presenting important news in a biased or overly dramatic way, which goes against the usual rules of fair and accurate journalism.

  Example: Death of actor Sushant Singh Rajput was swirled with sensationalism by media. The media's obsession with Sushant Singh Rajput's death transformed a tragic suicide into a relentless investigation, streamed live day after day, overshadowing critical matters. The Bombay High Court recognized the harm caused by trial by media, obstructing fair criminal case investigations. The media's role should be to inform, not to manipulate public sentiment.

- **Fake News:** Fake news can be defined as the deliberate representation of misinformation as legitimate news. It is a major ethical issue in journalism because it undermines public trust, spreads misinformation, and distorts reality. Though fake news is dominant in social media, mainstream news media channels are also not far behind.

Examples:

- o "UNESCO has declared 'Jana Gana Mana' best national anthem in the world."- is a widely circulated fake news over WhatsApp.
- o "President Kovind makes Twitter debut; gains 3 million followers in one hour."- was widely circulated over mainstream media channels which later turned out to be a fake news
- o Just before the 2016 US Presidential Elections, fake news propagating claims that Democrat candidate Hillary Clinton sold weapons to ISIS garnered more engagement that authentic news.

- **Paid News:** Paid news is a serious ethical issue in journalism where media outlets publish news and stories in exchange for money or other benefits without clearly disclosing it as advertising. This practice blurs the line between editorial content and advertisements, misleading the audience into believing the information is unbiased and independently reported. This practice is particularly prevalent during election campaigns when political parties seek to manipulate public opinion and gain an unfair advantage.
- **Plagiarism:** Plagiarism in journalism is the act of copying someone else's work—including words, ideas, or research—without giving proper credit. It is a serious ethical violation because it undermines journalistic integrity, deceives audiences, and disrespects the work of others.

  Journalists are expected to present original works and be honest about their sources. Plagiarism disregards the effort and intellectual labour of the original author. It damages journalists' reputation and credibility and can also have legal implications.
- **Advertorials:** Advertorials are a blend of advertisements and editorial content, designed to look like regular news articles while promoting a product, service, or brand. While they generate revenue for media outlets, they also raise ethical concerns because they can blur the line between objective reporting and paid promotion.

  They lack transparency and can mislead readers into believing they are consuming objective news instead of paid content. Advertorials risk sidelining important stories in favour of commercial interests, which can distort the public's understanding of key issues.
- **Partisan Reporting:** Partisan reporting refers to biased or one-sided journalism that promotes a particular political party, ideology, or agenda rather than providing neutral and objective coverage. This type of reporting often favours one viewpoint while discrediting or ignoring others, compromising the core journalistic value of impartiality.

  Example: The present scenario in India media is dominated by the views of ruling political party. More space and time is provided to the ruling party while subduing the opposition. All the important agendas such as employment, inflation, education, health, corruption, economic inequality, etc. are deliberately overshadowed by the agendas that create social tension or disturb harmony as they keep people diverted from real issues.
- **Sting Operation:** The ethical aspect of sting operation has been a long-debated issue. The main ethical frame that supports stings operations is that it must serve larger public interest and is done as a last resort when no other way of acquiring information is possible. However, sting operations, in most cases, flout these ethical guidelines and are done to take undue advantage.

  Sting operations are often done for business gains and not for public good. False scenarios are created, right to privacy of any individual or organization is violated and incomplete or unverified information is broadcasted that often causes irreparable damage. Some famous sting operations are *Operation West End* (2001) by Tehelka, *Operation Duryodhana* (2001) by Cobrapost and *Operation Karaoke* (2019) by Cobrapost.

MULTIPLE CHOICE QUESTIONS

1. Hard news is mostly

A. Spot news

B. Society news

C. Entertainment news

D. Filler news

2. The process of gathering, processing, and disseminating information to the public through various media is best described as:

A. News gathering B. Media management

C. Journalism D. Public relations

3. Journalism is
A. something that requires a professional degree or training
B. the medium of communication
C. bonded to some news organization
D. speculation and coverage of incidents and issues towards a broad audience

4. Who is primarily responsible for gathering and reporting news and information?
A. Editor-in-chief B. Publisher
C. Reporter D. Photographer

5. .... journalism refers to news reporting that is objective, impartial, and factual.
A. Yellow B. Investigative
C. Straight D. Sensational

6. .... journalism involves the use of opinion, analysis, and personal interpretation in news reporting.
A. Investigative B. Yellow
C. Opinionated D. Interpretative

7. The .... is the person or organization that owns and operates a media outlet.
A. Editor B. Publisher
C. Correspondent D. Reporter

8. The .... plays a large role in shaping public opinion.
A. Technology B. Media
C. Mind-set D. Science

9. Public opinion means:
A. Sum-total of confused and incoherent opinions held by different groups of citizens
B. Unanimous opinion of all the citizens
C. A definite opinion, which is the result of a process of clarification and co-ordination of views held by different persons
D. Majority opinion

10. The .... is the person who is responsible for the overall content and direction of a media outlet.
A. Editor-in-chief B. Publisher
C. Reporter D. Photographer

11. .... is the process of selecting and arranging news stories for publication or broadcast.
A. Fact-checking B. Editing
C. Reporting D. Broadcasting

12. Keith Rupert Murdoch is the founder, Chairman and CEO of ...., the world's second-largest media conglomerate.
A. The Economist B. The Dominion
C. The Daily mirror D. News Corporation

13. .... is the practice of gathering information from multiple sources to verify the accuracy and completeness of a news story.
A. Investigating B. Reporting
C. Fact-checking D. Sensationalizing

14. Kuldeep Nayar is well known for
A. fashion reporting
B. lifestyle reporting
C. investigative reporting
D. business reporting

15. .... is the process of conveying information through various media, such as print, broadcast, or digital.
A. Publishing B. Dissemination
C. Editing D. Reporting

16. .... is the practice of gathering news and information through direct observation or interviews.
A. Fact-checking B. Investigating
C. Reporting D. Editing

17. What does 'Berliner' mean?
A. Headline B. Newspaper format
C. Pull out quotes D. None of these

18. .... is the process of organizing and presenting information in a clear and concise manner.
A. Reporting B. Writing
C. Editing D. Fact-checking

19. .... is the practice of covering a specific topic or issue in depth over an extended period of time.
A. Feature writing
B. In-depth reporting
C. Investigative journalism
D. Opinion writing

20. As per the chronological order, what comes first in the newspaper format?
A. Columns B. headlines
C. Sub-heads D. Mast-heads

21. **Assertion (A):** Speed is the only crucial factor in news reporting.

Reason (R): Being the first to report a story is always more important than its accuracy.
A. Both A and R are true, and R is the correct explanation of A
B. Both A and R are true, but R is NOT the correct explanation of A
C. A is true, but R is false
D. A is false, but R is true

22. .... is the practice of using visual elements, such as photographs or graphics, to enhance the presentation of news and information.

A. Visual journalism
B. Feature writing
C. Investigative reporting
D. Opinion writing

23. Which among the following is/are included in the objections of journalism?

(a) Journalism provides an honest description of news.
(b) Journalists strictly follow the policy of freedom of speech and expression.
(c) Journalism is a service-oriented profession.
(d) Courage is an essential quality every journalist must possess.

A. both (a) and (b) B. (a), (b) and (c)
C. (b), (c) and (d) D. All the above

24. .... is the practice of gathering news and information from multiple sources and synthesizing it into a cohesive narrative.

A. Investigative reporting
B. Feature writing
C. Opinion writing
D. Sensational reporting

25. Which among the following is ***not*** true about the nature of journalism?

(a) Journalism is just limited to reporting.
(b) Journalists has to maintain ethics and standards.
(c) Journalism act as a liaison element.

A. Both (a) and (b) B. Both (b) and (c)
C. Both (a) and (c) D. All the above

26. Which one of the following news agencies is the oldest in the world?

A. Reuters (England)
B. Agence France - Presse (France) (AFP)
C. Deutsche Presse - Agentur (DPA)
D. Telegraph Agency of the Soviet Union (TASS), Russia

27. .... is the practice of gathering news and information from online and digital sources.

A. Online reporting
B. Digital journalism
C. Investigative journalism
D. Opinion writing

28. The most notable event in Indian journalism in 1948 was the formation of

A. Prasar Bharati B. UNI
C. Press Trust of India D. Press Guild

29. .... is the practice of reporting on events or issues that are ongoing or unfolding in real-time.

A. Investigative reporting
B. Feature writing
C. Breaking news
D. Opinion writing

30. Assertion (A): A good journalist needs strong communication skills.

Reason (R): Journalists must effectively convey information to their audience.

A. Both A and R are true, and R is the correct explanation of A.
B. Both A and R are true, but R is NOT the correct explanation of A.
C. A is true, but R is false.
D. A is false, but R is true.

31. Which of the following events significantly increased the role of television in political campaigning in the United States?

A. The Civil War
B. The 1960 Presidential debates (Kennedy vs. Nixon)
C. World War I
D. The Watergate scandal

32. The term "Watergate" refers to:

A. A major international treaty
B. A Supreme Court decision
C. A political scandal in the United States involving illegal activities by the Nixon administration
D. A global economic summit

33. Identify the correct chronological sequence of the following newspaper:

A. Amrita Bazar Patrika, Swarajya, The Hindustan Times, Deccan Herald
B. Swarajya, The Hindustan Times, Deccan Herald, Amrita Bazar Patrika
C. The Hindustan Times, Deccan Herald, Amrita Bazar Patrika, Swarajya
D. Deccan Herald, Amrita Bazar Patrika, Swarajya, The Hindustan Times

34. What role did investigative journalism play in the Watergate scandal?

A. It had no role; the scandal was uncovered solely by the government.
B. Journalists helped uncover and publicize the illegal activities.
C. Journalists tried to cover up the scandal.
D. Journalists focused only on the economic impact of the scandal.

35. Identify the correct chronological sequence of the following newspaper which were launched during freedom movement:

A. Digdarshan — Bangadoota — Samachar Darpan — Samvad Kaumudi

B. Bangadoota — Digdarshan — Samachar Darpan — Samvad Kaumudi

C. Samvad Kaumudi — Bangadoota — Samachar Darpan — Digdarshan

D. Digdarshan — Samachar Darpan — Samvad Kaumudi — Bangadoota

36. .... is the practice of investigating and reporting on issues that are not readily apparent or that have been hidden from public view.

A. Feature writing
B. Opinion writing
C. Investigative journalism
D. Sensational reporting

37. Journalism that promotes civic commitment and citizen participation in democratic processes is known as:

A. Advocacy Journalism
B. Public Journalism
C. Alternative Journalism
D. Counter media

38. .... is the practice of reporting on events or issues that have a significant impact on a community or society.

A. Investigative reporting
B. Community journalism
C. Opinion writing
D. Feature writing

39. Communist media philosophy believes in using the media for

A. Entertaining the masses
B. Planning sound objectives
C. Elevating public tastes
D. Counter revolutionary methods

40. Which of the following describes the concept of "media framing" in political reporting?

A. The use of statistics to analyze election results

B. The way media outlets present a story, influencing how audiences understand it

C. The legal regulations governing political advertising

D. The practice of journalists remaining completely neutral in their reporting

41. Bal Thackeray was a satirical ....

A. Scribe　B. Cartoonist
C. Correspondent　D. Editor

42. Selective presentation of facts and quotes in supports of certain opinions is referred to as

A. Cherry picking　B. Time craft
C. Propaganda　D. Selective publicity

43. What does 'sloppy copy' relate to?

A. pre-writing　B. editing
C. rough draft　D. publish

44. Good proof is concerned with

A. proofreading　B. editing
C. revising　D. All the above

45. .... is the practice of reporting on events or issues that are related to the government or political processes.

A. Political journalism
B. Investigative reporting
C. Opinion writing
D. Feature writing

46. What does the term embedded journalism refer to?

A. Journalists writing editorials for political parties

B. Reporters who investigate government corruption

C. Journalists attached to military units during conflict

D. Freelance journalists reporting from remote areas

47. The coverage of which war is often cited as an example of how embedded journalism can shape public perception?

A. The American Revolutionary War
B. The Vietnam War
C. The Gulf War and the Iraq War
D. World War II

48. A cardinal sin for a journalist is to

A. misspell a name.

B. disagree with an editor or news director.

C. publish a story that angers local officials.

D. reveal how decisions are made about what is newsworthy.

49. .... is the practice of reporting on events or issues that are related to the arts, culture, or entertainment.

A. Arts reporting
B. Cultural journalism
C. Entertainment reporting
D. Lifestyle journalism

50. In 1875, the Statesman was founded by
A. Rudyard Kipling
B. John Corbett
C. Robert Knight
D. James Silk Buckingham

51. Cloze is a method of
A. Editing B. Captioning
C. Readability D. Ending

52. .... is the practice of reporting on events or issues that are related to the sports or athletic sectors.
A. Sports reporting
B. Athletic journalism
C. Sporting events coverage
D. Fitness journalism

53. Assertion (A): Emotional involvement enhances a journalist's ability to report accurately.
Reason (R): Detachment allows for unbiased observation and analysis.
A. Both A and R are true, and R is the correct explanation of A.
B. Both A and R are true, but R is NOT the correct explanation of A.
C. A is true, but R is false.
D. A is false, but R is true.

54. .... is the practice of reporting on events or issues that are related to the environment or natural world.
A. Environmental journalism
B. Nature journalism
C. Green reporting
D. Eco-journalism

55. .... is the practice of reporting on events or issues that are related to the health or medical sectors.
A. Health reporting
B. Medical journalism
C. Healthcare coverage
D. Health and medical journalism

56. .... is the practice of reporting on events or issues that are related to the education or academic sectors.
A. Education reporting
B. Academic journalism
C. School coverage
D. Learning journalism

57. What is "fake news"?
A. News that disagrees with a person's political views
B. News reports that are factually incorrect and deliberately misleading
C. News from foreign sources
D. Old news stories

58. Assertion (A): Investigative journalism requires a high degree of persistence.
Reason (R): Uncovering hidden information often involves overcoming obstacles and challenges.
A. Both A and R are true, and R is the correct explanation of A.
B. Both A and R are true, but R is NOT the correct explanation of A.
C. A is true, but R is false.
D. A is false, but R is true.

59. .... is the practice of reporting on events or issues that are related to the social or cultural sectors.
A. Social journalism B. Cultural reporting
C. Lifestyle journalism D. Community news

60. .... is the practice of reporting on events or issues that are related to the military or defence sectors.
A. Military reporting
B. Defence journalism
C. Armed forces coverage
D. Security reporting

61. .... is the practice of gathering news and information through social media platforms.
A. Social news reporting
B. Social media journalism
C. Digital news gathering
D. Online reporting

62. Which was the first newspaper published in India?
A. Bengal Gazette B. Samachar Darpan
C. Mumbai Samachar D. The Times of India

63. Which was the first vernacular paper in India?
A. Bengal Gazette B. Samachar Darpan
C. Mumbai Samachar D. The Times of India

64. .... is the practice of reporting on events or issues that are related to technology and innovation.
A. Tech reporting
B. Innovation journalism
C. Technology journalism
D. Digital innovation coverage

65. Which was the oldest daily in India?
A. Bengal Gazette B. Samachar Darpan
C. Mumbai Samachar D. The Times of India

66. Which is the oldest English daily in India?
A. The Hindustan Times
B. The Statesman
C. The Times of India
D. The Indian Express

67. The Anandabazar Patrika, is rightly called the "........"
A. Voice of Bengal B. Noise of Bengal
C. Sound of Bengal D. Light of Bengal

68. .... is the practice of reporting on events or issues that are related to the criminal justice or law enforcement sectors.
A. Crime reporting
B. Justice journalism
C. Law enforcement coverage
D. Crime and justice journalism

69. .... is the practice of reporting on events or issues that are related to the science or technology sectors.
A. Scientific journalism
B. Technology reporting
C. Tech journalism
D. Science and technology journalism

70. .... is the practice of reporting on events or issues that are related to the business or financial sectors.
A. Business journalism B. Investigative reporting
C. Opinion writing D. Feature writing

71. .... is the practice of reporting on events or issues that have a global or international significance.
A. Feature writing B. Investigative journalism
C. Opinion writing D. Foreign correspondence

72. Identify the correct sequence of the following media related statutes:
A. The Working Journalists Act, the Copyright Act, the Contempt of Courts Act, the Criminal Procedure Code.
B. The Copyright Act, the Contempt of Courts Act, the Criminal Procedure Code, the Working Journalists Act.
C. The Contempt of Courts Act, the Working Journalist Act, the Criminal Procedure Code, the Copyright Act
D. The Criminal Procedure Code, the Working Journalists Act, the Contempt of Courts Act, the Copyright Act

73. .... is associated with the invention of printing.
A. Franklin B. Johannes Gutenberg
C. Charles Babbage D. Marconi

74. .... is the latest time at which a story can be accepted.
A. Dateline B. Deadline
C. Press time D. Print time

75. Leader writer is one who writes the ....
A. Main story B. Middle article
C. Editorial D. Edit page article

76. Condensing a story is generally referred to as in the newspaper offices.
A. Rewriting B. Miniaturizing
C. Shortening D. Boiling down

77. Title registration of newspaper is done by:
A. RNI B. DAVP
C. PIB D. IPRD

78. Hard news is:
A. Cultural news
B. Daily public news
C. Background information
D. Box

79. One- or two-word small headline appearing on the left-hand top of the story:
A. Topline B. Slug
C. Small head D. Top head

80. Copy editor is a synonym of:
A. Sub Editor B. News Editor
C. Copywriter D. Copyholder

81. Which news channel is one of the oldest public news broadcasters in India?
A. Zee News B. DD News
C. India Today D. News 24

82. The value of the Associated Press Stylebook is that it:
A. promotes consistency in newswriting and reduces errors.
B. tells reporters what constitutes fine writing and what does not.
C. gives reporters a template for all news stories they may write.
D. guides reporters in assuring that all stories will have a uniform political slant.

83. The main headline on the top of a page covering all columns is known as:
A. Blurb B. Lead
C. Banner D. Blow-up

84. Which news channel is owned by the India Today Group?
A. Republic TV B. Aaj Tak
C. NDTV India D. News Nation

85. Which news channel was founded by Rajat Sharma?
A. ABP News B. India TV
C. Zee News D. Total TV

86. What is the primary function of a news agency?
A. To publish its own newspapers
B. To broadcast television programs
C. To gather and distribute news to various media outlets
D. To conduct political polls

87. Sensation is the main feature of .... journalism.
A. Black B. Yellow
C. Red D. Blue

88. Obituaries should always be:
A. Posthumous B. Premature
C. Printed D. Passing through

89. **Assertion (A):** Ethical considerations are unimportant in journalism.

Reason (R): The primary goal of journalism is to attract a large audience, regardless of methods.
A. Both A and R are true, and R is the correct explanation of A.
B. Both A and R are true, but R is NOT the correct explanation of A.
C. A is true, but R is false.
D. A is false, but R is true

90. Letters to the editor are included in:
A. Sports page B. Last page
C. Editorial page D. Local page

91. Official Secrets Act was passed in:
A. 1923 B. 1922
C. 1924 D. 1925

92. Times of India was the first newspaper to appoint:
A. Editor B. Managing editor
C. Executive editor D. Ombudsman

93. A press run of a publication for one day:
A. Edition B. Publication
C. Imprint D. Pre-print

94. The Right to Information Act was enacted in:
A. 2004 B. 2003
C. 2006 D. 2005

95. Who among the following is a journalist?
A. Kapil Sibil B. M.J. Akbar
C. Kiran Bedi D. Girish Karnad

96. Xinhua News Agency is the official state-run news agency of which country?
A. Japan B. China
C. Russia D. India

97. Find the odd man:
A. The Hindu B. Times of India
C. Indian Express D. Business Line

98. What is the job of development reporter?
A. To help in creating awareness about the developmental issues
B. To inform readers, listeners & viewers about various plans
C. To create an atmosphere of understanding the objectives of the schemes
D. All the above

99. Mandatory deadline for the release of a story is called:
A. Hold B. Scoop
C. Release D. Embargo

100. A publication started by Mahatma Gandhi:
A. The Harijan B. Bombay Samachar
C. Indian Mail D. The Times of India

101. .... is the practice of reporting on events or issues that are related to the legal system and the courts.
A. Legal reporting
B. Court journalism
C. Law and order coverage
D. Legal proceedings reporting

102. .... is the practice of reporting on events or issues that are related to the real estate and housing sectors.
A. Real estate reporting
B. Housing journalism
C. Property news coverage
D. Housing market reporting

103. .... is the practice of reporting on events or issues that are related to the environmental and sustainability sectors.
A. Environmental reporting
B. Sustainability journalism
C. Green coverage
D. Eco-journalism

104. Which among the following is/are a type of lead?
A. Summary B. Descriptive
C. Question D. All the above

105. Which one of the following is most perishable?
A. A book
B. A newspaper
C. A magazine
D. All the above are equally perishable

106. Which of the following is an example of how media can influence election outcomes?

A. By providing accurate and unbiased information about all candidates
B. By focusing heavily on certain candidates while ignoring others
C. By refusing to cover political campaigns
D. By only publishing press releases from political parties

107. Which among the following is/are a type of column writing?

(a) Question and Answer
(b) Miscellaneous
(c) Editorial
(d) Specialized

A. Both (a) and (c) B. Only (d)
C. (a), (b), (c) and (d) D. (a), (c) and (d)

108. The word 'journalism' is derived from the .... word 'Diurnalis'.

A. Latin B. French
C. Italian D. English

109. Which of the following revolutions is often cited as the first to be significantly influenced by media, particularly the printing press?

A. The American Revolution
B. The French Revolution
C. The Glorious Revolution
D. The Russian Revolution

110. .... is a creative and a subject article, which is designed to entertain and inform readers.

A. News story B. Feature
C. Editorials D. None of these

111. What is "media literacy"?

A. The ability to use social media effectively
B. The ability to critically analyze and evaluate information presented by media
C. The skill of working in a television studio
D. The knowledge of how to operate a printing press

112. .... is an interesting story about a real incident or a person.

A. Metaphors B. Anecdotes
C. Feature D. None of these

113. Who edits local news?

A. Sub Editor B. Stringer
C. Bureau Chief D. Assistant Editor

114. Reuters, a major global news agency, was originally founded in which country?

A. United States B. France
C. Germany D. United Kingdom

115. The Pioneer was started in Allahabad in the year

A. 1901 B. 1865
C. 1890 D. 1923

116. What role did pamphlets and newspapers play in the American Revolution?

A. They had no significant impact
B. They helped to spread revolutionary ideas and mobilize public opinion
C. They primarily supported the British monarchy
D. They focused solely on economic issues

117. Name of an Indian news agency:

A. PTI B. CNN
C. AP D. AFP

118. .... is copy and pictures running over two pages in the middle of the newspaper.

A. News peg B. Centre spread
C. Bleed D. Middle

119. Which among the following is/are a mode of writing?

A. Expository B. Journalistic
C. Persuasive D. All the above

120. In India, inverted pyramid style of writing is followed in the print industry.

A. True B. False

121. Which technological development played a crucial role in disseminating information during the Russian Revolution?

A. The telegraph B. The radio
C. The printing press D. The internet

122. .... means delete or exclude a story or part of a story.

A. DL B. Kill
C. Exclude D. Reject

123. Which of the following is NOT a key quality of a good journalist?

A. Strong communication skills
B. Investigative skills
C. A tendency towards sensationalism
D. Ethical awareness

124. A journalist's ability to quickly adapt to changing circumstances and learn new technologies is known as:

A. Persistence B. Adaptability
C. Curiosity D. Courage

125. The ability to question facts and opinions, analyze data, and make thoughtful decisions is:

A. Critical thinking B. Objectivity
C. Integrity D. Humility

126. **Assertion (A):** Curiosity is a vital trait for a journalist.

Reason (R): Journalists need to ask questions and seek out information to tell compelling stories.

A. Both A and R are true, and R is the correct explanation of A.
B. Both A and R are true, but R is NOT the correct explanation of A.
C. A is true, but R is false.
D. A is false, but R is true.

127. Which of the following is NOT an example of a journalist's communication skills?

A. Writing clear and concise articles
B. Conducting effective interviews
C. Delivering news in a calm and unbiased manner
D. Using social media to promote personal opinions

128. The ability to maintain your integrity and stand by your values even when facing pressure is an example of:

A. Courage B. Humility
C. Objectivity D. Persistence

129. The ability to find and report stories that others might not find or ignore is an example of:

A. Persistence B. Curiosity
C. Analytical skills D. Investigative skills

130. The ability to maintain a neutral and balanced perspective when reporting on a story is:

A. Objectivity B. Curiosity
C. Integrity D. Humility

131. Which of the following is one of the largest international news agencies, headquartered in New York City?

A. Reuters
B. Agence France-Presse (AFP)
C. Associated Press (AP)
D. Xinhua News Agency

132. The ability to remain determined and keep pursuing a story despite obstacles is:

A. Courage B. Persistence
C. Adaptability D. Curiosity

133. A piece of news obtained and published by one newspaper before its competitors is known as:

A. Exclusive B. Runner
C. Scoop D. Expose

134. Daniel Boorstin coined the term:

A. Greenpeace B. Pseudo-event
C. Images D. Jackpot

135. Who won Ramon Magsaysay for journalism in 2019?

A. Ravish Kumar B. Ajit Anjum
C. Rajdeep Sardesai D. Karan Thapar

136. The ability to understand and extract relevant information from interviews is:

A. Interviewing skills B. Communication skills
C. Analytical skills D. Investigative skills

137. "The media's the most powerful entity on earth. They have the power to make the innocent guilty and to make the guilty innocent, and that's power. Because they control the minds of the masses" was said by:

A. Malcom X B. Albert Camus
C. Hugo Black D. Prannoy Roy

138. A journalist's ability to use technology and social media effectively for newsgathering and reporting is:

A. Digital literacy B. Technical savvy
C. Analytical skills D. Communication skills

139. The oldest established news agency in the world:

A. Reuters B. AFP
C. UPI D. AP

140. The nodal agency of the Government to disseminate the information to the print media in Government policies:

A. PIB B. Door Darshan
C. Akash Vani D. Films Division

141. Development Journalism is:

A. Pro-capitalist B. Pro- Third world
C. Neutral D. Anti-Third world

142. Who founded the Indian Languages Newspapers Association?

A. Mahatma Gandhi B. Bal Gangadhar Tilak
C. Mammen Mappillai D. Amritlal Sheth

143. The printing press was introduced in India during

A. The thirteenth century
B. The fourteenth century
C. The fifteenth century
D. The sixteenth century

144. UNI for Univarta and PTI for

A. PTI- Hindi B. Varta
C. PTI Varta D. Bhasha

145. When Mahatma Gandhi was in South Africa he started which newspaper?
A. Young India B. Indian Opinion
C. Reformer D. Hindustan

146. Famous quote "The press was to serve the governed, not the governors" was said by:
A. Albert Camus B. Hugo Black
C. Kuldip Nayar D. Amanda Crawford

147. Assertion (A): A journalist's role is solely to report facts.
Reason (R): Interpretation and analysis are not part of a journalist's responsibility.
A. Both A and R are true, and R is the correct explanation of A.
B. Both A and R are true, but R is NOT the correct explanation of A.
C. A is true, but R is false.
D. A is false, but R is true.

148. Which popular newspaper is published in Australia and known for its national coverage?
A. The New Zealand Herald
B. The Age
C. The Sydney Morning Herald
D. The Star

149. Mirat-ul-Akbar belonged to:
A. Aurobindo Ghosh
B. Maulana Abdul Kalam Azad
C. Raja Ram Mohan Roy
D. Syed Abdulla Brelvi

150. Red, Yellow and .... are primary colors.
A. Blue B. Black
C. White D. Violet

151. The purpose of a slugline on a news story is to
A. enable reporters to write the headlines for their stories.
B. help editors identify and track news stories as they are prepared for publication.
C. hit a news organization's enemies with an insult.
D. identify the political orientation of a news story.

152. Multimedia reporters who are mobile with audio, video recorders and camera are often referred to as ....
A. mobijourno B. mobile
C. mojos D. journos

153. 'Chief Minister resigned' is an example of:
A. Summary intro B. Common intro
C. Bullet intro D. None of these

154. Article 19 (1) (a) of the Constitution of India guarantees ....
A. Freedom of speech and expression
B. Freedom to assemble without arms
C. Freedom to possess property
D. Freedom to practice profession

155. Find the odd one
A. Spoken word B. Penny press era
C. Press relations D. Written words

156. Hicky's Gazette was started in
A. 1750 B. 1850
C. 1780 D. 1870

157. Lokmanya Tilak published
A. Kesari B. Indian Herald
C. Indian citizen D. Indian News

158. According to Article 19(2) of Indian Constitution, the state can impose reasonable restrictions on the exercise of the freedom of expression and speech in the interests of:
A. Public order
B. Contempt of Court
C. The security of the state
D. All the above

159. Al Ameen was started by:
A. Vakkom Moulavi
B. N P Mohamed
C. Mohammed Abdul Rahman
D. E Moidu Moulavi

160. Which was the first Indian-owned English Newspaper?
A. Bengal Herald B. Reformer
C. Bombay Herald D. Bengal Gazette

161. 'Vernacular Press Act 'was initiated by
A. Lord Canning B. Lord Minto
C. Lord Rippon D. Lord Lytton

162. The most authentic and dependable circulation figures of newspapers are published by
A. RNI B. UNI
C. ABC D. PIB

163. Which was the year of inauguration of the Times of India?
A. 1866 B. 1838
C. 1861 D. 1826

164. Which of the following is /are called as 'fourth estate'?
A. Print media B. Electronic media
C. Visual media D. All the above

165. Largest circulated Government publication is:
A. Employment News B. Kurukshetra
C. Suraksha D. Yojna

166. What was the name of Jawaharlal Nehru's newspaper for youth and political awareness?
A. National Herald B. Young India
C. Harijan D. Pioneer

167. Which one of the following is not a Malayalam newspaper?
A. Mathrubhumi B. Deshabhimani
C. Malayala Manorama D. None of these

168. Which of the following is ***not*** included in the list of domestic news agencies?
A. Press Trust of India
B. The Express News Service
C. The United News of India
D. Reuters

169. Citizen journalism is the practice of:
A. preparing stories that will help citizens vote in elections.
B. publishing only those stories that are of interest to politically active citizens.
C. collaborating with non-profit organizations to prepare news stories.
D. inviting readers and viewers to participate in the creation of news content.

170. Folio line gives details of:
A. Editorial staff B. Index of stories
C. Company D. Page numbers

171. 'Middle' means:
A. A type of headline
B. An amusing write-up on the editorial page
C. A kind of advertisement
D. A style of writing

172. The name of the writer in the newspaper is referred to as:
A. credits B. dateline
C. byline D. All the above

173. Imprint line means:
A. Type size B. Details of registration
C. A printing method D. Lead story

174. The very first story in the front page of the newspaper is termed as:
A. Lead B. Editorial
C. Feature D. Kicker

175. In journalism, a "mojo" is a:
A. journalist who has an unusual degree of sex appeal.
B. source who provides a journalist with a good-luck charm.
C. source who has the ability to bounce back from adversity.
D. journalist who carries her tools—computers, cameras, recorders—with her at all times.

176. Another name for Banner headline is:
A. Kicker head B. Line head
C. Crossline D. Hammer head

177. The other name of feature is:
A. Color story B. Entertainer
C. Brightener D. Lightner

178. National Press Day is on:
A. November 1 B. October 21
C. November 16 D. January 7

179. Match the following:
(a) Kheda Vartman 1. Gujarati
(b) Malayala Manorama 2. Bengali
(c) Anandabazar Patrika 3. Hindi
(d) Dainik Bhaskar 4. Malayalam
A. (a)-2, (b)-4, (c)-3, (d)-1
B. (a)-3, (b)-4, (c)-2, (d)-1
C. (a)-1, (b)-4, (c)-2, (d)-3
D. (a)-4, (b)-2, (c)-1, (d)-3

180. The New Trend in journalism:
A. Sensationalism B. Patriotism
C. Socialism D. Mechanism

181. The term fourth estate is coined by:
A. Edmund Burke B. Thomas Carlyle
C. Laski D. Henry Fayol

182. Freedom of press deals with:
A. Reporting
B. Editing
C. Freedom of expression
D. None of these

183. Editor is the person who is .... news for the newspaper or journal.
A. Reporting B. Editing
C. Collecting D. Publishing

184. Parliamentary proceedings (Protection of Publications) Act of 1956 is popularly known as:
A. Indira Gandhi Act
B. Contempt of Legislation Act
C. Feroze Gandhi Act
D. State Legislation Act

185. Find the odd man
A. The Hindu B. Times of India
C. Indian Express D. Business Line

186. Privacy is protected by laws relating to defamation under
A. The Constitution
B. Indian Penal Code
C. Press Council of India
D. Law of Torts

187. The Copyright Act was enacted in
A. 1957 B. 1959
C. 1956 D. 1958

188. The most popular Internet sites for Americans seeking news are those operated by
A. bloggers who have a clear political ideology.
B. bloggers who repackage news from traditional news organizations.
C. traditional news organizations, such as newspapers and TV stations.
D. web sites operated by companies not affiliated with traditional news media.

189. The Contempt of court Act was enacted in
A. 1973 B. 1972
C. 1971 D. 1970

190. Directive principles aim at establishing
A. Welfare state B. Socialist state
C. Gandhian state D. Ideal state

191. Fundamental duties have been added to the Constitution by inserting
A. Article 51 A B. Article 54 A
C. Article 53 A D. Article 52 A

192. Slander and libel are associated with:
A. Assault B. Defamation
C. Nuisance D. Hot news

193. Press and registration of books Act
A. 1871 B. 1867
C. 1869 D. 1873

194. According to Social responsibility Theory, who is responsible for the media content?
A. editors B. reporters
C. proprietors D. All the above

195. 'Amrita Bazar Patrika' was initially started as a vernacular weekly in which language?
A. Hindi B. Bengali
C. Urdu D. Marathi

196. **Assertion (A):** Adaptability is essential for journalists.
Reason (R): The media landscape is constantly changing, requiring journalists to learn new technologies and skills.
A. Both A and R are true, and R is the correct explanation of A
B. Both A and R are true, but R is NOT the correct explanation of A
C. A is true, but R is false
D. A is false, but R is true

197. Journalists start collecting answers to the questions of ....
A. 6W and 2H B. 5W and 2H
C. 5W and 1H D. 4W and 1H

198. Which among the following is true about the journalism as a profession?
(a) In 20th Century it was the extending organizations of profession.
(b) An increase in the social accountability that journalists should undertake.
(c) It was a growing literature that dealt with the problems of masses.
A. Only (a) B. Only (b)
C. Only (c) D. All the above

199. Yellow journalism is all about ....
A. exaggerations of news incidents
B. scandal-mongering
C. sensationalism of news stories
D. all of these

200. Which among the following is ***not*** included in the qualities of journalist?
A. irrational thoughts
B. high quality communication
C. obligation and promptness
D. professional personality

201. Which newspaper was started by M.M. Malaviya to serve the cause of the nation?
A. Hindustan Times B. The Leader
C. The Tribune D. The Pioneer

202. Which among the following is ***not*** true about the functions of journalism?
(a) It helps in changing public opinion.
(b) It acts as an agent of change.
(c) It enables decision making.
A. Only (a) B. Only (b)
C. Only (c) D. None of these

203. The essence of the journalism profession lies in ....
A. incidents and happenings
B. exploring the truth
C. both A and B
D. None of these

204. Media General's creation of a single center for its newspaper, television and Internet news organizations in Tampa, Fla., is an example of
A. conglomerate journalism
B. convergence
C. vertical integration
D. horizontal integration

205. What was the name of the revolutionary paper started by Bhagat Singh?
A. Kirti B. Vande Matram
C. Yugantar D. The Leader

206. Which among the following is included in the obligations of journalism?
A. unfurl truth B. allegiance to citizens
C. free from bias D. all of these

207. Which among the following is true about the duties of journalists?
(a) They must write reports as per the newspaper and agency standards.
(b) They have to follow press laws and ethics.
(c) They need to perform entry level work at a professional level.
A. Only (a) B. Only (b)
C. Only (c) D. All the above

208. Journalists need to differentiate between ....
A. marketing B. public relations
C. journalism D. All the above

209. What kind of research a journalist must perform?
A. Qualitative B. Quantitative
C. Both A and B D. None of these

210. Which English weekly was founded by Subhas Chandra Bose?
A. Young India B. Forward Bloc
C. The Forward D. Liberty

211. **Assertion (A):** Journalists should avoid challenging authority.
Reason (R): Maintaining good relationships with powerful figures is crucial for access to information.
A. Both A and R are true, and R is the correct explanation of A.
B. Both A and R are true, but R is NOT the correct explanation of A.
C. A is true, but R is false.
D. A is false, but R is true.

212. Who among the following is categorized under the type of journalist?
A. cameraman B. editor
C. reporter D. All the above

213. Who is a columnist?
A. One who write detailed stories on news.
B. One who writes daily reports on current happenings.
C. One who writes for a particular section pertaining to a specific theme or topic.
D. None of these

214. What was the name of the nationalist newspaper started by Lala Lajpat Rai?
A. Tribune B. Vande Matram
C. Punjabee D. The People

215. What makes Journalism - a tempting profession?
A. desire to be recognized and known
B. desire to write
C. desire to create awareness
D. All the above

216. Which among the following is *not* true about the skills of journalists?
A. They must have the ability to observe data on accurate lines.
B. Determination to get news out of people or society.
C. They need to be introvert in dealing with people.
D. Journalists must be keen about incidents in the surroundings.

217. Who was the editor of the newspaper 'Vande Matram'?
A. Bipin Chandra Pal
B. Sri Aurobindo Ghosh
C. Madam Bhikaiji Cama
D. Lala Lajpat Rai

218. In the questions below there are two statements labeled as Assertion (A) and Reason (R). which one of the following is correct?
Assertion (A): A newspaper is a mass-media tool.
Reason (R): Newspaper connects masses with pieces of information.
A. Both A and R are true, R is the correct explanation of A
B. Both A and R are true, R is not the correct explanation of A
C. A is true, R is false
D. A is false, R is true

219. News is ....
A. something that is extra-ordinary
B. a rare occurring event
C. something that is normal
D. Both A and B

220. From the following examples which one is considered as a news?
A. "a man bites a dog"
B. "a dog bites a man"
C. both A and B
D. None of these

221. Match the following elements of newsworthiness to their meanings.

(a) Timeliness	1. unusual or unexpected
(b) Proximity	2. Something that is new
(c) Prominence	3. geographical and psychological implications
(d) Human Interest	4. news about a prominent personality
(e) Bizarre	5. events that interest humans.

A. (a)-2, (b)-3, (c)-4, (d)-5, (e)-1
B. (a)-3, (b)-2, (c)-1, (d)-4, (e)-5
C. (a)-2, (b)-1, (e)-3, (d)-4, (c)-5
D. (a)-4, (b)-2, (c)-1, (d)-3, (e)-5

222. In the questions given below are two statements labeled as Assertion (A) and Reason (R). In the context of the two statements, which one of the following is correct?

Assertion (A): Worthiness of news depends on the consequences.

Reason (R): An outcome that makes people surprised or has a big impact on them.

A. Both A and R are true, R is the correct explanation of A
B. Both A and R are true, R is not the correct explanation of A
C. A is true, R is false
D. A is false, R is true

223. In the questions given below are two statements labeled as Assertion (A) and Reason (R). In the context of the two statements, which one of the following is correct?

Assertion (A): Journalism is considered as a tempting profession.

Reason (R): Journalists are known for their in-depth knowledge about events.

A. Both A and R are true, R is the correct explanation of A
B. Both A and R are true, R is not the correct explanation of A
C. A is true, R is false
D. A is false, R is true

224. In the questions given below are two statements labeled as Assertion (A) and Reason (R). In the context of the two statements, which one of the following is correct?

Assertion (A): Journalists face cut-throat competitions across their profession.

Reason (R): They compete to present the best stories.

A. Both A and R are true, R is the correct explanation of A
B. Both A and R are true, R is not the correct explanation of A
C. A is true, R is false
D. A is false, R is true

225. Match the following:

(a) Bleed	1. Illustration of the picture that runs into the edge of the page
(b) 20th century	2. Social accountability in journalism
(c) Reporters	3. Gathers information
(d) Whistle blowing	4. Investigative journalism

A. (a)-2, (b)-3, (c)-4, (d)-1
B. (a)-3, (b)-2, (c)-1, (d)-4
C. (a)-1, (b)-2, (c)-3, (d)-4
D. (a)-4, (b)-2, (c)-1, (d)-3

226. Match the following:

A. Newspaper	1. Tunisia Revolution
B. Journalism	2. Accountable to society
C. Jasmine Revolution	3. Readership

A. (a)-2, (b)-3, (c)-1
B. (a)-3, (b)-2, (c)-1
C. (a)-1, (b)-2, (c)-3
D. None of these

227. Which of the following is ***not*** a responsibility of a journalist?

A. professional responsibility
B. legal responsibility
C. ethical responsibility
D. None of these

228. Which major newspaper is published in Spain and is one of the country's newspapers of record?

A. Público B. El País
C. La Vanguardia D. ABC

229. Sensational, often irresponsible journalism is identified as

A. Parachute Journalism
B. Yellow Journalism
C. Neo-Journalism
D. Party Press

230. Which among the following is related to legal responsibilities of a journalists?

A. law of slander B. libel
C. Both A and B D. None of these

231. Which among the following is ***not*** a true statement?
A. Journalists act as a defender of democracy.
B. They are allowed to interfere in someone's private life if the matter is of public concern.
C. Identity of a major is always to be protected if they are accused.
D. Journalists are not allowed to expose the identity of a victim.

232. Which among the following is ***not*** true about the professional conduct of a journalist?
A. Journalists can make use of special investigation techniques to obtain information.
B. Opinions can be mixed with the information.
C. Confidentiality of the sources of information has to be maintained by journalist.
D. None of these

233. A .... is the defamatory statement that is made verbally.
A. backbiting B. misrepresentation
C. disparagement D. slander

234. The proportion of people who get their news from mobile devices was recently estimated at
A. about one-quarter B. about three-quarters
C. about two-thirds D. about half

235. News in leading media can lead to
A. change in stock prices
B. corporate collapses
C. resignation of senior office holders
D. all of these

236. Journalists recognize two types of news stories: hard and soft. In this regard:
A. "hard news" is about complicated topics, which are difficult to understand, and "soft news" is about things that are written in simple language.
B. "hard news" stories have long, complicated sentences, and "soft news" stories have short, simple sentences.
C. "hard news" is about serious topics and recent events, and "soft news" refers to human interest stories.
D. "hard news" stories are always 2,000 words or more, and "soft news" stories never exceed 500 words.

237. In journalism, "convergence" means
A. sharing facilities, newsgathering resources, personnel or content.
B. different news media all cover the same story in the same way.
C. the content of one newspaper is indistinguishable from that of any other newspaper.
D. news organizations are all striving to put the same ideological slant on news stories.

238. Which among the following is included in the tools of gathering news?
A. listening skills B. covering events
C. press conferences D. All the above

239. What among the following is ***not*** included in essentials of news stories?
A. lead B. angle
C. body D. None of these

240. Journalism is
A. something that requires a professional degree or training
B. is the medium of communication
C. is bonded to some news organization
D. speculation and coverage of incidents and issues towards a broad audience

241. Mistake in news reading is known as:
A. fluff B. foot in the door
C. ident D. lift

242. .... is a headline composed of single line.
A. Credit line B. Cut line
C. Catch line D. Cross line

243. Who is a famous columnist?
A. Bob Wood Word B. Khushwant Singh
C. Barkha Dutt D. Shobha De

244. Which among the following is/are included in the objections of journalism?
(a) Journalism provides an honest description of news.
(b) Journalists strictly follow the policy of freedom of speech and expression.
(c) Journalism is a service-oriented profession.
(d) Courage is an essential quality every journalist must possess.
A. Only (a), (b) and (c) B. Only (a) and (d)
C. Only (c) and (d) D. All the above

245. Which among the following is ***not*** true about the nature of journalism?
(a) Journalism is just limited to reporting.
(b) Journalists has to maintain ethics and standards.
(c) Journalism act as a liaison element.
A. Only (a) and (b) B. Only (b) and (c)
C. Only (a) and (c) D. All the above

246. A line of dots in printing is defined as:
A. kicker spots B. disjoints
C. leaders D. dotline

247. Another name for filler copy is:
A. casual copy B. time copy
C. hard copy D. slug copy

248. Which one of the following is ***not*** a Gujarati newspaper?
A. Bombay Samachar B. Matrubhumi
C. Gujarati Samachar D. Sandesh

249. Which of the following newspapers was started by Dadabhai Naoroji?
A. Voice of India B. Indian Opinion
C. The Bengalee D. Young India

250. **Assertion (A):** Journalists should always present information objectively.
Reason (R): Personal biases can distort the accuracy of reporting.
A. Both A and R are true, and R is the correct explanation of A.
B. Both A and R are true, but R is NOT the correct explanation of A.
C. A is true, but R is false.
D. A is false, but R is true.

251. Which among the following are included in the predicaments of journalism?
(a) Dealing with the issues related to National Security
(b) Intervention policy
(c) Non-discriminatory coverage
A. Only (a) and (b) B. Only (b) and (c)
C. Only (a) and (c) D. All the above

252. If a newspaper is of 280 x 430 mm, it is known as ....
A. tabloid size B. standard size
C. broadsheet size D. compact size

253. Forfeiture of any publication, containing prohibited contents, is permitted under
A. Finance Act, 1978
B. Criminal Procedure Code
C. Copyright Act
D. Press and Registration of Books Act

254. To choose the news items for the newspaper and to correct the language, spelling and remove all the unimportant sentences are the functions of
A. writer B. reporter
C. sub-editor D. None of these

255. Identify the correct sequence of newspaper format.
A. mast-head, headline, conclusion, body
B. body, conclusion, headline, mast-head
C. conclusion, headline, body, mast-head
D. mast-head, headline, body, conclusion

256. A journalist need not be .... while covering an event.
A. impartial B. meticulous
C. domineering D. inquisitive

257. Match the following.

List-I (Newspaper)	List-II (Language)
(a) Deshdoot	1. Bengali
(b) Udayavani	2. Malayalam
(c) Mathrubhumi	3. Kannada
(d) Dainik Pratidin	4. Marathi

A. (a)-1, (b)-2, (c)-3, (d)-4
B. (a)-4, (b)-3, (c)-1, (d)-2
C. (a)-3, (b)-4, (c)-2, (d)-1
D. (a)-4, (b)-3, (c)-2, (d)-1

258. Which of the following was considered as 'Gagging Act'?
A. Indian Penal Code
B. Indian Press Code
C. Vernacular Press Act
D. Press (Emergency) Powers Act, 1931

259. Which was the newspaper that Mahatma Gandhi edited in the year of 1919?
A. Indian Opinion B. The National Herald
C. The Pioneer D. Satyagraha

260. Times of India was the merger of which three papers?
A. Bombay Times, Standard, Telegraph
B. Standard, Telegraph, Mid-Day
C. Telegraph, Mid-Day, Chronicle
D. Mid-Day, Chronicle, Mathrubhumi

261. Which Newspaper logo bears "Let Truth prevail"?
A. The Statesman B. Times of India
C. The Tribune D. The Hindu

262. One reason for newspapers and magazines being no longer the only place for journalists is
A. technology and digitisation of information has made journalists redundant
B. all journalists have shifted to social media
C. online blogging sites have become popular with readers
D. None of these

263. 'Tabloid Journalism' is also called
A. Yellow Journalism
B. Red Journalism
C. White Journalism
D. None of these

264. Annie Besant was associated with which of the following newspapers?
A. The Bengalee
B. New India
C. The Amrita Bazar Patrika
D. The Tribune

265. Who started The Tribune?
A. Prem Bhatia
B. Dayal Singh Majithia
C. James Augustus Hickey
D. Master Tara Singh

266. Which of the following is NOT true about journalism today?
A. Stories created for one medium are likely to be found in other media.
B. Few people nowadays rely on journalists for information about important events.
C. The techniques for researching and writing stories continue to be important.
D. The tenets of good journalism—critical thinking, clear writing and organized presentation—remain the same.

267. The reach of print media is limited by the ....
A. language of its publication
B. literacy of the population
C. area in which it is distributed
D. All the above

268. Mahatma Gandhi was the editor of
A. Indian Opinion
B. Young India
C. Harijan
D. All the above

269. What is a house journal?
A. It is a magazine of a publishing group that is given free of cost to some readers
B. It is a private in-house magazine that is circulated among the members of a firm, industry or trade and it conveys the views of the management or other people working in that firm/industry/trade
C. It is a low-cost edition of a top-selling magazine that is sold to specific market niches at a low cost
D. None of these

270. Which newspaper was founded by Motilal Nehru?
A. The Hindu
B. The Leader
C. The Independent
D. The Bombay Chronicle

271. Who is a crime reporter?
A. A person who gives information to the media about police operations
B. A Journalist who writes news, views and articles about the crime scenario
C. A Journalist who covers the news related to criminal courts
D. A person who keeps in touch with the CBI and gives vital facts to the press about its operations

272. Identify the correct chronological sequence of the following newspapers that were launched during the freedom movement.
A. Bombay Herald, Madras Courier, Madras Gazette, Asiatic Mirror
B. Asiatic Mirror, Bombay Herald, Madras Courier, Madras Gazette
C. Madras Courier, Bombay Herald, Asiatic Mirror, Madras Gazette
D. Madras Gazette, Madras Courier, Bombay Herald, Asiatic Mirror

273. Which of the following is NOT true about journalism today?
A. A journalist needs a great deal of money to start a new news organization.
B. Journalists have a wider choice of career paths than in the past.
C. The journalism industry is evolving as people get their news in new ways.
D. Creative ideas for journalistic content and delivery systems are springing up everywhere.

274. Traditional news media—newspapers, magazines and broadcast news operations—provide what percentage of the factual information on the Internet?
A. 70 per cent
B. 55 per cent
C. 85 per cent
D. 90 per cent

275. The dateline on a news story indicates the
A. time when the story occurred.
B. place where the events described in the story took place.
C. date when the story was written.
D. date when the story should be published.

276. A news story is said to possess timeliness if it:
A. stresses events that have occurred in the last month.
B. includes anything that has been written within the last six hours.
C. stresses events that occurred today or yesterday.
D. has been read or heard by the reader within the last six hours.

277. Bias is most likely to appear in a news story when:
A. the reporter relies on multiple sources and gives abundant time or space to all sides of a controversy.

B. the reporter is writing about a topic that she or he already knows a lot about.

C. the reporter's story is reviewed by a large number of editors and supervisors.

D. the reporter relies on one source or gives disproportionate time to space to one side of a controversy.

278. The concept of proximity suggests that a news organization is likely to carry a story about a murder, if that crime:

A. involved a prominent person.

B. was committed locally.

C. occurred within the last 24 hours.

D. was unusually gruesome.

279. Which of the following is NOT true about journalism today?

A. Stories created for one medium are likely to be found in other media.

B. Few people nowadays rely on journalists for information about important events.

C. The techniques for researching and writing stories continue to be important

D. The smallest matters surrounding film personalities are often reported.

280. Which news value is prioritized in reporting the smallest matters surrounding film personalities?

A. prominence B. threshold

C. hypothesis D. meaningfulness

281. Stories that tug on the readers' heartstrings contain which feature?

A. human interest B. bizarre

C. threshold D. prominence

282. One reason news reporters sometimes use euphemisms is that they:

A. wish to avoid offending readers when they discuss sensitive and graphic topics such as death.

B. prefer using euphemisms to jargon.

C. are trying to avoid using clichés.

D. are trying to avoid sentences with excessive punctuation.

283. Reporters avoid clichés because they:

A. require too much originality, thought and time.

B. have been used so often they have lost their impact.

C. generally, cannot be understood by readers and viewers.

D. almost always shock or offend readers and viewers.

284. Which newspaper was started by Bal Gangadhar Tilak, a prominent leader of the Indian independence movement?

A. The Pioneer B. Kesari

C. The Tribune D. The Statesman

285. Which of the following should a summary news lead of a hard news story NOT try to do:

A. Provide the most important information

B. Stress what is unusual or interesting.

C. Convey the most recent information.

D. Start with a story

286. All trades and professions have jargon, but the problem jargon creates for news reporters is that it:

A. is sometimes used to mislead or confuse readers.

B. makes them look foolish in the eyes of their editors.

C. requires them to consult their dictionaries.

D. makes them look overeducated in the eyes of their readers.

287. What the reporter records while attending a certain event is:

A. bias B. personal observation

C. records D. stored sources

288. What should NOT be done while reporting Gender Based Violence?

A. Give details that would lead to identification of the survivor

B. Do not characterize offenders as inhuman monsters

C. Use images that reflect resilience and strength of the survivor

D. Be sensitive while interviewing survivors

289. Which of the following provide second-hand information and commentary from other researchers and include examples include journal articles, reviews, and academic books?

A. Primary sources B. Secondary sources

C. Cyber sources D. Personal sources

290. Which newspaper was started by Mahatma Gandhi to promote his philosophy of non-violence and social reform?

A. Young India B. Amrita Bazar Patrika

C. The Hindu D. Kesari

291. ……… is a story which is written so that the journalist can report more of a story which has already been published or broadcast.

A. Beat story B. Follow-up story

C. Journalism D. Headline

292. Which of the following is NOT the reason why follow-up stories needed?
- A. Journalists impose space and time limits on their reports which do not always reflect how important the event is in the real world
- B. So that the journalist can report more of a story which has already been published or broadcast
- C. To report those extra details can be new facts, later developments, reactions or new issues which have been raised by the original event.
- D. To discredit earlier stories that were reported on the same topic.

293. What is a disadvantage of beat reporting?
- A. Beats allow reporters to cover the subjects they are most passionate about
- B. Covering a beat also allows the reporter to build up expertise on a topic
- C. Spending time on a beat enables the reporter to build up a good collection of sources on that beat, so that they can get good stories and get them quickly
- D. Many reporters, after spending several years covering a beat, will crave a change of scenery and new challenges.

294. Which of the following is NOT a news value in crime beat reporting?
- A. Seriousness
- B. Unusual nature of the crime
- C. Size of the community
- D. Entertainment

295. Words like "flabbergast," "blizzard" and "GI" are examples of words that have become accepted in English but started as:
- A. clichés
- B. jargon
- C. euphemisms
- D. slang

296. Which of the following is a story structure in which the story unfolds through time; sequence and actions are the material of the investigation?
- A. Chronological
- B. Narratives
- C. Inverted Pyramid
- D. Processes

297. Which of the following is NOT among the kinds of details news organizations avoid including in their stories?
- A. unverifiable facts
- B. names of criminal suspects
- C. profanity
- D. grisly or gruesome photographs

298. Who is a person, usually an employee, who exposes information or activity within a private, public, or government organization that is deemed illegal, illicit, unsafe, or a waste, fraud, or abuse of taxpayer funds?
- A. Muckraker
- B. Journalist
- C. Whistleblower
- D. Reporter

299. ………….. means the action of searching out and publicizing scandal about famous people.
- A. Muckraking
- B. Beat journalism
- C. Crisis reporting
- D. Traditional journalism

300. Responsibility for securing the scene, preserving life and treating the wounded is the responsibility of
- A. First responders
- B. Mental health professionals
- C. Journalists
- D. All citizens

301. The media tends to cover power struggles in political parties, but fails to cover the ………….. of the power struggles.
- A. impact
- B. winner
- C. situation and location
- D. time

302. Veteran journalist and consultant Michael Marcotte says a news organization plays four key roles during a crisis, informing what is happening. Which of the following are the four key roles?
- A. what, who is affected, how things are changing, and what is the meaning.
- B. where, which prominent personality is affected, how things are changing, and why.
- C. where, who is affected, how things are changing, and why.
- D. graphic descriptions, who is affected, how things are changing, and why.

303. Which of the following is NOT an advantage in recording an interview?
- A. Easier to transcribe
- B. Allows for smooth flow of communication
- C. Does not record personal observation of the interviewer
- D. Minimises loss of information

304. The Press Council has stated that ………….. Act is vital for the media and its endeavour to be a watch dog of the society as there are few journalists who are able to break the iron curtain of the official non-cooperation.
- A. Right to Information
- B. Right to Investigation
- C. Right to Institution
- D. Right to Inspection

305. Citizen journalism does NOT involve
A. Private individuals
B. Amateur journalists
C. Traditional journalists
D. Consumers of traditional journalism

306. Maulana Abul Kalam Azad started his weekly, the .... on June 1, 1912.
A. Al Hilal B. Mirat-ul-Akbar
C. Madina D. Quami Awaz

307. Which of the following is NOT among the reasons journalists complain about a lack of objectivity in news releases?
A. The release describes an event or product that might interest the public
B. The release is laden with adjectives and puffery
C. The release is little more than a blatant advertisement
D. The release is telling the public what to do

308. What has NOT played a role in making citizen journalism more accessible to people worldwide?
A. social networking websites
B. media-sharing websites
C. increasing prevalence of cellular telephones
D. encouragement from professional journalism

309. Having a/an .... perspective(s) is an advantage of citizen journalism because it creates a clearer picture of the event.
A. multiple B. one
C. honest D. local

310. Which among the following is a magazine based on woman published by Malayala Manorama?
A. Vanitha B. Manorama
C. Mangalam D. Grihalakshmi

311. Which one of the following is the part of Indian Express Private Ltd.?
A. Jansatta
B. Lok Satta
C. Financial Express
D. All the Above

312. .... determines which party and politicians come to power, and which policies are adopted.
A. Neighbour's opinion
B. Husband's opinion
C. Public opinion
D. Individual opinion

313. Instead of ideological bias and manifestos, more media coverage is given to ....
A. speeches and inflammatory comments
B. funds and finance investigation of the parties
C. achievements and accolades
D. peaceful debates

314. Criticism of the press is that they are mostly owned and controlled by the ....
A. Capitalists B. Journalists
C. Editors D. Reporters

315. The term Agenda setting Theory of Media was postulated during the study of?
A. The second world war
B. Influence of media on gay rights
C. 1968 American Presidential Elections
D. The influence of Media on household rules

316. The Agenda Setting Theory was developed by two researchers named?
A. Max McCombs and Donald Shaw
B. Walter Lippmann and David price
C. Richard Wright and Rose Becker
D. Benard Cohen and Franklin Buck

317. Quite often, during the elections, media persons ignore to .... and buy into the claims of political parties and politicians.
A. wide traveling and direct contacts with people
B. internet research
C. office gossip
D. following television reports thoroughly

318. The best and only method for a journalist to assess public opinion is by ....
A. wide travelling and direct contacts with people
B. internet research
C. office gossip
D. following television reports thoroughly

319. If the media approaches an election with pre-conceived notions about a party's performance, it can lead to ....
A. shaping of an agenda where bright prospects of the party is reported
B. gatekeeping
C. political unrest
D. inactive audience

320. Which one of the following newspapers does ***not*** belong to Jagran Prakashan Ltd.?
A. Dainik Jagran B. Nai Duniya
C. Dainik Bhaskar D. All the above

321. Barack Obama ensured a victory for the Democrats in the U.S. Presidential election of ....
A. 2008 B. 2009
C. 2007 D. 2015

322. In which year did the Kargil Conflict take place?
A. 1965 B. 1974
C. 1993 D. 1999

323. What Caused the Arab Spring in Syria?
A. Khan Abdul Gaffar
B. Overthrow of President Bashar Al-Assad
C. Al-Fahid
D. Mohammed Bouazizi

324. Marginalisation refers to ....
A. Elite class of Society
B. Celebrities
C. Group of people who are removed from society
D. Youth of Society

325. Article 17 of Indian Constitution deals with?
A. Freedom of Movement
B. Freedom of Speech
C. Untouchability
D. Freedom to choose any religion

326. Press Registration act was passed in ....
A. 1866 B. 1867
C. 1868 D. 1869

327. Ramnath Goenka came up with Hindi newspaper, the name of the newspaper was ....
A. Janshakti B. Jansatta
C. Vandebharat D. Navbharat

328. How has the rise of social media affected political discourse?
A. It has led to more in-depth and thoughtful discussions.
B. It has created echo chambers and facilitated the spread of misinformation.
C. It has decreased political polarization.
D. It has made political campaigns less expensive.

329. Femina, a non-news fortnightly is published by
A. Benett Coleman & Co. Ltd.
B. Hindustan Times Group
C. Express Publications Ltd.
D. Express Publication (Bombay Ltd.)

330. UNI was established in ....
A. 1960 B. 1955
C. 1961 D. 1966

331. The first foreign news agency to start its operations in India was
A. Associated Press B. DPA
C. Reuters D. TASS

332. Widow in newspaper production refers to
A. isolated word B. useless headline
C. bad break D. tie break

333. IANS stands for ....
A. Indo – American News Service
B. International Agency of News Service
C. Indo – Asian News Source
D. Indo – Asian News Service

334. Throw line is
A. fragmented scenes of a large event
B. graphic representation
C. transition from one visual to another
D. a sentence in the news story that leads to a sound bite

335. Police story means:
A. newspaper's stand on an issue
B. opposing a police action
C. highlighting a day's events
D. correcting a blunder in the edition

336. In newspaper parlance, sacred cow means
A. highlighting an insane issue
B. using many adjectives
C. a favourable treatment to a story
D. management's favour to an employee

337. Which business house owns the Hindustan Times?
A. TATA group B. Birla group
C. Goenka group D. India Today group

338. Which popular newspaper is known for its in-depth reporting and is published in the United Kingdom?
A. The Wall Street Journal
B. USA Today
C. The Guardian
D. China Daily

339. Which influential newspaper is published in France and known for its comprehensive coverage of national and international news?
A. El País
B. Le Monde
C. Frankfurter Allgemeine Zeitung
D. The Globe and Mail

340. Which of the following is a prominent daily newspaper published in Germany?
A. Corriere della Sera
B. Folha de S.Paulo
C. Frankfurter Allgemeine Zeitung
D. The Australian

ANSWERS

1	2	3	4	5	6	7	8	9	10
A	C	D	C	C	D	B	B	C	A
11	**12**	**13**	**14**	**15**	**16**	**17**	**18**	**19**	**20**
B	D	C	C	B	C	B	B	B	D
21	**22**	**23**	**24**	**25**	**26**	**27**	**28**	**29**	**30**
D	A	D	B	C	B	B	C	C	A
31	**32**	**33**	**34**	**35**	**36**	**37**	**38**	**39**	**40**
B	C	A	B	D	C	B	B	C	B
41	**42**	**43**	**44**	**45**	**46**	**47**	**48**	**49**	**50**
B	A	C	B	A	C	C	A	B	C
51	**52**	**53**	**54**	**55**	**56**	**57**	**58**	**59**	**60**
C	A	D	A	D	A	B	A	C	A
61	**62**	**63**	**64**	**65**	**66**	**67**	**68**	**69**	**70**
B	A	B	C	C	C	A	D	D	A
71	**72**	**73**	**74**	**75**	**76**	**77**	**78**	**79**	**80**
D	A	B	B	C	D	A	B	B	A
81	**82**	**83**	**84**	**85**	**86**	**87**	**88**	**89**	**90**
B	A	C	B	B	C	B	A	D	C
91	**92**	**93**	**94**	**95**	**96**	**97**	**98**	**99**	**100**
A	D	A	D	B	B	D	D	D	A
101	**102**	**103**	**104**	**105**	**106**	**107**	**108**	**109**	**110**
A	A	A	D	B	B	C	A	B	B
111	**112**	**113**	**114**	**115**	**116**	**117**	**118**	**119**	**120**
B	B	A	D	B	B	A	B	D	A
121	**122**	**123**	**124**	**125**	**126**	**127**	**128**	**129**	**130**
C	B	C	B	A	A	D	A	D	A
131	**132**	**133**	**134**	**135**	**136**	**137**	**138**	**139**	**140**
C	B	A	B	A	A	A	A	B	A
141	**142**	**143**	**144**	**145**	**146**	**147**	**148**	**149**	**150**
B	B	D	D	B	B	D	C	C	A
151	**152**	**153**	**154**	**155**	**156**	**157**	**158**	**159**	**160**
B	C	A	A	B	C	A	D	D	D
161	**162**	**163**	**164**	**165**	**166**	**167**	**168**	**169**	**170**
D	C	B	D	A	A	D	D	D	D
171	**172**	**173**	**174**	**175**	**176**	**177**	**178**	**189**	**190**
A	C	B	A	D	D	A	C	C	A
181	**182**	**183**	**184**	**185**	**186**	**187**	**188**	**189**	**190**
B	C	B	C	D	B	A	C	D	A
191	**192**	**193**	**194**	**195**	**196**	**197**	**198**	**199**	**200**
A	B	B	D	B	A	C	D	D	A
201	**202**	**203**	**204**	**205**	**206**	**207**	**208**	**209**	**210**
B	D	C	B	A	D	D	D	C	C
211	**212**	**213**	**214**	**215**	**216**	**217**	**218**	**219**	**220**
D	D	C	D	D	C	B	A	D	A
221	**222**	**223**	**224**	**225**	**226**	**227**	**228**	**229**	**230**
A	A	B	A	C	B	D	B	B	C

231	232	233	234	235	236	237	238	239	240
C	B	D	B	D	C	A	D	D	D
241	242	243	244	245	246	247	248	249	250
A	D	D	D	B	C	B	B	A	A
251	252	253	254	255	256	257	258	259	260
D	A	B	C	D	C	D	C	A	A
261	262	263	264	265	266	267	268	269	270
B	C	A	B	B	B	D	D	B	C
271	272	273	274	275	276	277	278	279	280
B	C	A	C	B	C	D	B	B	A
281	282	283	284	285	286	287	288	289	290
A	A	B	B	D	A	B	A	B	A
291	292	293	294	295	296	297	298	299	300
B	D	D	D	D	B	B	C	A	A
301	302	303	304	305	306	307	308	309	310
A	A	C	A	C	A	A	D	A	A
311	312	313	314	315	316	317	318	319	320
D	C	A	A	C	A	A	A	A	C
321	322	323	324	325	326	327	328	329	330
A	D	B	C	C	B	B	B	A	C
331	332	333	334	335	336	337	338	339	340
C	A	D	D	A	C	B	C	B	C

EXPLANATORY ANSWERS

1. (A): Hard news is the kind of most important news that usually appears on the front page of newspapers. It is called spot news because it is reported immediately as it occurs and is always the latest one.

31. (B): Marshall McLuhan's concept of "the medium is the message" argues that the communication medium itself, rather than the content it conveys, shapes how we perceive and understand information. This idea was particularly relevant to the 1960 presidential debate between John F. Kennedy and Richard Nixon, as it was the first televised debate, influencing how the candidates were perceived and ultimately impacting the election outcome.

37. (B): Citizen journalism, also known as collaborative media, participatory journalism, democratic journalism, guerrilla journalism or street journalism, is based upon public citizens playing an active role in the process of collecting, reporting, analyzing, and disseminating news and information. Citizens participate in certain events or happenings giving their comments and opinions. Even some citizens give information and happenings to media about the things happening in their area.

51. (C): In the Cloze procedure, words are removed from a passage, and participants are asked to fill in the blanks using the context of the surrounding words. This method helps determine how easily a specific audience can understand and comprehend the material.

72. (A): The Working Journalists Act come in 1955. The Copyright Act come in 1957. The Contempt of Courts Act come in 1971. The Criminal Procedure Code was enacted in 1973 and came into force on 1 April 1974.

76. (D): In newspaper offices, "boiling down" refers to the process of condensing a story while retaining its essential points.

77. (A): RNI, or the Office of the Registrar of Newspapers for India, is a statutory body under the Ministry of Information and Broadcasting, responsible for regulating and overseeing the registration of newspapers and periodicals in India, established in 1956.

117. (A): PTI or the Press Trust of India Ltd., is the largest news agency in India. It is headquartered in New Delhi and is a nonprofit cooperative among more than 450 Indian newspapers. PTI was registered in 1947 and started functioning in 1949.

120. (A): Journalists term the inverted pyramid as a news writing activity. The inverted pyramid carries the most important facts on the top and give less importance to the least important facts. The first paragraph is known as lead and it contains the important facts such as who, what, when, where, why and how (**5**W's and **1** H). The introduction paragraph should not be dependent on the following paragraphs for any explanation.

139. **(B):** Agence France-Presse (AFP) is a French international news agency, one of the world's oldest and largest, headquartered in Paris. Founded in 1835 as Agence Havas, it's the world's oldest news agency, later becoming 'Agence France-Presse' in 1944.

140. **(A):** The Press Information Bureau (PIB) is a nodal agency of the Government of India, under the Ministry of Information and Broadcasting, tasked with disseminating information about government plans, policies, programs, initiatives, and achievements to the media (print, electronic, and web). It is available in 14 Indian official languages.

162. **(C):** The Audit Bureau of Circulations (ABC) of India, founded in 1948, is a non-profit circulation-audit organization. It certifies and audits the circulations of major publications, including newspapers and magazines in India.

197. **(C):** Before working on any story or news, journalist has to find out answers of the 5Ws (what, when, where, who, why) and 1H (how).

239. **(D):** Lead of the story is an opening paragraph of a news story that consists of 5Ws and 1H. Angle of the news story is the most vital part of the story where the interest of the story lies. Body is where all the facts and figures lies. All the three are included in the essentials of the news story.

247. **(B):** Filler copy is used to fill in the blank spaces in newspaper through quotations, articles, crossword puzzles, recipes, unusual facts, cartoons, etc. It is known as time copy because at time of dead line of publication fillers are used to fill the empty spaces.

248. **(B):** Matrubhumi is the Malayalam newspaper that is under the ownership of Matrubhumi Printing and Publishing Company Limited.

304. **(A):** The Right to Information (RTI) Act, 2005, is a landmark law in India that empowers citizens to access information from public authorities. It promotes transparency and accountability in government operations by granting citizens the right to seek information under the control of public authorities. The Act was enacted by Parliament and came into force on June 15, 2005.

306. **(A):** Al-Hilal was an Urdu weekly journal founded by Maulana Azad in Calcutta, India, to advocate for Indian nationalism and fight against British rule.

327. **(B):** Ramnath Goenka, the founder of The Indian Express, launched the Hindi newspaper Jansatta in 1983.

330. **(C):** United News of India is one of the main news agencies of India. It began its operation on 21 March, 1961 and was the first Indian news agency to serve the abroad subscribers in 1981.

CHAPTER-3

ADVERTISING AND TELEVISION PRODUCTION

ADVERTISING

ADVERTISING: CONCEPT AND DEFINITION

Advertising is a vital marketing tool helping to sell goods, services, images, and ideas through a channel of information and persuasion. It is a highly visible communication force in society. All of us receive many advertising messages daily. It is essential to the success of any type of business and industry.

Advertisement has become an integral part in today's marketing scenario. In earlier times, advertisement was not given as much emphasis as it is being given today. Non-business organizations such as government, college, and universities, and Public Service groups employ several advertising strategies to meet their organizational goals. It is one of the parts of the marketing and communication process.

Advertising convinces people to buy products. Advertising contains both information and persuasion. Today we can say advertising is a communication, marketing, public-relation, information and persuasion process. Advertising reaches us through a channel of communication referred to as a medium. It is usually aimed at a particular segment of the population called Target audience (Consumer and business).

The word advertising is a Latin word which means "*to turn attention of people to a specific thing*". It is a paid publicity.

Advertising

A common definition of advertising found in the text books and quoted in professional articles and discussion is as follows:

"Advertising is communicating with and influencing someone to do something—usually to buy a product or service—and often something to think" about?

The American Marketing Association has defined advertisement as 'any paid form of nonpersonal presentation and promotion of ideas, goods or services by an identified sponsor'. In other words, advertisement is the paid use of any channel of communication—radio, television, film, press, etc. to identify, explain or to urge the use of adoption of a product, service, or idea.

Advertising is a 'paid form' of communication intended to inform and influence a specific target group. The reasons for advertising are many and varied. An advertisement may be used to:

- announce a new product or service, or an idea/ concept
- urge and remind people to buy a product or service; or do something or think some thing
- announce a modification (price, ingredient, feature, packaging, special offer, etc.)
- announce a sponsorship
- recruit staff
- educate the public

- maintain sales; retrieve lost sales; enter new markets
- challenge competition (in terms of message or proposition)

Advertising also helps to build and maintain the 'brand image' of a product or service, and adds to its values (as perceived by the customers).

Advertising can be mainly classified as:

- Product Advertising;
- Institutional Advertising or Public Relations Advertising.

Product Advertising as the name itself suggests, is concerned with promoting sales of particular products; and Institutional Advertising is known by various other names also like 'Corporate Advertising'. 'Public Advertising' or 'Prestige Advertising', etc. The main objective of institutional advertising is to create awareness and favourable attitude of particular publics towards the institution as a whole. Although it does not seek to promote sales directly, it does help the sales also indirectly by establishing a good image e.g., by building up a reputation for reliable quality products, etc.

FEATURES OF ADVERTISING

Advertising has certain basic features. Few important ones are as follows:

- **Paid form:** Advertising is always a paid form of communication and hence, commercial in nature. Thus, advertising can easily be distinguished from publicity which is not paid for by the sponsor.
- **Non-personal presentation:** Advertising is a non-personal presentation. Whatever the form of presentation, advertising is always directed to a mass audience rather than to any individual.
- **Sell or promote ideas, goods and services:** Advertising is aimed at promoting and selling not only tangible and physical goods, but also ideas and services. Most often services like banking and insurance are sold through advertising.
- **Identified sponsor:** Advertising always has an identified sponsor. In other words, advertising discloses or identifies the source of the opinions and ideas it presents. On the other hand, the sponsor for publicity or propaganda can remain anonymous.
- **Mass Reach:** Advertising is a medium through which a large number of people over a vast geographical area can be reached at a time.
- **Inform and Persuade**: Advertising usually informs the potential consumer about products and services, their benefits and utilities. It also persuades the consumers to purchase such products and services. In short, advertising is the art of influencing human action and awakening of a desire to possess products and services.
- **Economical**: Advertising is an economical mode of communication. The total cost of advertising is spread over a large number of people and because of this, the per unit cost of reaching a prospective buyer is less as compared to other promotional techniques.

TYPES OF ADVERTISEMENT

Advertisers use various types of advertisements to reach their target consumers or to inform the public. Some of them are follows:

- **Print Advertising**: One of the first and longest-standing types of advertising methods is print. This promotion method allows you to advertise your brand in physical printed newspapers, magazines and brochures.
- **Broadcast Advertising**: Advertisers use TV and radio as medium to advertise their product and services. Both radio and Television have great reach. However, advertising on TV could be costly.
- **Outdoor Advertising**: Outdoor advertising refers to any advertising that reaches people when they're outside of their homes. This includes billboard ads, digital signage, transit ads (i.e. bus shelters, train ads, metro stop ads, etc.), and ads in sports venues.
- **Direct Mail Advertising**: Direct mail advertising involves all forms of ads that are delivered to a person's home through the mail. This includes brochures, catalogues, sales letters and newsletters.
- **Internet Advertising**: This type of advertising uses internet as the medium of propagation of message. Companies use Social media to promote their products and services. It is easy to track the sales and engagement on internet and optimization helps in extending the reach. It is also flexible in nature. e.g. Facebook ads, Twitter ads, Google Ads.
- **Public service advertising**: Public service advertising refers to advertisements that promote a cause or initiative rather than a product. This type of advertising often is used by government agencies or charitable organizations to educate consumers on health and safety topics.

- **Product placement advertising**: In this advertising, a company pays to have their product embedded in media content, such as a television show or movie. The content sometimes does not explicitly mention the product, but it is viewable by the audience. This method can help companies reach targeted groups more discreetly.
- **Guerrilla advertising**: Guerrilla advertising refers to less conventional methods that are generally low-cost and employ creative techniques to draw attention. For example, rather than advertising on a bus stop, a company may paint a mural on the sidewalk advertising their services.
- **Surrogate Advertising**: The word surrogate means a 'substitute'. This type of advertising refers to a form of advertisement that duplicates the brand image of one product to promote another product of the same brand. This type of advertising is mainly used by tobacco and liquor brands as their advertisements are banned. *For example:* Bacardi CDs, Bagpiper club soda, Kingfisher water, etc.

Cross-promotion

This form of advertising is a set of actions aimed at promoting products from different brands with similar audiences that are not in competition. It helps promote products and services, generate leads, boost sales, and establish brand awareness. *Example:* McDonald's and Coca-cola's partnership.

PSYCHOLOGICAL IMPACT OF ADVERTISEMENT

- Appeal to emotions like fear envy.
- Consciousness about appearance.
- Be a part of the 'crowd' of present times.
- Fun-loving.
- Comparison in status
- AIDCA Formula created - Attention Interest Desire Conviction and action- for change in buying behaviour.
- Impart conviction by engaging celebrities.

ADVERTISING APPEAL AND ITS TYPES

Advertising appeal is the persuasive technique used to attract the attention of consumers and influence their feelings towards a product, service, or idea. It's the underlying message that resonates with the audience's needs, wants, fears, or aspirations. The primary purpose of an advertising appeal is to target the consumer's wants or needs and motivate the target market to purchase a product or service.

There are several types of advertising appeals, and often, advertisements blend multiple appeals to create a more impactful message. Here are some of the common ones:

- **Emotional Appeal:** Emotional appeal is a persuasive technique in advertising that targets the audience's feelings and emotions to create a connection with the product or message. It taps into emotions like happiness, love, fear, sadness, excitement, or hope, aiming to influence how people perceive and respond to what's being advertised. *For example*: baby care products, invoking mothers' emotions to choose what is best for their babies.
- **Rational Appeal:** Rational appeal is a persuasive technique in advertising that uses facts, data, and logical reasoning to convince consumers. It appeals to the audience's sense of logic by presenting clear, factual information about a product's features, benefits, or advantages. *For example*: car advertisements often highlight fuel efficiency, safety ratings, durability, and price comparisons, providing solid reasons for why a customer should choose one vehicle over another based on measurable qualities.
- **Humour Appeal:** Humour appeal is an advertising technique that uses comedy and light-hearted situations to capture the audience's attention and make the message more memorable. *For example*: funny snack commercials often feature exaggerated, silly scenarios or clever jokes that leave a lasting impression while subtly promoting the product.
- **Fear Appeal:** Fear appeal is a persuasive advertising technique that creates a sense of fear, worry, or concern to encourage people to take action or exercise caution. These ads often highlight the negative consequences of certain behaviours or situations, aiming to influence decision-making by triggering a fear response. *For example*: Life insurance ads invoking fear of death, anti-smoking campaigns frequently show the serious health consequences of smoking.
- **Bandwagon Appeal:** Bandwagon appeal is an advertising technique that suggests that a product, service, or idea is popular and widely accepted, encouraging others to join in because "everyone is doing it". It plays on people's natural desire to fit in, belong, and be part of the majority. *For example*: advertisements might claim that a

product is the nation's top choice or the best-selling brand.

- **Sex Appeal:** Sex appeal is an advertising technique that uses suggestive imagery, attractive models, or sensual messages to grab attention and create interest in a product or brand. This approach often links the product with beauty, desirability, or romance, suggesting that using it can enhance one's appeal or attractiveness. *For example*: perfume or fashion ads often feature attractive models in glamorous, alluring settings, hinting that the product can help consumers achieve a similar sense of charm and desirability.
- **Scarcity Appeal:** Scarcity appeal is an advertising technique that creates a sense of urgency by suggesting that a product or opportunity is limited in availability or time. It plays on the fear of missing out (FOMO), encouraging consumers to act quickly before the chance disappears. *For example*: phrases like "Limited-time offer," "While supplies last," or "Only a few items remaining" are commonly used to drive urgency and motivate consumers to buy now rather than later.
- **Celebrity Endorsement Appeal:** Celebrity endorsement appeal is an advertising technique that features well-known personalities, such as actors, athletes, musicians, or influencers, to promote a product or brand. By associating a product with a famous face, advertisers aim to boost its credibility, popularity, and desirability. *For example*: sports stars endorsing sports shoes or energy drinks.
- **Moral Appeal:** Moral appeal is an advertising technique that targets the audience's sense of ethics, justice, and responsibility, encouraging them to support causes or make socially conscious choices. The goal is to inspire action or behavioural change in support of a greater good. *For example*: advertisements promoting environmental conservation, fair trade products, or charitable donations use moral appeal to motivate audiences. Similarly, public service campaigns against drunk driving, smoking, or littering rely on moral values to encourage responsible and ethical behaviour.
- **Adventure or Excitement Appeal:** Adventure or excitement appeal is an advertising technique that emphasizes thrilling, daring, and adventurous experiences associated with a product or service. This type of appeal connects products with feelings of exhilaration, exploration, and living life to the fullest. *For example*: travel advertisements often feature exotic destinations, extreme sports, or adventurous journeys.

VIDEO PRODUCTION

Video production encompasses the entire process of creating a video (TV shows/Film)—from concept planning to final release. It involves multiple stages, a variety of creative and technical roles, and significant coordination.

It broadly has three stages:

- Pre-Production
- Production
- Post-Production

Pre-Production Stage

In this stage, the seed of production is planted and initial foundation is laid. It involves:

- **Concept and idea:** Brainstorming ideas, adapting books, real-life stories, or original scripts.
- **Scriptwriting:** It includes a plot, story setting, dialogues, writing and refining the screenplay.
- **Budget:** Securing funding through studios, investors, or crowdfunding.
- **Crew and cast:** selecting actors for the roles and assembling the production crew, including the director of photography, sound recordist, costume designer, etc.
- **Scouting locations and set design:** Finding and securing suitable locations for filming and building or modifying sets to fit the story's requirements.
- **Storyboarding and Rehearsals:** Visualizing key scenes through drawings or digital illustrations and Working with the actors to refine their performances.

Production Stage

The production stage is where the actual filming process starts and the script comes to life.

- **Filming:** This is the stage where the director says lights, camera, and action. Capturing the scenes with actors, directors, and crew on set.

- **Cinematography**: It involves managing camera work, lighting, and visual style.
- **Sound Recording**: It involves capturing dialogue, background sound, and effects on set.

Post-Production Stage

It is the final stage where all the elements of the film come together, transforming raw footage into a polished masterpiece.

- **Editing**: In this stage, cutting and assembling of the footage is done to form a coherent narrative. Visual effects such as CGI, green screen compositing, etc. are added to fine-tune the film.
- **Sound Design:** A movie is incomplete without sound. This stage involves mixing sound, adding music, and creating sound effects.
- **Distribution & Marketing:** When the film is almost ready for the public, the marketing department comes into play. It is their job to take the film to the masses. Promoting the film through trailers, posters, interviews, and social media campaigns, and is later released through theatres, streaming platforms, or physical media.

MULTIPLE CHOICE QUESTIONS

1. According to the American Marketing Association, advertising is ....

A. any paid form of non-personal presentation of ideas, goods and services by an identified sponsor
B. To give public notice or to announce the publicity
C. A means of mass selling that has grown up parallel with and has been made necessary to mass production
D. None of these

2. .... is known as the father of advertisement.

A. George Gallup
B. David Ogilvy
C. Sir Martin Sorrell
D. Edward Whitehead

3. Which among the following is/are a feature of advertisement?

A. Mass Reach B. Economy
C. Impersonality D. All the above

4. .... is the first Indian Ad Agency.

A. Crayons advertising
B. Pressman advertising limited
C. Indian Advertising Agency
D. None of these

5. The Indian Society of Advertisers was formed in ....

A. 1951 B. 1950
C. 1948 D. 1962

6. Which among the following is/are the main players, involved in the communication of advertising?

A. Advertising Agencies
B. Mass Media Tools
C. Target Audience
D. All the above

7. .... is the main purpose of an advertisement.

A. Social role
B. Creating propaganda
C. Improvement of Sales
D. Both (A) and (C)

8. Match the following:

Types of Ad copy	Layout with their features
(*a*) Convincing	1. Elements of an advertising copy
(*b*) Topical	2. Characteristics of an ad copy
(*c*) Body Copy	3. Feature of an ad – layout
(*d*) White Space	4. Type of an ad – copy

A. (*a*)-4, (*b*)-1, (*c*)-3, (*d*)-2
B. (*a*)-2, (*b*)-4, (*c*)-1, (*d*)-3
C. (*a*)-2, (*b*)-1, (*c*)-3, (*d*)-4
D. (*a*)-3, (*b*)-4, (*c*)-1, (*d*)-2

9. Use of a simple language in advertisement, helps to grab the attention of the customers.

A. True B. False

10. Which among the following definition is given by Buck Rogers regarding Marketing?

A. The process of marketing is used by a firm to relate the creativity to the environment in which it sells its products or services.
B. Marketing is an art of selling products.
C. Only (A)
D. None of these

11. There are 3 Ps of marketing.

A. True B. False

12. With reference to the below diagram of Product Life Cycle, answer the following. If A is the introductory stage, B is the growth stage and D is the decline stage, what does C represent?

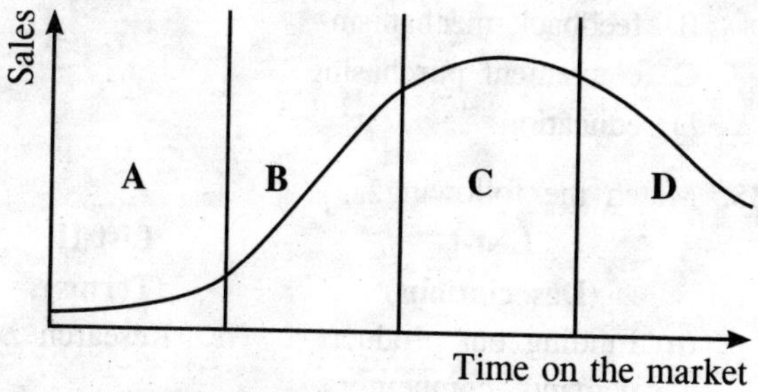

Product Life Cycle graph

A. Promotion stage
B. Maturity stage
C. Behavioural stage
D. None of these

13. .... is known as the father of public relations.
A. Ivy Lee
B. Thomas Jefferson
C. Edward Bernay
D. None of these

14. SWOT stand for ....
A. strength, weakness, opportunity, threat
B. scandal, weakness, opportunity, threat
C. skilfulness, weakness, opportunity, terror
D. None of these

15. Advertisement is a mass communication. It addresses to masses and it's a form of .... communication.
A. Personal B. Non-personal
C. Direct D. Indirect

16. .... is helpful in promotion of business by people and big industrialists who are promoting their goods and services through networking sites like Facebook, Twitter, etc.
A. Social media B. E-mail
C. Print D. Television

17. Creation of advertisement by an advertising agency involves activities like
A. copy writing
B. drawing photographs
C. making illustrations
D. All the above

18. What is the basic objective of market segmentation?
A. We want to identify target market niches
B. We want to define clearly such market niches as have similar **characteristics and features**
C. We want to divide the market into a few geographical sections so that logistics operations could be facilitated
D. **All** the above are true

19. If a firm advertises its own products in a magazine, this would be a/an
A. direct advertising effort
B. indirect advertising effort
C. both A and B
D. neither A nor B

20. Brand identity is followed by .... which is a reflection of what marketers' plan to send to the public.
A. brand value B. brand image
C. advertising D. brand personality

21. Advertising for .... is not allowed.
A. Liquor B. Washing powder
C. Cigarette D. Both A and C

22. There is a risk of client's resources getting wasted without proper
A. research
B. advertising campaign
C. advertising budget
D. media planning

23. AIDA is created by Elmo Lewis in:
A. 1898 B. 1910
C. 1912 D. 1913

24. Which of the following establishes relationship between clients and business entrepreneurs?
A. Market B. Advertising agency
C. Planning D. Products

25. Which of the following form is a process of advertising management?
A. Media strategy
B. Message development strategy
C. Evaluation of overall effectiveness of the advertising effort
D. All the above

26. To introduce new products to world of consumers is the main goal of
A. entertainment
B. advertising
C. boost the sales
D. online marketing

27. Which of the following is an example of product research?
A. Packaging research
B. Competitive product studies
C. New product acceptance and potential
D. All the above

28. Match the following:

List-I (Functions)	List-II (Departments)
(*a*) Preparing an attractive copy for its clients and customers	1. Art Department
(*b*) Preparing layouts and visuals for the clients	2. Research Department
(*c*) Producing final advertisements for the markets	3. Copy Department
(*d*) Carrying out research and applying in different ways	4. Production Department

A. (*a*)-1, (*b*)-2, (*c*)-3, (*d*)-4
B. (*a*)-4, (*b*)-3, (*c*)-2, (*d*)-1
C. (*a*)-2, (*b*)-4, (*c*)-1, (*d*)-3
D. (*a*)-3, (*b*)-1, (*c*)-4, (*d*)-2

29. Catalogues, magazines, newspaper and invitations to organisation-sponsored events are associated with the marketing mix activity of ....

A. manufacture B. production
C. promotion D. development

30. Understanding the different nuances of media is the role of a/an:

A. Advertising Agency
B. Media Planner
C. Research Analyst
D. Public Relations (PR)

31. The last stage of a PLC is:

A. maturity B. decline
C. introduction D. growth

32. Media research is a part of:

A. evaluating advertising research
B. strategic advertising research
C. marketing research
D. None of these

33. Advertising involves dissemination of information about a product or service to induce people to take actions beneficial to:

A. advertiser
B. sponsor
C. marketing manager
D. retailer

34. It is difficult to evaluate the impact of advertising message, as there is no immediate and accurate ....

A. legal environment
B. feedback mechanism
C. convenient purchasing
D. education

35. Match the following:

List-I (Descriptions)	List-II (Terms)
(*a*) Finding out product demand, competitors, etc.	1. Research
(*b*) Knowledge of prospect buyers	2. Know the target audience
(*c*) Evaluation of expenses on factors like media presentations, paper work etc.	3. Setting the budget
(*d*) Planning of colours, graphics etc to be used in advertisement	4. Deciding a proper theme

A. (*a*)-1, (*b*)-2, (*c*)-3, (*d*)-4
B. (*a*)-4, (*b*)-3, (*c*)-2, (*d*)-1
C. (*a*)-2, (*b*)-4, (*c*)-1, (*d*)-3
D. (*a*)-3, (*b*)-1, (*c*)-4, (*d*)-2

36. Brand assets include:

A. the name of the brand
B. reputation, relevance and loyalty
C. less quality complaints
D. All the above

37. Which of these media is ***not*** used for advertisement?

A. Newspapers B. Magazines
C. Billboards D. Notebooks

38. If the aim of promotion to introduce a new consumer product is to achieve high awareness levels, the firm will most likely make heavy use of .... in the promotional mix.

A. advertising B. sales promotion
C. publicity D. None of these

39. Which of the following is a step in the marketing process?

A. Finding a need
B. Conducting research
C. Setting a price and do mark testing
D. All the above

40. The first step in the marketing process is to:

A. find a need
B. test marketing
C. conduct research
D. build a relationship with customers

41. What purpose does an advertising copy serve?
A. Provides a degree of continuity in a brand's advertising
B. Helps a brand to achieve distinctiveness
C. Provides a common benchmark on which all concerned in the company and the agency can evaluate the merits of advertising submissions
D. All the above

42. For making advertisements more effective, the manufacturers improve .... and launch new products.
A. existing products
B. advertisement style
C. marketing channel
D. sponsors

43. The ultimate objectives of an advertising agency include:
A. helping advertisers to attain sales objectives
B. expand market share of the concerned company
C. provide long-term profitability
D. All the above

44. Which of these is ***not*** a characteristic of an advertisement?
A. Inspire a customer
B. Arouse a desire
C. Discourage the buyer
D. Convince the buyer

45. Advertisement provides information regarding product or idea in non-personal forms, as no face-to-face contact is involved between ....
A. marketer and retailer
B. jobber and wholesaler
C. buyer and seller
D. market manager and salesman

46. Advertising influences the mind of the consumers by creating desire and taste for:
A. old products B. same products
C. new products D. different products

47. .... refers to a brands' objective (functional) attributes in relation to other brands.
A. Brand position B. Product position
C. Brand relationship D. Both A and B

48. .... is a planned managerial process designed to oversee and control various advertising activities.
A. Marketing research
B. Media planning
C. Budgeting
D. Advertising management

49. Arrange the following in correct chronological order:
1. Marketing research
2. Media planning and budgeting
3. Advertising campaigns
4. Relationship with clients
A. 1, 2, 3, 4 B. 4, 3, 2, 1
C. 2, 4, 1, 3 D. 3, 1, 4, 2

50. .... includes all that is linked up in memory about the brand. It could be specific to attributes, features, benefits or looks of brand.
A. Brand attitude
B. Brand associations
C. Brand relationship
D. Brand image

51. The definition of marketing includes all except one of the following:
A. The need to earn a profit
B. The process of determining customer wants and needs
C. Profitably providing customers goods and services that meet their needs
D. An exchange between the organisation and a customer

52. Match the following:

List-I	List-II
(*a*) Retail advertising	1. Done across the country
(*b*) Outdoor advertising	2. Fortifies interest for general item or whole industry
(*c*) Demand based advertising	3. Billboard
(*d*) National advertising	4. Patronise a specific store

A. (*a*)-2, (*b*)-1, (*c*)-4, (*d*)-3
B. (*a*)-4, (*b*)-2, (*c*)-1, (*d*)-3
C. (*a*)-4, (*b*)-3, (*c*)-2, (*d*)-1
D. (*a*)-3, (*b*)-4, (*c*)-2, (*d*)-1

53. What influences the attitudes?
A. Value symbols
B. Events
C. Appeals through communication
D. All the above

54. What does management of advertisement need to play its role and perform its functions successfully?
A. Market B. Consumers
C. Agency D. Products

55. The advertisement of newspaper has a very short life span of ....

A. one day B. one week
C. one month D. one year

56. Major pricing strategies do not include

A. competition based pricing
B. customer values-based pricing
C. cost based pricing
D. discount and bonus pricing

57. Which of the following is ***not*** a function of advertising?

A. Informing the customer
B. Persuading the customer
C. Understanding the buying capacity of the customer
D. Reminding the customer for a repeat purchase

58. What is space marketing?

A. It is a tendency of the buyer to purchase the cheapest brand available in the market
B. It is the pre-purchase research activity carried out by a prospective customer
C. It is the promotional effort of the firm through which, it buys space in news-papers, and inserts its ad supplements in the newspapers to reach the readers of such newspapers
D. It is the set of those bargaining tools that a buyer uses to get the best deal from the seller

59. Which of these media need script for an advertisement?

A. Newspaper Advertisement
B. Classified Advertisement
C. Radio
D. Magazine

60. Match the following:

List-I (Functions)	List-II (Descriptions)
(*a*) Creation of advertisement	1. Making advertisement more appealing to attract buyers
(*b*) Advertising campaign	2. The process of managing publicity of a product
(*c*) Sales promotion	3. The process of expansion of sales of a product
(*d*) Public relations	4. Enhancing the goodwill between clients and other parties

A. (*a*)-1, (*b*)-2, (*c*)-3, (*d*)-4
B. (*a*)-4, (*b*)-3, (*c*)-2, (*d*)-1
C. (*a*)-2, (*b*)-4, (*c*)-1, (*d*)-3
D. (*a*)-3, (*b*)-1, (*c*)-4, (*d*)-2

61. Which of the following is ***not*** a basis for the demographic segment-action of a market?

A. Age B. Income
C. User Status D. Nationality

62. What is cognitive Dissonance?

A. The exhilarating experience in the mind of the customer a product of his choice
B. Post-purchase dissatisfaction that creeps into the mind of the consumer after he buys the product
C. A feeling of reassignment that is always present in the mind of the consumer (towards the products that he shuns)
D. None of these

63. An advertising agency studies and analyses collected information properly and draws conclusions for its research which help in:

A. planning advertisement campaign
B. selecting proper media
C. creating the required function
D. All the above

64. Brands are diversified because:

A. it is essential for brand survival
B. some brands have such a high awareness that those are perceived by customers to be in categories where they are not present
C. cost-cutting is possible by advertising products with the same brand name
D. All the above

65. What is world of mouth publicity?

A. The satisfied customer tells his friends and family about the services of the airline
B. A disgruntled sea traveller informs his boss that the airline he had used last Friday is lousy
C. A sales girl gives a beautiful registration from to a prospective tourist in the office of a travel agency
D. None of these

66. Which of the following is/are objectives of 'Advertising Campaigns'?

A. Inform people about the product
B. Convince people to buy the product
C. Make the product available to the customer
D. All the above

67. Arrange the different kinds of roles played by advertising agencies in correct chronological order.

1. Research on the company, products and reactions of the customers.
2. Market planning.

3. Production of creative materials.
4. Planning for the type of media to be used.

A. 1, 2, 3, 4 B. 4, 3, 2, 1
C. 2, 4, 1, 3 D. 3, 1, 4, 2

68. .... plays a crucial role in the management of advertising.
A. Evaluation of target market
B. Market
C. Advertising agency
D. Products

69. The image of brand is the .... with customer.
A. actual association
B. vision
C. positioning
D. personality traits

70. According to David Ogilvy, firms should
A. depend more upon sales promotion than upon sales advertising
B. depend more upon advertising than upon sales promotion
C. use advertising and sales promotion in equal proportions
D. use direct sales method to build the image of the brand

71. Pioneer advertising, consumer advertising and product advertising are
A. objective of advertising
B. types of advertising
C. marketing decisions in advertising
D. evaluation advertising

72. The Film Federation of India was formed in:
A. 1950 B. 1951
C. 1952 D. 1953

73. Advertisement through radio was very popular till the middle of last century because of:
A. its effectiveness
B. more popular than newspaper
C. mass reach
D. cost of advertisement

74. The phrase 'Newspaper goes to sleep' means:
A. goes for printing
B. take some rest
C. stops printing because a smaller number of readers
D. None of these

75. Which department of an advertising agency performs the functions of keeping constant contact with the media and the client?
A. Copy Department
B. Accounting and Finance Department
C. Media Department
D. Public Relations (PR) Department

76. Which of the following is ***not*** a part of marketing communication mix?
A. Advertising B. Public relations
C. Sales promotion D. Telemarketing

77. Identify the correct set of primary functions of advertising:
A. Creates demand, increases sales, affects seasonal fluctuations, Raises standard of living
B. Creates demand, supports salesmen, affects seasonal fluctuation, Raises standard of living
C. Furnish correct information, supports salesmen, affects seasonal fluctuation, Raises standard of living
D. Recruits best employees, creates demand, raises standard of living, Supports salesmen.

78. A television advertisement showing the safety features of the Volvo 240 DL would be best classified as which of the following?
A. Defensive advertising
B. Pioneer advertising
C. Product advertising
D. Societal war marketing

79. The most popular print media available to advertisers is ....
A. Newspapers B. Magazine
C. Pamphlet D. Emails

80. Advertising profession needs intense knowledge of:
A. communication B. marketing
C. products D. consumers

81. Media buying is a process of:
A. advertising management
B. marketing research
C. message development
D. target market

82. How is a brand name different from a brand mark?
A. The brand name has legal protection but a brand mark does not
B. A brand name can be uttered but a brand mark cannot be
C. A brand name is visible but a brand mark is not
D. A brand name is recognised by the targeted customer but a brand mark is not

83. Which of the following is a non-advertising function of an advertising agency?
A. Designing the product
B. Designing the product's package
C. Designing trademarks
D. All the above

84. Arrange the following in correct chronological order of process of research.
1. Limitations of a product
2. Present and future market possibilities
3. Buyers' preferences
4. Competition in the market
A. 1, 2, 3, 4 B. 4, 3, 2, 1
C. 2, 4, 1, 3 D. 3, 1, 4, 2

85. Advertising creates employment, as it increases the volume of sales and:
A. production B. marketing
C. promotion D. new products

86. DAGMAR Model was created by
A. Elma Lewis B. Russell Colley
C. G Marconi D. None of these

87. Right branding increases of the product, which should be more than that of the generic product.
A. consumer revolt B. market share
C. profit D. value

88. Which of these contain no illustrations or logos?
A. Television
B. Magazine
C. Classified advertisements
D. Cinema

89. Identify the correct components of print advertisement.
A. Headline, Signature line, Standing details, Illustrations
B. Headline, Bodycopy, Motion picture, Subscriber
C. Motion picture, Subscriber, Bodycopy, Brand
D. Umbrella brand, Headline, Illustrations, Signature line

90. Strategic media planning is a complex challenge because advertisers must use their knowledge of
A. demographics
B. psychographics
C. behavioural characteristics
D. all of these

91. "Advertising is any paid form of non-personal presentation and promotion of ideas, goods and services by an identified person". Who stated this?
A. Australian Marketing Association
B. European Marketing Association
C. China Marketing Association
D. American Marketing Association

92. Comparing past sales and advertisement, trying for new experiments, measuring sale difficulties are:
A. objective of advertising
B. models of advertising
C. evaluation of advertising
D. developing strategy

93. According to some critics, the most potent tool of media imperialism is
A. newspaper B. radio
C. magazine D. television

94. The underlying theme or idea in advertisement is known as:
A. spam B. phishing
C. message D. marketing

95. Advertising has been criticized because:
A. it motivates consumers to try new products
B. it generates the demand not needed by consumers
C. it is high-profile and glossy and therefore, it enthrals to win customers
D. All the above

96. "Through newspaper any firm can reach literate customers only". It's a
A. nothing related to illiterate customers
B. advantage of newspaper
C. drawback of newspaper
D. no problem in such advertising

97. In the process of new product development, the commercialisation step would follow:
A. business analysis
B. test marketing
C. screening and evaluation of ideas
D. generation of new product ideas

98. The basic idea behind advertise is:
A. to control the market
B. to increase business by selling goods or services
C. to trap the customers
D. to inform the consumers

99. Which department of an advertising agency performs the function of assembling the typographic design patterns, engraved photos, illustrations, copy, etc?
A. Production Department
B. Art Department
C. Copy Department
D. Office Management Department

100. Arrange the following activities related to creation of advertisement in correct chronological order.

1. Effective advertisement message
2. Layout
3. Drawing photographs
4. Copy writing

A. 1, 2, 3, 4 B. 4, 3, 2, 1
C. 2, 4, 1, 3 D. 3, 1, 4, 2

101. Arrange the following in correct chronological order.

1. Setting an advertising budget
2. Development of advertising objectives
3. Fixing advertising objectives
4. Determining the target market

A. 1, 2, 3, 4 B. 4, 3, 2, 1
C. 2, 4, 1, 3 D. 3, 1, 4, 2

102. Advertising agencies in general provide services like

A. creative development
B. promotional campaigns
C. public relations
D. All the above

103. Who is known as the 'Father of Indian Cinema'?

A. Tomey
B. J. F. Madan
C. Dada Saheb Phalke
D. Natraj Mudaliar

104. From the perspective of sales, advertisements are required for:

A. profit B. loss
C. increasing sales D. decreasing sales

105. Identify the correct set of terminology used in advertising and branding.

A. Umbrella brand, Logo, Identified sponsor, Online advertising
B. Umbrella brand, Concept, Identified sponsor, Logo
C. Logo, Definition, Online advertising, Concept
D. Concept, Definition, Logo, Identified sponsor

106. When colours in an advertisement are not harmonious, it is identified as

A. non-structured
B. parallel colouring
C. marginal colouring
D. out of register

107. Selecting time, choosing media types, deciding on reach of frequency and media vehicle for advertisements are part of:

A. Media strategy
B. Media execution
C. Selecting media
D. Measuring communication

108. Lower costs, greater global advertising coordination consistent worldwide image are the .... of international marketing decision.

A. Standardization drawbacks
B. Advertisement regulations
C. Standardization benefits
D. Typical responses

109. Catalogues, magazines, newspaper and invitations to organization-sponsored events are associated with the marketing mix activity of ....

A. Manufacture B. Production
C. Promotion D. Development

110. Advertisement is a type of ....

A. Outdoor marketing
B. Indirect marketing
C. Share marketing
D. Transaction marketing

111. Advertising is a non-personal process but must be written or printed in words .... advertise and helps in the sale of the product.

A. Salesman B. Sponsors
C. Marketer D. Marketing manager

112. Advertising is not flexible as the message is once fixed it can't be altered again and again according to the ....

A. Advertiser B. Sponsor
C. Customer D. Marketer

113. Advertising is generally criticized because the cost involved in making ads are generally ....

A. High B. Low
C. Medium D. Equal to the production

114. Levels of differentiation, market share, product lifecycle stage, correlating promotional spending and brand sales are part of .... in advertising.

A. Objective of advertising
B. Models of advertising
C. Evaluation of advertising
D. Developing strategy

115. Direct mail advertising is suitable in case of

A. Retailer
B. Wholesaler
C. Personal selling
D. Share broker

116. ....is helpful in promotion the businesses people and big industrialists are promoting their goods and services through networking sites like Facebook, Twitter etc.

A. Social media B. Email
C. Radio D. Television

117. In advertisements we generally see a warning for cigarettes that "Smoking is Injurious to health". It's an example of

A. Advertising
B. Monopoly in market
C. Legal environment
D. Entertainment

118. Selecting style, tone, words for making ads are part of

A. Message strategy
B. Message execution
C. Selecting media
D. Measuring communication

119. "Think globally, act locally" is a global advertising strategies and local advertising programs under .... of international marketing decision.

A. Standardization drawbacks
B. Advertisement regulations
C. Standardization benefits
D. Typical responses

120. Digital marketing is same as

A. Marketing through emails
B. Marketing on Social media
C. Online ads
D. All the above

121. The numbers of readers who can recall of seeing advertisement is referred to as

A. net recall B. gross recall
C. noting score D. recall score

122. Creating innovative and new ideas, identifying customers benefit, selecting specific appeals for advertisements are the part of

A. Message strategy
B. Message execution
C. Selecting media
D. Measuring communication

123. What does the term PLC stand for?

A. Product life cycle
B. Production life cycle
C. Product long cycle
D. Production long cycle

124. PLC in marketing represents two main challenges. 1st an organization must be good at developing new product to replace old ones and 2nd it must be good at ....

A. Functioning B. Marketing
C. Selling D. Adapting

125. Which of the following is ***not*** a characteristic of "Market Introduction Stage" in PLC?

A. Demands has to be created
B. Costs are low
C. Makes no money at this stage
D. Slow sales volume to start

126. The most important performance dimension for product development project is

A. Time to market B. Time to target
C. Time to consumer D. Time to seller

127. The Advertising Standards Council of India was formed in

A. 1975 B. 1985
C. 1995 D. 2005

128. As the volume of advertising is getting more and more expanded it is becoming difficult to make advertising messages heard by the target prospects. This will affect the .... of advertising.

A. Social values
B. Preference
C. Effectiveness
D. More than one of the above

129. Personal selling is ***not*** targeted towards

A. Mass audiences
B. Personal contact
C. Two-way communication
D. Quick feedback

130. Which media is useful for illiterate consumers?

A. Print media B. Broadcast media
C. Posters/Hoardings D. Transit means

131. .... advertisement is a small, graphic links placed on a web page.

A. Banner B. Buttons
C. Website D. E-mail

132. What kind of advertising involves kiosks, events and Tradeshows?

A. Print advertising
B. Outdoor advertising
C. Covert advertising
D. Public service advertising

133. After the introductory stage, the advertising spiral moves towards:

A. The retentive stage
B. The neo-pioneering stage
C. The competitive stage
D. The rejection stage

134. Re-marketing is related with creating demand for ....

A. Fresh products
B. Non-usable products
C. Low quality products
D. Renewed use of products

135. Comparing the attributes of two or more brands of advertising is called:

A. Persuasive advertisement
B. Informative advertisement
C. Reminder advertisement
D. Inducing advertisement

136. The basis of the cost of publicity on television media is:

A. Time B. Place
C. Production D. Colour

137. Surrogate Advertising refers:

A. Advertising Indirectly
B. Advertising Directly
C. Both A and B
D. None of these

138. When a product or brand is embedded in entertainment and media then it is known as which of the following?

A. Covert advertising
B. Guerilla advertising
C. Surrogate advertising
D. Mail advertising

139. Pay-per-click (PPC) is also known as

A. Mobile Advertising
B. Guerrilla Advertising
C. Paid Search Advertising
D. None of these

140. What is the primary purpose of Google Ads?

A. To increase video streaming speeds
B. To generate organic search results
C. To create static websites
D. To drive targeted traffic through paid advertising

141. What is a keyword in Google Ads?

A. A type of ad format
B. A hidden HTML code
C. A word or phrase that triggers ads
D. A Google search algorithm

142. Which metric in Google Ads measures how often a user takes a desired action on your website?

A. ROI B. CPC
C. Conversion Rate D. Bounce Rate

143. Which bidding strategy is commonly associated with Search Advertising?

A. Enhanced CPC
B. Cost Per Click (CPC)
C. Cost Per Acquisition (CPA)
D. Cost Per Impression (CPM)

144. Match the following movies with their achievements.

(a) Mother India	1. First Indian film in Guiness Book of World Record
(b) Kaagaz Ke Phool	2. First colorized film
(c) Mughal-E-Azam	3. First Oscar nomination for best Foreign language film
(d) Yaadein	4. First 75 mm cinema scope film

A. (a)-2, (b)-3, (c)-1, (d)-4
B. (a)-3, (b)-4, (c)-2, (d)-1
C. (a)-2, (b)-1, (c)-4, (d)-3
D. (a)-4, (b)-3, (c)-2, (d)-1

145. Advertising is affected by which forces?

A. Economic B. Social
C. Technology D. All the above

146. DAGMAR model meaning:

A. Defining advertising goals for measured advertising results
B. Defining attention and goals for measure attractive results
C. Advertising goals for measured attractive results
D. None of these

147. Which one is *not* a type of advertising copy?

A. Scientific copy
B. Narrative copy
C. Product copy
D. Personality copy

148. .... means doing what the advertiser and the advertisers peers believe is morally right in a given situation.

A. Social advertising
B. Ethical advertising
C. Legal advertising
D. Physical advertising

149. Which of the following advertising types involves placing promotional messages in newspapers and magazines?
A. Broadcast advertising
B. Online advertising
C. Print advertising
D. Outdoor advertising

150. Advertisements shown on television and radio fall under which category?
A. Direct mail advertising
B. Broadcast advertising
C. Native advertising
D. Guerrilla marketing

151. Which type of advertising utilizes platforms like Facebook, Instagram, and Google?
A. Outdoor advertising
B. Influencer marketing
C. Online advertising
D. Product placement

152. Billboards and posters alongside roads are examples of:
A. Print advertising
B. Direct mail advertising
C. Outdoor advertising
D. Native advertising

153. Sending flyers and catalogues directly to people's homes is known as:
A. Guerrilla marketing
B. Direct mail advertising
C. Product placement
D. Influencer marketing

154. When a brand's product is subtly featured in a movie scene, this is an example of:
A. Native advertising B. Outdoor advertising
C. Product placement D. Influencer marketing

155. Collaborating with a popular social media figure to promote a product is known as:
A. Broadcast advertising
B. Guerrilla marketing
C. Influencer marketing
D. Direct mail advertising

156. Creating sponsored articles that look like regular content on a news website is an example of:
A. Print advertising
B. Native advertising
C. Outdoor advertising
D. Product placement

157. Using unconventional tactics like flash mobs to promote a brand fall under:
A. Online advertising
B. Direct mail advertising
C. Guerrilla marketing
D. Broadcast advertising

158. Which of the following can be considered a form of broadcast advertising?
A. A banner ad on a website
B. A flyer delivered to your door
C. An advertisement shown before a movie starts in a cinema
D. A sponsored post on Instagram

159. Generally, position of the Logo in an advertisement is at
A. Top left side B. Top right side
C. Bottom right side D. Bottom left side

160. Meaning of the "Signature of Advertiser" is
A. Brand name B. Logo
C. Illustration D. Slogan

161. The fastest growing medium of advertising is
A. Internet B. Television
C. Radio D. Magazines

162. Advertising on television impacts more because
A. It has a huge reach
B. Products can be demonstrated.
C. Advertisement of a product is repeated
D. All the above

163. Email of a commercial message is a method of advertising which is
A. Direct marketing B. Indirect marketing
C. Pyramid marketing D. None of these

164. Prime time of advertising on television is a time between
A. 7.00 A.M. to 10.00 A.M.
B. 1.00 PM to 4.00 P.M.
C. 7.00 P.M. to 10.00 P.M.
D. Only Sunday Evening

165. Financial budget for advertising is decided as
A. Percentage of sales method
B. Competitors' expenditure method
C. Share of the market method
D. All the above

166. Bursting method of advertising is
A. Advertising in a particular season
B. Advertising in a particular period
C. Advertising throughout the year
D. Advertising every alternate month

167. Identify the correct "Target Audience" from the following for "2-minute noodles"
A. CEO of automobile manufacturing company
B. College students
C. Housewife
D. Cricket player

168. In 'all-you-can-afford' method of budget allocation for advertising
A. A fixed budget is provided.
B. A percentage of previous sales budget is provided.
C. Budget is provided after considering spend for production and operations.
D. Budget is allocated depending on charges by advertising company.

169. Meaning of advertising campaign is
A. Advertisements having same theme
B. Advertisements published within specific period
C. Product advertising using different media but with unified approach
D. All the above

170. During decline stage of a product in its Life Cycle
A. It requires huge spend on advertising.
B. It requires high spend on advertising.
C. It requires comparatively lesser spend on advertising.
D. It requires no spend on advertising.

171. An innovative advertisement
A. Creates a good impact on the minds of the people.
B. Has a great recall value.
C. Helps in retaining brand name in minds of people for a long time.
D. All the above

172. Creative advertisement
A. Requires extra spending of money
B. Gives competitive edge over the competitor.
C. Does not increase product recall and therefore product demand
D. Focusses on advertisement rather than on product.

173. Meaning of USP is
A. United States Pharmacopoeia
B. Union of State Paramedicos
C. Unique Selling Proposition
D. United State of Paraguay

174. One of the most important selling points of a water filter is
A. Price
B. Warranty of the product
C. After-sales-service
D. Number of branches of the company

175. The advertisement
A. Can challenge a competitor product.
B. Can make unsubstantiated claims.
C. Can employ animals or birds.
D. None of these

176. One of the following factors of advertisement is provided by client to the advertising agency's creative team. Identify the same –
A. Plant layout B. Creative pitch
C. Creative brief D. Financial budget

177. Creative advertisement establishes the following of a product –
A. Essence B. Identity
C. Life cycle D. Sale worthiness

178. Advertisement of Insurance Policy is an example of which buying motive?
A. Love and affection of family.
B. Economy or gain.
C. Fear
D. Health

179. Copy normally includes the following elements in an advertisement
A. Main headline and tagline
B. Product name
C. Company name and signature
D. All the above

180. "Reason-why" copy of the advertisement is also known as
A. Soft sell copy
B. Hard sell copy
C. Educational copy
D. Descriptive copy

181. Advertisement should be
A. Simple
B. Memorable
C. Inviting to look at
D. All the above

182. An advertisement showing a happy family enjoying a vacation to promote a travel agency is using which type of appeal?
A. Rational Appeal
B. Humour Appeal
C. Emotional Appeal
D. Bandwagon Appeal

183. Highlighting the kilometres per litre and safety features of a new car in an advertisement is an example of:
A. Fear Appeal
B. Rational (Logical) Appeal
C. Sex Appeal
D. Nostalgia Appeal

184. A commercial for a snack food that uses funny situations and characters to make viewers laugh is employing:
A. Celebrity Endorsement Appeal
B. Adventure/Excitement Appeal
C. Humour Appeal
D. Bandwagon Appeal

185. Anti-smoking advertisements that depict the negative health consequences of smoking are using:
A. Emotional Appeal
B. Rational (Logical) Appeal
C. Fear Appeal
D. Nostalgia Appeal

186. An advertisement stating that "millions of people have switched to our brand" is an example of:
A. Sex Appeal
B. Celebrity Endorsement Appeal
C. Bandwagon Appeal
D. Adventure/Excitement Appeal

187. Perfume commercials often feature attractive models in alluring settings. This is an example of:
A. Humour Appeal
B. Sex Appeal
C. Fear Appeal
D. Rational (Logical) Appeal

188. When a famous athlete promotes a brand of sports drink, which advertising appeal is being used?
A. Nostalgia Appeal
B. Bandwagon Appeal
C. Celebrity Endorsement Appeal
D. Emotional Appeal

189. Advertisements for adventure tours that showcase thrilling activities like skydiving or white-water rafting are using:
A. Rational (Logical) Appeal
B. Adventure/Excitement Appeal
C. Fear Appeal
D. Humour Appeal

190. A candy bar commercial that uses imagery and music from past decades to evoke warm memories is employing:
A. Sex Appeal
B. Celebrity Endorsement Appeal
C. Nostalgia Appeal
D. Bandwagon Appeal

191. Which advertising appeal aims to connect with the audience's feelings, such as happiness or sadness?
A. Rational Appeal
B. Humour Appeal
C. Emotional Appeal
D. Fear Appeal

192. An ad for a new software that emphasizes its efficiency and time-saving features is using a:
A. Bandwagon Appeal
B. Rational (Logical) Appeal
C. Sex Appeal
D. Adventure/Excitement Appeal

193. A light-hearted commercial with a funny storyline to promote a household cleaner is using:
A. Fear Appeal
B. Humour Appeal
C. Nostalgia Appeal
D. Celebrity Endorsement Appeal

194. Insurance commercials that highlight the potential financial devastation of unforeseen events are using:
A. Emotional Appeal
B. Fear Appeal
C. Bandwagon Appeal
D. Rational (Logical) Appeal

195. An advertisement for a new social media platform that claims "everyone is joining now" is using:
A. Sex Appeal
B. Bandwagon Appeal
C. Nostalgia Appeal
D. Adventure/Excitement Appeal

196. Fashion advertisements that focus on the attractiveness of the models wearing the clothing are often using:
A. Humour Appeal
B. Sex Appeal
C. Fear Appeal
D. Celebrity Endorsement Appeal

197. When a well-known chef promotes a brand of kitchen appliances, it's an example of:
A. Nostalgia Appeal
B. Bandwagon Appeal
C. Celebrity Endorsement Appeal
D. Emotional Appeal

198. Tourism advertisements showcasing extreme sports in exotic locations are using:
A. Rational (Logical) Appeal
B. Adventure/Excitement Appeal
C. Fear Appeal
D. Humour Appeal

199. Commercials were introduced on Doordarshan on ....
A. 1st December, 1976
B. 1st January, 1976
C. 31st January, 1976
D. 31st March, 1975

200. A commercial for a classic car that features vintage footage and music is employing:
A. Sex Appeal
B. Celebrity Endorsement Appeal
C. Nostalgia Appeal
D. Bandwagon Appeal

201. Which appeal relies on presenting factual information and logical reasoning to persuade consumers?
A. Emotional Appeal
B. Rational (Logical) Appeal
C. Humour Appeal
D. Fear Appeal

202. An advertisement encouraging consumers to buy products made with sustainable practices is using which type of appeal?
A. Social Appeal B. Scarcity Appeal
C. Moral Appeal D. Testimonial Appeal

203. An advertisement showing a group of popular students using a particular brand of backpack is employing:
A. Moral Appeal B. Scarcity Appeal
C. Social Appeal D. Testimonial Appeal

204. Public service announcements that highlight the dangers of texting while driving utilize which advertising appeal?
A. Testimonial Appeal
B. Scarcity Appeal
C. Social Appeal
D. Moral Appeal

205. Campaigns urging people to donate to a disaster relief fund are examples of:
A. Social Appeal
B. Moral Appeal
C. Scarcity Appeal
D. Testimonial Appeal

206. Promotions that emphasize the "exclusive membership" associated with a product are using:
A. Testimonial Appeal
B. Moral Appeal
C. Social Appeal
D. Scarcity Appeal

207. Promotions that state "Offer Ends This Weekend!", "Only 5 Units Left!" are employing which type of appeal?
A. Testimonial Appeal
B. Scarcity Appeal
C. Social Appeal
D. Moral Appeal

208. An advertisement featuring customer reviews and star ratings for a product is using:
A. Scarcity Appeal
B. Social Appeal
C. Testimonial Appeal
D. Moral Appeal

209. A public service announcement against drunk driving featuring a heartfelt story from a victim uses a combination of which appeals?
A. Moral and Scarcity
B. Moral and Emotional
C. Social and Emotional
D. Testimonial and Moral

210. An advertisement for an eco-friendly product that also features positive reviews from environmental experts uses a combination of which appeals?
A. Social and Scarcity
B. Moral and Testimonial
C. Scarcity and Testimonial
D. Social and Moral

211. A luxury watch advertisement showing a successful entrepreneur wearing it and stating "Limited Edition" combines which appeals?
A. Moral and Scarcity
B. Social and Moral
C. Social and Scarcity
D. Testimonial and Moral

212. The role of a film .... involves overseeing the entire production process.
A. producer B. editor
C. director D. cinematographer

213. The process of selecting and assembling shots into a coherent sequence is known as ....
A. cinematography B. directing
C. editing D. production design

214. In film and TV production, lighting sets the .... for a scene, influencing its emotional impact.

A. pace B. mood
C. setting D. tone

215. The raw, unedited footage captured during filming is commonly referred to as ....

A. dailies B. rushes
C. raw footage D. both (A) and (B)

216. Effective .... design enhances the auditory experience in films and TV shows.

A. visual B. sound
C. set D. costume

217. The individual responsible for creating and coordinating characters' wardrobe in a film is the ....

A. set designer B. makeup artist
C. costume designer D. hair stylist

218. What is 'Prasar Bharati'?

A. a private company owning TV channels
B. a telecom company owning a large mobile network
C. an advertising and public relation wing of the central govt.
D. an autonomous body for public radio and TV broadcasting

219. A .... is the written document detailing the story, dialogue, and scene descriptions of a film.

A. synopsis B. treatment
C. screenplay D. storyboard

220. The process of recording audio elements for a film or TV show is called ....

A. audio mixing B. sound design
C. sound recording D. voice-over

221. The term .... encompasses the strategies used to promote and market a film or TV show.

A. distribution B. exhibition
C. promotion D. advertising

222. Vladimir Zworykin was associated with the invention of

A. Colour printing B. Radio
C. Television D. Internet

223. An .... shot is commonly used to establish the setting or location of a scene.

A. close-up B. establishing
C. medium D. over-the-shoulder

224. The .... is responsible for creating visual concepts and scenes in a film or TV show.

A. cinematographer
B. editor
C. production designer
D. art director

225. .... refers to the process of capturing live-action footage using a camera.

A. Animation B. Filming
C. Rendering D. Compositing

226. The term .... describes the process of adjusting the colour tones in post-production.

A. visual effects B. sound editing
C. colour grading D. motion graphics

227. The role of a .... involves managing the financial and business aspects of a film or TV production.

A. director B. producer
C. editor D. unit production manager

228. The .... is responsible for composing and arranging the musical score in a film.

A. sound designer B. composer
C. music supervisor D. orchestrator

229. In filmmaking, a .... shot captures a character's facial expression, emphasizing emotions.

A. wide B. medium
C. close-up D. long

230. The process of adding visual effects or graphics to a film is known as ....

A. cinematography
B. CGI (Computer-Generated Imagery)
C. set design
D. Foley

231. The .... is the first edited version of a film, usually shown to producers for feedback.

A. final cut B. director's cut
C. rough cut D. assembly cut

232. A .... is a shot where the camera moves parallel to the ground, following a subject.

A. pan shot B. tilt shot
C. tracking shot D. zoom shot

233. The .... is responsible for coordinating and managing the technical aspects of a film shoot, including camera operation and lighting.

A. gaffer B. best boy
C. cinematographer D. key grip

234. In film and TV production, ... involves planning and organizing all aspects of a project.
A. production B. post-production
C. pre-production D. development

235. The .... is the final version of a film after all editing and post-production work is complete.
A. rough cut B. director's cut
C. final cut D. assembly cut

236. The .... is responsible for designing and creating special makeup effects for characters.
A. makeup artist
B. hair stylist
C. special effects makeup artist
D. prosthetic artist

237. The process of creating a film's .... involves combining dialogue, sound effects, and music.
A. sound design B. sound recording
C. audio mix D. Foley

238. A .... is a short segment of a film that is shot and edited before the actual production begins, often to test ideas.
A. trailer B. scene study
C. pre-visualization D. sizzle reel

239. .... is the process of adding subtitles or captions to a film or TV show.
A. Dubbing B. Subtitling
C. Voice-over D. Transcription

240. The .... is responsible for managing the day-to-day operations on a film set.
A. Director
B. Producer
C. First assistant director
D. Second assistant director

241. The .... is the person responsible for overseeing the continuity of props and costumes during filming.
A. Costume designer
B. Prop master
C. Script supervisor
D. Production coordinator

242. .... involves assembling all the elements of a film, including sound, music, and visuals.
A. Pre-production B. Production
C. Post-production D. Distribution

243. The .... is the process of capturing additional footage after the main shooting is complete.
A. Pick-up shot
B. Reshoot
C. Second unit photography
D. Overtime shooting

244. A .... is a shot taken from a high angle, looking down on the subject.
A. Low-angle shot B. Eye-level shot
C. High-angle shot D. Dutch angle

245. The .... is responsible for selecting and acquiring locations for a film or TV production.
A. Set designer
B. Location manager
C. Location scout
D. Production designer

246. .... is the process of recording the actors' lines during filming.
A. ADR (Automated Dialogue Replacement)
B. Voice-over recording
C. Dialogue recording
D. Sound mixing

247. The .... is responsible for creating and applying prosthetics and special effects makeup.
A. Makeup artist B. Special effects artist
C. Prosthetics artist D. Character designer

248. The .... is the final step in post-production, ensuring that the colours are consistent throughout the film.
A. Colour grading
B. Colour correction
C. Visual effects compositing
D. Mastering

249. The .... is responsible for capturing the director's vision through the camera lens.
A. Gaffer
B. Cinematographer
C. Key grip
D. Director of photography

250. The .... is the person responsible for coordinating and executing stunts in a film.
A. Fight choreographer
B. Action director
C. Stunt performer
D. Stunt coordinator

251. .... is the process of planning and organizing the shots and scenes in a film.
A. Storyboarding B. Shot listing
C. Scene breakdown D. Shot composition

252. A .... is a shot taken from a low angle, looking up at the subject.
A. High-angle shot B. Eye-level shot
C. Low-angle shot D. Bird's-eye view

253. The .... is responsible for creating the visual design and style of a film.
A. Set decorator
B. Art director
C. Production designer
D. Visual effects supervisor

254. The .... is responsible for ensuring that the costumes remain consistent throughout the film.
A. Costume designer
B. Wardrobe supervisor
C. Costume continuity supervisor
D. Seamstress

255. .... refers to the process of recording additional dialogue or sound effects after filming is complete.
A. Sound mixing
B. Sound editing
C. ADR (Automated Dialogue Replacement)
D. Foley

256. The .... is responsible for coordinating and managing the cast and crew on a film set.
A. Director
B. Producer
C. Production manager
D. Unit production manager

257. The .... is responsible for creating and coordinating the overall visual elements of a film.
A. Art director B. Cinematographer
C. Set designer D. Production designer

258. Who is responsible for providing the funding for a film production?
A. Director B. Executive Producer
C. Actor D. Screenwriter

259. Which of the following is NOT a stage in the film production process?
A. Distribution B. Post-production
C. Pre-production D. Production

260. What is the primary importance of having a unified team in film production?
A. To reduce the budget of the film.
B. To ensure smooth communication and efficient workflow towards a shared creative vision.
C. To allow individual departments to work independently without interference.
D. To guarantee that each team member gets equal recognition.

261. Who is primarily responsible for providing the financial resources necessary for a film production?
A. The director
B. The cinematographer
C. The producer(s)
D. The editor

262. What is the name of the stage in film production that involves detailed planning, script breakdown, location scouting, casting, and overall preparation before filming begins?
A. Production B. Post-production
C. Pre-production D. Development

263. What term is used to describe the collaborative effort of various individuals with different specialized jobs working together to create a final film?
A. Individual brilliance
B. Hierarchical structure
C. Collective endeavour
D. Independent filmmaking

264. What is the primary role of a Line Producer in film production?
A. To secure financing for the film.
B. To oversee the creative aspects of the film.
C. To manage the budget and day-to-day physical production of the film.
D. To direct the actors on set.

265. What is the main responsibility of a Production Manager in film production?
A. To write the screenplay.
B. To manage the overall organization of the production, including schedules, logistics, and personnel.
C. To operate the camera and lighting equipment.
D. To edit the film footage.

266. What is the primary role of a Director of Photography (DP) in film production?
A. To direct the actors' performances.
B. To manage the film's budget.
C. To be responsible for the visual look of the film, including camera operation, lighting, and composition.
D. To design the sets and costumes.

267. Who is primarily responsible for developing the overall visual design concept of a film, including sets, costumes, and locations?
A. The Director of Photography
B. The Costume Designer
C. The Production Designer
D. The Art Director

268. What is the primary responsibility of a Sound Recordist on a film set?
A. To design the film's sound effects.
B. To mix the audio tracks in post-production.
C. To capture clear and high-quality audio during filming, including dialogue and ambient sound.
D. To compose the film's musical score.

269. Who is generally considered the primary individual leading the creative aspects of a film production?
A. The Producer
B. The Director
C. The Director of Photography
D. The Editor

270. Who is responsible for finding the script, hiring a director and talent, and securing finance?
A. Executive Producer
B. Director
C. Production Assistant
D. Producer

271. What is a CTB?
A. It's a type of lighting used in film.
B. It's a type of camera.
C. It's something you put on a light to change the colour temperature.
D. None of these

272. In filmmaking, what is the purpose of a "key grip" on set?
A. To operate the camera
B. To design the costumes
C. To manage lighting and grip equipment
D. To direct the actors

273. Independent organization of creative people for advertisement and promotional tools are called
A. Advertisement Makers
B. Advertisement Creators
C. Advertisement Developers
D. Advertisement Agency

274. Which among the following is ***not*** a function of ad agency?
A. Conduct market analysis
B. Develop advertising plans
C. Develop media strategy
D. Collect feedback from target audience

275. An Ad copy which informs the target group the fact that the manufacturer is established enough to give them the right goods is?
A. institutional copy B. straight selling copy
C. educational copy D. expository copy

276. Marketing management must make four important decisions when developing an advertising program. All of the following would be among those decisions except:
A. Setting advertising objectives
B. Conducting advertising culture audit
C. Setting the advertising budget
D. Developing advertising strategy

277. If a copy tells openly and directly all the features of a product or a service with the help of suitable pictures, photos and diagrams to impress a customer, it is called?
A. descriptive copy
B. educational copy
C. straight selling copy
D. expository copy

278. The central theme of an advertisement that motivates the consumer to make a purchase decision is?
A. Advertising appeal
B. Advertisement script
C. Slogan
D. Headline

279. .... is used heavily when introducing a new product category.
A. Persuasive advertising
B. Inferential advertising
C. Reminder advertising
D. Informative advertising

280. Keeping consumers thinking about the product is the objective for which type of advertising?
A. Informative advertising
B. Psychological advertising.
C. Reminder advertising
D. Persuasive advertising

281. .... is a self-regulatory voluntary organization of the advertising industry
A. Securities and Exchange Board of India
B. Reserve Bank of India (RBI)
C. Medical Council of India
D. Advertising Standards Council of India (ASCI)

282. Point of Purchase Ads are also known as
A. In-Store Advertising
B. Built-in Advertising
C. Green Advertising
D. Stock Advertising

283. Airline frequent flyers schemes are
A. Promotion mix B. Fulfilment cost
C. Loyalty schemes D. Direct marketing

284. The promotion tool that may include coupons, contests, premiums, and other means of attracting consumer attention is best described as being which of the following?
A. Advertising
B. Personal selling
C. Public relations
D. Sales promotion

285. What is one of the primary goals of reminder advertising?
A. maintain customer relationships
B. build brand preference
C. correct false impressions
D. inform the market of a price change

286. Which of these types is a hidden advertisement?
A. Surrogate B. Competitive
C. Comparative D. Industrial

287. A short and striking or memorable phrase used in advertising is called
A. logo B. slogan
C. brand image D. sign

288. POP is an abbreviation of
A. Purchase of product
B. Point of purchase
C. Property of product
D. Priority of purchase

289. Pride appeal is which type of appeal?
A. Rational B. Informative
C. Emotional D. Non information

290. A specific coordinated advertising effort on behalf of a particular product or service that extends for a specified period of time
A. Campaign B. Trial
C. Commercial D. Marketing

291. Levels of differentiation, market share, product lifecycle stage, correlating promotional spending and brand sales are part of .... in advertising.
A. Objective of advertising
B. Models of advertising
C. Evaluation of advertising
D. Developing strategy

292. Which of the following is a characteristic of single-camera production?
A. Uses multiple cameras to shoot the same action.
B. Requires less editing time.
C. Gives more control over each shot.
D. Is primarily used for live events.

293. What is the function of a video switcher or vision mixer in multi-camera production?
A. To record sound from all cameras.
B. To control the lighting setup.
C. To select which camera's output goes on air or for recording.
D. To provide power to the cameras.

294. Which of the following is NOT a typical characteristic of Electronic News Gathering (ENG)?
A. Well-planned production.
B. Use of camcorders and microphones.
C. Focus on gathering news content for television.
D. Speed is a key element.

295. Which stage of production involves activities like budgeting, location hunting, and casting?
A. Production
B. Post-production
C. Pre-production
D. Final production

296. What is the purpose of a treatment in the pre-production process?
A. It is the final script used for shooting.
B. It is a graphical representation of an idea.
C. It is a narrative inscription of the production.
D. It is a detailed shooting schedule.

297. Who is responsible for the visual look of a film, including camera operation and lighting?
A. Production Designer
B. Art Director
C. Director
D. Director of Photography (DoP)

298. Audio-visual content is NOT produced for:
A. Movie theatres
B. Television channels
C. Online platforms
D. Print media

299. What has democratized audio-visual production?
A. Movie theatres
B. Television channels
C. Technology
D. YouTube

300. What is a common tool used by ordinary people to produce videos?
A. Professional video cameras
B. DSLRs and smartphones
C. Film cameras
D. Studio equipment

301. The basic process of production is:
A. Different for each type of production
B. The same for all types of production
C. Only for high-budget productions
D. Only for amateur productions

302. What varies according to the level of production?
A. The basic production process
B. The scale of activities
C. The need for planning
D. The need for personnel

303. Audio-visual productions can be classified based on:
A. The number of cameras
B. Location of shooting
C. Production objectives
D. All the above

304. Single-camera production uses:
A. One camera B. Multiple cameras
C. No camera D. Robotic cameras

305. Single-camera shooting is popular in:
A. Feature films B. Short films
C. News gathering D. All the above

306. A disadvantage of single-camera production is:
A. Less repetition B. Less shooting time
C. More editing time D. Less editing time

307. Multi-camera production involves:
A. One camera B. More than one camera
C. No camera D. Virtual cameras

308. Multi-camera production is used for:
A. Studio interviews B. Sports broadcasts
C. Reality shows D. All the above

309. What device is crucial in multi-camera shoots?
A. A single camera
B. Video switcher/vision mixer
C. Microphone
D. Lighting equipment

310. In a multi-camera setup, each camera has:
A. A dedicated microphone
B. A dedicated monitor
C. A dedicated light
D. A dedicated actor

311. The vision mixer allows you to:
A. Select any camera for broadcasting
B. Control camera angles
C. Adjust lighting
D. Operate microphones

312. A director's command to switch cameras might be:
A. "Zoom in camera-1"
B. "Pan camera-2"
C. "Take camera-3"
D. "Focus camera-4"

313. A major advantage of multi-camera production is:
A. More shooting time
B. Less shooting time
C. More editing time
D. Requirement of less equipment

314. A disadvantage of multi-camera production is:
A. Requirement of less crew
B. Requirement of more equipment
C. Easier lighting setup
D. More interesting lighting

315. ENG stands for:
A. Electronic News Gathering
B. Electronic Natural Gathering
C. Electrical News Gathering
D. Electronic National Gathering

316. The main objective of ENG is:
A. To produce creative content
B. To gather news content quickly
C. To produce high-quality dramas
D. To shoot live events

317. EFP stands for:
A. Electronic Film Production
B. Electronic Field Production
C. Electrical Film Production
D. Electrical Field Production

318. Unlike ENG, EFP is:
A. Not well-planned
B. Well-planned
C. Used for news gathering
D. A one-man team operation

319. Examples of EFP include:
A. Shooting sports events
B. Award shows
C. Big conferences
D. All the above

320. The film production process includes the following stages:
A. Pre-production
B. Production
C. Post-production
D. All the above

321. Which stage is considered the foundation of a production?

A. Production B. Post-production
C. Pre-production D. Editing

322. A well-managed pre-production does NOT:

A. Make production smooth
B. Save time
C. Increase costs
D. Save money

323. What is the first step in pre-production?

A. Script writing B. Budgeting
C. Idea generation D. Location hunting

324. A mind map is:

A. A written script
B. A graphical representation of an idea
C. A shooting schedule
D. A list of equipment

325. What are the two basic questions to keep in mind while developing an idea?

A. What is the budget? and Who is the director?
B. What is the shooting location? and What equipment is needed?
C. What is the main purpose? and Who is the target audience?
D. What is the cast? and What is the crew?

326. Lightman is the member of

A. Production team B. Direction team
C. Cast team D. None of these

327. What is known as lazy bones?

A. headphones B. newspapers
C. TV remotes D. mobile phones

328. Which among the following is the first talking film?

A. Raja Harishchandra B. Bhakta Prahlada
C. Alam Ara D. None of these

ANSWERS

1	2	3	4	5	6	7	8	9	10
A	B	D	C	A	D	D	B	A	C
11	**12**	**13**	**14**	**15**	**16**	**17**	**18**	**19**	**20**
B	B	C	A	B	A	D	B	A	B
21	**22**	**23**	**24**	**25**	**26**	**27**	**28**	**29**	**30**
D	D	A	B	D	B	D	D	C	B
31	**32**	**33**	**34**	**35**	**36**	**37**	**38**	**39**	**40**
B	B	A	B	A	B	D	A	D	A
41	**42**	**43**	**44**	**45**	**46**	**47**	**48**	**49**	**50**
D	A	D	C	C	C	D	D	A	B
51	**52**	**53**	**54**	**55**	**56**	**57**	**58**	**59**	**60**
A	C	D	C	A	D	C	C	C	A
61	**62**	**63**	**64**	**65**	**66**	**67**	**68**	**69**	**70**
C	B	D	D	A	D	A	C	A	B
71	**72**	**73**	**74**	**75**	**76**	**77**	**78**	**79**	**80**
B	B	C	A	C	D	A	C	A	B
81	**82**	**83**	**84**	**85**	**86**	**87**	**88**	**89**	**90**
A	B	D	C	A	B	D	C	A	D
91	**92**	**93**	**94**	**95**	**96**	**97**	**98**	**99**	**100**
D	C	D	C	B	C	B	B	A	B
101	**102**	**103**	**104**	**105**	**106**	**107**	**108**	**109**	**110**
B	D	C	C	A	D	A	C	C	B
111	**112**	**113**	**114**	**115**	**116**	**117**	**118**	**119**	**120**
B	C	A	D	D	A	C	B	D	D
121	**122**	**123**	**124**	**125**	**126**	**127**	**128**	**129**	**130**
C	A	A	D	B	A	B	C	A	B

131	132	133	134	135	136	137	138	139	140
A	B	C	D	A	A	A	A	C	D
141	142	143	144	145	146	147	148	149	150
C	C	B	B	D	A	C	B	C	B
151	152	153	154	155	156	157	158	159	160
C	C	B	C	C	B	C	C	A	B
161	162	163	164	165	166	167	168	169	170
A	D	A	C	D	B	B	D	D	C
171	172	173	174	175	176	177	178	189	190
D	B	C	C	D	D	B	C	D	B
181	182	183	184	185	186	187	188	189	190
D	C	B	C	C	C	B	C	B	C
191	192	193	194	195	196	197	198	199	200
C	B	B	B	B	B	C	B	B	C
201	202	203	204	205	206	207	208	209	210
B	C	C	D	B	C	B	C	B	B
211	212	213	214	215	216	217	218	219	220
C	C	C	B	D	B	C	D	C	C
221	222	223	224	225	226	227	228	229	230
C	C	B	C	B	C	B	B	C	B
231	232	233	234	235	236	237	238	239	240
C	C	C	C	C	C	C	C	B	C
241	242	243	244	245	246	247	248	249	250
C	C	B	C	C	C	C	B	D	D
251	252	253	254	255	256	257	258	259	260
B	C	B	C	C	C	D	B	A	B
261	262	263	264	265	266	267	268	269	270
C	C	C	C	B	C	C	C	B	D
271	272	273	274	275	276	277	278	279	280
C	C	D	D	A	B	C	A	D	C
281	282	283	284	285	286	287	288	289	290
D	A	C	D	A	A	B	B	C	C
291	292	293	294	295	296	297	298	299	300
D	C	C	A	C	C	D	D	C	B
301	302	303	304	305	306	307	308	309	310
B	B	D	A	D	C	B	D	B	B
311	312	313	314	315	316	317	318	319	320
A	C	B	B	A	B	B	B	D	D
321	322	323	324	325	326	327	328		
C	C	C	B	C	A	C	C		

EXPLANATORY ANSWERS

5. (A): The Indian Society of Advertisers was established in the year 1951. It represents the interests of all the organizations which are interested in marketing, advertising etc. It tries to promote the rights of its members and also try to protect the consumers by ensuring that the advertising and marketing communications are conducted effectively. It aims to maintain the ethics and economic discipline in advertising.

11. (B): Market mix consist of 4 Ps – product, price, place and promotion.

12. (B): The product life cycle describes the stages a product goes through from its introduction to the market until its eventual removal. It typically includes the *introduction, growth, maturity, and decline stages.*

23. (A): The AIDA marketing model stands for Awareness, Interest, Desire, and Action, in that order.

45. (C): The correct option is (C) Buyer and seller, as advertisements aim to communicate directly with potential buyers about products or ideas. This relationship emphasizes the non-personal nature of advertising, distinguishing it from direct interactions in sales. Advertisements are designed to inform and persuade customers about products in various media formats.

86. (B): The DAGMAR model defines the four steps of an effective advertising campaign as causing awareness, comprehension, conviction, and action. The model stresses defining the segment of the market that the campaign seeks to reach.

127. (B): The Advertising Standards Council of India (ASCI) was formed in 1985. It was established by professionals from the advertising and media industry to keep Indian ads decent, fair, and honest. Over the years, ASCI has played a crucial role in regulating advertising content and protecting consumer interests in India.

137. (A): Surrogate advertising is prominently seen in cases where advertising a particular product is banned by law. Advertisements for products like tobacco, cigarettes, or alcohol that are injurious to health are prohibited by law in several countries.

142. (C): Conversion Rate indicates the percentage of users who perform a specific action, like making a purchase or signing up.

143. (B): In Search Advertising, Cost Per Click (CPC) is a widely used bidding strategy where advertisers pay for each click their ad receives.

271. (C): CTB stands for Colour Temperature Blue. It's a type of lighting gel or filter used in film, photography, and stage lighting to convert warmer light sources (like tungsten) to a cooler, more bluish colour temperature, often resembling daylight.

272. (C): The Key Grip is the head of the grip department on a film set. Their primary responsibility is to work closely with the Director of Photography (DP) to shape and control the lighting by using various grip equipment such as flags, nets, and diffusion. They also oversee camera support and movement.

275. (A): Institutional copy focuses on building the reputation and goodwill of the advertiser (the manufacturer) rather than directly selling a specific product or service. By highlighting the manufacturer's established nature, the ad aims to instil trust and confidence in the target group, implying that they are reliable and capable of providing "the right goods."

317. (B): Electronic Field Production (EFP) is a term in the television industry that refers to video production conducted outside of a formal studio, in a practical location or special venue. It leverages both ENG (electronic news gathering) and studio techniques, focusing on capturing high-quality video in real-world settings. EFP is used for various events, including sports, concerts, award shows, and conferences.

CHAPTER-4

RADIO

REPORTING FOR RADIO

Of all mediums, Radio is most affordable and has a wider reach in the society. According to UNESCO It is "the mass medium that reaches the widest audience in the world". It is also the easiest form of broadcasting to produce. Radio is also called 'Theatre of Mind' and is quite popular among those who cannot read and write. It can transmit on a local level, in regional language, addressing issues of importance to local listeners.

The radio newscast is consumed sequentially. Listeners have to wait. Even if, listeners are bored by one part of the newscast, they cannot skip forward to the next segment or news. Therefore, it is important for a newscast to be interesting and captivating.

Radio news listeners are hardly, attentive. Usually, people listen to radio while doing something else. The radio listeners are often driving, working, or engaged in some task other than absorbing the latest news. Hence radio news stories are told in familiar words combined into sentences, which run at comfortable lengths in a conversational style.

The radio news writing style includes the choice of simple words with short declarative sentences. Clarity in both sentence length and word choice is important in radio news reporting. Sentences must be crisp and short. Since the listeners have no opportunity to go back and hear it again.

Sentences in a radio news story generally contain just one idea and do not contain multiple clauses and internal clauses. Jargons or highly technical words are also avoided. Radio news is shorter than newspaper news and hence requires comprehension and filtration of facts while writing the news.

Communication over radio depends on the message transmitted through sound to a listener who has to first listen and then interpret it to grasp the message. Not only the verbal expression of the communicator, but also the listening and understanding capacity of the listener is involved in an effective communication. To achieve this, the message has to be designed carefully.

Like any other medium, Radio production also has three stages namely: pre-production, production and post production. However, the writing and elements of radio program vary.

WRITING FOR RADIO

The production of any radio program starts with ideation. Writing is a crucial element in this phase. It ensures weaving of the thought flow and content progression of a radio program.

- First of all, when it comes to radio, you listen to a person who is not seen
- The person speaks from a script written down earlier
- You feel that the person is talking to you
- The person sounds friendly and you have no problem in understanding what is being said
- You can call the language, or the words used in a radio script as the spoken word as against the written word or the printed word used in the print media

- Unlike the printed word, which is written for the eye, the spoken word is written for the ear.

Main characteristic of spoken word are:

- Though it is written, it is spoken
- It is written for the ear not the eye
- It is heard only once. The listener normally does not get a second chance to listen.

It is conversational and should therefore sound like one and have the following qualities:

- It should be simply worded without any difficult or unfamiliar words.
- The sentences should be short and simple and not complex.
- There should be only one idea in a sentence and not many ideas.
- Though there are thousands of listeners, the written material should be meant for just one listener. So, it should be speaking to one person.
- The words chosen should denote the exact meaning and not be vague or abstract. The words should make pictures in the minds of the listeners.
- Abbreviations or short forms should be avoided. If an abbreviation is used, then its full form should be given.
- If the script consists of big numbers, it can be rounded off to the nearest whole number.
- While referring to more than one person, avoid using 'he' or 'she'. It can confuse the listeners.

Elements of Radio Production

- **Studio:** A sound proof and technologically rich studio is necessary to record and broadcast programs.
- **Microphones:** Microphones are necessary to record audio. They amplify or in other words, increase the volume of your voice.
  - ❑ **Unidirectional:** This microphone picks up sound from one direction.
  - ❑ **Bi- directional**: The voice or sound is picked up from two directions. If you are recording an interview in a radio studio, you may use this type of a microphone.
  - ❑ **Omni- directional microphone**: It picks up sound from all directions.
- **Sound Effects**: Sound effects give meaning and sense of location to a program. Most importantly, it gives realism.
- **Music:** Music is the soul of radio. They not only play music to entertain people. Music forms the signature tunes for many programs broadcasted.
  - ❑ Music adds color and life to any spoken word program.
  - ❑ Music can break monotony.
  - ❑ Music is used to give the desired effect of happy or unhappy situations, fear or joy.
  - ❑ Music can suggest scenes and locations.
- **Artificial Echo**: An echo is used in radio programs. This is a technical input.
- **Filter or Distort**: If you listen to someone speaking to you on phone, the voice will not sound normal. This sort of effect called distort is produced using technology.
- **Human Voice**: The main stay in any radio program is the human voice. There are two aspects of the use of human voice in radio production. Firstly, there has to be a well written script to be spoken and then someone has to speak or read it before a microphone in studio.

Broadcast Script Writing

Broadcast script writing means writing for radio and television. It can also be explained as writing for ears and eyes. It is different from print media. In the print media, one can write even difficult words and sometime some long sentences with some complex construction. But in broadcast script writing, we have to use simple and short sentences. There are **five key principles** for broadcast script writing:

1. It is spoken

We should remember that we are not writing a piece of written literature. So we should be natural and use the words you know the meaning and which are in your spoken vocabulary.

Use the spoken words of everyday speech. Do not be afraid to use the same words twice or thrice if required. The broadcast style must be natural.

Example: Do not write like: The Road is not motorable INSTEAD WRITE LIKE;

The Road is blocked or closed.

In Broadcast scripts, do not use abbreviations. Write full words.

We cannot write Like: Don't, That's, they're, won't, isn't INSTEAD WRITE AS:

Do not, That is, They are, Would not, Is not, etc.

2. *It is immediate*

Broadcast scripts are considered to be written in immediate format. For Radio and Television, information is considered immediate. Broadcast is a "NOW" medium. But in print we can publish even history or something which is not immediate.

Example: Do not write: The Chief Executive said today the country's economy was booming. INSTEAD WRITE LIKE:

The chief executive says the country's economy is booming.

3. *It is person to person*

At a time thousands of people would be listening or watching your scripts to be delivered from radio or television, but they should feel that they are attached to this script or drama or any information.

These scripts develop friendship with listeners and viewers. When we broadcast any script, we should adopt a friendly tone. Use language normally your audience use, to speak and understand.

4. *It is heard once*

When we write a script for Radio and Television, we should keep in mind that the words, dialogue spoken are heard once and they can not be referred back as in case of print media. In the print media, we can again read the words we do not understand or miss them. So, always use easy, simple short sentence and understandable language and words. Clarity must be observed. Do not write confusing words. Leave out superfluous information. The idea must be grasped. Use only one idea in one sentence.

5. *It is sound/picture*

You should know that your scripts are delivered through sound in case of radio and sound and picture in case of television. Your words are a bridge between you and your audience. Do not use vague or ambiguous language in script writing.

Punctuation is absolutely vital. When eyes see a mark on page, the brain reacts in a certain way and the sentences, dialogues are delivered in a right way. Always your first sentence should be catchy and attractive.

KNOWLEDGE OF GRAMMAR AND PUNCTUATION

Audiences hold media and strategic communication professionals to a high standard when it comes to knowledge of grammar and punctuation. Here are a few basic grammar and punctuation rules:

- **Use active, not passive voice.** Active voice helps with clarity and concise writing. For e.g. *(Passive voice: The press release was completed by Ashok. Active voice: Ashok completed the press release.)*
- **Understand word choice and meaning**:
  - ❑ affect, effect
  - ❑ its, it's
  - ❑ they're, their, there
  - ❑ accept, except
- **Be aware of comma uses**:
  - ❑ Set off modifiers (words or clauses that provide further description) for e.g. *The bureaucrat, who works for the government, arrived late to the meeting.*
  - ❑ Separate an introductory phrase or word for e.g. *While studying, I listened to music.*
  - ❑ Before a conjunction for e.g. *I want to go, but I have to study.*
  - ❑ When writing a series of items (three or more) for e.g. *She bought shoes, food, and a bag.*

COMPILATION OF RADIO NEWS

Pool Copy

All incoming news, after editing, is put into the pool which split into news categories such as Home, Foreign, Parliament and Sports. Inclusion of an item in the pool means: (*a*) the news which is broadcast worthy, (*b*) it has already been written in broadcast style and (*c*) any linkages and backgrounding required has been done. The entire pool copy is distributed among all editors compiling different bulletins. Home as well as External. The editors preparing the pool copy also look after the important developing stories and constantly go on revising and updating them. They also prepare round ups of important events and happenings such as riots, floods, disturbance, and whatever is in the news. The News Room has four shifts during a day and each shift issues its own pool copy, during morning, day time, evening and night.

Compiling News Bulletins

The compiling editors further select and prune the news items, keeping in view the duration of each bulletin and the interest of the target audience. They prepare the bulletins and, together with the headlines, send them to the Language Units and the External Services Units where they are translated and put out in their languages.

Selecting the Headlines

Having prepared the bulletin; the editor has to decide which items apart from the lead story are to be headlined. There is only one criterion: which are the items that will interest the largest number of listeners.

Use of Spoken Language in the News Bulletins on Radio

As the news on the radio moves fast without the facility of recall, which is possible, though, in the case of newspapers, whatever is broadcast, must be clear, precise and to the point. Sentences should be short and direct without sub clauses. Brevity is essential as a minute of broadcast time can take about 100 words, thus giving an editor the choice of about 1000 to 1100 words (in a 10-minute news bulletin) to cover world, national and regional news. There is a great constraint of space in radio, hence broadcast news must be big and important and should be put in crisp and easily understood language.

Clarity through the use of simple words

There should be no need for a dictionary while listening to a radio bulletin. It should be in words which are common in everyday speech. For .example, "The work has started" and not "the work has commenced". "The play has ended" and not "terminated".

The words chosen should create visual images in the mind. "Roads are under water" or "The telegraph poles have been uprooted" or "The bridges have been washed away" sound better than "The communications have been disrupted".

Short Sentences

While writing news for the radio, we should not use long sentences. Avoid subordinate clauses; they are rarely used in every day conversation.

The attention of an average radio listener cannot be held for long: so the sentences as well as the paragraphs have to be short. Avoid a sentence which is longer than 18 to 20 words.

Present Tense

Wherever possible, use the present tense. Broadcasts on radio should appear to the listener to be happening at that moment. Instead of saying "the new generator was switched on yesterday" say "The new generator has been switched on". Instead of saying "The Prime Minister said today that the country's economy is booming", write "The Prime Minister says the country's economy is booming".

PREPARATION FOR THE RADIO COMMENTARY AND FEATURES

In the audio medium, voice, sound effects and music are the critical elements which gain the listeners attention and hold it. The spoken word is crucial to a radio feature or a commentary. Special attention has to be paid to what is said and the tone in which it is uttered. A radio commentator is both the eyes and ears of the listener. A commentator creates verbal pictures in the minds of the receivers by simply combining the spoken world with music and sound effects in a creative fashion.

It is a creative capsule presentation of an equally creative area or theme. Narration is a crucial element of a radio feature. The spoken word is liberally supported by sound effects and music.

Commentary is an art and its successful practice depends on attention to a special technique-descriptive power and narrative style. This is possible only when one has the capacity to notice the finer details and also express them in simple but evocative terms. Without preliminary preparation, the commentators would find themselves in serious trouble. The best plans can be thrown out of gear by some unforeseen circumstance say a new twist to the event.

An intelligent and resourceful commentator will be able to place his thoughts and ideas across without much difficulty. In order to evoke a vivid word picture, one would require alert human faculties, and a vast knowledge of men and matters gathered through extensive reading and intense involvement in the social, political and cultural developments in the country.

In short, a radio commentary describes an occasion or event in vivid words. The attempt is always to verily transport the distant listeners to the scene of action or attention. Naturally, the commentators has to be all ears and eyes to perform the job perfectly.

A radio commentator/feature narrator must have certain essential physical characteristics. In using the word physical, we imply the personality of the commentator as reflected in the credence and vibration of speech delivery which actually holds the key to success on the job.

Broadcaster's Voice and Microphone Manners

Whether one is a commentator, interviewer, newsreader or announcer, one must take care of one's voice. To make a beginning, one needs to breathe correctly, enunciate clearly and attend to the vocal rhythm in order to ensure a liquid stream of pure sound.

Speech Rhythm

Rhythm is the life blood of speech. Without this (very important input) speech becomes lifeless and mechanical. Nothing kills a broadcast more surely than the monotony of delivery. Remember, words are the fuel of speaker's thoughts, and rhythm is the oil that lubricates that vehicle. Therefore, the broadcaster's sound not only sends messages, but also ensures that the listener is persuaded by it. Again, every broadcast has to be kept alive and this is mainly achieved by correct emphasis, stress, and pause in the speech.

Language

It is important to remember that the language must be understandable to the majority of the listeners.

Usually, a listener reacts quickly to the broadcaster's manner. There are a few thumb rules which a broadcaster would do well to follow. We shall enumerate these rules here.

- Do not patronise the listeners. At least, for having taken the trouble to listen to you, the listeners ought to be treated with courtesy.
- Be friendly without being familiar. Do not take the listeners for granted. Do not shout or preach Speak impressively confidently and with dignity.
- Finally, be yourself and not what you would like the listeners to think you are. While the listener is seldom deceived you may flounder and reveal your true colours sooner rather than later.

The art of writing a production script for the radio very often lies in the art of knowing what not to say. It is said in BBC TV circles that a commentator is paid as much to comment as to keep quiet.

Avoid Padding

The term 'Padding' refers to the filling out of a sentence, publication, etc., with superfluous matter.

While preparing the script for a radio programme, we must not pad out the narration. As a rule, avoid, using unnecessary words, and admitting irrelevant contexts or distantly related topics in the script. One dull patch can imperil the broadcaster's hold on the listeners.

TIPS FOR A GOOD RADIO SCRIPT

- **Keep the Script/Commentary Moving:** The shorter your sentences and crisper your narration, the greater will be the commentary's impact. While padding has to be avoided at all costs, repetition of the main points is permitted and even necessary. This you can do towards the end of the programme in the form of a summary. It is to ensure that all the points that you want your listeners to remember are, in fact, briefly expressed again.
- **Enliven the Script/Commentary:** The wider your vocabulary, the more visual are your images. And this, in turn, helps you to vary your form and have a firm hold over listeners/audience.
- **Be Completely Natural:** It is very life of your broadcast that you read aloud your narration/script/ commentary as you write, if it is not off-the-cuff broadcast, e.g., running commentary. If it sounds natural, as though you were talking, you are on the right line. If on the other hand, it sounds like formal written language, you will immediately know you are off-the-track. Get your friends and well-wishers to help you with their reactions. This tried and tested method will be of immense help to you in improving your performance.
- **Keep Cliches Out:** This applies to hackneyed phrases as much as to journalistic ones. The microphone only reinforces their staleness. It is only radio journalism at its worst.
- **Keep on Looking for the Needs of the Market:** It is well to remember that broadcasting is essentially a family affair. Good taste is what matters and should be the main criterion. The writer's script should be simple and conjure visual rather than oral images in the listeners mind. Remember: short sentences and short words are always more effective than long-winded and pedantic phrases.
- **Do not Talk Down to the Audience:** In any programme where the spoken word dominates in a running commentary or any other—one must take precaution against any slip of the tongue that would offend a listener. Be professional when you have to explain some matter. Do not sound like the know-all teacher talking down to the students.

LANGUAGE OF THE RADIO COMMENTARY AND FEATURE

The language of speech (the spoken word) differs considerably from the language of writing (the written word). The differences arise in the

- vocabulary,
- sentence length,
- sentence structure,
- density of distribution of information,
- writer speaker's intention and attitude to the subject and toward the listeners.

The important factors which make or break a commentary are:

- stress on syllables
- accent of one's speech
- amount of information
- actual, speed of delivery.

One must take into account the varying spans of memory and levels of comprehension of different listeners. Clarity of both content and actual narration is thus essential.

One must remember that it is an individual's memory and comprehension that we deal with. Listeners generally cannot turn to anybody for explanation. Neither can they be expected to have reference books at hand. Therefore, all the necessary aids to remember and comprehension are, generally built into the programme material. Scripts for radio commentary and features ought to be written with this vital factor in view. The narrators too must be chosen with due care and given instructions about the required pace of narration, style of delivery, etc.

The radio is an audio medium. The secret of the ideal radio broadcast is the unexpressed will to woo listeners to stay tuned for the entire programme by simply providing the right fare. A good radio feature or running commentary is one that strives to describe the subject or phenomenon cogently and comprehensively.

A radio feature and commentary is written in words that create appropriate atmosphere and concrete pictures in the listener's mind. It is by improving the script and presenting it creatively that a radio feature writer and commentator makes even the most complex subject appear simple. It is in their hands to make listening a gainful and lasting pleasure. They have only to wield their power correctly to endear themselves to their audience.

RADIO STATION

A Radio station is a place where radio programmes are recorded, produced and are transmitted from. In a radio station, there are three different wings. These are:

- Programme Wing
- Engineering Wing
- Administration Wing

While the first two wings are responsible for running a radio station's broadcasts, the administrative wing provides all the support that is required for the functioning of the station.

RADIO STUDIO

A radio studio is a specialized workspace designed for producing and broadcasting audio content. It consists of various technical, acoustic, and operational components that ensure high-quality transmission and seamless workflow. It typically includes:

- **Broadcast Console**: The main control panel for mixing and managing audio signals.
- **On-Air/Live Studio:** Where presenters, hosts, and guests communicate live with the audience.
- **Microphones**: High-quality mics for clear voice transmission.
- **Headphones & Speakers**: For monitoring audio output.
- **Computers & Software**: Used for editing, recording, and streaming.
- **Telephone Hybrid**: Allows live call-ins from listeners.
- **Production Room:** Used for recording, editing, and pre-producing audio content.
- **Soundproofing**: Ensures high audio quality by minimizing external noise. Uses materials like acoustic foam, heavy drapes, and double-glazed windows.
- **Absorption Panels**: Minimize echoes and reverberation, improving audio clarity.
- **Bass Traps**: Reduce low-frequency build-up for balanced sound.
- **Diffusers**: Help in evenly distributing sound waves to avoid dead spots.

Essential Equipment in a Radio Studio

A. Audio Equipment

- **Microphones**:
  - ❑ Dynamic Microphones (e.g., Shure SM7B, Electro-Voice RE20) – durable and good for live radio.
  - ❑ Condenser Microphones – used in voiceovers and pre-recorded segments due to higher sensitivity.
  - ❑ Lavalier and Headset Microphones – for hands-free broadcasting.
- **Microphone Accessories**:
  - ❑ Pop Filters – reduce plosive sounds.
  - ❑ Shock Mounts – prevent vibrations from affecting the recording.
  - ❑ Boom Arms – allow flexible microphone positioning.
- **Mixing Console (Audio Mixer)**:
  - ❑ Controls microphone levels, equalization (EQ), and audio routing.
  - ❑ Digital and analog mixers are available (e.g., Behringer X32, Allen & Heath ZED-14).
- **Headphones and Monitors**:
  - ❑ Closed-back headphones for presenters (e.g., Audio-Technica ATH-M50X, Beyerdynamic DT 770).
  - ❑ Studio monitors for accurate audio playback.
- **Audio Processors**:
  - ❑ Compressors, limiters, and equalizers for enhancing sound quality.
  - ❑ Noise gates to minimize unwanted background noise.

B. Broadcasting Equipment

- **Playout Software**: Automates music and ad scheduling (e.g., RadioBOSS, StationPlaylist, Zetta).
- **Telephony System**:
  - ❑ Used for live caller interaction.
  - ❑ Hybrid systems connect telephone audio to the mixer.
- **Broadcast Delay Unit**: Provides a short delay to filter inappropriate content before transmission.
- **Transmitter and Antenna**: Sends the radio signal over FM/AM frequencies.
- **Streaming Encoder**: Converts audio for online streaming (e.g., Shoutcast, Icecast).

C. Computers and Software

- **Digital Audio Workstation (DAW)**: Software for recording and editing (e.g., Adobe Audition, Audacity, Pro Tools).
- **Automation Software**: For scheduling playlists, jingles, and news bulletins.
- **Remote Broadcasting Software**: Allows presenters to go live from different locations (e.g., Cleanfeed, Source-Connect).

RADIO JOCKEY (RJ)

A Radio Jockey (RJ) is the voice of a radio station, responsible for engaging listeners, presenting music, conducting interviews, and providing entertainment, news, and information. They create a strong connection with the audience through their personality, communication skills, and content delivery.

Key Responsibilities of a Radio Jockey

- **Hosting and Presenting Shows:** A Radio Jockey conducts live or pre-recorded radio programs, engaging listeners through conversations, stories, and discussions. They introduce and play songs, advertisements, and station jingles, creating an entertaining and interactive experience for the audience.
- **Content Creation and Planning:** A Radio Jockey prepares scripts, show outlines, and talking points while researching trending topics, news, and audience interests to keep the content relevant and engaging. They also create unique segments, contests, and interactive sessions to captivate listeners and enhance audience participation.
- **Engaging with Listeners:** A Radio Jockey takes live calls, messages, and social media interactions, ensuring active audience participation. They organize audience polls, requests, and shout-outs to keep listeners engaged. Through personal engagement and interactive communication, they build a loyal listener base.
- **Conducting Interviews:** A Radio Jockey hosts celebrity interviews, expert talks, and guest segments, bringing diverse perspectives to the audience. They prepare insightful questions and moderate discussions to ensure engaging and informative conversations.
- **Technical and Broadcasting Tasks:** A Radio Jockey operates basic audio equipment like microphones and mixers while working with radio automation software to schedule content efficiently.

They ensure smooth transitions between segments, advertisements, and music, maintaining a seamless listening experience.

- **Promoting the Radio Station:** A Radio Jockey represents the station at events, promotions, and public appearances, strengthening the station's presence. They engage in social media marketing and collaborations to connect with a wider audience. Additionally, they create podcasts or digital content to extend their reach beyond traditional radio broadcasting.

Skills Required for a Radio Jockey

- **Communication Skills:** A Radio Jockey should possess a clear, expressive, and engaging voice, essential for capturing audience attention. They should have the ability to modulate their tone and style based on the content, ensuring effective communication and an engaging listening experience.
- **Creativity and Spontaneity:** A Radio Jockey should have the ability to think quickly on-air to handle unexpected situations with confidence and spontaneity. They should also be able to create unique and entertaining show formats to keep the audience engaged and entertained.
- **Sense of Humor and Wit:** It is important for a Radio Jockey to know how to keep the show lively and engaging while handling interactions with humor and confidence, ensuring an enjoyable experience for the audience.
- **Technical Knowledge:** A good understanding of studio equipment, mixers, and playout software, is a must for Radio Jockey, along with basic editing and sound production skills to ensure high-quality broadcasts.
- **Awareness and Research Abilities:** It is important for a Radio Jockey to keep up with trends, news, and audience interests to stay relevant and engaging. They must also research topics thoroughly to facilitate informative and meaningful discussions.
- **Time Management:** A Radio Jockey must possess strong time management skills to ensure the show runs smoothly within scheduled slots. They carefully manage talk time between songs, advertisements, and segments to maintain a balanced and well-structured broadcast.

MULTIPLE CHOICE QUESTIONS

1. How did radio broadcasts affect public perception during revolutions in the 20th century?
A. They decreased the spread of propaganda
B. They allowed for immediate dissemination of information and leaders' speeches
C. They had minimal impact compared to print media
D. They were primarily used for entertainment purposes

2. Which of the following is included in the technique of electronic media?
A. production B. transmission
C. reception D. all of these

3. Which one of the following is considered as the cheapest source of information?
A. Internet B. Television
C. Radio D. All the above

4. Who was the one to send first radio signals?
A. Heinrich Hertz
B. Nikola Tesla
C. Guglielmo Marconi
D. Thomas Edison

5. .... invented the first theoretical model of Radio.
A. Nikola Telsa
B. Guglielmo Marconi
C. Thomas Edison
D. Elon Musk

6. Radio broadcasting in India was started in .... in the year 1923.
A. Calcutta B. Bombay
C. Madras D. None of these

7. Indian Broadcasting Service was later named as ....
A. BIG FM B. Club FM
C. Vividh Bharti D. AIR

8. When was the first music program transmitted from AIR?
A. 1932 B. 1936
C. 1952 D. 1957

9. The World radio is celebrated on ....
A. January 14 B. February 13
C. April 13 D. January 30

10. In the year 1930, All India Radio was known as ....
A. Akashvani
B. Indian Broadcasting Company
C. Indian Broadcasting Service
D. Vividh Bharati

11. Vividh Bharati is also known as ....
A. Commercial Broadcasting Service
B. Commercial Broadcasting Company
C. Commercialized Broadcasting Service
D. Mercantile Broadcasting Company

12. Match the following:

(a) 1st news bulletin broadcast from AIR	1. 20 July 1952
(b) Central News Organization came into existence on	2. 19 January 1936
(c) 1st National program of music broadcast from AIR	3. 3 October 1957
(d) Vividh Bharati was started on	4. 1 August 1937

A. (a):2, (b):3, (c):4, (d):1
B. (a):3, (b):2, (c):1, (d):4
C. (a):2, (b):4, (c):1, (d):3
D. (a):3, (b):1, (c):2, (d):4

13. .... inaugurated the Bombay station of Indian broadcasting Company.
A. Lord Mountbatten
B. Lord Irwin
C. Lord Dalhousie
D. Lord Chelmsford

14. Calcutta station of Indian Broadcasting Company was inaugurated on ....
A. 26 August, 1927 B. 23 July, 1927
C. 1 April, 1930 D. 31 July, 1934

15. Match the following:

(a) 1st November, 1967	1. Inauguration of 1st ever FM service from Madras
(b) 1st April, 1976	2. Introduction of hourly news bulletins
(c) 23 July, 1977	3. Introduction of commercials from Vividh Bharati
(d) 15 August, 1985	4. Doordarshan separated from AIR

A. (a):2, (b):3, (c):1, (d):4
B. (a):4, (b):2, (c):3, (d):1
C. (a):3, (b):1, (c):4, (d):2
D. (a):3, (b):4, (c):1, (d):2

16. When did Prasar Bharati came into existence?
A. 23 November 1996
B. 23 November 1997
C. 26 January 1998
D. 29 August 1999

17. Match the following:

(a) 2 May 1996	1. Launch of Kisan Vani program from 12 stations
(b) 26 January 2004	2. Launch of AIR online information service on internet
(c) 1 April 2004	3. Launch of AIR's first ever digital satellite home service
(d) 27 February 2002	4. Launch of classical music channel at Bangalore

A. (a):4, (b):1, (c):3, (d):2
B. (a):3, (b):2, (c):1, (d):4
C. (a):2, (b):4, (c):1, (d):3
D. (a):1, (b):3, (c):2, (d):4

18. Choose the correct statement.
A. 12th November 2001 is declared as The Public Service Broadcasting Day to celebrate the inauguration of Museum of Radio and Doordarshan.
B. 12th November 1947 is declared as The Public Service Broadcasting Day to celebrate Gandhiji's visit to AIR.
C. 10th October 1947 is declared as The Public Service Broadcasting Day to celebrate Gandhiji's visit to AIR.
D. 12 November 1946 is declared as The Public Service Broadcasting Day to celebrate Gandhiji's visit to AIR.

19. FM Radio was first introduced by AIR in:
A. Delhi B. Madras
C. Bombay D. Calcutta

20. .... is India's first private FM radio station.
A. Red FM B. Big FM
C. Radio City D. Radio One FM

21. Which among the following are the most common uses of music in radio?
A. Acts as a background to a scene or narration
B. Acts as a theme for a drama series
C. To create mood
D. All the above

22. What style of language is primarily used in radio scripts?
A. Formal B. Conversational
C. Technical D. Poetic

23. Radio scripts must create what for the listeners?
A. Charts B. Imagery
C. Graphs D. Dialogues

24. Which voice is most preferred in radio script writing?
A. Passive voice B. Active voice
C. Third-person voice D. Indirect voice

25. What type of sentences should be used in radio scripts?
A. Complex and long
B. Simple and short
C. Passive and indirect
D. Technical and detailed

26. What should radio script writers avoid?
A. Emotional words
B. Vivid imagery
C. Technical jargon
D. Short sentences

27. Why is conversational language important for radio?
A. It sounds academic
B. It engages listeners
C. It is easier to write
D. It looks professional

28. A good radio script should be designed for the audience to:
A. Read
B. Watch
C. Hear and imagine
D. Memorize

29. What writing approach helps listeners easily visualize?
A. Analytical writing
B. Descriptive writing
C. Technical writing
D. Legal writing

30. Which of the following is NOT a characteristic of a radio script?
A. Simple sentences
B. Active voice
C. Heavy technical terms
D. Conversational style

31. How should technical terms be handled in radio scripts?
A. Used heavily
B. Ignored completely
C. Avoided or simplified
D. Explained in detail

32. Radio writing aims to be:
A. Complex B. Visual
C. Scholarly D. Formal

33. Active voice ensures the writing is:
A. Slow
B. Dull
C. Immediate and clear
D. Technical

34. Why are simple sentences preferred in radio?
A. They are easier to write
B. They are easier to understand
C. They are more impressive
D. They sound technical

35. What is a disadvantage of passive voice in radio writing?
A. It makes the writing stronger
B. It slows down understanding
C. It increases clarity
D. It helps visualization

36. Good radio writing should avoid:
A. Rhythm
B. Natural tone
C. Long complex clauses
D. Imagination

37. Radio scripts should primarily focus on:
A. Vocabulary richness
B. Complex sentence structure
C. Clear communication
D. Technical elaboration

38. What technique helps radio scripts stay interesting?
A. Use of jargon
B. Use of passive sentences
C. Use of conversational phrases
D. Use of complicated terminology

39. Which of the following would improve imagery in a radio script?
A. Long technical explanations
B. Vivid, sensory descriptions
C. Complicated words
D. Academic tone

40. A radio script must allow the listener to:
A. Analyse deeply
B. Visualize easily
C. Memorize facts
D. Read multiple times

41. How should the tone of a radio script be?
A. Distant
B. Casual and friendly
C. Formal and stiff
D. Academic and heavy

42. Using active voice in radio helps:
A. Slow down the pace
B. Hide the subject
C. Make sentences more direct
D. Make it complicated

43. The best radio writing is:
A. Visual and conversational
B. Textual and technical
C. Dense and difficult
D. Scholarly and detached

44. Why is it important to avoid jargon in radio scripts?
A. It makes the program more specialized
B. It confuses the audience
C. It attracts a wider audience
D. It simplifies concepts

45. What happens if a radio script uses complex words?
A. Increases engagement
B. Makes listening harder
C. Helps listener memory
D. Creates better imagery

46. Imagery in radio is created through:
A. Charts B. Words and descriptions
C. Pictures D. Videos

47. Radio scripts must be written with the idea that the audience is:
A. Reading the script
B. Watching a screen
C. Only listening
D. Reading subtitles

48. Which of the following should a radio script always maintain?
A. Legal terminology
B. Reader-friendly format
C. Listener-friendly format
D. Heavy analytical data

49. To create imagery, radio writers must:
A. Use descriptive language
B. Use factual data
C. Quote statistics
D. Avoid adjectives

50. A common mistake in radio writing is:
A. Keeping sentences short
B. Overloading information
C. Creating images
D. Using an active voice

51. The listener's understanding is maximized when scripts are:
A. Complex and technical
B. Friendly and vivid
C. Academic and passive
D. Deep and analytical

52. A device that converts sound waves into electrical signals is called a:
A. Speaker B. Microphone
C. Amplifier D. Sound Mixer

53. Which microphone type is most sensitive and captures detailed sounds?
A. Dynamic B. Ribbon
C. Condenser D. Carbon

54. Which microphone is rugged and ideal for live use?
A. Condenser B. Dynamic
C. Ribbon D. Lavalier

55. A microphone that requires phantom power is usually a:
A. Dynamic mic B. Condenser mic
C. Ribbon mic D. USB mic

56. Phantom power typically supplies:
A. 12V B. 24V
C. 48V D. 120V

57. A small microphone clipped to clothing is called:
A. Shotgun mic B. Lavalier mic
C. Condenser mic D. Ribbon mic

58. Which mic is best for recording interviews in noisy environments?
A. Ribbon mic B. Shotgun mic
C. Dynamic mic D. Parabolic mic

59. Ribbon microphones are known for their:
A. Durability B. Fragility
C. Loudness D. Battery operation

60. What type of mic has a long tube design for directional recording?
A. Lavalier mic B. Shotgun mic
C. Ribbon mic D. Handheld mic

61. USB microphones connect directly to:
A. Audio interfaces B. Speakers
C. Computers D. Amplifiers

62. An amplifier is used to:
A. Reduce sound
B. Record video
C. Increase audio signal strength
D. Tune radio frequency

63. Amplifiers boost the signal for:
A. Radio waves
B. Microphones and speakers
C. Light signals
D. Video feeds

64. A preamplifier boosts a weak microphone signal to:
A. Final output B. Line level
C. Phantom power D. Broadcast level

65. Amplifiers mainly affect:
A. Colour B. Sound
C. Image D. Data

66. Which amplifier is used specifically for microphones?
A. Power amp B. Line amp
C. Preamp D. Subwoofer amp

67. A sound mixer is used to:
A. Record videos
B. Combine audio signals
C. Boost video quality
D. Transmit internet signals

68. Which control on a mixer adjusts the input level of a channel?
A. Fader B. Crossfader
C. Reverb D. Equalizer

69. A function on a mixer that adjusts bass, midrange, and treble is:
A. Gain B. Pan
C. EQ (Equalizer) D. Delay

70. What is "pan" control in mixers?
A. Adjusts frequency
B. Sends audio left or right
C. Mutes a channel
D. Enhances bass

71. A basic component of any mixer is:
A. Monitor B. Channel strip
C. Radio antenna D. Recording tape

72. What type of mixer can automatically adjust levels?
A. Manual mixer B. Analog mixer
C. Digital mixer D. Rotary mixer

73. In radio, mixers are used for:
A. Only live music
B. Combining microphone, phone, and sound effects inputs
C. Broadcasting movies
D. Only voice recording

74. The section controlling overall output level is called:
A. Channel B. Master fader
C. Reverb D. Gate

75. What device converts electrical signals into sound?
A. Microphone B. Amplifier
C. Speaker D. Sound mixer

76. Studio monitors are designed to:
A. Enhance bass
B. Accurately reproduce sound
C. Increase volume
D. Colour the sound

77. What type of speakers are used for professional audio monitoring?
A. Home theatre speakers
B. PA speakers
C. Studio monitors
D. Bluetooth speakers

78. Speakers used in a radio studio are usually:
A. Portable
B. Wireless
C. Near-field monitors
D. Open-air megaphones

79. What part of the speaker moves to produce sound?
A. Magnet B. Cone
C. Coil D. Frame

80. Audio recording refers to capturing:
A. Light signals B. Video frames
C. Sound waves D. Electrical currents

81. In digital recording, audio is captured as:
A. Magnetic waves B. Light rays
C. Binary code D. Watermarks

82. What device captures audio for editing and broadcasting?
A. Transmitter B. Recorder
C. Antenna D. Modulator

83. Which format is commonly used for audio files?
A. JPEG B. MP3
C. MPEG D. PNG

84. A high-quality, lossless audio file format is:
A. WAV B. MP4
C. JPEG D. MOV

85. Multi-track recording allows:
A. Only one instrument
B. Recording multiple sources independently
C. Editing text
D. Enhancing brightness

86. A DAW stands for:
A. Digital Audio Workstation
B. Digital Antenna Wire
C. Dynamic Audio Writer
D. Direct Audio Web

87. Which microphone is best for voice-over work?
A. Dynamic B. Ribbon
C. Condenser D. Shotgun

88. In recording, clipping occurs when:
A. Audio is too quiet
B. Audio signal is distorted due to overload
C. Audio is muted
D. Audio is amplified correctly

89. An audio interface connects microphones to:
A. Antennas
B. Computer recording software
C. Batteries
D. Amplifiers

90. What tool removes background noise during recording?
A. Equalizer B. Noise gate
C. Amplifier D. Mixer

91. The sample rate in digital recording refers to:
A. Frame rate of videos
B. Number of times sound is captured per second
C. Size of the speaker
D. Bit rate of internet

92. Dynamic microphones are:
A. Fragile B. Expensive
C. Durable D. Directional

93. Condenser microphones are:
A. Insensitive B. Sensitive
C. Rough D. Heavy

94. Shotgun mics are:
A. Omnidirectional B. Highly directional
C. Wireless D. Fragile

95. Lavalier mics are:
A. Heavy and bulky
B. Wall-mounted
C. Tiny and wearable
D. Always wireless

96. Phantom power is:
A. 12V B. 24V
C. 48V D. 96V

97. A preamp boosts:
A. Speaker output B. Mic signals
C. Sound cones D. Battery life

98. Master fader controls:
A. Pan settings B. Effects volume
C. Overall volume D. Input sensitivity

99. EQ in a mixer adjusts:
A. Track speed B. Frequencies
C. Recording time D. Bit rate

100. An audio interface connects:
A. Speakers to each other
B. Mic to computer
C. Radio tower to studio
D. Two microphones

101. Studio monitors are used for:
A. Broadcasting B. Accurate listening
C. Signal boosting D. Audio effects

102. In Radio without lap or pause called
A. sibilance B. segue
C. simulcast D. slip start

103. The World Association of Community Radio Broadcasters was launched in
A. Brazil B. Sri Lanka
C. Canada D. Argentina

104. The major objective of a community radio station is
A. infotainment
B. entertainment
C. economic profit
D. social inclusion

105. **Assertion (A):** Mass media audiences are acknowledged of their presence, but scant attention is paid to them.

Reason (R): Because mass media are an institutionalised product of a corporate society, it is easy to examine them rather than their audiences.
A. Both (A) and (R) are true.
B. Both (A) and (R) are true, but (R) is not the correct explanation of (A).
C. (A) is true, but (R) is false.
D. (A) is false, but (R) is true.

106. Clipping in audio means:
A. Perfect sound B. Audio distortion
C. Silent signals D. Echo creation

107. WAV files are:
A. Compressed B. Lossless
C. Low quality D. Always small-sized

108. Sound mixers are used to:
A. Boost radio frequency
B. Store audio files
C. Combine multiple audio inputs
D. Print sound waves

109. Sound cones are parts of:
A. Microphones B. Mixers
C. Speakers D. Cables

110. Binary code in audio refers to:
A. Analog recording
B. Digital recording
C. Mono output
D. AM transmission

111. Overloading mic input causes:
A. Boosted bass B. Clearer sound
C. Clipping D. Stereo widening

112. Which mic pattern captures sound equally from all directions?
A. Cardioid B. Bidirectional
C. Omnidirectional D. Hypercardioid

113. A cardioid microphone picks up sound best from:
A. Back B. Side
C. Front D. Top

114. Directionality in microphones affects:
A. Output voltage B. Pickup pattern
C. Size D. Price

115. Boom microphones are typically mounted on:
A. Walls B. Long poles
C. Cables D. Desks

116. An equalizer is used to adjust:
A. Audio frequencies
B. Transmission range
C. Mic distance
D. Battery life

117. A pop filter helps to:
A. Increase bass
B. Reduce plosive sounds
C. Enhance volume
D. Delay echo

118. A limiter in recording ensures:
A. Echo effect
B. No signal exceeds maximum level
C. Longer recording time
D. Lower file size

119. Near-field monitors are placed:
A. Far from listener
B. Close to listener
C. Next to microphone
D. Inside walls

120. The term broadcasting refers to ....
A. various media technologies
B. a device which produces radio waves
C. airborne transmission of radio and TV waves
D. None of these

121. Earlier, ... was considered to be the backbone of the communication industry.
A. Radio B. Television
C. Internet D. All the above

122. A radio station consists of 2 wings.
A. True
B. False

123. Audio compression helps to reduce:
A. Audio clarity
B. Dynamic range
C. Noise
D. Echo

124. Crossfade in mixing creates:
A. A new track
B. Smooth transition between sounds
C. Silence
D. Audio distortion

125. What is the main job of a radio jockey?
A. Write newspapers
B. Read news bulletins
C. Engage and entertain the audience
D. Film advertisements

126. A radio jockey often acts as a:
A. News anchor
B. Host and storyteller
C. Technician
D. Cameraman

127. One important responsibility of an RJ is:
A. Delivering lectures
B. Keeping the audience tuned in
C. Editing newspapers
D. Managing TV content

128. Which among the following statements regarding working of a radio station is/are correct?
A. A radio studio is similar to a dark room which is used for taking photographs.
B. The main technical area of the radio station is the control room.
C. A 1KW transmitter is usually installed within the locality of the studio.
A. Both A and C B. A, B and C
C. Only B D. None of these

129. A good RJ must have a strong sense of:
A. History B. Mathematics
C. Timing D. Painting

130. An RJ's role includes:
A. Conducting cooking shows
B. Writing novels
C. Conducting interviews
D. Teaching classes

131. Radio jockeys must frequently:
A. Travel overseas
B. Write movie scripts
C. Announce upcoming programs
D. Do live reporting from the field

132. A key part of a radio jockey's role is:
A. Playing music and entertaining
B. Publishing newspapers
C. Filming videos
D. Editing books

133. An RJ often works with:
A. Photographers and artists
B. Scientists and engineers
C. Music directors and producers
D. Politicians and activists

134. .... was India's first community radio operation from a university.
A. Suryan FM B. Anna FM
C. Kongu FM D. Loyola FM

135. RJs are also responsible for:
A. Promoting station events
B. Managing movie sets
C. Making advertisements
D. Editing documentaries

136. A successful RJ creates a sense of:
A. Isolation
B. Personal connection with listeners
C. Academic authority
D. Formality

137. A good radio jockey must master:
A. Drawing skills B. Singing skills
C. Spoken language D. Dance moves

138. Writing skills are important for:
A. Filing taxes
B. Composing music
C. Preparing scripts and notes
D. Designing graphics

139. Which among the following is/are a type of radio station?
A. National radio B. Satellite radio
C. Internet radio D. All the above

140. An RJ must have excellent:
A. Drawing and painting
B. Pronunciation and diction
C. Fashion sense
D. Gymnastics

141. Radio production has three steps – pre production, production and post production.
A. True
B. False

142. To engage listeners, an RJ must use a:
A. Formal tone
B. Conversational tone
C. Robotic tone
D. Aggressive tone

143. Active listening skills help an RJ during:
A. Advertisement writing
B. Interviews
C. Music mixing
D. Outdoor reporting

144. A radio jockey must be skilled at:
A. Quick thinking and improvisation
B. Slow and steady speech
C. Long pauses
D. Memorizing poetry

145. Match the following:

(a) Programme Personnel	1. program wing
(b) Radio Announcer	2. planning production
(c) Station Engineer	3. convey feelings
(d) Station Director	4. technical work

A. (a):3, (b):1, (c):4, (d):2
B. (a):4, (b):2, (c):1, (d):3
C. (a):2, (b):3, (c):4, (d):1
D. (a):1, (b):4, (c):3, (d):2

146. Humour is important for an RJ because it:
A. Confuses listeners
B. Keeps the show lively
C. Disrupts flow
D. Sounds unprofessional

147. A good RJ is usually:
A. Boring and dull
B. Energetic and enthusiastic
C. Quiet and shy
D. Monotonous

148. Radio formats are classified into 2 parts.
A. True
B. False

149. One important speaking skill for RJs is:
A. Singing loudly
B. Speaking fast
C. Modulation of voice
D. Whispering

150. Public speaking ability helps an RJ to:
A. Write novels
B. Build confidence on-air
C. Dance on stage
D. Operate studio equipment

151. Knowledge of current affairs helps an RJ:
A. Pass university exams
B. Stay relevant
C. Cook better
D. Avoid news

152. Storytelling skills allow an RJ to:
A. Confuse the audience
B. Fill time
C. Captivate the audience
D. Ignore facts

153. A radio jockey must avoid:
A. Humour
B. Sound effects
C. Monotonous speaking
D. Listener interaction

154. Which among the following is/are a part of the spoken word on a radio?
A. Magazine programs
B. Radio features
C. Radio drama
D. All the above

155. Clear articulation ensures:
A. Lower ratings
B. Faster speaking
C. Better understanding
D. Stronger signals

156. A good RJ maintains a balance between:
A. Singing and dancing
B. Talking and walking
C. Speaking and listening
D. News and sports

157. .... are used for radio transmission.
A. Short waves B. Medium waves
C. Long waves D. None of these

158. To create connectedness, an RJ should:
A. Use formal terms
B. Use inclusive language ("we", "us")
C. Avoid emotional words
D. Talk only about facts

159. Which among the following sentences is/ are correct?
A. Phone-in program is also known as the interactive programming.
B. Radio stations like BBC and Voice of America are available on internet.
C. Radio bridge is a part of the IT based on radio formats.
D. An informal script format enables the announcer to maintain a friendly relation with the listeners.
A. Only C B. Both B and D
C. Both A and D D. A, B, C and D

160. A major audience-related skill for RJs is:
A. Speed reading B. Empathy
C. Singing talent D. Graphic design

161. Interacting with callers helps an RJ to:
A. Reduce airtime
B. Fill show gaps
C. Build rapport
D. Avoid technical work

162. One way to engage listeners is through:
A. Long speeches
B. Live contests
C. Pre-recorded shows
D. Ignoring feedback

163. Which among the following is/are a type of interview?
A. Vox Pop B. Interpretative
C. Personal D. All the above

164. Personal anecdotes shared on air:
A. Make the RJ relatable
B. Bore the audience
C. Waste time
D. Cause confusion

165. Social media is used by RJs to:
A. Block criticism
B. Post selfies
C. Extend audience interaction
D. Avoid studio work

166. A radio jockey must always sound:
A. Serious B. Approachable
C. Arrogant D. Formal

167. Audience feedback helps an RJ to:
A. Change shows B. Enter contests
C. Improve content D. Ignore opinions

168. A radio jockey must avoid sounding:
A. Cheerful B. Judgmental
C. Confident D. Clear

169. Creating mental imagery through words:
A. Confuses listeners
B. Delays the show
C. Strengthens connection
D. Encourages noise

170. Using real-life examples on air helps:
A. Break station rules
B. Audience relates to content
C. Confuse listeners
D. Reduce preparation

171. Asking questions to listeners promotes:
A. Silence B. Participation
C. Confusion D. Complaints

172. An RJ should always encourage:
A. One-way communication
B. Silence
C. Audience opinions
D. Ignoring reactions

173. When responding to messages, an RJ should:
A. Be sarcastic B. Use abbreviations
C. Be respectful D. Be dismissive

174. A sense of humour helps in:
A. Ending shows early
B. Losing listeners
C. Lightening tense moments
D. Avoiding facts

175. RJs must know how to use:
A. Microphones properly
B. Cameras professionally
C. Lights and filters
D. Editing photos

176. Knowing the use of a sound mixer helps:
A. Control audio quality
B. Select songs
C. Operate the phone
D. Schedule ads

177. RJs must understand:
A. Mic positioning
B. Video editing
C. Song lyrics
D. Studio lighting

178. Adjusting levels is important to:
A. Avoid distortion
B. Increase ratings
C. Change tracks
D. Enter commercials

179. Phantom power is needed for:
A. Ribbon microphones
B. Dynamic microphones
C. Condenser microphones
D. Shotgun microphones

180. A basic knowledge of speakers helps in:
A. Reading news
B. Broadcasting video
C. Changing lights
D. Monitoring output

181. An RJ uses a DAW for:
A. Editing pre-recorded shows
B. Playing ads live
C. Broadcasting weather
D. Changing mic stands

182. Audio compression tools help to:
A. Lower mic volume
B. Balance sound levels
C. Edit video files
D. Compress paper files

183. A radio jockey must be familiar with:
A. On-air console operation
B. Bookkeeping
C. Camera lenses
D. Advertisement sales

184. Volume faders on the mixer are used to:
A. Control sound levels
B. Change track order
C. Turn off studio lights
D. Edit scripts

185. RJs often record segments using:
A. Still cameras
B. Video cameras
C. Teleprompters
D. Audio recorders

186. Backup recording ensures:
A. No data is lost
B. Louder sound
C. Faster show
D. Audience interaction

187. Equalization adjusts:
A. Schedule
B. Time slots
C. Frequency balance
D. Mic height

188. Understanding gain helps an RJ to:
A. Set optimal input levels
B. Increase audience
C. Get promotions
D. Boost advertising

189. Knowledge of headphones helps:
A. Monitor sound clearly
B. Avoid interviews
C. Adjust studio lights
D. Schedule events

190. Using monitors during a live show helps:
A. Avoid feedback
B. Increase reverb
C. Broadcast online
D. Adjust lighting

191. An RJ should know basic:
A. Scriptwriting only
B. Troubleshooting techniques
C. Acting skills
D. Software coding

192. Proper mic etiquette involves:
A. Speaking at correct distance
B. Wearing headphones backward
C. Eating during show
D. Turning off faders

193. Pop filters are used to:
A. Reduce echo
B. Increase bass
C. Edit songs
D. Eliminate plosive sounds

194. USB microphones are:
A. Always condenser mics
B. Wireless only
C. Easy to connect to computers
D. Hard to install

195. Dynamic mics are preferred for:
A. Recording choirs
B. Film dubbing
C. Instrumental music only
D. Live shows

196. Condenser mics are good for:
A. Studio recordings
B. Outdoor interviews
C. Street shows
D. Background music

197. An RJ should understand:
A. Signal flow in the studio
B. Traffic control
C. Ad design
D. Graphic layout

198. Audio interfaces connect:
A. Speakers to cameras
B. Mics to computers
C. Lights to mixers
D. Phones to microphones

199. Adjusting bass and treble affects:
A. Listener count
B. Show time
C. Audio clarity
D. Power supply

200. Audio file formats commonly used are:
A. MP3 and WAV
B. PDF and DOC
C. MP4 and JPEG
D. ZIP and EXE

201. Knowing file formats helps in:
A. Choosing best audio quality
B. Managing phone calls
C. Decoding scripts
D. Organizing studio lights

202. An RJ should save recordings:
A. Without filenames
B. On one computer only
C. In multiple backup formats
D. After every show only

203. Good knowledge of equipment ensures:
A. Smooth broadcast
B. Great writing skills
C. Fast script memorization
D. Better music taste

204. Basic technical skills in radio equipment help an RJ:
A. Use social media
B. Write long reports
C. Choose fashion styles
D. Handle emergencies

205. Which of the following is ***not*** a type of sound effect?
A. Fader B. Contextual
C. Descriptive D. Commentative

206. Identify the correct chronological order of international radio stations that were launched.
A. BBC, Voice of America, Radio Moscow, United Nations Radio
B. BBC, United Nations Radio, Voice of America, Radio Moscow
C. BBC, Radio Moscow, Voice of America, United Nations Radio
D. BBC, Radio Moscow, United Nations Radio, Voice of America

207. Short wave frequencies are used for radio communication of
A. short distance
B. long distance
C. location specific distance
D. specific distance

208. Why radio is deemed a passive media?
A. People watch TV commentaries with keen interest, but do not listen to radio commentaries with keen interest
B. People have small radio sets but large TV sets and that is why, they are not actively involved in the listening process (in radio listening)
C. People actively take part in media like Internet and give it full attention, but they listen to radio while they complete their daily chores
D. Radio is an aural media and hence, it is passive

209. If you have to record the interview in a windy area, you should use a
A. microphone without a wind filter
B. microphone with a wind filter
C. microphone with mounting stand
D. None of these

210. Which one of the following is the major element of radio production?
A. Sound Effects B. Texts
C. Optimiser D. Basics

211. Which one of the following is a type of microphone?
A. Basic Microphone
B. Stagnant mike
C. Omni-directional
D. Large Microphone

212. Characteristics of Radio is
A. The Speed of Radio
B. Radio is inexpensive
C. A radio receiver is portable
D. All the above

213. Radio is the theatre of the .... and TV is the theatre of the ....
A. individual; group
B. soul; consciousness
C. mind; home
D. society; home

214. If you want to record the message of a person on the footpath (for radio), you should use a/an
A. omni-directional microphone
B. hyper-cardioid microphone
C. cardioid microphone
D. anyone of these

215. Match the following

(a) December 16, 2004	1. Vividh Bharati Services started.
(b) November, 1999	2. This day declared as The Public Service Broadcasting Day
(c) October 3, 1957	3. AIR launched a daily Malayalam Service for the Gulf Region
(d) November 12, 1947	4. Inauguration of DTH Service of AIR & Doordarshan.

A. (a):4, (b):3, (c):1, (d):2
B. (a):3, (b):2, (c):1, (d):4
C. (a):2, (b):4, (c):1, (d):3
D. (a):3, (b):1, (c):2, (d):4

216. Amateur Radio is also known as?
A. Home Radio B. Pocket Radio
C. Fun Radio D. Ham Radio

217. Community Radio is
A. Homogenous B. Uniform
C. Mixed D. None of these

218. Which among the following is/ are a type of radio station?
A. National Radio B. Satellite radio
C. Internet Radio D. All the above

219. Control Room in a radio studio is a
A. Administration wing
B. Technical area
C. Announcement room
D. Conference room

220. Functionaries of a radio station
A. Station director
B. Station engineer
C. Programme personnel
D. All the above

221. Match the following:

Date	Event
(a) 26 January 2004	1. Launch of Kisan Vani program from 12 stations
(b) 27 February 2002	2. Launch of AIR online information service on the internet
(c) 2 May 1996	3. Launch of AIR's first-ever digital satellite home service
(d) 1 April 2004	4. Launch of classical music channel in Bangalore

A. (a)-4, (b)-3, (c)-2, (d)-1
B. (a)-2, (b)-1, (c)-3, (d)-4
C. (a)-1, (b)-2, (c)-3, (d)-4
D. (a)-3, (b)-4, (c)-1, (d)-2

222. The first radio programme in India was broadcasted by the Radio Club of:
A. Delhi B. Bombay
C. Madras D. Lucknow

223. AIR is also termed as:
A. Akashvani B. Social Equity
C. FMs D. All of These

224. Which is one of the best-known services of AIR?
A. Stereo B. Liberalisation
C. Vividh Bharati D. None of these

225. Red FM 93.5 is owned by:
A. Sun Group
B. Anil Dhirubhai Ambani Group
C. Entertainment Network Limited
D. None of these

226. 'Suno Sunao Life Banao' is the famous slogan of which FM channel?
A. Red FM B. Big FM
C. Radio Mirchi D. None of these

227. Vividh Bharati was started in:
A. 1972 B. 1958
C. 1957 D. None of these

228. In radio, the term FM stands for:
A. Frequency Modulation
B. Frequency Modification
C. Frank Mode
D. Frank Mass

229. Yuva Vani service was started from where?
A. Delhi B. Jammu
C. Chennai D. Goa

230. Akashvani broadcast programmes to:
A. urban B. rural
C. all over nation D. None of these

231. Which of the following is an ethic that should be followed in radio reporting?
A. Truth and Accuracy
B. Accountability
C. Fairness and Impartiality
D. All the above

232. Which one of the software is used to edit radio programmes?
A. Adobe Audition
B. Adobe Dreamweaver
C. Zingle
D. Adobe Photoshop

233. What is the term for the static or noise heard on a radio when no station is tuned in?
A. Interference B. Crosstalk
C. Feedback D. White noise

234. Which radio station is known for its slogan "The Voice of America" and broadcasts news and information worldwide?
A. BBC Radio
B. Radio Free Europe
C. Voice of America (VOA)
D. Radio Moscow

235. What is the name of the first commercially successful radio network in the United States, founded by David Sarnoff?
A. NBC (National Broadcasting Company)
B. ABC (American Broadcasting Company)
C. CBS (Columbia Broadcasting System)
D. FOX (Fox Broadcasting Company)

236. What are the major 3 components of a radio programme?
A. Spoken Word or human voice
B. Music
C. Sound Effects
D. All of these

237. The modulation technology that is used for analogue radio transmission in MW and SW is:
A. Amplitude Modulation
B. Frequency Modulation
C. Generic Modulation
D. High Modulation

238. Radio News is also edited according to which form?
A. Vessel B. Inverted Pyramid
C. Join Line D. None of these

239. Which radio station format is characterized by talk shows, discussions, and debates on various topics?
A. Classical B. News/Talk
C. Country D. Jazz

240. The opening lines of the story, called:
A. Body B. Extract
C. Lead D. Resume

241. Which media is suitable for a Communication Campaign for an illiterate population?
A. Radio B. Newspaper
C. Pamphlets D. Digital

242. Who coined the term "Pay Radio"?
A. Chad Dyner
B. Walter Benjamin
C. Hans Magnus Enzensberger
D. David Pogue

243. What is the full form of VHF?
A. Very High Frequency
B. Very Heavy Frequency
C. Versatile Heavy Frequency
D. Various High Frequency

244. VHF is transmitted through:
A. Amplitude Modulation
B. Frequency Modulation
C. Average Modulation
D. Frequent Modulation

245. In radio broadcasting, what is the purpose of an "advertising jingle"?
A. To host talk shows
B. To play music
C. To promote products or services
D. To announce news headlines

246. The private radio stations as well as Community Radio Stations broadcast in:
A. FM mode B. AM mode
C. KW mode D. RW mode

247. Radio News Bulletins are typed in:
A. 14 font B. 12 font
C. 16 font D. 10 font

248. The first community radio station in Asia was set up in
A. The Philippines B. South Korea
C. Vietnam D. India

249. In which year was the first World Radio Day observed?
A. 2012 B. 2013
C. 2014 D. 2015

250. What is the theme of World Radio Day 2025?
A. Radio and Sports
B. Radio and Diversity
C. Radio and Education
D. Radio and Climate Change

251. Which organization is responsible for the organization of World Radio Day?
A. United Nations
B. World Health Organization
C. World Trade Organization
D. International Atomic Energy Agency

252. Which country is credited with the invention of radio?
A. Germany B. France
C. Italy D. United Kingdom

253. Which type of radio waves are used for FM radio broadcasts?
A. AM waves B. SW waves
C. VHF waves D. UHF waves

254. Which radio station is known as the "world's oldest continuously broadcasting radio station"?
A. BBC Radio 1
B. KDKA-AM
C. Radio Nacional de España
D. WGY-AM

255. What is the term used to describe the process of sending a radio signal to a distant location by reflecting it off the ionosphere?
A. Refraction B. Reflection
C. Diffraction D. Scattering

256. Which type of radio technology is commonly used in modern smartphones?
A. AM radio B. FM radio
C. DAB radio D. Internet radio

257. What was the first radio station to broadcast a regular schedule of programs?
A. KDKA-AM B. WGY-AM
C. BBC Radio D. Nacional de España

258. In which decade was the transistor radio invented?
A. 1930s B. 1940s
C. 1950s D. 1960s

259. What is the name of the radio program that famously caused a panic in the United States in 1938 by portraying Martian Invasion?
A. The War of the Worlds
B. The Shadow
C. The Lone Ranger
D. The Mercury Theatre on the Air

260. Which is the world's largest radio network?
A. NTS Radio B. NPR Radio
C. BBC Radio 6 D. All India Radio

261. Which radio station is known for its famous call sign "This is London" during World War II broadcasts?
A. Radio Moscow
B. BBC Radio
C. Radio Free Europe
D. Radio Vichy

262. What is the term for the interference that occurs when two radio signals on nearby frequencies mix and produce unwanted noise?
A. Crosstalk B. Feedback
C. Interference D. Static

263. Which radio format is known for playing contemporary and popular music, often targeting younger audiences?
A. News/Talk B. Classical
C. Top 40 D. Jazz

264. What radio station famously broadcast the message "Houston, we've had a problem here" during the Apollo 13 mission?
A. NASA Radio B. KDKA-AM
C. BBC Radio D. WGY-AM

265. Which British radio show is known for its long-running music interviews and desert island theme?
A. Desert Island Discs
B. The Archers
C. Top Gear
D. BBC Talk Hour

266. "This American Life" is produced in which country?
A. United States B. Canada
C. UK D. Australia

267. Which genre best fits "This American Life"?
A. Narrative journalism
B. Comedy
C. Horror
D. Talk show

268. "The Archers" is a famous radio soap opera from:
A. United Kingdom B. USA
C. Australia D. Canada

269. Who narrated and produced "War of the Worlds"?
A. Edward R. Murrow
B. Ira Glass
C. Orson Welles
D. Howard Stern

270. Which U.S. shock jock is known for "The Howard Stern Show"?
A. Howard Stern B. Rush Limbaugh
C. Casey Kasem D. Larry King

271. Which radio countdown show was hosted by Casey Kasem?
A. American Top 40
B. Billboard Hour
C. Chart Countdown
D. Pop Tracks

272. "Radiolab" is best described as a show that focuses on:
A. News
B. Politics
C. Comedy
D. Science and philosophy

273. "BBC Radio 1" is popular for its focus on:
A. Contemporary music and youth culture
B. Oldies
C. Documentaries
D. News only

274. "Fresh Air" is a talk show on which U.S. radio network?
A. NPR (National Public Radio)
B. ABC
C. BBC
D. CNN

275. Who is the host of "Fresh Air"?
A. Sarah Koenig
B. Ira Glass
C. Terry Gross
D. Jad Abumrad

276. "Serial," a hit investigative podcast/radio show, primarily deals with:
A. Music B. Sports
C. Fiction D. True crime

277. Which podcast helped revolutionize modern audio storytelling and podcasts?
A. Serial
B. The Daily
C. Fresh Air
D. BBC World Update

278. "The Moth Radio Hour" features:
A. True personal stories told live
B. Fictional storytelling
C. Politics
D. News summaries

279. What is "BBC World Service" known for?
A. Global news and analysis
B. Music
C. Comedy
D. Sports

280. Which Australian radio show gained fame for its comedy sketches and social satire?
A. Aussie Live
B. Hamish & Andy
C. The Outback Hour
D. Koala FM

281. Which is a famous Indian radio show known for storytelling?
A. Yaadon Ka Idiot Box
B. Hello India
C. Filmy Talk
D. AIR Update

282. "Car Talk" was a popular American radio show focused on:
A. Food
B. Travel
C. Automotive advice with humour
D. Finance

283. What is "The Daily" by The New York Times?
A. Gaming
B. Drama
C. Comedy
D. News podcast/show

284. "All Things Considered" is a flagship news program by:
A. NPR B. BBC
C. Fox D. CBS

285. Who is a well-known host associated with "This American Life"?
A. Rick Dees B. Ira Glass
C. Roman Mars D. Jon Stewart

286. "Hardtalk" is a hard-hitting interview program on:
A. CNN B. BBC Radio
C. NPR D. Sky News

287. "Prairie Home Companion" is famous for blending:
A. Music, stories, and humour
B. Horror
C. Politics
D. Science

288. The show "No Such Thing As A Fish" comes from the creators of:
A. QI (Quite Interesting)
B. Top Gear
C. BBC News
D. Mythbusters

289. "Invisibilia" explores:
A. The invisible forces that shape human behaviour
B. War
C. Politics
D. Animals

290. "The Breakfast Club" is a popular morning radio show in:
A. UAE B. South Africa
C. UK D. USA

291. "Loveline" was a radio call-in show about:
A. Relationships and mental health
B. Cars
C. Travel
D. Music

292. "Desert Island Discs" has guests select:
A. Eight songs they'd take to a desert island
B. Books
C. Foods
D. TV shows

293. Which radio station is famous for the tagline "Bajaate Raho"?
A. Radio Mirchi B. Red FM
C. Big FM D. Radio One

294. "Sunne Ka Maza Hi Kuch Aur Hai" is the signature tagline of which station?
A. Radio City
B. Radio Mirchi
C. Fever FM
D. Red FM

295. Which radio station markets itself with the tagline "Feel the Fever"?
A. Big FM
B. Fever FM
C. Radio One
D. Red FM

296. "Aapka Number 1" is the well-known tagline for which radio station?
A. Red FM
B. Radio Mirchi
C. Big FM
D. Fever FM

297. Which station uses the tagline "Where the youth connect" to appeal to a younger audience?
A. Radio City
B. Fever FM
C. Radio One
D. Big FM

298. The energetic call to "Bajaate Raho" primarily encourages listeners to:
A. Keep their phones on
B. Continuously enjoy great music
C. Stay tuned for news updates
D. Tune into talk shows

299. The tagline "Sunne Ka Maza Hi Kuch Aur Hai" suggests what kind of experience on Radio Mirchi?
A. A uniquely enjoyable sound experience
B. A focus on celebrity interviews
C. An emphasis on international music
D. A relaxed, slow-paced show

300. What does the slogan "Feel the Fever" imply about the programming on Fever FM?
A. It features low-tempo music
B. It plays high-energy, trending tracks
C. It is dedicated to talk shows
D. It focuses on regional folk music

301. By using the tagline "Aapka Number 1," Big FM positions itself as:
A. The station with the fewest listeners
B. The top choice for its audience
C. A station that broadcasts only retro music
D. The most expensive radio channel

302. Which tagline directly targets the young generation by emphasizing connection?
A. "Bajaate Raho"
B. "Where the youth connect"
C. "Feel the Fever"
D. "Sunne Ka Maza Hi Kuch Aur Hai"

303. Red FM's "Bajaate Raho" can best be interpreted as an invitation to:
A. Keep the music playing non-stop
B. Listen to news round-ups
C. Participate in talk shows
D. Call in for contests

304. The tagline "Sunne Ka Maza Hi Kuch Aur Hai" highlights Radio Mirchi's:
A. Extraordinary audio experience
B. Focus on live sports coverage
C. Emphasis on listener calls
D. Commitment to classical music

305. **Assertion (A):** Radio plays are different from TV plays because radio plays have no actors in them.

Reason (R): Because radio is a blind medium.
A. Both (A) and (R) are correct, but (R) is not the correct explanation of (A)
B. Both (A) and (R) are correct and (R) is the correct explanation of (A)
C. (A) is correct, but (R) is false
D. (A) is false, but (R) is correct

306. Which pairing of radio station and tagline is correct?
A. Red FM — "Feel the Fever"
B. Big FM — "Aapka Number 1"
C. Radio One — "Sunne Ka Maza Hi Kuch Aur Hai"
D. Fever FM — "Where the youth connect"

307. Which of the following taglines is NOT correctly matched with its radio station?
A. Red FM — "Bajaate Raho"
B. Radio Mirchi — "Sunne Ka Maza Hi Kuch Aur Hai"
C. Big FM — "Your World, Your Station"
D. Fever FM — "Feel the Fever"

308. The merits of radio advertising are
A. Human touch
B. Not mass coverage
C. Not selectivity
D. Group Coverage

309. A large amount of ………. advertising is for retailers, local businesses and for promotions.
A. newspaper B. magazines
C. radio D. television

ANSWERS

1	2	3	4	5	6	7	8	9	10
B	D	C	C	A	B	D	C	B	C
11	12	13	14	15	16	17	18	19	20
A	C	B	A	D	B	C	B	B	C
21	22	23	24	25	26	27	28	29	30
D	B	B	B	B	C	B	C	B	C
31	32	33	34	35	36	37	38	39	40
C	B	C	B	B	C	C	C	B	B
41	42	43	44	45	46	47	48	49	50
B	C	A	B	B	B	C	C	A	B
51	52	53	54	55	56	57	58	59	60
B	B	C	B	B	C	B	B	B	B
61	62	63	64	65	66	67	68	69	70
C	C	B	B	B	C	B	A	C	B
71	72	73	74	75	76	77	78	79	80
B	C	B	B	C	B	C	C	B	C
81	82	83	84	85	86	87	88	89	90
C	B	B	A	B	A	C	B	B	B
91	92	93	94	95	96	97	98	99	100
B	C	B	B	C	C	B	C	B	B
101	102	103	104	105	106	107	108	109	110
B	B	C	D	A	B	B	C	C	B
111	112	113	114	115	116	117	118	119	120
C	C	C	B	B	A	B	B	B	C
121	122	123	124	125	126	127	128	129	130
A	C	B	B	C	B	B	B	C	C
131	132	133	134	135	136	137	138	139	140
C	A	C	B	A	B	C	C	D	B
141	142	143	144	145	146	147	148	149	150
A	B	B	A	C	B	B	B	C	B
151	152	153	154	155	156	157	158	159	160
B	C	C	D	C	C	A	C	D	B
161	162	163	164	165	166	167	168	169	170
C	B	D	A	C	B	C	B	C	B
171	172	173	174	175	176	177	178	179	180
B	C	C	C	A	A	A	A	C	D
181	182	183	184	185	186	187	188	189	190
A	B	A	A	D	A	C	A	A	A
191	192	193	194	195	196	197	198	199	200
B	A	D	C	D	A	A	B	C	A
201	202	203	204	205	206	207	208	209	210
A	C	A	D	A	C	B	C	B	A
211	212	213	214	215	216	217	218	219	220
C	D	C	A	A	D	A	D	B	D
221	222	223	224	225	226	227	228	229	230
A	B	A	C	A	B	C	A	A	C
231	232	233	234	235	236	237	238	239	240
D	A	D	C	A	D	A	B	B	C

241	242	243	244	245	246	247	248	249	250
A	D	A	B	C	A	A	A	A	D
251	**252**	**253**	**254**	**255**	**256**	**257**	**258**	**259**	**260**
A	A	C	B	B	D	C	C	A	D
261	**262**	**263**	**264**	**265**	**266**	**267**	**268**	**269**	**270**
B	C	C	A	A	A	A	A	C	A
271	**272**	**273**	**274**	**275**	**276**	**277**	**278**	**279**	**280**
A	D	A	A	C	D	A	A	A	B
281	**282**	**283**	**284**	**285**	**286**	**287**	**288**	**289**	**290**
A	C	D	A	B	B	A	A	A	D
291	**292**	**293**	**294**	**295**	**296**	**297**	**298**	**299**	**300**
A	A	B	B	B	C	C	B	A	B
301	**302**	**303**	**304**	**305**	**306**	**307**	**308**	**309**	
B	B	A	A	D	B	C	A	C	

EXPLANATORY ANSWERS

8. (C): AIR was launched formally in 1936 with the aim of transmitting news to the people but later on in 1952 it came up with its first music program.

13. (B): The first radio broadcast in India, and therefore the Bombay Station of the Indian Broadcasting Company, was inaugurated on July 23, 1927. This private company, the Indian Broadcasting Company, made the first ever news bulletin in the country on the air from Bombay. The Indian Broadcasting Company was later taken over by the government and renamed All India Radio in 1936.

18. (B): Mahatma Gandhi, father of the nation, had stepped inside the Broadcasting House on November 12, 1947 to address the refugees. The refugees belonged to Pakistan and were camping in Haryana. AIR organized a special speech for Gandhi from its studios. That was Gandhi's first and last visit to AIR.

19. (B): FM broadcasting in India began on July 23, 1977, with the inauguration of the first FM service in Chennai (then Madras) by All India Radio (AIR).

20. (C): Radio City Bangalore is India's first private FM radio station. It was started on July 3, 2001.

122. (B): A radio station consists of three or four wings - program wing, administrative wing, sales wing, and engineering wing.

148. (B): Radio formats are classified into three parts – spoken word, music and sound effects.

217. (A): Community Radio is generally considered a form of local broadcasting that caters to the specific interests and needs of a particular community, often characterized by a degree of homogeneity in its audience and programming.

251. (A): The day was designated by UNESCO on the 3rd of November, 2011, during its 36th conference. The primary purpose of World Radio Day is to celebrate radio technology, raise awareness about the importance of radio, and encourage international cooperation in radio broadcasting. This day serves as a platform to recognize the power of radio as a medium for communication, education, and entertainment. By celebrating radio technology, raising awareness about its significance, and promoting international cooperation, World Radio Day aims to highlight the enduring relevance and impact of radio in today's digital age.

254. (B): KDKA (1020 kHz) is a class A, clear channel, AM radio station, licensed to Pittsburgh, Pennsylvania, owned and operated by Audacy, Inc. It traces its beginning to its broadcast of the Harding-Cox presidential election results on the evening of November 2, 1920.

CHAPTER-5

CINEMA

HISTORY OF CINEMA

History of cinema is long and having started from simple photographic experiments, it has now evolved into a sophisticated and multi-billion-dollar visual storytelling business today.

The late 19th century saw crucial technological advancements that led to the creation of cinema. Eadweard Muybridge in his experiments in the 1870s, captured sequential images of a horse in motion using multiple cameras, demonstrating the possibility of recording movement. In 1891, Thomas Edison and William K.L. Dickson invented the Kinetoscope, a peep-show device which enabled one person at a time to view moving pictures.

Lumerie Brothers

The first public exhibition of commercial motion picture is attributed to Lumerie brothers. In 1895, the Lumerie brothers, Auguste and Louis, developed the Cinématographe, a device that could record, develop, and project films. It combined the functions of a camera, film processor, and projector in one compact unit. On December 28, 1895, they screened short films in Paris and it is widely considered the birth of cinema. The Lumière brothers created a series of short, documentary-style films, which they called "actualities." These films often depicted real-life events and scenes, such as workers leaving the Lumière factory, a crowd watching a train arrive, and a baby's lunch. They travelled the world, showcasing their films and the Cinématographe.

Robert Flaherty

Robert Flaherty (1884-1951) was a highly influential American filmmaker often credited as the "father of documentary film." Flaherty's Nanook of the North (1922) is widely considered the first commercially successful feature-length documentary film. This demonstrated the potential for non-fiction film to engage audiences with narratives centered on real people and their environments.

Flaherty's work laid the foundation for ethnographic filmmaking. He immersed himself in the cultures he documented, spending extended periods living with the Inuit for Nanook and the people of Samoa for Moana (1926) and the Aran Islands for Man of Aran (1934). This immersive approach, emphasizing observation and participation, became a benchmark for filmmakers seeking to understand and represent different cultures.

Despite the debates surrounding his methods, Flaherty's work had a profound influence on the development of the documentary genre. He demonstrated the commercial viability of non-fiction features and inspired countless filmmakers to explore the world and its people through a cinematic lens.

John Grierson

John Grierson, a Scottish filmmaker, made indelible contributions in world of cinema. He is a towering figure in the history of cinema, particularly in the realm of documentary filmmaking. In 1926, while working as a film critic in the United States, Grierson coined the term "documentary" in a review of Robert Flaherty's film *Moana*. He used it to describe films that offered a "creative treatment of actuality." This single act provided a name and a framework for a new genre of filmmaking focused on the realistic portrayal of the world.

Upon returning to Britain in 1927, Grierson became a driving force behind the establishment of the British Documentary Film Movement. He believed that film could be a powerful tool for social education and democratic understanding.

Grierson's own film, *Drifters* (1929), a silent film about the lives of North Sea herring fishermen, is considered a landmark in documentary history. He encouraged filmmakers to move beyond simply recording reality and to shape and interpret their material creatively to convey a specific message or perspective. He famously said, "Art is not a mirror, but a hammer."

Dada Saheb Phalke

Though Lumiere brothers were first to introduce India to cinema when they showcased motion pictures in 1896, Dadasaheb Phalke is regarded as the 'father of Indian Cinema' for making first film in India. In 1913, Phalke wrote, directed, produced and released *Raja Harishchandra* in Bombay, that became India's first film. It was a silent film incorporating English, Marathi, and Hindi title cards. His pioneering efforts laid the very foundation of the massive film industry that India boasts today.

Before Phalke, filmmaking in India primarily consisted of recording stage plays. *Raja Harishchandra* was the first film to have an indigenously developed narrative and screenplay, establishing the concept of cinematic storytelling in India.

Phalke was a self-taught filmmaker who experimented with various aspects of the craft. His films often featured mythological themes, bringing popular stories to life on the screen in a visually engaging manner. In a career spanning nearly two decades (until 1937), Phalke directed and produced an impressive 95 feature films and 27 short films. His notable works include *Mohini Bhasmasur* (1913), *Satyavan Savitri* (1914), *Lanka Dahan* (1917), *Shri Krishna Janma* (1918), and *Kaliya Mardan* (1919).

In recognition of his monumental contributions, the Government of India established the Dadasaheb Phalke Award in 1969. This is the highest award in Indian cinema, presented annually to individuals for their lifetime contribution to the growth and development of Indian cinema.

CINEMA GENRES

Film genres are categories used to classify movies based on similarities in their narrative elements, themes, visual style, emotional tone, and target audience. Understanding film genres is crucial for filmmakers, critics, and audiences as it provides a framework for analysing and appreciating the diverse world of cinema.

Genre Theory

Genre theory in film is a framework for understanding how films are categorized into different types based on shared conventions, narrative elements, themes, visual styles, and audience expectations. It's not just about labelling movies; it's a way of analysing how these categories function within the film industry, for audiences, and in reflecting and shaping culture.

What Defines a Genre?

Genre categorization isn't always clear-cut, but theorists often look at a combination of factors:

- **Narrative Conventions:** Recurring plot structures, common character arcs, and familiar story elements. For example, a romantic film emphasizes the formation of a romantic relationship and, as a rule, has a ''happily ever after ending".
- **Thematic Elements:** Underlying ideas and messages that are prevalent in a group of films. Horror films frequently explore themes of death, fear, and the unknown.
- **Character Archetypes:** Recurring character types with familiar traits and roles. The femme fatale in noir films or the comedic sidekick are examples.
- **Setting:** Typical locations and time periods associated with a genre. Science fiction often takes place in the future or in space, while historical dramas are set in specific past eras.
- **Visual and Audio Style:** This includes the distinctive look, cinematography, special effects, costumes, and music commonly associated with a particular genre. These elements work together to create the mood and atmosphere that audiences expect. For example, horror films often use dark lighting, eerie sound effects, sudden loud noises, and unsettling music to build suspense and evoke fear.
- **Style and Techniques:** Distinctive filmmaking techniques, such as lighting (low-key lighting in noir), camera work (sweeping landscapes in epics), and editing styles.
- **Audience Expectations:** The preconceived notions and desires that viewers bring to a film based on its genre. Knowing a film is a romantic comedy sets up certain expectations for tone and outcome.

Why is Genre Theory Important?

- **For Filmmakers:** Genres provide a blueprint and a set of expectations to work with. Filmmakers can choose to adhere to conventions for familiarity or subvert them for innovation. Genre can also be a useful tool in the screenwriting process, helping to structure narratives and develop characters.
- **For Audiences:** Genres act as a guide, helping viewers choose films they are likely to enjoy based on past experiences. Genre labels create expectations and provide a framework for understanding and discussing films.
- **For the Industry:** Genre is crucial for marketing and distribution. It allows studios to target specific demographics and position films effectively. Video rental stores (in the pre-streaming era) and streaming platforms use genre categories to organize their content.
- **For Critics and Scholars:** Genre theory provides a framework for analyzing films within a cultural and historical context. It helps in understanding how genres evolve, reflect societal values, and engage with other texts.

TYPES OF FILM GENRES

- **Action:** Action films are all about delivering thrills, excitement, and high-stakes situations, often featuring a hero who battles against overwhelming odds. These movies are designed to keep audiences on the edge of their seats with fast-paced storytelling and intense physical sequences. The core elements of action films include spectacular stunts, high-speed chases, hand-to-hand combat, shootouts, and dramatic explosions. The conflict between good and evil is central, with the hero using courage, skill, and quick thinking to overcome danger and save the day. Some examples:
  - ❑ *Mission Impossible*
  - ❑ *Die hard*
  - ❑ *The Raid Redemption*
- **Adventure:** Adventure films take audiences on exciting journeys to exotic lands, filled with quests for hidden treasures, daring missions, and thrilling escapades. These stories are built around the spirit of exploration and discovery, often leading characters into unknown or dangerous territories. The core elements of adventure films include exotic locales, ancient mysteries, dangerous obstacles, and a constant sense of excitement and the unknown. Some examples:
  - ❑ *Indiana Jones*
  - ❑ *National Treasure*
  - ❑ *Tomb Raider*
  - ❑ *The Mummy*
- **Comedy:** Comedy films are designed to amuse and entertain audiences by making them laugh, using a variety of comedic techniques. These films often revolve around humorous situations, misunderstandings, or quirky characters that create moments of joy and light-heartedness. The core elements of comedy include humour, witty dialogue, slapstick physical comedy, satire, and character-based humour. Some examples include:
  - ❑ *Dumb and Dumber*
  - ❑ *The Hangover series*
  - ❑ *Dhol*
  - ❑ *Hera Pheri*
- **Drama:** Drama films take audiences on emotional journeys, often focusing on complex characters, realistic conflicts, and serious themes. These films often explore important issues like family, love, loss, identity, injustice, or social challenges, aiming to connect with viewers on a heartfelt and thought-provoking level. The core elements of drama include character development, emotional depth, and believable conflicts, whether personal, social, or moral. Some examples include:
  - ❑ *The Pursuit of Happyness*
  - ❑ *Forrest Gump*
  - ❑ *A Beautiful Mind*
  - ❑ *Sholay*
- **Fantasy:** Fantasy films invite audiences to escape into worlds filled with magic, mythical creatures, and the impossible. These stories transport viewers to imaginary realms where the laws of reality are replaced by enchantment and wonder. The core elements of fantasy include magic, supernatural forces, legendary heroes, and mythical beings, often set in richly imagined worlds. At the heart of many fantasy films is a battle between good and evil, with brave characters embarking on epic quests, facing dark powers, and uncovering ancient secrets. Fantasy offers a sense of adventure and wonder, where anything is possible. Examples include:
  - ❑ *Harry Potter series*
  - ❑ *The Lord of the Rings*
  - ❑ *The Chronicles of Narnia*
  - ❑ *The Sorcerer's Apprentice*

- **Horror:** Horror films are designed to scare, unsettle, and thrill audiences, often making them jump out of their seats. These films build intense suspense and fear, using eerie settings, creepy visuals, and chilling sound effects to create an atmosphere of dread. The core elements of horror include supernatural forces, monsters, psychological terror, and encounters with the unknown. Many horror films explore dark themes like death, isolation, evil, and the fear of the unseen, tapping into human anxieties and primal fears. Some famous horror movies are:
  - *The Exorcist*
  - *The Conjuring*
  - *Pari*
  - *The Wailing*
- **Mystery:** Mystery films invite audiences to put on their detective hats and unravel a puzzle, often trying to solve it before the characters themselves do. These stories are built around secrets, hidden clues, and unexpected twists, keeping viewers guessing until the very end. The core elements of mystery include suspense, investigation, and a gradual uncovering of the truth, frequently revolving around crimes, disappearances, or unexplained events. Some intriguing mystery movies are:
  - *Gone Girl*
  - *Bhool Bhulaiyaa*
  - *Drishyam*
  - *Prisoners*
- **Romance:** Romance films center around heartfelt connections, blossoming love, and the emotional journeys of relationships. These stories focus on the joys and struggles that come with falling in love, highlighting the chemistry and passion between characters. The core elements of romance include romantic relationships, deep emotional connections, love, passion, and sometimes heartbreak. Some famous romantic movies include:
  - *The Notebook*
  - *La La land*
  - *A Walk to Remember*
  - *Love Aaj Kal*
- **Science Fiction (Sci-Fi):** Science fiction (sci-fi) films invite audiences to explore the possibilities of the future, advanced technology, and the mysteries of space. These films often imagine worlds shaped by scientific breakthroughs, futuristic inventions, and encounters with alien life. The core elements of sci-fi include futuristic technology, space travel, extraterrestrial beings, and scientific speculation, frequently paired with bold visual effects and imaginative settings. Examples:
  - *Star Wars*
  - *The Matrix*
  - *Interstellar*
  - *Tenet*
- **Thriller:** Thriller films are designed to keep audiences on the edge of their seats with suspense, excitement, and constant tension. These movies build a sense of anticipation and uncertainty, often placing characters in dangerous or high-stakes situations where the outcome is uncertain. The core elements of thrillers include suspense, unexpected plot twists, psychological tension, and a fast-paced storyline. Some spine-chilling thrillers include:
  - *The Silence of the Lambs*
  - *Fresh*
  - *The Prestige*
  - *Fight Club*

Beyond these main genres, there are many subgenres and hybrid genres that blend elements to create unique cinematic experiences. Many filmmakers don't want to limit their film to just one genre and hence blends in two or more genres together. Most of the films in today's generation are hybrid genre movies; Just think of any of your favourite films from the new age cinema and there is a high chance of it being a hybrid film. Joaquin Pheonix starrer *Her* (2013) is a blend of sci-fic and romance. *Crazy Stupid, Love* (2011) is a romantic-comedy.

CINEMA AND SOCIAL CHANGE

Cinema is not just a form of entertainment, but also a powerful tool for social change. Through storytelling, visuals, and emotion, films have the ability to influence public opinion, raise awareness about important issues, challenge stereotypes, and inspire action. From silent films to modern digital cinema, movies have reflected and shaped the values, struggles, and hopes of societies.

Cinema's impact on society can be profound and it derives change by:

- **Raising Awareness:** Cinema often reflects the society we live in. Films bring attention to social issues such as poverty, gender inequality, racism, environmental problems, mental health, and human rights. By portraying these realities on screen, cinema educates audiences and sparks conversations. Movies like *Pink* and *Article 15* are its classic examples.

- **Challenging Stereotypes and Norms:** Society often reels under norms and stereotypes that are hard to challenge. Cinema holds power to question outdated social norms and stereotypes, offering new perspectives on gender roles, caste, religion, sexuality, and identity. It often acts as a mirror to society, highlighting prejudice and inequality. Movies like English Vinglish and Queen discuss gender stereotypification in society.
- **Inspiring Movements and Change:** Certain films have inspired social movements and policy changes by mobilizing public support. Powerful narratives can emotionally connect audiences with issues, motivating them to advocate for justice or contribute to causes. *The Square* (2013), a documentary about the Egyptian Revolution, not only documented the events but also served as a tool for mobilizing activists.
- **Giving a Voice to the Marginalized:** Films can amplify the voices of underrepresented communities, offering them a platform to tell their stories and share their struggles with a broader audience. Movies like *Jai Bhim* portrays the ordeal of the backward communities in society.
- **Preserving and Promoting Culture:** Cinema also helps in preserving cultural heritage and promoting diversity by showcasing traditions, languages, and lifestyles that might otherwise be overlooked or forgotten. Classic Indian films like *Do Bigha Zamin* (1953) and *Mother India* (1957) reflected the hardships and resilience of rural India.

GOLDEN AGE OF INDIAN CINEMA

The 1950s has led film historians to refer to this glorious time as the golden age of Indian Cinema. Film makers created authored and individual works while sticking strictly within the set conventions of the films. The example of Mahatma Gandhi and Prime Minister Nehru's vision of the newly independent nation was also highly influential throughout the decade, and many excellent Urdu poets and writers worked with film makers in the hope of creating a cinema that would be socially meaningful. It is no surprise that the 1950s is regarded today as the finest period in Indian cinema, and the era has profoundly influenced generations of Indian film makers in a way that no other decade has done since. The best directors of the time, including Mehboob Khan, Bimal Roy, Raj Kapoor and Guru Dutt, brought new depth to established themes. They drew on the wide spectrum of cinema stories, but brought to them a personal vision. The films of the late 1940s, 1950s and early 1960s were lyrical and powerful and dealt with themes including the exploitation of the poor by rich landlords (DO BIGHA ZAMEEN, 1953), the importance of sacrifice and honour (MOTHER INDIA), survival in the big city (BOOT POLISH, 1954), untouchability (SUJATA, 1959), the changing role of the woman (Mr. and Mrs. 55, 1955), urban vs rural morality (SHREE 420, 1955), nature vs nurture (AWAARA, 1951), dilemas faced by modern Indians (ANDAZ, 1949), materialism vs spiritualism (PYAASA, 1957) and the importance of destiny (CHAUDHVIN KA CHAND, 1960). These films show a complex and sophisticated mix of characters, plots, ideas and morals. The important film makers of this period not only made commercially successful works but also mastered the language of cinema. They understood how performance, photography, editing and above all, music could be used to create a new aesthetic. It was around this time that Indian films started to receive regular worldwide distribution, and films such as AWAARA made by Raj Kapoor and his co-star Nargis major celebrity in places as far afield as Russia and China. Mehboob's AAN (1952, AKA MANGALA, Daughter of India) and MOTHER INDIA (Perhaps the best known Indian films of all) also won large audiences beyond the Indian sub continent.

One of the most important things that happened in the fifties was the appearance of Satyajit Ray on the film scene. He gave us his famous **Apu Trilogy** (a set of 3 inter-connected films) during this period — **Pather Panchali** in 1954, **Aparajito** in 1957 and **Apur Sansar** in 1959. His **Jalsaghar** appeared in 1958.

A great director, P.C. Barua, maker of **Devdas** died in 1951.

Raj Kapoor's **Awara** became a great hit in the Soviet Russia in 1954. The same year Bimal Roy's **Do Bigha Zamin** won awards at the International Film Festivals at Cannes and Karlovy Vary. In 1956 Ray's **Pather Panchali** won an award at Cannes. In 1957, his **Aparajito** won an award at Venice. K.A. Abbas made **Munna** that was widely praised at Edinburgh festival in 1955. This was the first Indian film without songs or dances. **Kaagaz ke Phool** of Guru Dutt marked the start of widescreen production. Films Division's **Jaipur** won the first award for a documentary at Venice in 1951.

The Film Enquiry Committee's report came in 1951. Its important recommendations were the creation of a Film Finance Corporation, Film Institute for training and a Film Export Corporation.

The Film Federation of India was formed in 1951. In 1952 was held the first International Film Festival in India. In 1954, National Awards for films were instituted.

Great colour films appeared during the same fifties. Sohrab Modi's *Jhansi Ki Rani* was the first colour film in 1953. Shantaram's *Jhanak Jhanak Payal Baje* appeared in 1955 and Mehboob's *Mother India* in 1957.

Raj Kapoor (*Aag, Barsaat, Shri 420*), Satyajit Ray, Guru Dutt (*Baazi, Pyasa, Kaagaz ke Phool*) and Kamal Amrohi **(Mahal, Dawa)** were the great new names during this period.

In the sixties, K. Asif's *Mughal-e-Aazam* was a period (historical) film on a grand scale, with spectacular sets (1960). *Ganga Jamuna* was another great success. Raj Kapoor's *Sangam* set the trend for shooting abroad.

The **Film Finance Corporation was formed in 1960** to finance and encourage new, young and creative film makers. The **Film Institute of India** was created in **1961 at Poona** to train young talented people in different aspects of film. The Indian Motion Pictures Export Corporation was established in 1963. The **National Film Archive of India was established at Pune in 1964.** In **1966 Dadasaheb Phalke Award was instituted** to honour people for their outstanding contribution to Indian cinema. **Devika Rani** was the first film personality to receive the Phalke award in 1967. Mrinal Sen's **Bhuvan Shome**, financed by the Film Finance Corporation, won several awards. It was also a commercial success. Phalke's birth centenary was celebrated in 1970.

In 1971, India was producing the largest number of films in the world. *Calcutta'71* (1971) was an example of the film taking notice of the current politics. This film was made by Mrinal Sen. *Garam Hawa* of M.S. Sathyu was funded by the Film Finance Corporation and won several awards. *Ankur* in 1974 was the first film of Shyam Benegal and was a great success.

NEW WAVE CINEMA OR PARALLEL CINEMA

The new wave cinema (or parallel or alternative or "the other" or art cinema) which started with **Bhuvan Shome** was carried further by its creator, **Mrinal Sen** and others like Shyam Benegal, Sathyu, Basu Chatterji, Satyajit Ray and others. *Rajnigandha* of Basu Chatterji was a very successful film of this "wave" in 1974.

During the 1950s and the 1960s, intellectual filmmakers and story writers became frustrated with musical films. To counter this, they created a genre of films which depicted reality from an artful perspective. Most films made during this period were funded by state governments to promote an authentic art genre from the Indian film fraternity. Parallel cinema films are low-budget and carry high artistic value. It usually has a dedicated audience as it does not impress every viewer with same effect.

The most famous Indian "neo-realist" was the Bengali film director *Satyajit Ray*, followed by *Shyam Benegal*, *Mrinal Sen*, *Adoor Gopalakrishnan* and *Girish Kasaravalli*. Ray's most famous films which formed The ***Apu Trilogy*** were produced on a shoestring budget of Rs. 150,000 ($3000). The three films won major prizes at the Cannes, Berlin and Venice Film Festivals, and are today frequently listed among the greatest films of all time.

The Indian new wave changed Indian cinema forever. Though mainstream Indian cinema still consists of dancing, this new wave pushed the way and allowed new Indian directors like Mira Nair, Deepa Mehta, and Mani Ratnam to make thought provoking dramas.

Raj Kapoor made *Bobby* in 1973. This film on teenage love became very popular. A great spectacle *Sholay* (1975) was shot in 70 mm. Amjad Khan, a heartless dangerous dacoit, became a star overnight. The film set a new trend in multi-star films, spectacular locations and scenes and violence. Side by side films with offbeat, uncommon theme and treatment like Mahesh Bhatt's *Janma* and *Daddy* were also produced. In the late eighties and the early nineties, a new trend of love between the very young started as in films such as *Main Ne Pyar Kiya*, *Ashiqi* and *Love Story*. New young artists acted as heroes and heroines.

Low-budget production was a defining characteristic of Indian Parallel Cinema, often necessitating creative solutions and reliance on film festivals and art house cinemas for distribution. Parallel cinema films often prioritized content and realism over star power, allowing for less expensive casting. Limited budgets encouraged filmmakers to use local actors, locations, and crews, fostering a sense of authenticity. In 1960, the Union government set up the Film Finance Corporation to encourage low budget filmmaking, which benefitted several filmmakers, including those from the Film and Television Institute of India in Pune. This led to a resurgence of directors, actors, technicians and a new political audience. A number of these filmmakers were united in their concern for aesthetics and representation of social issues ranging from poverty to social injustice, feudal power structures and exploitation of lower castes and women.

Another maestro of this parallel cinema movement was Shyam Benegal. It was Shyam Benegal's films that brought commercial success to parallel cinema, especially his uprising trilogy – *Ankur* (1974), *Nishant* (1975) and *Manthan* (1976) – that would break through to audiences in cinema halls. His films communicated the truths about women, caste, religion and social injustice and also discussed stories of political empowerment.

Trilogy's first film *Ankur* (1974), set in a village, follows the story of a young woman, Lakshmi, who is sexually assaulted by a landlord's son and then dies in childbirth. The film explores the stark power dynamics of the rural setting and the plight of marginalized women. *Nishant* (1975), which means "target," tells the story of a young woman who is abducted and forced into a feudal family, while a group of young men, led by a young man named Kumar, are sent to steal the woman back. The film explores themes of social injustice, violence, and the power of the individual within a larger social context. The last of the trilogy - *Manthan* (1976), meaning 'churning,' inspired by the groundbreaking milk cooperative movement by Dr Verghese Kurien that transformed India into one of the largest milk producers in the world and the challenges it faces. The film highlights the struggles of the rural poor and their fight for economic independence, while also touching upon issues of gender inequality and the potential of cinema for social change.

The iconic *Manthan* (1976) was made with a meagre budget of Rs 10 lakhs. It is touted as India's first crowd funded film produced by 500,000 farmers of Gujarat by contributing Rs. 2/- each towards the production of the film.

Though Benegal's style of film making was more accustomed to neo-realist cinema, he was proficient enough to shape his style depending on the subject and it was women who were often at the centre of many of his best films – be it in front of the screen (such as actor Shabana Azmi) or behind it (such as writer Shama Zaidi).

MULTIPLE CHOICE QUESTIONS

1. The National Film Awards were established in ....

A. 1950 B. 1948
C. 1953 D. 1965

2. The National Film Archive of India has the responsibility ....

A. of screening the movies
B. of preserving the movies
C. justify the rates of entertainment tax
D. None of these

3. Which of the following is a function of cinema?

A. Entertainment B. Catharsis
C. Education D. All the above

4. The New Indian Wave Movement is also known as ....

A. Art cinema B. Parallel cinema
C. Both A and B D. None of these

5. In 1896, the Lumiere films were shown in ..... .

A. Delhi B. Kolkata
C. Chennai D. Mumbai

6. Who are considered the pioneers of the motion picture?

A. Lumiere Brothers
B. Edison and Ford
C. D.W. Griffith and Phalke
D. John Grierson and Flaherty

7. What was the name of the first publicly screened film by the Lumiere Brothers in 1895?

A. Train Comes to the Station
B. Workers Leaving the Lumière Factory
C. Moving Train
D. Cinematographe

8. What was the major invention of the Lumière Brothers?

A. Kinetoscope B. Cinematographe
C. Vitascope D. Zoetrope

9. What made the Cinematographe unique?

A. It could film, develop, and project
B. It could record sound
C. It was portable but couldn't project
D. It was used only for still photos

10. Which year is considered the birth year of cinema?

A. 1888 B. 1895
C. 1903 D. 1910

11. The Lumiere brothers are credited with:

A. inventing the first film camera
B. developing the first sound film
C. pioneering the use of special effects
D. showing the first projected moving pictures to a paying audience

12. In what country did the Lumiere Brothers begin their work?

A. United Kingdom B. France
C. Germany D. Italy

13. Which movie create Milestone in history of world cinema?

A. *The Birth of a Nation*
B. *The Wrestlers*
C. *Titanic*
D. *Alam Ara*

14. D.W. Griffith is best known for:
A. Editing techniques B. Political cinema
C. Comedy films D. Musical dramas

15. Which film by Griffith is considered highly controversial but technically revolutionary?
A. *The Gold Rush* B. *Birth of a Nation*
C. *Metropolis* D. *The Kid*

16. What technique did Griffith popularize?
A. Stop motion B. Montage theory
C. Cross-cutting D. Split screen

17. A significant contribution of D.W. Griffith to filmmaking was his mastery and popularization of:
A. Long, static takes
B. Early sound technology
C. Parallel editing, close-ups, and other cinematic techniques
D. The use of minimal sets and natural lighting

18. What was a major criticism of *'Birth of a Nation'*?
A. Poor sound quality
B. Racist content
C. Short runtime
D. Historical inaccuracy

19. Griffith's work influenced which future film style?
A. Expressionism
B. Realism
C. Hollywood narrative continuity
D. Documentary realism

20. D.W. Griffith's film *'Intolerance'* was notable for its:
A. Use of only one central storyline
B. Complex narrative structure spanning different historical periods
C. Minimalist aesthetic and focus on character psychology
D. Purely comedic approach to historical events

21. D.W. Griffith's film *'Broken Blossoms'* is known for its:
A. Grand scale and epic storytelling
B. Intimate and tragic narrative
C. Use of groundbreaking animation techniques
D. Its optimistic and comedic tone

22. .... movie introduced the elements of imagination in films.
A. *The Birth of a Nation*
B. *A Trip to the Moon*
C. *La Voltige*
D. None of these

23. Dadasaheb Phalke is known for ....
A. producing first full-length motion picture in India
B. making the first short film in India
C. making the first color film in India
D. None of these

24. Dada Saheb Phalke's film *Lanka Dahan* was significant for:
A. Being his first silent film
B. Featuring double roles played by the same actor
C. Its extensive use of early special effects
D. Being a contemporary social commentary

25. The first film to win the Academy Award for Best Picture was:
A. *The Birth of a Nation*
B. *All Quiet on the Western Front*
C. *Wings*
D. *Grand Hotel*

26. The first Indian talkie is ....
A. *The Melody of Love*
B. *Alam Ara*
C. *Bombay Talkies*
D. *Amar Jyoti*

27. The first color movie of India was ....
A. *Amar Jyoti*
B. *Kisan Kanya*
C. *Krishna Jamuna*
D. None of these

28. The period from 1940 -1950 is described as the "Golden Age of Indian Cinema".
A. True
B. False

29. Satyajit Ray entered the cinema through the movie ....
A. *The Lonely Wife*
B. *Three Daughters*
C. *Distant Thunder*
D. *Pather Panchali*

30. *Apu Sansar* is the second part of the Apu Trilogy.
A. True
B. False

31. What was John Grierson's most famous early documentary?
A. *Moana*
B. *Nanook of the North*
C. *Night Mail*
D. *Man with a Movie Camera*

32. John Grierson believed film should serve what purpose?

A. Commercial entertainment
B. Historical reenactment
C. Social education and reform
D. Religious instruction

33. Grierson's philosophy emphasized the potential of cinema to:

A. Primarily entertain the masses
B. Critically examine and interpret society
C. Create elaborate fictional worlds
D. Focus solely on aesthetic innovation

34. What government did Grierson work with to create documentaries?

A. Indian Government
B. French Republic
C. British Government
D. U.S. Congress

35. Grierson's work led to the establishment of which institution?

A. Hollywood Studios
B. National Film Board of Canada
C. BBC
D. UNESCO

36. John Grierson believed that documentary films should primarily serve as:

A. A form of pure artistic expression
B. A tool for social education and reform
C. A means of escapism and entertainment
D. A platform for individual storytelling

37. The genre Mumbai Noir is ....

A. the reflection of the economic issues of Mumbai
B. the reflection of the political issues of Mumbai
C. the reflection of the social issues of Mumbai
D. None of these

38. .... is the first film in South India.

A. *Valli Thiru-Manam*
B. *Keechaka Vadham*
C. *Nandanar*
D. *Balayogini*

39. National Award is constituted in the year ....

A. 1953 B. 1954
C. 1956 D. 1957

40. .... was the first film to win a National Award in 1955.

A. *Khuj* B. *Joymati*
C. *Piyali Phukan* D. *Bristi*

41. Initially there were only two categories of certification for films.

A. True
B. False

42. CBFC was set up in ....

A. 1945 B. 1955
C. 1948 D. 1950

43. .... is known as the Father of Indian cinema.

A. Hiralal Sen
B. Dadasaheb Phalke
C. Satyajit Ray
D. All of these

44. What inspired Dadasaheb Phalke to make films?

A. Edison's invention
B. Foreign cinema
C. A screening of "Life of Christ"
D. British newsreels

45. What is Robert Flaherty known as?

A. Father of Silent Films
B. Father of Hollywood
C. Father of Documentary
D. Pioneer of Sound Film

46. Flaherty's first and most famous documentary is:

A. *Night Mail*
B. *Moana*
C. *Nanook of the North*
D. *Man of Aran*

47. A key characteristic of Flaherty's filmmaking approach was:

A. His use of hidden cameras and candid filming
B. His collaborative relationship with his subjects and focus on their lives
C. His emphasis on fast-paced editing and urban environments
D. His creation of staged scenes presented as reality without subject involvement

48. Robert Flaherty often spent extended periods living with his subjects to:

A. Manipulate their stories for dramatic effect
B. Gain their trust and understanding of their culture
C. Impose his own narrative onto their lives
D. Avoid the need for extensive research

49. What was a criticism of Flaherty's documentaries?

A. Too long
B. Not factual
C. Staged and dramatized scenes
D. Shot on a phone

50. "Moana" was filmed in which region?
A. Greenland B. Canada
C. Samoa D. Alaska

51. What technique did Flaherty popularize?
A. Fast cutting B. Docufiction
C. Animation D. Stop motion

52. Which film movement was known for its realistic portrayal of everyday life in post-war Italy?
A. German Expressionism
B. French New Wave
C. Italian Neorealism
D. Hollywood Classicism

53. The biggest film studio of India is ....
A. Ramoji Film Studio
B. AVM Studio
C. Volvo Studio
D. Indian artist Studio

54. Which of the following is/are a genre of the film?
A. Comedy B. Adventure
C. Horror D. All the above

55. When a photograph is edited to adjust the color balance, it is called
A. color separation
B. color gradation
C. color constancy
D. color correction

56. The film 'Lawrence of Arabia' belongs to the genre of:
A. crime B. detective
C. epic D. comedy

57. A psychographic characteristic of film audience is:
A. income B. age
C. gender D. need for status

58. William Edward Green was primarily known for his work in:
A. Indian cinema
B. British experimental film
C. German expressionism
D. Italian neorealism

59. What medium did William Edward Green use for experiments?
A. Film noir
B. Animated cells
C. Silent film
D. Time-lapse photography

60. William Edward Green's contributions are recognized for:
A. Narrative drama
B. Realist performance
C. Technical innovation
D. Sound design

61. William Edward Green's work laid the groundwork for:
A. CGI effects B. Cinematic illusion
C. Color film D. Film schools

62. William Edward Green's influence is seen in:
A. Modern musicals
B. Experimental and art films
C. War documentaries
D. Biopics

63. In film making, panning shots can be described as visual
A. art B. convergence
C. speechless D. paradigms

64. The Children's Film Society of India was established in
A. 1966 B. 1955
C. 1944 D. 1946

65. The Film Division of India was established in
A. 1947 B. 1948
C. 1949 D. 1950

66. What is the work of NFDC?
A. Encouraging the concept of low budget films
B. Discouraging the concept of low budget films
C. Encouraging the high budget films
D. Completing the high budget films

67. The Directorate of Film Festivals (DFF) was set up by the Government of India in
A. 1971 B. 1972
C. 1973 D. 1974

68. The National Film Development Corporation (NFDC) was incorporated in
A. 1973 B. 1974
C. 1975 D. 1976

69. Documentaries are mostly:
A. Fictional B. Non-fictional
C. Dramatic D. None of these

70. Cinema is the mirror of ....
A. Society B. People
C. Nation D. None of these

71. .... is involved in all the film plots.
A. Action B. Sex
C. Romance D. All of these

72. The aim of the non-commercial movies is:
A. business B. giving social message
C. awards D. None of these

73. The word 'Cinema' was coined in
A. The United States
B. The Soviet Union
C. Great Britain
D. France

74. Which cinema is produced for the business purpose?
A. Commercial cinema
B. Non-commercial cinema
C. Both A and B
D. None of these

75. Match the following:

List-I (Film)	List-II (Director)
(*a*) *Kaaghaz Ke Phool*	1. Bimal Roy
(*b*) *Do Bigha Zameen*	2. Muzaffar Ali
(*c*) *Mother India*	3. Guru Dutt
(*d*) *Umrao Jaan*	4. Mehboob Khan

A. (*a*)-1, (*b*)-2, (*c*)-3, (*d*)-4
B. (*a*)-3, (*b*)-1, (*c*)-4, (*d*)-2
C. (*a*)-4, (*b*)-3, (*c*)-2, (*d*)-1
D. (*a*)-1, (*b*)-4, (*c*)-3, (*d*)-2

76. Which among the following movies belong to the comedy genre?
A. *The Dictator*
B. *Barfi*
C. *The Hateful Eight*
D. *The Silence of Others*

77. The Dadasaheb Phalke Award was instituted by the Government of India
A. 1969 B. 1960
C. 1935 D. 1958

78. Identify correct sequence of Satyajit Ray films:
A. *Pather Panchali, Aparajito, Apur Sansar, Charulata*
B. *Apur Sansar, Pather Panchali, Aparajito, Charulata*
C. *Pather Panchali, Charulata, Apur Sansar, Aparajito*
D. *Aparajito, Pather Panchali, Charulata, Apur Sansar*

79. The Hindi film songs are present in Hindi Cinema right from the first sound film?
A. *Pather Panchali*
B. *Raja Harishchandra*
C. *Alam Ara*
D. *Shirhin Farhad*

80. Match the following:

List-I (Film)	List-II (Director)
(*a*) *Charulata*	1. Bimal Roy
(*b*) *Subbarna Rekha*	2. Satyajit Ray
(*c*) *Saheb Bibi Ghulam*	3. Ritwik Ghatak
(*d*) *Prem Patra*	4. Guru Dutt

A. (*a*)-1, (*b*)-2, (*c*)-3, (*d*)-4
B. (*a*)-2, (*b*)-3, (*c*)-4, (*d*)-1
C. (*a*)-3, (*b*)-2, (*c*)-1, (*d*)-4
D. (*a*)-4, (*b*)-3, (*c*)-2, (*d*)-1

81. Who was the director of social epic film *Mother India* (1957)?
A. Mehboob Khan B. Guru Dutt
C. Bimal Ray D. Satyajit Ray

82. All the channels of DD switched to the digital transmission mode from
A. December, 2003 B. January, 2004
C. April, 2003 D. November, 2003

83. The liberalization led to the emergence of .... in Indian cinema.
A. pop culture
B. regional cinema
C. international actors
D. all of these

84. The movies which consist of a wide classification of non-fictional motion pictures that are aimed to show and represent the facts, aspects and realities of society are
A. epic B. documentary
C. melodrama D. horror

85. The movie 'Sign of Leo' (1962) belongs to which National Cinema Movement?
A. French New Wave Cinema
B. British New Wave Cinema
C. German Expressionist
D. None of these

86. .... is the supreme medium to express yesterday, today and tomorrow with its own unique language.
A. cinema B. radio
C. newspaper D. television

87. At present, the box-office collections of Indian cinemas have been steadily increasing due to
A. rise in the ticket price
B. increase in number of theatres
C. increase in print of films
D. All the above

88. Consider the following statements and select the correct one:
1. Indian cinema has always been a reflection of Indian society.
2. Indian commercial cinema started from the 1960 onwards.
3. Indian commercial cinemas are made only in Hindi.

A. Only 1 B. Only 2
C. Both 1 and 2 D. Both 2 and 3

89. Match the following:

List-I (Director)	List-II (Film)
(a) Mrinal Sen	1. *Madhumati*
(b) Ritwik Ghatak	2. *Raat Bhore*
(c) Shyam Benegal	3. *Nishant*
(d) Satyajit Ray	4. *Pather Panchali*

A. (a)-2, (b)-1, (c)-3, (d)-4
B. (a)-1, (b)-2, (c)-3, (d)-4
C. (a)-4, (b)-3, (c)-2, (d)-1
D. (a)-1, (b)-3, (c)-4, (d)-2

90. Which one of the following directors is known as the 'greatest showman of Hindi Cinema'?
A. Raj Kapoor
B. Dadasaheb Phalke
C. Mehboob Khan
D. Satyajit Ray

91. The non-commercial cinemas are not noticed as commercial cinemas because of ....
A. big star B. big director
C. low budget D. None of these

92. The director of famous film *3 Idiots* is ....
A. Rajkumar Hirani
B. Karan Johar
C. Yash Chopra
D. Prakash Jha

93. Which director had applied the 'Rasa Method' of classical Sanskrit drama to movie?
A. Dadasaheb Phalke
B. Raj Kapoor
C. Satyajit Ray
D. Mrinal Sen

94. One of the most famous German Expressionist films 'Metropolis' (1927) was directed by
A. Fritz Lang B. GW Pabst
C. Robert Wiene D. FW Murnau

95. Who among the following movie director discarded the song and dance motif in its effort to stand apart from mainstream cinema?
A. Bimal Roy
B. Satyajit Ray
C. Mrinal Sen
D. None of these

96. Which of the following is an example of sit com (situation Comedy)?
A. *De Dana Dan*
B. *Garam Masala*
C. *Golmaal*
D. All of these

97. Commercial cinema is made in which languages?
A. Hindi
B. All regional language of India
C. Both A and B
D. None of these

98. The famous director during 'Italian Neo Realistic Cinema Movement', was
A. Federico Fellini B. Fritz Lang
C. Robert Wiene D. Ken Loach

99. Which among the following are the major characteristics of Italian-neorealism?
(a) Usage of non-professional actors
(b) Usage of Schüfftan process
(c) Documentary style of film making
(d) Shooting at outdoor location
(e) Discontinuity editing

Choose the correct answer from the options given below:
A. (a), (c) and (d) B. (b), (c) and (d)
C. (d) and (e) D. (a), (b), (c) and (e)

100. Match the following:

List-I (Director)	List-II (Film)
(a) Yash Chopra	1. *Kabhi-Kabhi*
(b) Karan Johar	2. *My name is Khan*
(c) Raj Kumar Hirani	3. *3 Idiots*
(d) Prakash Jha	4. *Gangajal*

A. (a)-3, (b)-2, (c)-1, (d)-4
B. (a)-4, (b)-2, (c)-1, (d)-3
C. (a)-3, (b)-4, (c)-2, (d)-3
D. (a)-1, (b)-2, (c)-3, (d)-4

101. Who among the following is the director of movie "Bandit Queen"?
A. Prakash Jha
B. David Dhawan
C. Shekhar Kapoor
D. None of these

102. Which among the following film director was honored with 'Bharat Ratna'?
A. Dadasaheb Phalke B. Satyajit Ray
C. Ritwik Ghatak D. Shyam Bengal

103. John Grierson coined the term
A. Feature film B. Documentary
C. Short Feature D. Drama of life

104. From the 1960s onwards Indian films had become the primary source of entertainment for the urban masses because of ....
A. Technicolor affordable
B. Regular features of Indian films
C. Both A and B
D. None of these

105. The debut film of Dadasaheb Phalke was
A. *Raja Harishchandra*
B. *Lanka Dhan*
C. *Kaliya Mardan*
D. *Sri Krishna Janma*

106. **Assertion (A):** The Indian film industry represents a splintered semiotics of inter-cultural integration.
Reason (R): Films in India frequently project sub-cultural themes to exhibit identity integration.
A. Both (A) and (R) are true
B. Both (A) and (R) are true, but (R) is not the correct explanation of (A)
C. (A) is true, but (R) is false
D. (A) is false, but (R) is true

107. Match the following:

List-I (Shot)	List-II (Feature)
(a) Close Up	1. Complete view of subject from waist up
(b) Full Shot	2. Complete view of subject
(c) Mid Shot	3. Face of the subject
(d) Extreme Long Shot	4. Large amount of landscape

A. (a)-(2), (b)-(1), (c)-(3), (d)-(4)
B. (a)-(3), (b)-(1), (c)-(2), (d)-(4)
C. (a)-(3), (b)-(2), (c)-(1), (d)-(4)
D. (a)-(2), (b)-(3), (c)-(4), (d)-(1)

108. Who directed the ten-part television mini-series *'Samvidhaan: The Making Of The Constitution of India'*?
A. Suman Das
B. Gautam Ghosh
C. Shyam Benegal
D. Dr. Chandraprakash Dwivedi

109. Match the following:

List-I (National Award for Best Actor)	List-II (Film)
(a) Riddhi Sen	1. *Nagar Kirtan*
(b) Premji	2. *Paar*
(c) Vikram Gokhale	3. *Anumati*
(d) Naseeruddin Shah	4. *Piravi*

A. (a)-(2), (b)-(4), (c)-(1), (d)-(3)
B. (a)-(1), (b)-(4), (c)-(3), (d)-(2)
C. (a)-(3), (b)-(1), (c)-(2), (d)-(4)
D. (a)-(4), (b)-(3), (c)-(2), (d)-(1)

110. **Assertion (A):** Films division is encouraging and promoting a culture of film making in India.
Reason (R): Films division is not the main film making organization of the government of India.
A. Both A and R are true but R is NOT the correct explanation of A
B. A is true but R is false
C. A is false but R is true
D. Both A and R are false

111. Which among the following genre is/are represents the real-life experiences?
A. Action cinema
B. Biographical cinema
C. Adventure cinema
D. Science fiction

112. Identify the correct sequence of cinematic process.
A. Direction, Scripting, Cinematography, Editing, Poet Production
B. Cinematography, Direction, Scripting Editing, Post Production
C. Scripting, Direction, Cinematography, Editing, Post Production
D. Editing, Scripting, Direction, Cinematography, Post Production

113. The director of famous film *Bahubali : The Beginning* (2015):
A. Mahesh Bhatt B. Karan Johar
C. S.S. Rajamouli D. Aditya Chopra

114. Which of the following films marked Anurag Kashyap's directorial debut?
A. *Gangs of Wasseypur*
B. *Black Friday*
C. *No Smoking*
D. *Dev.D*

115. A level shot is
A. above the head of the subject
B. in the line of the eyes of the subject
C. a bird's eye view of the scene
D. a worm's eye view of the scene

116. The famous screen writer of 1970s was ....
A. Salim Khan B. Javed Akhtar
C. Both A and B D. None of these

117. From the 1960s onwards Indian films had become the primary source of entertainment for the urban masses because of ....
A. Technicolor affordable
B. Regular features of Indian films
C. Both A and B
D. None of these

118. Who is known as first lady of Indian cinema?
A. Nargis Datt B. Devika Rani
C. Laxmi Rai D. Bhanu Athaiya

119. Who among the following was the first Indian woman producer and director in Indian cinema?
A. Fatma Begum B. Alam Ara
C. Savitri Devi D. Damini Seth

120. How do movies impact our societies?
A. Movies mirror culture
B. Movies shape culture
C. Movies teach us history
D. All the above

121. What genre is "Sherlock Holmes" film?
A. Comedy B. Mystery
C. Horror D. Fantasy

122. Match the following:

List-I	List-II
(a) *Imagi Nigthem*	1. First Oriya film
(b) *Bhakta Prahlad*	2. First Bengal feature film
(c) *Sita Bibaha*	3. First Manipuri film
(d) *Bilwamangal*	4. First Telugu Talkie

A. (a)-(3), (b)-(4), (c)-(1), (d)-(2)
B. (a)-(2), (b)-(4), (c)-(3), (d)-(1)
C. (a)-(4), (b)-(2), (c)-(3), (d)-(1)
D. (a)-(2), (b)-(1), (c)-(4), (d)-(3)

123. The Dadasaheb Phalke Awards were introduced in which year?
A. 1975 B. 1961
C. 1965 D. 1969

124. Who made the first animated film in 1906?
A. Walt Disney
B. J. Stuart Blackton
C. William Horner
D. J. A. Ferdinand Plateau

125. Who among the following was the first Indian musician to receive the Ramon Magsaysay Award?
A. Ustad Alla Rakha
B. Lata Mangeshkar
C. MS Subbulakshmi
D. Pandit Ravi Shankar

126. The Emmy Awards, seen in the news, are presented for excellence in which of the following fields?
A. Music B. Literature
C. Cinema D. Television industry

127. Which one of the following films did Satyajit Ray make for children?
A. *Pather Panchali* B. *Sonar Kella*
C. *Aparajito* D. *Ashani sanket*

128. Who among the following is the first Indian to get an Oscar Award?
A. Bhanu Athaiya B. Satyajit Ray
C. AR Rahman D. Resul Pookutty

129. Which singer entered the Guinness World Records for the most single studio recordings?
A. Asha Bhosale
B. Mohammad Rafi
C. Lata Mangeshkar
D. Kishore Kumar

130. Name the first actor to win the Oscar Awards.
A. Emil Jannings
B. Lionel Barrymore
C. Warner Baxter
D. Charlie Chaplin

131. Who was the first recipient of Dadasaheb Phalke Award?
A. Raj Kapoor B. Prithviraj Kapoor
C. Devika Rani D. Guru Dutt

132. Which is the first narrative feature film in India?
A. *Pundalik*
B. *Raja Harishchandra*
C. *Alam Ara*
D. *Sant Tukaram*

133. Which is the first golden jubilee film of India?
A. *Pundalik*
B. *Alam Ara*
C. *Sant Tukaram*
D. *Raja Harishchandra*

134. Which is the first Sanskrit film?
A. *Shankaracharya*
B. *Bhagavad Gita*
C. *Gunda*
D. *Margazhi Raagam*

135. Which is the first telefilm of India?
A. *Sadgati* B. *Pather Panchali*
C. *Pikoo* D. *Bala*

136. Which is the first serialised animation film in India?
A. Ek Anek Aur Ekta
B. Ghayab Aya
C. Kittu
D. Motu Patlu

137. Who among the following invented the cinematograph?
A. Lumiere Brothers
B. Mani Sethna
C. Dada Saheb Phalke
D. Dhirendra Nath Ganguly

138. Which of the following the first foreign film was demonstrated in India?
A. *Magic Lamp*
B. *Arrival of the train*
C. *Life of Christ*
D. *Sea Birth*

139. He is known for creating the montage:
A. Edwin S. Porter
B. Sergie Eisenstein
C. George Eastman
D. Douglas Fairbanks

140. Neorealist films focus on the .... in the present day after WW II.
A. High class B. Middle class
C. Lower class D. None of these

141. ....won Oscar award for Best Foreign Film in 1949.
A. Bicycle Thieves
B. Breathless
C. Offside
D. Marriage of Maria Braun

142. The famous movie 'The Bicycle Thieves' takes place in ....
A. Iran B. Rome
C. Greece D. Japan

143. The psychological thriller and neo-noir film 'Memento' is directed and written by .... in 2000.
A. Akira Kurosawa
B. Christopher Nolan
C. Victor Fleming
D. Alfred Hitchcock

144. 'Gone With the Wind' is set in the American South during the .... War.
A. I World B. II World
C. Civil D. Falklands War

145. Popular commercial Indian cinema is one of the most maligned and criticized of cinemas and is often referred to as ....
A. Hollywood B. Bollywood
C. Mollywood D. Tollywood

146. .... is a Latin American film movement that started in the 1960-70s which decries neocolonialism, the capitalist system, and the Hollywood model of cinema as mere entertainment to make money.
A. Asian cinema
B. Indian cinema
C. Swedish cinema
D. Third cinema

147. The headquarters of the National Centre of Films for Children and Young People (NCYP) is situated at
A. Pune B. Chennai
C. Mumbai D. Kolkata

148. From which year did the Indian Government sponsor the National Film Awards?
A. 1972 B. 1971
C. 1973 D. 1980

149. Non-Fiction film means:
A. Artificial B. Dreams
C. Reality D. Imagination

150. Who is called the father of Indian talkie film?
A. Ardeshir Irani B. Dadasaheb Phalke
C. Satyajit Ray D. Hiralal Sen

151. Which is the First 70 MM film of India?
A. *Awaara* B. *Shree 420*
C. *Pyaasa* D. *Around the World*

152. Which was the first Cinemascope Film?
A. *Kagaz Ke Phool*
B. *Mughal-e-Azam*
C. *Pyaasa*
D. *Awaara*

153. In which year was Satyajit Ray's first film released?
A. 1955 B. 1956
C. 1965 D. 1966

154. The first Hit film of India is ....
A. *Raja Harishchandra*
B. *Lanka Dahan*
C. *Chandralekha*
D. *Devdas*

155. First song-less film of India is ....
A. *Naujawan*
B. *Neecha Nagar*
C. *The Apu Trilogy*
D. *Awaara*

156. First Cinema Theatre of India is ....
A. Elphinstone Palace
B. Swatantra Theatre
C. Fireweavers Theatre
D. Tulsi Theatre

157. First film festival of India was held at ....
A. Mumbai B. Calcutta
C. Delhi D. Goa

158. Film 'Gone with the wind' released in?
A. 1934 B. 1939
C. 1940 D. 1941

159. Satyajit Ray, A.R. Rahman and Priyanka Chopra are all ....
A. National Film Award winners
B. Film Fare Winners
C. Academy Award winners
D. Bengali-language writers

160. Who developed the first workable motion picture camera?
A. Matthew Brady
B. Thomas Edison
C. George Eastman
D. William Dickson

161. The Lumière brothers are known for ....
A. creating a celluloid film that could capture movement
B. inventing a disk that would add sound to movies
C. developing the first projector and first movie house
D. shooting the first feature-length foreign movie shown in the U.S

162. Most independent filmmakers rely on .... to get their films noticed and sold for distribution.
A. movie theater B. film festival
C. Hollywood D. Bollywood

163. *Sholay* movie screenplay by ....
A. Salim-Javed B. Shailendra
C. Divender D. Bhupinder

164. What does film noir mean?
A. Dark film B. Foreign film
C. Night film D. Old film

165. Fantasy films were strong at the turn of the 21st Century because of ....
A. the death of personal cinema.
B. the death of realistic cinema.
C. the emergence of digital effects.
D. massive economic recession.

166. Which decade signaled the mainstream financial success of independent films?
A. 2000s B. 1990s
C. 1980s D. 1970s

167. The Cinematography Act of ....
A. 1950 B. 1951
C. 1952 D. 1953

168. After WWII, what change (if any) took place in the frequency of American movie attendance?
A. Less frequent
B. About the same
C. More frequent
D. None of these

169. Studios controlling distribution and exhibition, as well as production ....
A. Horizontal integration
B. Vertical integration
C. Monopoly
D. Oligopoly

170. What is a panning?
A. A camera mover
B. A heavy tripod
C. A remote flash
D. A camera case

171. Vertical turning of the camera is called ....
A. tilt B. pan
C. arc D. fade

172. Which of these is NOT a fiction?
A. Novel B. Short Stories
C. Short Films D. Auto-biography

173. .... is a non-linear editing system.
A. Final Cut Pro B. Photoshop
C. Motion D. Color

174. .... plays a much stronger role in the manipulation and a factor to altering time.
A. Post-production B. Film editing
C. Filmmaking D. Bollywood

175. Which of the following are the types of sound in the cinema?
A. Loudness, Pitch, Timbre.
B. Speech, Music, Ambient Sound.
C. Rhythm, Fidelity, Space
D. Time, Perspective, Quality.

176. An editing Dip to Black transition called as ..... .
A. A Zoom B. A Dissolve
C. A Cut D. A Wipe

177. Only takes which are vetted by the continuity person and/or script supervisor are printed and are sent to the ....
A. Film editing B. Post-production
C. Filmmaking D. Bollywood

178. Production schedule is normally created and managed by the ....
A. Assistant director
B. Unit production manager
C. Production assistant
D. Film crew

179. Which of the following is not a transition?
A. Fast Zoom B. Fade in
C. Fade out D. Zoom

180. A working title, sometimes called a production title, is the temporary name of a product or project used during its development, usually a ...., novel, video game, or music album.
A. Independent film
B. Film
C. Film Making
D. Movie theatre

181. The first attempt at editing a movie is the?
A. Production Cut B. Quick Edit
C. Rough Cut D. Editors

182. A shot which reveals extreme detail of the subject is ....
A. big close-up B. close-up
C. master shot D. medium shot

183. The two different locations and sets of action together called ....
A. Parallel editing
B. Simple editing
C. Montage editing
D. Linear editing

184. Parallel cinema consists of ....
A. action, romance, comedy all together.
B. serious content of realism and naturalism
C. representing change in psyche and condition of everyday life
D. representing truth and reality, not overtly using filmic artifice

185. Which of the following is/are common themes in film noir?
A. The meaninglessness of life.
B. Futility of individual action.
C. Arbitrariness of social justice.
D. All the above

186. Which of the following is/are characteristic of film noir?
A. Low-key lighting.
B. High contrast photography.
C. Deep focus cinematography
D. All the above

187. Bollywood film with the highest number of songs is ....
A. *Neel Kamal*
B. *Indrasabha*
C. *Alam Ara*
D. *Kisan Khanya*

188. U stands for ....
A. Unrestricted Public Exhibition
B. Unrestricted Exhibition
C. Unrestricted
D. Unrestricted Public

189. UA stands for ....
A. Unrestricted Public Exhibition - but with a word of caution that Parental discretion required for children below 12 years
B. Restricted to adults
C. Unrestricted Public Exhibition
D. Restricted to any special class of persons

190. CBFC stands for ....
A. Control Board of Film Censors
B. Central Board of Film making Censors
C. Central Board of Film Certification
D. Control Board of Film Cut

191. What is the literal meaning of melodrama?
A. A drama accompanied by music
B. A tragic drama
C. An unbelievable drama
D. None of these

192. Star lighting aims to ....
A. make all characters equally well lit
B. make the lead performer pop off the screen with more light
C. frame all characters with light to distinguish them from the setting
D. None of these

193. Which of the following shot is called as bust shot?
A. close up B. extreme close up
C. long shot D. medium close up shot

194. Which of the following includes the setting, the lighting, and the distance between the subject and the camera?
A. Mise-en-scene B. Segmentation
C. Dramatic unities D. Modernism

195. A .... shot makes a character look less powerful.
A. high angle B. low angle
C. perspective shot D. subjective shot

196. .... is a structural analysis of a film's narrative.
A. Mise-en-scene B. Segmentation
C. Dramatic unities D. Modernism

197. The technique of making transitions between shots as unnoticeable as possible is called ....
A. Mise-en-scene
B. Segmentation
C. Dramatic unities
D. Seamless editing

198. *The Apur Sansar* film by Satyajit Ray was in the year ....
A. 1955 B. 1959
C. 1954 D. 1957

199. A .... is a combination of text and graphic that represents a studio.
A. copyright B. logo
C. trademark D. All the above

200. What does "genre" mean in film?
A. Editing technique
B. Category of film
C. Lighting method
D. Dialogue style

201. Genre theory in cinema primarily focuses on:
A. The technical aspects of filmmaking
B. Categorizing films based on shared conventions, themes, and styles
C. Analyzing the director's individual artistic vision
D. The historical context of film production

202. Who is one of the key theorists associated with genre theory?
A. D.W. Griffith B. Rick Altman
C. Steven Spielberg D. Quentin Tarantino

203. A genre typically includes:
A. Costumes
B. Setting
C. Themes and conventions
D. All the above

204. Genre helps filmmakers by:
A. Limiting creativity
B. Giving structure and audience expectation
C. Ensuring awards
D. Preventing editing

205. Action films are primarily characterized by:
A. Humorous situations and witty dialogue
B. High-energy sequences, stunts, and conflicts
C. Exploration of deep emotional themes and character development
D. Set in the American West with cowboys and gunfights

206. Which of the following is a classic example of an action film?
A. *Singin' in the Rain*
B. *The Good, the Bad and the Ugly*
C. *Die Hard*
D. *Casablanca*

207. Which of the following Bollywood films is a classic example of the action genre?
A. *Dilwale Dulhania Le Jayenge*
B. *Sholay*
C. *Barfi!*
D. *Taare Zameen Par*

208. Western films are typically set in:
A. Medieval Europe
B. The American West during the 19th century
C. Futuristic dystopian societies
D. Urban environments with organized crime

209. A recurring motif in Western films is often:
A. A love triangle between wealthy socialites
B. The conflict between civilization and the wilderness
C. Musical numbers integrated into the plot
D. Supernatural elements and magical realism

210. Which actor is famous for classic Western films?
A. John Wayne B. Jim Carrey
C. Tom Hanks D. Johnny Depp

211. Which of the following is a well-known Western film?
A. *Pulp Fiction*
B. *La La Land*
C. *High Noon*
D. *The Shawshank Redemption*

212. While Bollywood doesn't have a strong tradition of pure Westerns, which film, with its dacoit setting, can be seen as having some thematic similarities?
A. *Dil Se..*
B. *Sholay*
C. *Hum Aapke Hain Kaun..!*
D. *Khakee*

213. What is the primary aim of a comedy film?
A. To scare the audience
B. To make people laugh
C. To document real events
D. To explain history

214. Slapstick, satire, and romantic comedy are all subgenres of:
A. Crime B. Comedy
C. Drama D. Musical

215. Which of the following is a comedy film?
A. *Saving Private Ryan*
B. *Dumb and Dumber*
C. *Schindler's List*
D. *Gladiator*

216. Which Bollywood film is widely considered a classic comedy?
A. *Devdas*
B. *Andaz Apna Apna*
C. *Lagaan*
D. *Kabhi Khushi Kabhie Gham*

217. Crime films often revolve around:
A. Lighthearted romantic relationships
B. The activities of criminals and law enforcement
C. Epic battles and historical conflicts
D. Imaginative and fantastical worlds

218. Film noir is a subgenre of:
A. Western B. Crime
C. Musical D. Historical

219. Which Bollywood film blends elements of crime and action effectively?
A. *Bajrangi Bhaijaan*
B. *Satya*
C. *Kabhi Alvida Naa Kehna*
D. *Queen*

220. Which film is a classic example of the crime genre?
A. *The Godfather*
B. *Frozen*
C. *The Lion King*
D. *Avatar*

221. Which of the following is a characteristic element of crime films?
A. Singing and dancing performances
B. Moral ambiguity and suspense
C. Cowboys, horses, and saloons
D. Elaborate historical costumes and settings

222. Drama films typically focus on:
A. Over-the-top action sequences
B. The development of characters and their emotional journeys
C. Humorous situations and comedic timing
D. The exploration of fantastical and magical elements

223. Which of the following is a well-known drama film?
A. *The Princess Bride*
B. *Forrest Gump*
C. *Toy Story*
D. *The Sound of Music*

224. Which Bollywood film is a well-known example of the drama genre, often exploring complex human relationships?
A. *Dhoom* B. *Mother India*
C. *Mr. India* D. *Amar Akbar Anthony*

225. Fantasy and science fiction genres often involve:
A. Realistic portrayals of everyday life
B. Elements of the supernatural, magical, or technologically advanced
C. Historical events and figures
D. Musical numbers and dance sequences

226. Which of the following is an example of a science fiction film?
A. *The Lord of the Rings : The Fellowship of the Ring*
B. *Star Wars : A New Hope*
C. *Pride and Prejudice*
D. *Gladiator*

227. Historical films are set in:
A. Imaginary worlds with mythical creatures
B. The past and often depict real events or figures
C. Contemporary urban environments
D. The distant future with advanced technology

228. Accuracy and authenticity are often important considerations in which genre?
A. Fantasy B. Animation
C. Romance D. Historical

229. Which film is an example of a historical movie?
A. *Braveheart* B. *Home Alone*
C. *The Hangover* D. *Spider-Man*

230. Which Bollywood film can be categorized as a historical drama?
A. *Dil Chahta Hai*
B. *Jodhaa Akbar*
C. *Chennai Express*
D. *Munna Bhai M.B.B.S.*

231. Animation films are characterized by:
A. The use of live actors in real-world settings
B. The creation of moving images through various techniques like drawing, stop-motion, or CGI
C. A focus on musical performances and elaborate choreography
D. Their setting in the American West

232. Which of the following is a popular animated film?
A. *Titanic* B. *The Lion King*
C. *Seven Samurai* D. *Psycho*

233. Romance films primarily explore:
A. High-octane action and thrilling suspense
B. Romantic love and relationships between characters
C. Humorous situations and comedic misunderstandings
D. The lives of criminals and their pursuit by law enforcement

234. A common expression in romance films is often:
A. A lone hero facing insurmountable odds
B. The journey of self-discovery in a historical setting
C. Overcoming obstacles to find or maintain love
D. Musical numbers that advance the plot

235. Which of these is a romance movie?
A. *The Fast and the Furious*
B. *The Notebook*
C. *Alien*
D. *Inception*

236. Which Bollywood film is a beloved example of the romance genre?
A. *Gangs of Wasseypur*
B. *Dilwale Dulhania Le Jayenge*
C. *Don*
D. *PK*

237. Musical films prominently feature:
A. Extended dialogue sequences and minimal action
B. Song and dance numbers integrated into the narrative
C. Dark and gritty themes with moral ambiguity
D. Settings in the American West with cowboys and outlaws

238. Which is a well-known musical film?
A. *Rocky* B. *La La Land*
C. *The Revenant* D. *Jaws*

239. Genre conventions can be:
A. Rigid and unchanging over time
B. Fluid and subject to innovation and subversion
C. Determined solely by the film's budget
D. Irrelevant to the audience's understanding of the film

240. Which genre would most likely feature superheroes?
A. Crime B. Comedy
C. Action D. Romance

241. Romantic comedies blend elements of:
A. Romance and horror
B. Romance and comedy
C. Comedy and fantasy
D. Romance and documentary

242. "3 Idiots" is best categorized under which genre?
A. Horror B. Historical
C. Comedy-Drama D. Musical

243. Genres evolve over time due to:
A. Technology
B. Audience preferences
C. Cultural shifts
D. All the above

244. The blending of different genres can result in:
A. More traditional and predictable films
B. Hybrid genres that offer new and unexpected experiences
C. Films that fail to appeal to any specific audience
D. The complete disappearance of established genre categories

245. Which Bollywood movie is a well-known crime thriller?
A. *Kabir Singh* B. *Drishyam*
C. *Chennai Express* D. *Lagaan*

246. Which genre often explores themes of good versus evil and features heroes and villains?
A. Comedy B. Action
C. Romance D. Musical

247. Documentaries differ from fiction genres because they:
A. Use CGI
B. Are humorous
C. Present factual content
D. Feature magical realism

248. "Gully Boy" is an example of which film genre?
A. Musical Drama B. War
C. Horror D. Western

249. Which genre often uses humor to critique social norms or political figures?
A. Drama B. Comedy
C. Fantasy/Sci-Fi D. Romance

250. Films in this genre often explore complex human emotions and relationships in realistic settings.
A. Action B. Drama
C. Western D. Musical

251. Which genre is best known for futuristic settings and advanced technology?
A. Historical B. Western
C. Sci-fi D. Crime

252. Which of the following is a fantasy/sci-fi film from Bollywood?
A. *Zindagi Na Milegi Dobara*
B. *Ra.One*
C. *Queen*
D. *Badhaai Ho*

253. Which of these genres typically involves singing and dancing as a core component?
A. Action B. Musical
C. Thriller D. Western

254. The Parallel Cinema movement in India is primarily known for its focus on:
A. Lavish sets and glamorous stars
B. Socially relevant themes and realistic narratives
C. Escapist entertainment and commercial success
D. Grand historical epics and mythological tales

255. What was a common theme in Parallel Cinema?
A. Superhero battles
B. Village and agrarian issues
C. Intergalactic warfare
D. Mythological stories

256. The acting style in Parallel Cinema typically emphasized:
A. Over-the-top melodrama
B. Lip-syncing to playback singers
C. Stylized theatrical performances
D. Naturalism and realism

257. Parallel Cinema in India emerged as a counterpoint to:
A. Hollywood blockbusters
B. The dominant mainstream Bollywood cinema
C. European art films
D. Silent films

258. A key characteristic of Parallel Cinema's production process was:
A. Low budget and emphasis on content over spectacle
B. High budget and extensive special effects
C. Reliance on established commercial formulas
D. Exclusive shooting in foreign locations

259. Shyam Benegal is a significant director associated with:
A. Early silent films
B. The Parallel Cinema movement
C. Bollywood masala films of the 1980s
D. Animated feature films

260. Which social issue is highlighted in Shyam Benegal's 'Manthan'?
A. Space exploration
B. Dairy cooperative movement
C. Urban nightlife
D. Political espionage

261. Which of the following films was directed by Shyam Benegal and is considered a key work of Parallel Cinema?
A. *Dilwale Dulhania Le Jayenge*
B. *Ankur*
C. *Sholay*
D. *Kabhi Khushi Kabhie Gham*

262. The film 'Nishant', directed by Shyam Benegal, critically examines:
A. The beauty of rural landscapes
B. Power structures and exploitation in rural society
C. The joys of urban life
D. The history of Indian cinema

263. One of the primary motivations of Parallel Cinema was to:
A. Win international awards only
B. Entertain without meaning
C. Portray societal problems authentically
D. Showcase lavish sets

264. Satyajit Ray, though with his own distinct style, also contributed significantly to cinema that aligned with the sensibilities of:

A. Mainstream commercial cinema
B. The Parallel Cinema movement
C. Hollywood musicals
D. European experimental films

265. The Apu Trilogy, directed by Satyajit Ray, includes the films:
A. *Ankur, Nishant, Manthan*
B. *Pather Panchali, Aparajito, Apur Sansar*
C. *Deewaar, Trishul, Shakti*
D. *Mr. India, Nagina, Lamhe*

266. Satyajit Ray's films in the Apu Trilogy primarily explore:
A. Mythology
B. Urban fantasy
C. Human struggle and rural life
D. Supernatural powers

267. Mrinal Sen's films often revolved around:
A. Historical fiction
B. Personal memoirs
C. Urban discontent and class struggles
D. Musical comedies

268. Ritwik Ghatak's films are known for their:
A. Lighthearted comedic themes
B. Intense exploration of social and political turmoil, often related to the partition of India
C. Lavish musical sequences
D. Focus on escapist fantasy worlds

269. Which element is NOT typical in Parallel Cinema?
A. Natural lighting
B. Non-professional actors
C. Song-and-dance sequences
D. Social commentary

270. Which of the following actors was frequently associated with the Parallel Cinema movement?
A. Amitabh Bachchan
B. Naseeruddin Shah
C. Shah Rukh Khan
D. Salman Khan

271. Shabana Azmi and Smita Patil were prominent actresses known for their work in:
A. Mainstream romantic comedies
B. Parallel Cinema films addressing social issues
C. Bollywood action thrillers
D. Historical epics

272. The low budget production of Parallel Cinema films often resulted in:
A. Technically inferior quality
B. A greater focus on strong narratives and acting
C. Over-reliance on special effects
D. Limited distribution and reach

273. 'Ankur' (1974) was directed by:
A. Satyajit Ray
B. Mrinal Sen
C. Shyam Benegal
D. Raj Kapoor

274. 'Pather Panchali' is part of the:
A. Ray Trilogy
B. Ghatak Trilogy
C. Bollywood Superhits
D. South Indian Cinema

275. 'Ashani Sanket' directed by Satyajit Ray deals with:
A. Partition
B. Bengal famine
C. Indian independence
D. School reforms

276. Shabana Azmi made her debut in:
A. *Manthan* B. *Ankur*
C. *Nishant* D. *Mandi*

277. The Apu Trilogy does NOT include:
A. *Pather Panchali*
B. *Aparajito*
C. *Charulata*
D. *Apur Sansar*

278. 'Bhuvan Shome' is considered the beginning of:
A. Parallel Cinema
B. Musical Comedy
C. Romantic Drama
D. Horror Films

279. 'Meghe Dhaka Tara' is a film by:
A. Satyajit Ray
B. Shyam Benegal
C. Ritwik Ghatak
D. Basu Chatterjee

280. Ritwik Ghatak's film 'Meghe Dhaka Tara' deals with the themes of:
A. A lighthearted family drama
B. The tragic consequences of the partition of Bengal
C. A futuristic science fiction story
D. A grand musical spectacle

281. Parallel Cinema often received support from:
A. Major Bollywood studios
B. Government funding bodies and film societies
C. International commercial distributors
D. Private financiers seeking high returns

282. Mrinal Sen's 'Bhuvan Shome' was produced by:
A. Rajshri Productions
B. Film Finance Corporation
C. Zee Studios
D. Netflix

283. Which of Shyam Benegal's films explores the issue of caste discrimination?
A. *Ankur* B. *Manthan*
C. *Junoon* D. *Bhumika*

284. The character of Apu in Satyajit Ray's trilogy grows from a child in rural Bengal to:
A. A wealthy businessman in Bombay
B. A struggling writer in Calcutta
C. A powerful political leader
D. A famous Bollywood actor

285. Actor who was prominently seen in Parallel Cinema:
A. Om Puri
B. Rajesh Khanna
C. Amitabh Bachchan
D. Dharmendra

286. 'Manthan' was crowd-funded by:
A. Government of India
B. Dairy farmers of Gujarat
C. Bollywood producers
D. Foreign investors

287. Parallel Cinema provided a platform for filmmakers to explore:
A. Only light entertainment
B. Complex social realities and human conditions
C. Pure fantasy and escapism
D. Solely historical narratives

288. The reach and influence of Parallel Cinema, while not as commercially dominant as mainstream Bollywood, was significant in:
A. Completely replacing mainstream cinema
B. Shaping a more diverse and socially conscious film culture
C. Primarily influencing international audiences
D. Having no lasting impact on Indian filmmaking

289. 'Pather Panchali' won:
A. No awards
B. Best Bollywood Song award
C. Several international film awards
D. Academy Award

290. Which of the following films by Shyam Benegal features an ensemble cast exploring various social issues?
A. *Kalyug* B. *Ankur*
C. *Manthan* D. *Bhumika*

291. 'Agantuk' was directed by:
A. Mrinal Sen
B. Shyam Benegal
C. Ritwik Ghatak
D. Satyajit Ray

292. Ritwik Ghatak's 'Subarnarekha' is about:
A. A war hero
B. Displacement after Partition
C. A Bollywood actress
D. Indian mythology

293. Satyajit Ray's film 'Charulata' is an adaptation of a novella by:
A. Munshi Premchand
B. Rabindranath Tagore
C. Sarat Chandra Chattopadhyay
D. Khushwant Singh

294. Mrinal Sen's film 'Ek Din Pratidin' explores the anxieties of a family when:
A. Their business flourishes unexpectedly
B. Their daughter mysteriously disappears
C. They win a large sum of money
D. They inherit a vast estate

295. Who among the following is NOT a key figure in Parallel Cinema?
A. Satyajit Ray
B. Ritwik Ghatak
C. Karan Johar
D. Mrinal Sen

296. Parallel Cinema often prioritized ……… over star power.
A. Visual effects
B. Strong scripts and performances
C. Elaborate costumes
D. Foreign locations

297. The Parallel cinema movement aimed to create a cinema that was more:
A. Removed from social realities
B. Engaged with the socio-political context of India
C. Focused on pure entertainment value
D. Imitative of Western cinematic trends

298. Parallel Cinema often used:
A. High-end CGI
B. Lavish costumes
C. Real locations
D. Foreign sets

299. What kind of actors were often cast in Parallel Cinema?
A. Big stars only
B. Non-actors or newcomers
C. Singers
D. Models

300. Funding for Parallel Cinema often came from:
A. Bollywood producers
B. Government institutions
C. Reality shows
D. YouTube channels

301. Parallel Cinema had strong links with:
A. Literary works
B. Soap operas
C. Western musicals
D. Detective fiction

302. The primary audience for Parallel Cinema was:
A. Children
B. Urban and intellectual viewers
C. Tourists
D. Sports fans

303. Who is regarded as the father of Parallel Cinema in India?
A. Raj Kapoor B. Mrinal Sen
C. Satyajit Ray D. Bimal Roy

304. Which film inspired a new wave of socially conscious filmmakers?
A. *Sholay*
B. *Pather Panchali*
C. *Hum Aapke Hain Koun*
D. *Amar Akbar Anthony*

305. Hugo Munsterberg stated that film was the Art of the:
A. Heart B. Ear
C. Mind D. Man

306. The dialogues in Parallel Cinema were often:
A. Over-dramatic
B. Realistic and subtle
C. Poetic only
D. Dubbed in English

307. Who acted in *Nishant*, *Manthan*, and *Bhumika*?
A. Amitabh Bachchan
B. Smita Patil
C. Nargis
D. Saira Bano

308. Which actress was known for her powerful portrayals of women in Shyam Benegal's films?
A. Madhuri Dixit
B. Shabana Azmi
C. Sridevi
D. Kajol

309. The term "Art Cinema" in India is synonymous with:
A. Cultural movies
B. Commercial blockbusters
C. Parallel Cinema
D. Mythologicals

310. Which genre did Parallel Cinema mostly avoid?
A. Fantasy
B. Political
C. Social drama
D. Historical

311. One key challenge faced by Parallel Cinema was:
A. Lack of stars
B. Distribution and reach
C. Excessive marketing
D. Overloaded VFX

312. Satyajit Ray's films often showcased a deep understanding of:
A. Advanced technology
B. Human psychology and social dynamics
C. Grand historical narratives
D. Elaborate musical traditions

313. Known as the Wizard of Menlo Park and the inventor of the first commercial camera:
A. Thomas A. Edison
B. George Smith
C. W. K. L. Dickson
D. Charles Francis

314. George Melies is known as the father of:
A. Special Effects
B. After Effects
C. Cinematographe
D. Zoetrope

ANSWERS

1	**2**	**3**	**4**	**5**	**6**	**7**	**8**	**9**	**10**
C	B	D	C	D	A	B	B	A	B
11	**12**	**13**	**14**	**15**	**16**	**17**	**18**	**19**	**20**
D	B	A	A	B	C	C	B	C	B
21	**22**	**23**	**24**	**25**	**26**	**27**	**28**	**29**	**30**
B	B	A	B	C	B	B	A	D	B
31	**32**	**33**	**34**	**35**	**36**	**37**	**38**	**39**	**40**
C	C	B	C	B	B	C	B	B	C
41	**42**	**43**	**44**	**45**	**46**	**47**	**48**	**49**	**50**
A	D	B	C	C	C	B	B	C	C
51	**52**	**53**	**54**	**55**	**56**	**57**	**58**	**59**	**60**
B	C	A	D	D	C	D	B	D	C
61	**62**	**63**	**64**	**65**	**66**	**67**	**68**	**69**	**70**
B	B	D	B	B	A	C	C	B	A
71	**72**	**73**	**74**	**75**	**76**	**77**	**78**	**79**	**80**
C	B	D	A	B	A	A	A	C	B
81	**82**	**83**	**84**	**85**	**86**	**87**	**88**	**89**	**90**
A	B	A	B	A	A	D	C	A	A
91	**92**	**93**	**94**	**95**	**96**	**97**	**98**	**99**	**100**
A	A	C	A	B	D	C	A	A	D
101	**102**	**103**	**104**	**105**	**106**	**107**	**108**	**109**	**110**
C	B	B	C	A	B	C	C	B	A
111	**112**	**113**	**114**	**115**	**116**	**117**	**118**	**119**	**120**
B	C	C	B	B	C	C	B	A	D
121	**122**	**123**	**124**	**125**	**126**	**127**	**128**	**129**	**130**
B	A	D	B	C	D	B	A	A	A
131	**132**	**133**	**134**	**135**	**136**	**137**	**138**	**139**	**140**
C	A	C	A	A	B	A	C	B	C
141	**142**	**143**	**144**	**145**	**146**	**147**	**148**	**149**	**150**
A	B	B	C	B	D	C	C	C	A
151	**152**	**153**	**154**	**155**	**156**	**157**	**158**	**159**	**160**
D	A	B	B	A	A	A	B	A	D
161	**162**	**163**	**164**	**165**	**166**	**167**	**168**	**169**	**170**
C	B	A	A	C	B	C	A	B	A
171	**172**	**173**	**174**	**175**	**176**	**177**	**178**	**189**	**190**
A	D	A	B	B	B	A	A	D	B
181	**182**	**183**	**184**	**185**	**186**	**187**	**188**	**189**	**190**
C	A	A	B	D	D	B	A	A	C
191	**192**	**193**	**194**	**195**	**196**	**197**	**198**	**199**	**200**
A	B	D	A	A	B	D	B	B	B
201	**202**	**203**	**204**	**205**	**206**	**207**	**208**	**209**	**210**
B	B	D	B	B	C	B	B	B	A
211	**212**	**213**	**214**	**215**	**216**	**217**	**218**	**219**	**220**
C	B	B	B	B	B	B	B	B	A
221	**222**	**223**	**224**	**225**	**226**	**227**	**228**	**229**	**230**
B	B	B	B	B	B	B	D	A	B
231	**232**	**233**	**234**	**235**	**236**	**237**	**238**	**239**	**240**
B	B	B	C	B	B	B	B	B	C

241	242	243	244	245	246	247	248	249	250
B	C	D	B	B	B	C	A	B	B
251	252	253	254	255	256	257	258	259	260
C	B	B	B	B	D	B	A	B	B
261	262	263	264	265	266	267	268	269	270
B	B	C	B	B	C	C	B	C	B
271	272	273	274	275	276	277	278	279	280
B	B	C	A	B	B	C	A	C	B
281	282	283	284	285	286	287	288	289	290
B	B	A	B	A	B	B	B	C	A
291	292	293	294	295	296	297	298	299	300
D	B	B	B	C	B	B	C	B	B
301	302	303	304	305	306	307	308	309	310
A	B	B	B	C	B	B	B	C	A
311	312	313	314						
B	B	A	A						

EXPLANATORY ANSWERS

3. (D): One of the functions of the Cinemas is called catharsis. It helps the audiences to remove the negative thoughts and emotions. Sometimes, the audience relate themselves to the characters of the movies and thus, they let out their emotions by weeping, laughing etc.

10. (B): The year widely considered the "birth of cinema" is 1895. On December 28, 1895, the Lumiere brothers, Auguste and Louis, held the first public commercial screening of their "Cinematographe" films in Paris, France. This event marked the beginning of cinema as a public art form, with audiences experiencing moving images on a large screen for the first time.

27. (B): *Kisan Kanya* was a 1937 Hindi Cinecolor feature film which was directed by Moti Gidwani and produced by Ardeshir Irani of Imperial Pictures. It is largely remembered by the Indian public on account of it being India's first indigenously made color film.

28. (A): Most of the critically approved Indian films were produced during the golden age. Some these movies include *Pyaasa, Kaagaz Ke Phool*, *Awaara* and *Shree 420*. Some of the epic movies such as *Mother India*, *Mughal-e-Azam* were also produced during this era. The movie *Mother India*, was directed by Mehboob Khan and was nominated for the Best Foreign Language film in the Academy Award. Bimal Roy popularized the theme of reincarnation in with his movie *Madhumati*.

30. (B): *Apu Sansar* is the third part of Satyajit Ray's Apu Trilogy. The first part being the *Pather Panchali* (1955) and the second one is the *Aparajito* (1956).

38. (B): *Keechaka Vadham* was the first film in South India as well as the first silent film of Tamil film industry. It was made by R. Nataraja Mudaliar in 1916. The story is based on Mahabharata, which is an Indian epic.

41. (A): Earlier there were two categories of certification under the Central Board of Film Certification – 'A' and 'U'. Later on, two other categories – 'UA' and 'S' were added in June 1983.

66. (A): The National Film Development Corporation of India (NFDC) based in Mumbai is the central agency established in 1975, to encourage high quality Indian cinema. It functions in areas of film financing, production and distribution and under the Ministry of Information and Broadcasting, Government of India. The primary goal of the NFDC is to plan, promote and organize an integrated and efficient development of the Indian film industry and foster excellence in cinema.

102. (B): Satyajit Ray was honored with Bharat Ratna for lifetime achievement in cinema in 1992.

105. (A): Raja Harishchandra, which was released in the year 1913 was Dadasaheb Phalke's debut film and also India's first full-length feature film.

124. (B): J. Stuart Blackton is considered the father of American animation. He co-founded the Vitagraph

Company of America, a pioneering studio in the silent film era. His 1906 film "Humorous Phases of Funny Faces" is one of the earliest examples of animation.

125. (C): Indian Carnatic singer MS Subbulakshmi was from Madurai, Tamil Nadu. She was the very first artist to ever get the Bharat Ratna. In 1974, she became the first artist from India to earn the Ramon Magsaysay award. In 1966, she was the first Indian to perform before the UN General Assembly.

128. (A): Bhanu Athaiya became the first Indian to win an Academy Award in 1983 for designing the costumes for Richard Attenborough's Gandhi.

130. (A): Emil Jannings was the first actor to win the Oscar Awards. He won the award for the movie- *The Last Command* and *The Way of All Flesh*.

135. (A): Satyajit Ray adapted Munshi Prem Chand's Short Story 'Sadgati' for Doordarshan in 1981. It is said to have been the first tele-film produced by Doordarshan, with Om Puri, Smita Patil and Mohan Agashe in the lead roles.

139. (B): A montage is a film editing technique in which a series of short shots are sequenced to condense space, time, and information.

147. (C): The headquarters of the National Centre of Films for Children and Young People (NCYP), the former name of the Children's Film Society, India (CFSI), is located in Mumbai.

152. (A): Cinemascope was a widescreen film format popular from the 1950s to 1960s, known for its wide aspect ratio and the use of anamorphic lenses.

187. (B): The Bollywood film with the highest number of songs is Indrasabha (1932), a musical film that had 72 songs.

278. (A): Mrinal Sen's film 'Bhuvan Shome' is considered a landmark in the early stages of Parallel Cinema.

314. (A): George Melies experimented with techniques such as stop-motion animation, double exposure, and hand-painted color to create magical and fantastical scenes. His film 'A Trip to the Moon' (1902) is a prime example of his groundbreaking use of special effects.

CHAPTER-6

SOCIAL MEDIA

SOCIAL MEDIA

Social media refers to websites and applications that facilitates community-based communication through the sharing and collaboration of information, ideas, multimedia content in real-time.

Over the past decade, social media has evolved beyond being just a tool for connecting with friends and family. It now serves as a platform for news dissemination, entertainment, and even commerce, becoming a significant part of both personal lives and business operations.

In the business world, social media serves as a key tool for marketing, product promotion, customer service, and engagement. Businesses use these platforms to communicate with customers and gather feedback.

As per the research of Kepios, there were 5.24 billion social media users around the world at the start of January 2025, equating to 63.9 percent of the total global population. There is an annualized growth of 4.1 percent, at an average rate of 6.5 new users every single second.

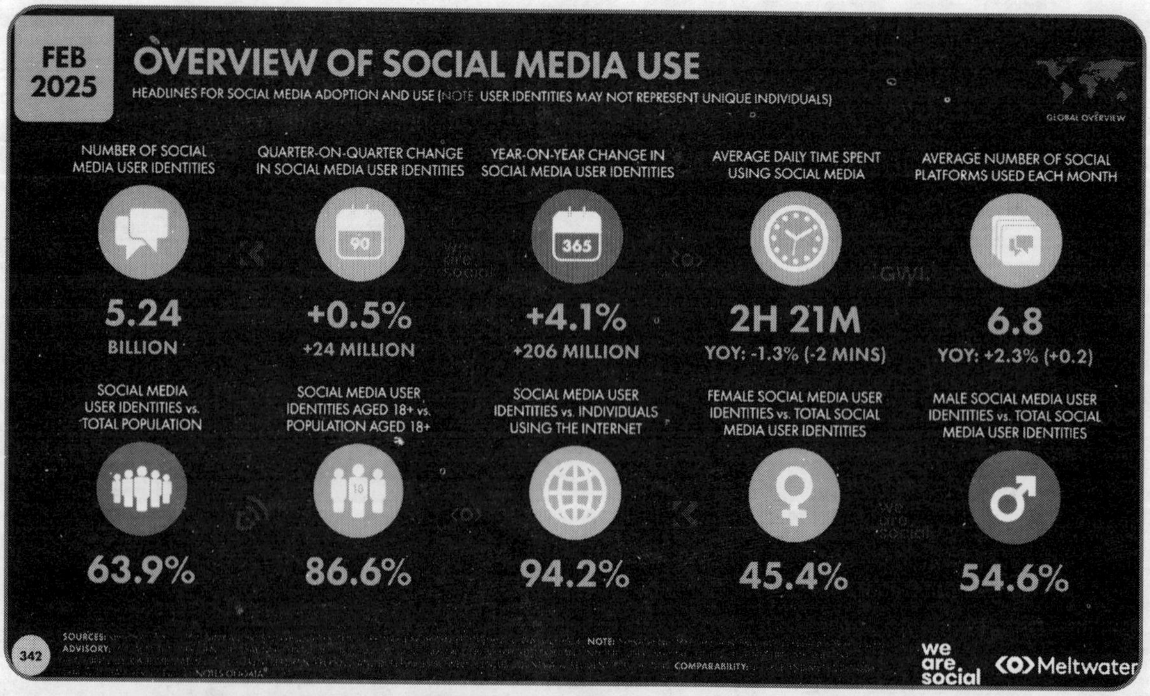

SOURCE: Kepios Analysis

TYPES OF SOCIAL MEDIA PLATFORMS

Social media serves varied interests depending on users interests and needs. There are different types of social media services that cater to different needs and accommodate various types of content. While some platforms have common features, others are more specific in their use and the kind of services offered. While some can use social media for recreational purposes, others might need it to support their business needs. Social media offers an economical option for creating brand awareness, communicating with customers, building a niche audience and increasing sales.

Social media platforms can be categorized based on their purpose, user engagement, and content type. Below are the four main types of social media platforms with examples:

- **Social networks platforms:** These focus on connecting people, building relationships, and sharing personal or professional updates. They focus more on person-to-person conversations. Aside from personal conversations, these platforms encourage knowledge sharing. Examples include Facebook, LinkedIn, and Twitter.
- **Media Sharing platforms:** These platforms center around sharing visual content like photos or videos. Examples include YouTube, Instagram and TikTok.
- **Discussion and Community platforms:** These platforms facilitate discussions, allowing users to ask questions and get answers from the community members. These platforms spark conversations based on shared interests or out of curiosity. Examples include Quora and Reddit.
- **Blogging & Publishing platforms:** These platforms allow sharing of long-form written content, articles, and opinions. Examples include WordPress and Medium.
- **Business and Review platforms:** These platforms focus on enabling business networking, enhancing customer engagement, and collecting consumer feedback. Popular examples include Yelp, Google My Business, and Trustpilot.
- **Live streaming platforms:** These platforms are designed for broadcasting live video content and interacting with audiences in real time. YouTube Live, Facebook Live and Instagram Live are its examples.
- **Social shopping platforms:** These platforms merge e-commerce with social networking, making it easier for users to discover and purchase products within social media environments. Examples include Facebook Marketplace, and Instagram Shopping are its examples.
- **Private and messaging platforms:** These platforms prioritize direct communication through one-on-one or group messages. WhatsApp, Telegram and Messenger are its examples.

ROLE OF SOCIAL MEDIA IN DEMOCRACY

The term 'Democracy' implies equal participation and media works an instrument in its facilitation. The emergence of social media platforms has transformed people's participation in democracy. It has given voice to people to put forth their opinions and engage in discussions on any ongoing issue. While traditional media is run and governed by the media professionals, social media is more democratic in nature as it is run by the people. It has a larger reach, quicker transmission and is easily accessible. Social media enables mass participation and also provides for instant updates and feedbacks.

However, it too has a few downsides as well. On the flip side, due to its organic and unregulated nature, and rapid information sharing, it is a potent medium for the spread of misinformation. On several instances, its misuse has led to spread of fake news, led to communal tension and have even destabilized governments, compromising the spirit of democracy. Moreover, as these social media platforms work on algorithm, they can create echo chambers, where people only see stuff that confirms what they already believe, making it harder to have constructive conversations and find common ground.

ROLE OF SOCIAL MEDIA IN CREATING COLLECTIVE IDENTITIES

Social media plays a significant role in creating collective identities. Collective identity refers to a shared sense of belonging to a group with common interests, values, or goals. Social media helps in the creation and strengthening of such identities by creating communities, sharing information, building narratives and enabling cyber activism.

Sharing information online is like a digital campfire where folks gather and realize they're not alone in their thoughts, feelings, or passions. When someone posts about an issue they care about, or shares a personal story that resonates with others, it can spark a chain reaction. People chime in with their own experiences, offer support, and suddenly, a sense of "us" starts to bubble up. These online interactions can solidify shared beliefs and values, which are really the building blocks of any collective identity.

Cyber Activism (Digital Activism)

Cyber Activism utilizes the collective identity and channels it into action. Social media platforms become the organizing hub for movements. Sharing information about a cause, a petition, or an upcoming protest can spread like wildfire. People who identify with the cause connect online, coordinate their efforts, and amplify their message in ways that were much harder before. Use of Hashtags on Twitter and Instagram have proven to be a powerful digital tool to empower and unite people around a specific issue, creating a virtual space for discussion and mobilization. Social media platforms such as WhatsApp, Telegram, and Twitter enable rapid coordination of protests and events. Movements like the Arab Spring, Fridays for Future, and #EndSARS were significantly amplified through online engagement, allowing people to unite and act collectively across geographical boundaries.

Black Lives Matter Campaign (*Source: WIKIMEDIA COMMONS*)

Moreover, cyber activism serves as a means of applying pressure on authorities. Online petitions, widely circulated videos, and coordinated social media campaigns can generate enough public attention to compel governments, institutions, and corporations to respond. In many cases, the threat of online backlash or "cancel culture" prompts swift reactions from public figures and brands, showcasing the tangible impact of digital activism in today's interconnected world.

CYBERCRIME

Cybercrime refers to illegal activities conducted using computers, networks, or digital devices, typically over the internet. These crimes may target individuals, organizations, or governments and often involve theft, fraud, harassment, or damage to data and systems.

Types of Cybercrime

The spectrum of cybercrime is broad, encompassing various methods and targets. Some common types include:

- **Malware Attacks:** This involves the use of malicious software (like viruses, worms, ransomware, spyware) to damage computer systems, steal data, or disrupt operations.
- **Phishing and Social Engineering:** These tactics rely on deceiving individuals into revealing sensitive information like passwords, credit card details, or personal data. Phishing often involves fraudulent emails, messages, or websites that mimic legitimate entities.
- **Data Breaches:** These occur when sensitive or confidential information is accessed or disclosed

without authorization. This can happen through hacking, insider threats, or accidental exposure.

- **Identity Theft:** This involves stealing someone's personal information (like their Social Security number, bank account details, or credit card numbers) to commit fraud or other crimes in their name.
- **Cyberstalking and Harassment:** Using electronic communication to harass, threaten, or intimidate someone. This can include sending abusive messages, spreading rumors online, or monitoring someone's online activities without their consent.
- **Denial-of-Service (DoS) and Distributed Denial-of-Service (DDoS) Attacks:** These attacks aim to disrupt the normal functioning of a website or online service by overwhelming it with a flood of traffic from a single source (DoS) or multiple sources (DDoS).
- **Financial Fraud:** This includes a range of activities like online banking fraud, credit card fraud, investment scams, and e-commerce fraud.
- **Intellectual Property Theft and Piracy:** Illegally copying, distributing, or using copyrighted material, software, or other forms of intellectual property.
- **Cyber Espionage:** Nation-states or organizations may engage in cyber espionage to gain unauthorized access to sensitive information from other governments or companies for strategic or economic advantage.
- **Cryptojacking:** Secretly using someone else's computing resources to mine cryptocurrency without their knowledge or consent.

Causes of Cybercrime

- Lack of digital literacy and awareness
- Inadequate cybersecurity measures
- Accessibility of hacking tools and dark web markets
- Financial gain or political motives
- Weak law enforcement in cyberspace

Impacts of Cybercrime

- Financial Loss – Victims may lose money, suffer business losses, or incur costs to recover data.
- Loss of Privacy – Personal or sensitive information may be exposed or misused.
- Reputation Damage – A company's or individual's image can be harmed by online attacks or data leaks.
- Emotional Distress – Victims may suffer anxiety, fear, or mental trauma.
- National Security Risks – Cyberattacks on defence, banking, or infrastructure can threaten national safety.

NETIQUETTES

Netiquette is a blend of the words "network" and "etiquette". It refers to the rules and guidelines for appropriate and respectful behavior when communicating online. Just like social etiquette governs behavior in real life, netiquette ensures that interactions in the digital world are civil, polite, and productive.

Importance of Netiquette

- **Promotes Respectful Communication:** Encourages users to treat others kindly and consider different viewpoints.
- **Prevents Misunderstandings:** Clear and respectful communication reduces conflict and confusion in digital conversations.
- **Builds a Positive Online Environment:** Helps maintain a supportive and inclusive digital community.
- **Protects Privacy and Security:** Educates users on safe online behaviour and respecting personal boundaries.
- **Enhances Professionalism:** Especially important in emails, virtual meetings, and online classrooms.

Key Principles of Netiquette

- **Think Before You Post:** Always pause before posting, commenting, or sharing content. Ensure your words are not offensive, misleading, or hurtful. Once posted online, content can be hard to erase.
- **Be Respectful and Courteous:** Treat others the way you want to be treated. Avoid using harsh language, sarcasm, or insults—even in disagreement.
- **Use Proper Language and Grammar:** Using clear, professional language helps avoid misunderstandings. Avoid excessive slang, ALL CAPS (which is considered shouting), and unnecessary emojis in formal settings.
- **Respect Others' Privacy:** Do not share someone else's personal information, photos, or conversations without permission. Always ask before tagging people or sharing content involving them.

- **Avoid Spamming and Trolling:** Do not post irrelevant or repetitive content in forums, chats, or comment sections. Avoid provoking others intentionally or starting arguments.
- **Give Credit Where It's Due:** Always acknowledge sources when sharing articles, images, or ideas that are not your own. Plagiarism is unethical, even online.
- **Stay On Topic:** In discussions or forums, keep your comments relevant to the subject being discussed. This keeps conversations productive and focused.
- **Be Mindful of Tone:** Written text lacks tone and facial expressions, so choose your words carefully to avoid sounding rude or aggressive. Use punctuation to add clarity.
- **Be Inclusive and Avoid Discrimination:** Avoid posting or supporting content that is racist, sexist, homophobic, or discriminatory in any way. Support diversity and inclusivity.
- **Follow Platform Rules and Guidelines:** Every website or platform has its own rules. Read and follow these to ensure you are using the space appropriately.

MULTIPLE CHOICE QUESTIONS

1. Match the following:

(*a*) Twitter	1. Mark Zuckerberg
(*b*) Facebook	2. Dick Costolo
(*c*) LinkedIn	3. Jeff Weiner
(*d*) Google	4. Larry Page

A. (*a*)-1, (*b*)-4, (*c*)-2, (*d*)-3
B. (*a*)-4, (*b*)-2, (*c*)-3, (*d*)-1
C. (*a*)-2, (*b*)-1, (*c*)-3, (*d*)-4
D. (*a*)-4, (*b*)-1, (*c*)-3, (*d*)-2

2. Popular social network(s) for news are:
A. Facebook B. Twitter
C. Instagram D. All of these

3. Which of the following is NOT a Social Media Platform?
A. Facebook B. Twitter
C. Instagram D. Google

4. In ...., we create our online communication sites through which we can share information, images, ideas, audio and video files, as well as other content with our friends, family members, and business partners.
A. Search Engines B. Social Media
C. Google Images D. Google Search

5. What is the name of the parent company of Facebook and Instagram?
A. Meta Platforms, Inc.
B. Amazon
C. Google
D. Microsoft

6. .... content through social media (videos and written text) allows us to disseminate information.
A. Networking B. Publishing
C. Marketing D. Advertising

7. What is the primary purpose of hashtags in social media?
A. To mark keywords or topics for easy searchability.
B. To indicate sarcasm or irony in a post.
C. To identify the author of a post.
D. To categorize posts based on their sentiment.

8. Which of the following social media platforms is best suited for professional networking and job hunting?
A. Instagram B. Facebook
C. LinkedIn D. Snapchat

9. YouTube was launched in which year?
A. 1980 B. 1993
C. 2001 D. 2005

10. What is Social Media Marketing (SMM)?
A. Only about sharing photos
B. Promoting products and services using social media platforms
C. Only focusing on email marketing
D. Creating blogs on websites

11. Why is Social Media Marketing important for businesses?
A. To create long PDFs
B. To avoid traditional advertising
C. To replace email marketing entirely
D. To build brand awareness and engage with customers

12. Which social media platform is often the first choice for B2B companies to connect with professionals?
A. Instagram
B. TikTok
C. LinkedIn
D. Snapchat

13. What does the term 'Call to Action' (CTA) mean in social media marketing?
A. A button that tracks video views
B. A feature that redirects users to product pages or signup links
C. A tool to analyse video quality
D. A button to create graphics

14. What is User-Generated Content (UGC), and why is it valuable in social media marketing?
A. Content created by social media influencers
B. Content made by brands
C. Content shared by social media users themselves
D. Only blog posts from experts

15. Social Media Marketing helps improve –
A. Brand Awareness B. Product Visibility
C. Both A and B D. None of these

16. What is the primary purpose of social media platforms?
A. Providing weather updates
B. Facilitating online shopping
C. Connecting people and fostering communication
D. Providing medical advice

17. Which of the following is a Social Media Classification tool?
A. Social Publishing
B. Social Networking
C. Photo-based Social Networking
D. All the above

18. Which social media tool or feature is ideal for quick interactions and short-lived engagement?
A. LinkedIn Groups B. Instagram Stories
C. Pinterest Boards D. Facebook Newsfeed

19. What is Social Listening, and how does it help brands?
A. Sending promotional emails
B. Monitoring online interactions to gather insights about brand sentiment
C. Creating product catalogues
D. Ignoring customer engagement

20. What are Social Media Campaigns, and how do they work?
A. Randomly posting content without a strategy
B. Strategic, planned initiatives with specific goals and outcomes
C. Only creating product advertisements
D. Ignoring follower engagement

21. What key metric indicates the effectiveness of your social media strategy?
A. Reach
B. Engagement Rate
C. Click-Through Rate (CTR)
D. All of the mentioned

22. What is "Social Media Advertising"?
A. Free organic posts
B. Only for sharing company news
C. Promoted or sponsored content on social platforms
D. Creating long blogs

23. What does ROI (Return on Investment) mean in social media marketing terms?
A. Number of followers
B. Total likes on a post
C. Money invested compared to revenue generated
D. Length of video content

24. What is A/B testing in social media advertising?
A. Posting content at random
B. Running two variations of an ad to see which one performs better
C. Ignoring follower comments
D. Using only Instagram influencers

25. Why is 'content diversification' important in social media marketing?
A. To focus only on one type of content
B. To provide a variety of content types to engage a wider audience
C. To reduce the overall quality of content
D. To complicate the content strategy

26. What does the term "Virality" mean in social media marketing?
A. Deleting content after low engagement
B. Posting less frequently
C. Creating irrelevant content
D. Sharing content that goes viral and spreads quickly online

27. What is the benefit of 'live streaming' on social media for brands?
A. To avoid real-time interaction
B. To provide a more authentic and interactive experience
C. To solely focus on recorded content
D. To reduce audience reach

28. What is Social Proof in Social Media Marketing?
A. Content only created by influencers
B. Testimonials, reviews, and interactions showing brand trust
C. Long-form written content
D. Posting content without interaction

29. Why is Social Media Marketing necessary?
A. Business growth can be achieved through cost-effective techniques.
B. Our search engine rankings are improved as a result of it.
C. We can enhance the authority of our brands with it.
D. All the above

30. User interface has become a critical issue with digital media and the Internet because
A. Digital media is very new and has not had the time to evolve.
B. Rapid advances in technology radically alter any user-interface assumptions that are made.
C. Varying computer standards mean not all technology is accepted.
D. All the above

31. Posting deliberately obnoxious or provocative messages in online discussion groups is known as
A. Phishing B. Trolling
C. Sock-puppeting D. Spamming

32. What is the primary goal of influencer marketing?
A. Collaborating with individuals with a large social media following
B. Avoiding social media entirely
C. Selling products only through traditional channels
D. Focusing solely on television ads

33. What is a sponsored post in influencer marketing?
A. A link to a news article
B. A post where influencers promote a product in exchange for payment
C. A personal diary entry by the influencer
D. A social media account introduction

34. Why do brands work with micro-influencers instead of celebrities with millions of followers?
A. No interaction with followers
B. Higher costs of celebrity marketing
C. Poor social media presence of celebrities
D. More genuine engagement with niche audiences

35. What is a 'Profile Picture' used for in social media marketing?
A. To display a random image
B. To identify and differentiate profiles
C. To track user location
D. To measure website traffic

36. What is an influencer's primary responsibility in an influencer marketing campaign?
A. Neglect social media trends
B. Create and share content promoting a brand's products or services
C. Create traditional advertisements
D. Focus solely on press releases

37. What is the role of a Brand Ambassador in influencer marketing?
A. A person solely focused on radio promotions
B. Someone representing a brand long-term
C. A content writer for blogs
D. A traditional newspaper spokesperson

38. Why do brands use influencer marketing campaigns on multiple social media platforms?
A. To avoid traditional email marketing
B. To eliminate the need for professional advertisements
C. To reduce the overall campaign costs
D. To maximize reach and engagement across diverse audiences

39. Through the creation of various types of content (videos, blogs, infographics, etc.), ………… helps promote our business, increase traffic to our website, customer engagement, and brand awareness. Share photos using social networking sites using Facebook, Instagram, Twitter, LinkedIn, etc.
A. Social Publishing
B. Social Networking
C. Social Media Marketing
D. Photo-based Social Networking

40. What is a major benefit of working with influencers for brand promotion?
A. Higher costs with guaranteed returns
B. Complete reliance on traditional media
C. Instant sales results
D. Increased brand visibility and consumer trust

41. What is "Cross-Promotion" in influencer marketing?
A. Creating a single post for multiple platforms
B. Influencers sharing content across various social media channels
C. Hiring influencers only for offline promotions
D. Using only radio and print media

42. What is the term for partnering with influencers who have a highly niche but dedicated audience?
A. Nano Engagement
B. Mass Influencing
C. Niche Influencer Marketing
D. Micro-targeting

43. What is the primary challenge brands face when collaborating with influencers?
A. Ineffective radio campaigns
B. High printing costs
C. Lack of email subscribers
D. Inconsistent influencer content quality and trust issues

44. Why do influencers often collaborate with affiliate marketing programs?
A. To ignore social media engagement
B. To conduct offline promotions
C. To earn commissions on product sales through affiliate links
D. To make online calls

45. What is the primary reason brands use social media influencers over traditional advertising channels?
A. Fewer opportunities for creativity
B. Higher cost
C. Lack of measurable results
D. Faster reach and engagement with targeted audiences

46. Which platform is most commonly used by affiliates to promote products?
A. Facebook B. Twitter
C. YouTube D. All of the mentioned

47. What is Instagram primarily known for?
A. Text-heavy blogging
B. Video conferencing
C. Visual content sharing (photos and videos)
D. Only audio updates

48. What feature on Instagram is most helpful for e-commerce brands to sell their products directly?
A. Instagram Reels
B. IGTV
C. Instagram Shopping
D. Instagram Bio

49. How does Instagram Stories help in engaging followers?
A. By sharing long-form PDFs
B. By posting text-heavy updates
C. By creating temporary, interactive content
D. By blocking audience interactions

50. What is the purpose of Instagram Reels in marketing?
A. To share audio-only podcasts
B. To create short and entertaining videos
C. To conduct long webinars
D. To write product descriptions

51. What insights can Instagram Analytics provide to marketers?
A. Only the number of likes
B. Information about followers, engagement, and demographics
C. Personal contact details of followers
D. Random snapshots of Instagram trends

52. How does Instagram Paid Promotion help in reaching your target audience?
A. It discourages brand interactions
B. It allows for precise targeting and engagement through Ads Manager
C. It only focuses on influencers' content
D. It ignores the importance of visual storytelling

53. How do hashtags help in growing an Instagram account?
A. They delete irrelevant photos
B. They organize content and make it discoverable
C. They reduce follower engagement
D. They prevent tagging of other accounts

54. Which of these is the main benefit of affiliate marketing for businesses?
A. Pay-for-performance model
B. Increased upfront costs
C. Higher product prices
D. Less customer interaction

55. Which platform is famous for short, looped video content and viral trends?
A. Facebook B. LinkedIn
C. TikTok D. Medium

56. What does CPA stand for in affiliate marketing terms?
A. Content Promotion Agreement
B. Cost Per Action
C. Central Partner Association
D. Customer Purchase Agreement

57. What is Affiliate Marketing?
A. A traditional offline retail business model
B. A direct email campaign strategy
C. A method of inventory storage
D. A partnership where individuals promote products and earn a commission

58. What does the term 'Pay Per Click' (PPC) mean in affiliate marketing?
A. Affiliates get paid for each ad click
B. None of the mentioned
C. Affiliates get a commission for website traffic
D. Affiliates get paid for each purchase

59. Reddit is best described as a:
A. Microblogging site
B. Content aggregator and discussion platform
C. Video streaming site
D. Professional forum

60. WhatsApp is primarily used for:
A. Blogging B. Messaging and calling
C. Job applications D. Video production

61. Why do brands prefer working with multiple affiliates instead of a single one?
A. Making contracts less formal
B. Avoiding content creation altogether
C. Higher costs with a single partnership
D. Diversifying traffic sources and boosting reach

62. Which of the following platforms is ideal for creating and maintaining personal blogs?
A. Twitter B. Medium
C. YouTube D. Pinterest

63. Which action is considered a conversion in affiliate marketing?
A. A sale, signup, or product download
B. Following a brand's Instagram account
C. Clicking on an affiliate link
D. A user liking a social media post

64. What is Facebook Marketing?
A. Only sharing photos and videos
B. Promoting brands and businesses through Facebook platforms
C. Sending personal messages only
D. Posting comments on other users' profiles

65. What is the main purpose of Facebook Ads Manager?
A. Creating personal stories
B. Managing and optimizing ad campaigns
C. Sending automated messages
D. Posting memes and photos

66. Which Facebook campaign objective should you choose to drive traffic to your website?
A. Lead Generation
B. Engagement
C. Brand Awareness
D. Traffic

67. Why do marketers use Facebook Groups as part of their strategy?
A. Only for personal chatting
B. Building a community and driving engagement
C. Sending random friend requests
D. Posting automated text links

68. What is CPM (Cost Per Mille) in Facebook Ads?
A. Cost for 100 impressions
B. Cost of buying new followers
C. Cost for 1000 impressions
D. Cost for email subscriptions

69. Which tool consolidates all Facebook business assets, users, and permissions in one place?
A. Instagram Creator Studio
B. Business Suite
C. Video Ad Creator
D. Content Scheduler

70. Why is engagement important in a Facebook ad campaign?
A. Increases 'likes' on a personal post
B. Encourages shares, comments, and overall interaction
C. Hides company links
D. Prevents ad tracking

71. How do marketers use the term ROI (Return on Investment) in Facebook campaigns?
A. Cost of sending friend requests
B. Profit earned from ad expenses
C. Engagement rates only
D. Number of video shares

72. Clubhouse is a platform focused on:
A. Text chats
B. Audio conversations
C. Video reels
D. Status updates

73. What is the primary benefit of using hashtags in Twitter marketing?
A. Boost visibility and engagement of tweets
B. Increase character count
C. Reduce ad costs
D. Automatically tag influencers

74. Which type of ad campaign is designed to increase followers on Twitter?
A. Follower campaign
B. Video views
C. Engagement campaign
D. App installs

75. What makes Twitter a microblogging site?
A. Use of videos
B. Limited character posts
C. Only audio posts
D. Paid subscriptions

76. What does the blue checkmark next to a Twitter account indicate?
A. The account is verified
B. The account has over 10,000 followers
C. The account is active
D. The account has high engagement

77. What is the term for targeting specific users with promoted tweets based on their interests?
A. Hashtag targeting
B. Behaviour targeting
C. Interest targeting
D. Contextual targeting

78. Which metric measures the number of times users interact with a tweet?
A. Retweets
B. Engagement
C. Click-through rate
D. Impressions

79. What is the main benefit of using Twitter Analytics?
A. Tracking audience engagement and performance metrics
B. Scheduling tweets
C. Automatic content creation
D. Gaining more followers

80. How can you track the effectiveness of your Twitter ad campaigns?
A. By checking the number of likes on tweets
B. Counting the followers gained during the campaign
C. Using Twitter Analytics and campaign metrics
D. Manually reviewing replies and retweets

81. Which of these is considered a best practice for engaging tweets?
A. Avoid questions in tweets
B. Use trending hashtags and visuals
C. Always schedule tweets at night
D. Post tweets without visuals

82. What is a Twitter Poll used for?
A. Increasing ad conversions
B. Measuring tweet impressions
C. Conducting surveys and gaining audience insights
D. Promoting sponsored content

83. What does "Impressions" mean in Twitter Analytics?
A. The number of hashtags used
B. The number of retweets a post gets
C. The number of times a tweet is seen
D. The number of followers gained

84. Tumblr combines blogging with:
A. Live streaming
B. Audio forums
C. Social networking features
D. Online courses

85. Which of these platforms is mostly used for live game streaming?
A. YouTube B. Instagram
C. Twitch D. Reddit

86. Telegram is known for its:
A. Video content
B. Public channels and secret chats
C. Job recommendations
D. Short dance videos

87. What type of platform is Discord?
A. Podcast publishing
B. Messaging and community platform
C. Blogging platform
D. Music sharing site

88. Which platform is often used to showcase professional portfolios, especially by designers?
A. Dribbble B. WhatsApp
C. Clubhouse D. Telegram

89. Which of the following platforms is used to publish long-form writing and articles?
A. Twitter B. Snapchat
C. Medium D. Instagram

90. What is LinkedIn mainly designed for?
A. Music streaming
B. Photo sharing
C. Video sharing
D. Social networking and job searching

91. What is a LinkedIn Company Page used for?
A. Posting short videos
B. Uploading personal photos
C. Showcasing a brand's products and services
D. Sharing personal updates

92. What are LinkedIn InMail messages used for?
A. Advertising services
B. Sending emails outside LinkedIn
C. Creating job listings
D. Communicating directly with prospects and clients

93. What is the main objective of LinkedIn Sponsored Content?
A. To create long-form blog content
B. To create memes
C. To drive traffic to your website and promote events
D. To share personal stories

94. Which type of content is best suited for LinkedIn posts?
A. Personal selfies
B. Memes and entertainment videos
C. Professional insights, news, and articles
D. Short TikTok-style clips

95. How does LinkedIn Pulse benefit marketers and professionals?
A. It allows short video uploads
B. It provides a platform for sharing personal updates
C. It enables sharing long-form content and thought leadership articles
D. It removes spelling errors in text

96. Why do marketers prefer LinkedIn for B2B marketing efforts?
A. It's better suited for casual personal sharing
B. It maintains a professional environment ideal for B2B interactions
C. It's primarily entertainment-focused
D. It encourages spam interactions

97. How do LinkedIn Events help businesses with marketing and engagement?
A. By providing free music and entertainment videos
B. Through short video campaigns
C. By hosting webinars, product launches, and professional networking events
D. By automatically curating content

98. Why is LinkedIn considered an essential tool for job seekers?
A. It focuses on sports news
B. It only shares memes
C. It provides job listings and networking opportunities
D. It's only about entertainment

99. What is Content Scheduling, and why is it useful in social media marketing?
A. Only creating video content
B. Posting everything at random times
C. Planning and scheduling posts in advance across various platforms
D. Ignoring brand storytelling

100. Why do businesses prefer using Instagram for visual marketing?
A. The platform only supports text posts
B. No video integration features
C. It has limited photo upload options
D. Instagram is known for high interaction rates with visual content

101. What is an ethical approach to email marketing?
A. Sending unsolicited emails to random users
B. Ignoring GDPR compliance
C. Providing a clear unsubscribe option and obtaining user consent
D. Spamming all website visitors

102. What is Cross-Promotion in social media marketing?
A. Ignoring social media analytics
B. Ignoring brand consistency
C. Avoiding customer interactions
D. Promoting content across multiple social media channels simultaneously

103. Which Facebook campaign objective is best for collecting contact information of potential clients?
A. Engagement
B. Brand Awareness
C. Lead Generation
D. Video Views

104. What is the benefit of receiving positive reviews on platforms like Google?
A. They improve website security
B. They increase domain authority
C. They reduce the website loading time
D. They help rank your business higher in local search results

105. Social media is considered part of new media because:
A. It is broadcast-only
B. It is controlled by government
C. It allows user-generated content
D. It is only available in newspapers

106. Streaming platforms like YouTube and Netflix represent:
A. Print-only media
B. Passive viewing
C. Converged digital media
D. Single-format content

107. Online platforms that allow individuals to share their thoughts, opinions, and creations are examples of:
A. Media monopolies
B. Participatory media
C. Legacy media
D. Corporate media

108. When a podcast episode is transcribed and shared as a blog post, this is an example of:
A. Media redundancy
B. Content repurposing across media
C. Decreased audience engagement
D. Limited information reach

109. Live streaming of news on TV and simultaneously on YouTube is an example of:
A. Content duplication
B. Cross-platform broadcasting
C. Isolation broadcasting
D. Asynchronous content

110. The spread of memes across platforms is a form of:
A. Formal communication
B. Corporate media
C. Participatory culture
D. Institutional content

111. A tweet linking to a blog shows:
A. Independent media use
B. Hyperlink convergence
C. Static linking
D. Content lock

112. Social networks are organized primarily around ....
A. People B. Forums
C. Discussions D. Interests

113. What is the name for Face book's ranking algorithm?
A. Face Rank B. Mock Rank
C. Page Rank D. Edge Rank

114. Which of the following is example of micro blogging?
A. Google+ B. Facebook
C. Twitter (now X) D. Instagram

115. .... is a major issue connecting to social media
A. Privacy and Security
B. Internet addiction
C. Digital Plagiarism
D. All the above

116. Facebook was founded in the year:
A. 2002 B. 2003
C. 2004 D. 2005

117. Facebook was founded by:
A. Jack Dorsey B. Noah Glass
C. Biz Stone D. Mark Zuckerberg

118. Twitter was founded in the year:
A. 2004 B. 2005
C. 2006 D. 2007

119. The small messages that can be read and written on Twitter are known as:
A. Tweeks B. Tweezers
C. Tweets D. TwitThis

120. Using Twitter has the disadvantage of limiting messages to .... characters.
A. 120 B. 240
C. 140 D. 280

121. LinkedIn was founded in the year:
A. 2001 B. 2002
C. 2003 D. 2004

122. Pinterest was founded in the year:
A. 2007 B. 2008
C. 2009 D. 2010

123. Which of the following is an image-pinning website?
A. Twitter B. Instagram
C. Pinterest D. Snapchat

124. Which of the following is/are the advantage(s) of using Pinterest?
A. Brand awareness and website traffic are its two main purposes of it.
B. A visually appealing business profile and news can be created by using its user-friendly platform.
C. Our website gets more traffic at a low cost through its visually rich social network.
D. All the above

125. A pin is an idea users .... on Pinterest.
A. Create B. Find
C. Save D. All the above

126. YouTube was created in the year:
A. 2004 B. 2005
C. 2006 D. 2007

127. Which of the following is a free video-sharing platform created in the year 2005?
A. Instagram B. Facebook
C. YouTube D. LinkedIn

128. Video series, ... are the main YouTube content types.
A. Podcasts B. Infographics
C. Presentations D. All the above

129. Which of the following is the second largest search engine?
A. YouTube B. Google
C. Yahoo D. None of these

130. Which of the following is/are the advantage(s) of using YouTube?
A. New technologies can be learned easily and quickly through it.
B. Products are promoted and sold worldwide as a result of it.
C. Traffic from qualified sources can be acquired for free through this service.
D. All the above

131. ………… combine on YouTube.
A. Content marketing
B. Social Media Marketing
C. Both A and B
D. None of these

132. A notable feature of ………… is the disappearance of messages and content.
A. Facebook B. YouTube
C. Snapchat D. None of these

133. Through their Facebook page, ………… introduced a strategy that allows consumers to suggest new variants of their existing products, so customers are not only able to enjoy click-ins and photographs from marketers, but can also interact with Facebook users in real-time.
A. Starbucks B. TikTok
C. Instagram D. Snapchat

134. TikTok was launched in the year –
A. 2017 B. 2018
C. 2019 D. 2020

135. Which of the following strategies does not come in Social Media Management?
A. Set the goal
B. Know nothing about your targeted audience
C. Research the competition
D. Set brand guidelines

136. Which of the following is/are a/the type(s) of ad that could be run on SM?
A. Storewide discounts
B. New product promotions
C. New customer deals
D. All the above

137. By automating several tasks across social networks, which of the following SMM tools makes our business processes more efficient?
A. PostPlanner B. Agorapulse
C. Chattypeople D. SocialOomph

138. Facebook updates are scheduled with ………… , which increases customer engagement.
A. Chattypeople B. SocialOomph
C. PostPlanner D. Agorapulse

139. Which of the following feature(s) is/are available in Agorapulse?
A. Social Media inbox
B. Publishing and scheduling
C. Monitoring
D. All the above

140. Which of the following is compatible with Messenger?
A. Chattypeople B. SocialOomph
C. PostPlanner D. Agorapulse

141. Global movements like #MeToo spread rapidly due to:
A. Local campaigns
B. Newspaper circulation
C. Social media platforms
D. Private letters

142. Which tool allows instant feedback to events?
A. Printed letters
B. Online comment sections
C. TV reporting
D. Posters

143. Online forums and social media allow:
A. Passive audiences
B. Delayed reactions
C. Immediate public opinion sharing
D. Government-only views

144. What feature of social media supports rapid opinion formation?
A. Paid subscriptions
B. Upvote/downvote systems
C. Fax machines
D. Offline conversations

145. Which event showed massive public opinion through hashtags?
A. Radio launches
B. Independence Day parades
C. Arab Spring
D. Olympic Games

146. Opinion leaders on social media can influence:
A. Only their locality
B. Only newspapers
C. Large-scale public discourse
D. Archived media only

147. Which app is known for real-time public discussion?
A. Photoshop B. Telegram
C. Twitter/X D. Excel

148. Social media can be used by governments to:
A. Ignore public B. Spread propaganda
C. Avoid elections D. Stop elections

149. Which Social Media Platform introduced the concept of "Fleets", similar to Instagram stories and Snapchat snaps?
A. TikTok B. LinkedIn
C. Naukri D. X (Twitter)

150. What is the length of the videos uploaded on Facebook?
A. 30 sec B. 90 sec
C. 120 sec D. 240 sec

151. What does a verified account indicate on social media platforms like Twitter and Instagram?
A. The account belongs to a public figure or organization and is authenticated
B. The account has a high number of followers
C. The account is used for advertising
D. The account is frequently used

152. Consider the following statements:
1. Social media is useless for professionals.
2. LinkedIn Profile can only be maintained by professionals.
3. Students Should not create LinkedIn Profile.
A. Only 1 is correct B. Only 2 is correct
C. All are correct D. All are incorrect

153. Which one Generally DOES NOT consider itself as a social media platform?
A. Facebook B. Twitter
C. LinkedIn D. Wikipedia

154. Which of the following in communication of internet is a process of transferring real-time messages between users that facilitates private chat room atmosphere?
A. Collaboration B. Remote access
C. File sharing D. Instant messaging

155. Which of the following is the parent company of Instagram?
A. Google B. Android
C. Meta D. Microsoft

156. The internet service that provides 'audio' and 'video' conversations is called:
A. Chat
B. E-mail
C. Video Conferencing
D. Voice Call

157. In the world of Facebook and Twitter, ESN stand for ....
A. Enterprise Social Networking
B. Entrepreneur Special Networking
C. Enterprise Special Networking
D. Essential Social Networking

158. Which of the following is NOT an instant messaging software?
A. Twitter B. Signal
C. Telegram D. WhatsApp

159. Which of the following is NOT an example of a voice chat system?
A. Google Meet B. Zoom
C. Facebook D. Apple Facetime

160. Tapping or clicking on the smiley face icon along the bottom of the screen in Facebook Messenger is used to ....
A. Send a quick like
B. Send photos
C. Send stickers
D. Send videos

161. .... is a person who has subscribed to an account in order to receive all updates from social media.
A. Moderator B. Follower
C. Author D. Friend

162. In social media, ... is a form of engagement in which a user replies to your social media post.
A. Likes B. Friend
C. Subscription D. Comment

163. Which among the following given below is correct in context of privacy issues in social media and online platforms?
A. The sharing on social media especially by children must be monitored at all times.
B. The addiction of social media does not hamper the academic performance of a student.
C. Rumours and fake news cannot put the administration at risk.
D. Mishandling of social media cannot create tension in the law and order.

164. Most blogs contain short, informal articles called ....
A. Blog reels B. Blog posts
C. Blog column D. Blog shots

165. The company Meta Inc. owns
A. Facebook, LinkedIn, YouTube
B. Facebook, WhatsApp, Instagram
C. Facebook, LinkedIn, Instagram
D. YouTube, WhatsApp, Instagram

166. A cookie is a file on the user's browser that uniquely identifies ....
A. the advertiser B. the buyer
C. the seller D. the user

167. Cyber consumers are not ....
A. heterogeneous B. segmented
C. mass D. homogeneous

168. What is the term for a social media post that goes viral, being widely shared and discussed?

A. Trending B. Overheating
C. Memorable D. Popularizing

169. Social media allows users to share which types of content?

A. Text, images, videos, and live streams
B. Songs and movies only
C. Physical products for sale
D. Personal identification information

170. How do businesses and organizations use social media?

A. For offline marketing only
B. For increasing shipping costs
C. For connecting with their target audience, marketing, and customer service
D. For promoting social isolation

171. Which of the following term is associated with Internet/e-Mail?

A. Plotter B. Slide presentation
C. Bookmark D. Pie chart

172. In the context of social media, what does the term "engagement" refer to?

A. The number of followers a user has
B. Interactions such as likes, comments, shares, and retweets on posts
C. The amount of time spent online
D. The number of posts made regularly

173. What is a challenge associated with social media?

A. Lack of internet connection globally
B. Increased privacy protection
C. Cyberbullying and misinformation
D. Reduced usage of smartphones

174. How does social media transcend geographical boundaries?

A. By providing free internet access globally
B. By allowing users to communicate in different languages
C. By enabling users from different locations to connect and interact virtually
D. By displaying satellite images of the Earth

175. Social media has become a catalyst for what types of change?

A. Political and economic change
B. Social and cultural change
C. Medical breakthroughs
D. Technological advancements

176. What is cybercrime?

A. Crime involving chemicals
B. Crime that occurs in cyberspace using computers
C. Physical theft
D. None of these

177. Which of the following is an example of cyber bullying?

A. Posting positive comments
B. Sending anonymous threats online
C. Creating educational content
D. Watching YouTube videos

178. Online stalking involves:

A. Physical surveillance
B. Repeated unwanted attention through the internet
C. Door-to-door visits
D. None of these

179. Trolling is defined as:

A. Fishing on the internet
B. Posting inflammatory content to provoke people
C. Sharing news updates
D. Cyber security

180. Which of the following is a form of online fraud?

A. Phishing
B. Reading emails
C. Downloading songs
D. Watching movies

181. Which law in India governs cybercrimes?

A. IT Act, 2000
B. Penal Code Act
C. Data Usage Act
D. Digital Law 1995

182. Phishing is aimed at stealing:

A. Identity B. Cars
C. Pets D. Furniture

183. Which government body deals with cyber security in India?

A. TRAI B. CERT-In
C. CBSE D. UIDAI

184. Which is a common platform for cyber bullying?

A. Email B. Social media
C. Forums D. All the above

185. Cyber stalking can result in:

A. Emotional trauma
B. Identity theft
C. Fear of being watched
D. All the above

186. Sending fake emails to extract personal info is known as:
A. Trolling B. Cyberbullying
C. Phishing D. Stalking

187. Cyber defamation is:
A. Hacking into someone's account
B. Stealing personal data
C. Posting false information to harm reputation
D. Spreading malware

188. Which of these is a type of cybercrime?
A. Vandalism B. Identity theft
C. Trespassing D. Assault

189. Trolling on the internet is usually done to:
A. Educate people
B. Provide helpful information
C. Provoke emotional responses
D. Facilitate constructive discussions

190. Which of the following is ***not*** a cybercrime?
A. Physical theft B. Hacking
C. Online fraud D. Cyber stalking

191. Which Act includes provisions for punishment for cyber bullying in India?
A. Indian Penal Code (IPC)
B. Consumer Protection Act
C. IT Act, 2000
D. Companies Act

192. Online frauds can include:
A. Credit card fraud B. Lottery scams
C. Phishing D. All the above

193. A cyber-criminal may use:
A. Malware
B. Emails
C. Social engineering
D. All the above

194. Online impersonation is a form of:
A. Hacking B. Identity theft
C. Trolling D. Cyberbullying

195. The punishment for cyber stalking under IPC is:
A. Fine only
B. Imprisonment up to 1 year
C. Imprisonment up to 3 years
D. Life imprisonment

196. What does 'DoS attack' stand for?
A. Denial of Service
B. Data Over System
C. Digital Operating System
D. Direct Online Security

197. A keylogger is a type of:
A. Firewall B. Spyware
C. Antivirus D. Adware

198. Cyber extortion typically involves:
A. Stealing personal information
B. Damaging computer hardware
C. Demanding money to prevent data leak
D. Sending spam emails

199. Online scams promising prizes are:
A. Lottery frauds
B. Phishing attacks
C. Malware distribution
D. Denial-of-service attacks

200. Sextortion is:
A. Hacking social media accounts
B. Distributing viruses
C. Identity theft
D. Blackmail using intimate content

201. Which law punishes cyber terrorism in India?
A. Indian Penal Code (IPC)
B. Information Technology Act, 2008
C. Section 66F of IT Act
D. Cyber Security Act

202. Cyber grooming refers to:
A. Befriending minors for exploitation
B. Stealing online passwords
C. Spreading false rumours online
D. Online harassment

203. Using someone's photo without consent online is:
A. Defamation B. Privacy invasion
C. Stalking D. Trolling

204. Data breach refers to:
A. Loss of computer hardware
B. Damage to software
C. Unauthorized access to data
D. Website malfunction

205. What is the penalty for identity theft under the IT Act?
A. Fine only
B. 3 years imprisonment and fine
C. 5 years imprisonment
D. Life imprisonment

206. Which of the following can be used to report cybercrimes in India?
A. reportcybercrime.in
B. https://www.google.com/search?q= indiancybercrime.com

C. cybercrimehelpline.org
D. cybercrime.gov.in

207. Cyber trolls are often:
A. Identified individuals
B. Government officials
C. Anonymous users
D. Corporate entities

208. What is cyber forensics?
A. Investigation of digital crimes
B. Prevention of cyber attacks
C. Development of cybersecurity software
D. Ethical hacking practices

209. Spoofing is:
A. Stealing data online
B. Distributing malware
C. Pretending to be someone else online
D. Launching DDoS attacks

210. Which type of cybercrime involves ransom?
A. Phishing
B. Ransomware
C. Identity theft
D. Cyber stalking

211. Online harassment laws are covered under:
A. IT Act and IPC
B. Consumer Protection Act
C. Copyright Act
D. Data Protection Act

212. Publishing fake news online may lead to:
A. Social unrest
B. Damage to reputation
C. Legal consequences
D. All the above

213. A secure website URL begins with:
A. http://
B. https://
C. www.
D. ftp://

214. What is cyber-squatting?
A. Hacking into websites
B. Installing spyware
C. Registering domain names to resell at a higher price
D. Sending spam emails

215. India's National Cyber Crime Reporting Portal is managed by:
A. Ministry of Information and Broadcasting
B. Ministry of Electronics and Information Technology
C. Reserve Bank of India
D. Ministry of Home Affairs

216. Which of the following best describes the role of social media in a democracy?
A. Entertainment only
B. Enhancing political debates
C. Reducing public participation
D. Censoring opposition

217. Social media allows citizens to directly interact with which of the following?
A. Celebrities only
B. International agencies
C. Political leaders and institutions
D. Educational boards

218. What term is used when citizens use social media to organize protests or express dissent?
A. Cyber trolling
B. Online gaming
C. Cyber activism
D. Media manipulation

219. Which major political event was significantly influenced by Twitter and Facebook in the Arab world?
A. Brexit
B. Arab Spring
C. Vietnam War
D. Gulf War

220. Social media platforms provide ....
A. Controlled speech
B. Real-time public opinion
C. Official government announcements only
D. Political party funding

221. What is meant by 'collective identity' in the context of social media?
A. Identity theft
B. Formation of shared values and beliefs
C. Creation of fake profiles
D. Personal branding

222. Which platform is widely used to form communities with shared ideologies?
A. Instagram
B. Facebook Groups
C. Snapchat
D. Netflix

223. Hashtags on Twitter are an example of:
A. Cybercrime
B. Misinformation
C. Symbolic identity and information categorization
D. Meme culture

224. Which of the following is a known cyber activist group?
A. Instagram
B. Anonymous
C. Meta
D. LinkedIn

225. Sharing of memes and visuals related to a cause is a form of:
A. Meme trolling
B. Cyber journalism
C. Visual activism
D. E-commerce

226. Which campaign used social media to raise awareness on sexual harassment and assault?
A. Save Water B. #MeToo
C. Make in India D. Clean India

227. Which feature helps social media users to mobilize quickly for protests or campaigns?
A. Paid advertisements
B. Notifications and tagging
C. Online quizzes
D. Business analytics

228. Digital petitions are primarily shared on platforms like:
A. Snapchat B. Change.org
C. TikTok D. Spotify

229. Which Indian movement used Twitter hashtags to demand justice for a rape victim?
A. Beti Bachao
B. Justice for Nirbhaya
C. Skill India
D. Ujjwala Yojana

230. Cyber activism is effective because:
A. It is always anonymous
B. It ensures legal action
C. It helps gather support instantly
D. It increases online shopping

231. Social media is sometimes referred to as the "fifth estate" for its influence in public affairs. Which of the following is the correct term?
A. Fourth power B. Digital authority
C. Fifth estate D. Public sphere

232. Online petitions contribute to which form of democracy?
A. Representative democracy
B. Participatory democracy
C. Direct democracy
D. Liberal democracy

233. Political campaigns use social media primarily to:
A. Limit public debate
B. Control information flow
C. Reach large audiences quickly
D. Avoid media scrutiny

234. Youth-driven political engagement on Instagram is an example of:
A. Traditional activism
B. Digital civic participation
C. Apathy among young voters
D. Political polarization

235. Twitter polls are an example of:
A. Authoritarian control
B. Elite opinion
C. Censored feedback
D. Crowd-sourced opinion

236. Social media boosts freedom of expression through:
A. Censored content
B. Delayed information
C. Real-time, user-generated content
D. Limited public access

237. Online communities such as Reddit help build:
A. Social isolation
B. Political apathy
C. Collective identity
D. Cultural uniformity

238. Social media strengthens democracy by:
A. Reducing transparency
B. Increasing transparency and accountability
C. Centralizing political power
D. Limiting public discourse

239. WhatsApp groups used for awareness on voting reflect:
A. Top-down propaganda
B. Elitist mobilization
C. Controlled information dissemination
D. Grassroots mobilization

240. A challenge of using social media in activism is:
A. Lack of public engagement
B. Limited information sharing
C. Spread of misinformation
D. Reduced political participation

241. Which of the following is an example of online activism?
A. Watching television news
B. Reading a newspaper editorial
C. Signing a digital petition
D. Attending a traditional rally

242. Fake news on political matters undermines:
A. Public trust in social media
B. Informed public decision-making
C. Political participation
D. All the above

243. The ability to go "live" on platforms enhances:
A. Censorship
B. Controlled broadcasting
C. Direct citizen reporting
D. Limited public access

244. Sharing protest locations in real-time helps in:
A. Decreasing mobilization
B. Slow information spread
C. Centralized control
D. Rapid mobilization

245. TikTok has been used as a platform for:
A. Political satire and awareness
B. Limiting political discourse
C. Censoring political views
D. Discouraging youth engagement

246. Social media echo chambers result in:
A. Balanced viewpoints
B. Diverse opinions
C. Reinforced biased opinions
D. Objective analysis

247. "Twitter diplomacy" refers to:
A. International treaties signed on Twitter
B. Public debates among citizens on Twitter
C. Government censorship of Twitter
D. Government-to-public communication via Twitter

248. The Arab Spring is an example of:
A. Decline in social media influence
B. Social media-enabled uprising
C. Government control of social media
D. Reduced political engagement

249. Troll armies on social media can:
A. Promote civil discourse
B. Encourage respectful debate
C. Foster online harmony
D. Intimidate opposition voices

250. Anonymous blogging helps in:
A. Spreading misinformation
B. Centralized control of information
C. Whistleblowing
D. Reduced accountability

251. #BlackLivesMatter began as a:
A. Political party
B. Hashtag movement for racial justice
C. Government initiative
D. Media campaign

252. Which of these supports building online identities?
A. Profile creation and bio customization
B. Censoring user information
C. Restricting user interaction
D. Enforcing anonymity

253. Activists use Instagram stories to:
A. Limit public awareness
B. Share brief updates and calls to action
C. Control information flow
D. Avoid audience engagement

254. Sharing of news and personal opinions creates:
A. A passive media environment
B. A controlled media system
C. Participatory media culture
D. A uniform information landscape

255. Real-time updates during elections on social media help:
A. Obscure public opinion
B. Delay information dissemination
C. Limit voter turnout
D. Track public sentiment

256. What does "netiquette" stand for?
A. Network etiquette
B. Internet license
C. Cyber passport
D. Communication protocol

257. Why are netiquettes important?
A. They regulate data usage
B. They ensure respectful and effective communication online
C. They enhance hardware performance
D. They boost download speed

258. Which of the following best describes netiquette?
A. Set of online marketing strategies
B. Informal rules for online behaviour
C. Software development methods
D. Legal internet policies

259. Which of these is a goal of netiquette?
A. Internet censorship
B. Online advertising
C. Promoting respectful interaction
D. Tracking online users

260. Netiquette applies to which platforms?
A. Only emails
B. Only social media
C. Only forums
D. All online communication platforms

261. Which of the following shows proper identification in emails?
A. Sending anonymous messages
B. Using real name and contact info in signature
C. Using pseudonyms
D. Skipping subject lines

262. When joining a new online forum, you should:
A. Stay anonymous
B. Use offensive usernames
C. Introduce yourself respectfully
D. Share private information

263. In professional communication, netiquette suggests using:
A. Memes
B. Formal titles and your real name
C. Fake identities
D. Slang

264. Why is it important to identify yourself online?
A. To spam users
B. To ensure transparency and trust
C. To track emails
D. To create fake profiles

265. Which is not recommended for email identification?
A. Full name
B. Email signature
C. Nicknames like "DarkKnight"
D. Contact information

266. Respecting online privacy means:
A. Sharing passwords
B. Reading others' messages
C. Not sharing someone else's info without consent
D. Saving personal data

267. Which action violates privacy online?
A. Asking permission before posting
B. Sharing private chats without consent
C. Sending direct messages
D. Using strong passwords

268. A good netiquette example regarding privacy:
A. Tagging people in posts without asking
B. Publishing someone's photo without permission
C. Asking before sharing others' content
D. Sharing all private conversations

269. What should you do if someone shares your private content without permission?
A. Ignore it
B. Report or contact them respectfully
C. Share their info too
D. Delete your account

270. Netiquette encourages protecting whose privacy?
A. Only celebrities
B. Everyone
C. Only friends
D. Government officials

271. Online communication should be:
A. Vulgar and expressive
B. Rude to make a point
C. Polite and professional
D. Ambiguous

272. Which of the following is acceptable language online?
A. Profanity
B. Abusive language
C. Polite and clear expressions
D. Caps lock shouting

273. What is the problem with typing in ALL CAPS?
A. It improves visibility
B. It is considered shouting
C. It helps with grammar
D. It shows emphasis only

274. Netiquette suggests using appropriate imagery to:
A. Offend others
B. Communicate respectfully
C. Spread propaganda
D. Encourage spam

275. Which image is considered inappropriate online?
A. Inspirational quotes
B. Offensive memes
C. Nature photos
D. Educational infographics

276. What is spam?
A. Useful messages
B. Unwanted and repeated messages
C. Helpful advertisements
D. Security emails

277. Sending mass emails without consent is considered:
A. Marketing
B. Spam
C. Formal communication
D. Teamwork

278. Why should spam be avoided?
A. It entertains users
B. It promotes content
C. It disrupts communication and annoys users
D. It's legal everywhere

279. Which of these is NOT spam?
A. Personalized email updates
B. Unsolicited ads
C. Repetitive messages
D. Random links in comments

280. Posting the same comment repeatedly is an example of:
A. Encouragement B. Spam
C. Netiquette D. Promotion

281. You receive an offensive message. What should you do?
A. Reply with abuse
B. Ignore it
C. Report and block the sender
D. Forward to others

282. You accidentally post incorrect info. You should:
A. Blame someone B. Delete silently
C. Post a correction D. Leave it

283. Someone uses inappropriate language in a group. What's ethical?
A. Support them
B. Join the talk
C. Report or correct respectfully
D. Ignore forever

284. Best way to maintain online reputation is to:
A. Troll others
B. Stay inactive
C. Follow netiquette
D. Post controversial content

285. An appropriate profile photo should:
A. Be offensive
B. Include nudity
C. Be respectful and clear
D. Be anonymous

286. Flaming is:
A. Respectful debate
B. Angry, abusive online messages
C. Sharing memes
D. Posting updates

287. A respectful disagreement should include:
A. Sarcasm
B. Personal attacks
C. Facts and courtesy
D. Caps lock rants

288. Before joining an online forum, it's polite to:
A. Troll moderators
B. Understand rules and etiquette
C. Spam links
D. Argue with admins

289. Which behaviour demonstrates poor netiquette?
A. Respectful discussion
B. Sharing useful links
C. Spreading rumours
D. Proper grammar use

290. The golden rule of netiquette is:
A. Talk only to friends
B. Post often
C. Treat others as you want to be treated
D. Be anonymous always

291. What does 'organic reach' mean in social media?
A. The number of paid ads
B. The reach obtained through non-paid means
C. The geographical reach of posts
D. The number of posts published

292. What is the main benefit of using 'Facebook Insights' for a business page?
A. To change the page's design
B. To track and analyse the performance of your content
C. To increase the page's loading speed
D. To add more friends to your profile

293. Why is 'engagement rate' important in social media marketing?
A. It reduces the effectiveness of posts
B. It is unrelated to marketing success
C. It indicates how actively users interact with your content
D. It only counts the number of negative comments

294. What is the purpose of 'Instagram Stories'?
A. To permanently store data
B. To share content that disappears after 24 hours
C. For text-only posts
D. To increase website loading times

295. What does 'organic content' mean on social media?
A. Content that is only about organic farming
B. Paid promotional posts
C. Content naturally shared without paid promotion
D. Posts containing only images

296. What is a 'social media content calendar'?
A. A tool to track competitors' posts
B. A schedule for posting content on social media platforms
C. A calendar that marks social media holidays only
D. A diary for recording personal events

297. What does 'boosting a post' mean on platforms like Facebook?
A. Deleting a post
B. Reducing the visibility of a post
C. Paying to increase the reach and visibility of a post
D. Posting the same content repeatedly

298. Why is video content effective in social media marketing?
A. It's the only type of content allowed on social media
B. Videos tend to be more engaging and shareable than other content forms
C. Video content is cheaper to produce than photos
D. Videos are easier to create than written content

299. What is 'user-generated content' in social media marketing?
A. Content created by the social media platform itself
B. Content created and shared by users, often featuring or promoting a brand
C. Only negative reviews and comments
D. Content exclusively created by professional marketers

300. Why is it important to have a 'consistent brand voice' across social media platforms?
A. To confuse the audience
B. To ensure your brand is easily recognizable and relatable
C. To comply with social media regulations
D. To limit creativity in posts

301. What is 'social listening' in social media marketing?
A. Ignoring customer feedback and comments
B. Broadcasting messages without engaging with the audience
C. Monitoring and analysing conversations around your brand and industry
D. Focusing only on posting content without observing its impact

302. Arrange the following social media platforms on the basis of highest to lowest popularity in India (FICCI Report, 2020)
(*a*) Facebook (*b*) WhatsApp
(*c*) FB Messenger (*d*) YouTube
(*e*) Instagram
A. (*b*), (*a*), (*d*), (*c*), (*e*)
B. (*d*), (*b*), (*a*), (*c*), (*e*)
C. (*d*), (*a*), (*b*), (*e*), (*c*)
D. (*b*), (*a*), (*d*), (*e*), (*c*)

303. Write the chronological order of Social Media Platforms:
(*a*) YouTube (*b*) Facebook
(*c*) Tumblr (*d*) Instagram
(*e*) Twitter
A. (*a*), (*b*), (*c*), (*d*), (*e*)
B. (*e*), (*a*), (*d*), (*c*), (*b*)
C. (*c*), (*d*), (*b*), (*a*), (*e*)
D. (*b*), (*a*), (*e*), (*c*), (*d*)

304. Which social media platform has introduced a limit to viewing the posts to fix data scraping?
A. Facebook B. Twitter
C. Instagram D. Snapchat

305. Which Union Ministry released 'Endorsements Know-hows!' guide for celebrities, influencers and virtual influencers on social media?
A. Ministry of Consumer Affairs, Food and Public Distribution
B. Ministry of Home Affairs
C. Ministry of External Affairs
D. Ministry of Defence

306. Which country has introduced a bill that aims to ban social media access for children under 16 years of age?
A. India B. Nepal
C. Australia D. Canada

307. Which country recently passed the "Online Safety Amendment (Social Media Minimum Age) Bill 2024"?
A. Australia B. India
C. France D. Bangladesh

308. Which state has decided to create a fact-checking unit to curb fake news on social media?
A. Karnataka B. Kerala
C. Tamil Nadu D. West Bengal

309. Which ministry has proposed prohibiting the advertising of online betting sites on social media platforms such as Facebook, Instagram, and YouTube?
A. Ministry of Social Justice and Empowerment
B. Ministry of Micro, Small, and Medium Enterprises
C. Ministry of Home Affairs
D. Ministry of Electronics and IT

310. 'Blue subscriber service' is a premium service of which social media company?
A. Facebook B. Twitter
C. WhatsApp D. Instagram

311. Which social media platform company has announced a new facility named 'Circles'?
A. Facebook B. Twitter
C. Telegram D. Instagram

ANSWERS

1	2	3	4	5	6	7	8	9	10
C	D	D	B	A	B	A	C	D	B
11	12	13	14	15	16	17	18	19	20
D	C	B	C	C	C	D	B	B	B
21	22	23	24	25	26	27	28	29	30
D	C	C	B	B	D	B	B	D	B
31	32	33	34	35	36	37	38	39	40
B	A	B	D	B	B	B	D	C	D
41	42	43	44	45	46	47	48	49	50
B	C	D	C	D	D	C	C	C	B
51	52	53	54	55	56	57	58	59	60
B	B	B	A	C	B	D	A	B	B
61	62	63	64	65	66	67	68	69	70
D	B	A	B	B	D	B	C	B	B
71	72	73	74	75	76	77	78	79	80
B	B	A	A	B	A	C	B	A	C
81	82	83	84	85	86	87	88	89	90
B	C	C	C	C	B	B	A	C	D
91	92	93	94	95	96	97	98	99	100
C	D	C	C	C	B	C	C	C	D
101	102	103	104	105	106	107	108	109	110
C	D	C	D	C	C	B	B	B	C
111	112	113	114	115	116	117	118	119	120
B	B	D	C	D	C	D	C	C	D
121	122	123	124	125	126	127	128	129	130
B	C	C	C	D	B	C	D	A	D
131	132	133	134	135	136	137	138	139	140
C	C	A	B	B	D	D	C	D	A
141	142	143	144	145	146	147	148	149	150
C	B	C	B	C	C	C	B	D	D
151	152	153	154	155	156	157	158	159	160
A	D	D	D	C	C	A	A	C	C
161	162	163	164	165	166	167	168	169	170
B	D	A	B	B	D	D	A	A	C
171	172	173	174	175	176	177	178	189	190
C	B	C	C	B	B	B	B	B	A
181	182	183	184	185	186	187	188	189	190
A	A	B	D	D	C	C	B	C	A
191	192	193	194	195	196	197	198	199	200
C	D	D	B	C	A	B	C	A	D
201	202	203	204	205	206	207	208	209	210
D	A	B	C	B	D	C	A	C	B
211	212	213	214	215	216	217	218	219	220
A	D	B	C	D	B	C	C	B	B
221	222	223	224	225	226	227	228	229	230
B	B	C	B	C	B	B	B	B	C
231	232	233	234	235	236	237	238	239	240
C	B	C	D	D	C	C	B	D	C

241	242	243	244	245	246	247	248	249	250
C	B	C	D	A	C	D	B	D	C
251	252	253	254	255	256	257	258	259	260
B	A	B	C	D	A	B	B	C	D
261	262	263	264	265	266	267	268	269	270
B	C	B	B	C	C	B	C	B	B
271	272	273	274	275	276	277	278	279	280
C	C	B	B	B	B	B	C	A	B
281	282	283	284	285	286	287	288	289	290
C	C	C	C	C	B	C	B	C	C
291	292	293	294	295	296	297	298	299	300
B	B	C	B	C	B	C	B	B	B
301	302	303	304	305	306	307	308	309	310
C	C	D	B	A	C	A	A	D	B
311									
B									

EXPLANATORY ANSWERS

5. (A): Meta Platforms, Inc. is the parent company of Facebook and Instagram. Originally founded as Facebook, Inc. by Mark Zuckerberg in 2004, the company was renamed Meta in October 2021 to emphasize its broader vision beyond social media—especially its focus on building the "metaverse," a virtual shared space integrating augmented and virtual reality. Meta owns and operates major platforms like Facebook, Instagram, WhatsApp, and Oculus, making it one of the most influential tech conglomerates globally.

10. (B): Social Media Marketing (SMM) involves using social media platforms like Instagram, Facebook, LinkedIn, etc., to promote products and services. Strategies include sharing content, engaging followers, running paid campaigns to drive traffic, sales, and brand awareness.

73. (A): Hashtags expand a tweet's reach by associating it with trending or popular topics, increasing its visibility to a broader audience.

91. (C): A LinkedIn Company Page allows businesses to showcase their services, share company updates, and engage with followers.

96. (B): LinkedIn's professional user base and networking opportunities make it the top choice for B2B marketing. It offers direct engagement with decision-makers and relevant business interactions.

98. (C): Digital marketing involves promoting products or services through digital channels like search engines, social media, email, websites, and more, reaching a larger and more diverse audience efficiently.

99. (C): Content scheduling tools (like Hootsuite or Buffer) allow marketers to plan, organize, and distribute content across multiple platforms at optimal times, ensuring consistency and greater reach.

118. (C): Twitter was created in March 2006 by Jack Dorsey, Noah Glass, Biz Stone, and Evan Williams, and was launched in July of that year.

303. (D): Here is the chronological order of the social media platforms based on their launch dates:

1. Facebook - 2004
2. YouTube - 2005
3. Twitter - 2006
4. Tumblr - 2007
5. Instagram - 2010

304. (B): Twitter applied the following temporary limits. Verified accounts are limited to reading 6000 posts per day, Unverified accounts to 600 posts per day, New unverified accounts to 300 per day.

CHAPTER-7

NEW MEDIA

New media refers to forms of communication in the digital world, primarily online via the internet. It encompasses a wide range of technologies, practices, and content that rely on digital devices and the internet for creation, distribution, and consumption. Think of it as the evolution of media beyond traditional forms like print newspapers, radio, and television.

A defining characteristic of new media is its ability to utilize multimedia elements such as video and audio to create engaging, easily shareable content across different platforms. New media is constantly evolving ways that we consume and create content. It encompasses various digital technologies, including social media, streaming services, and mobile devices. With these new technologies, anyone can easily and quickly share their ideas, opinions, or creations with the world. Unlike traditional media, which primarily includes print and broadcast media, new media is interactive, allowing users to engage in two-way conversations and participate in online communities. It is a powerful tool transforming how we communicate, work, and play.

Key Characteristics of New Media

Some of the key characteristics of New media include:

- **Digital:** Information is represented in binary code (0s and 1s), allowing for easy manipulation, storage, and transmission.
- **Interactive:** Unlike traditional one-way media, new media often allows for user input, feedback, and participation. Think of commenting on a social media post or controlling a video game character.
- **Hypertextual:** Information is often linked in a non-linear way, allowing users to navigate through content based on their interests via hyperlinks, like on websites.
- **Networked:** New media is often connected through the internet, enabling global communication and the formation of online communities.
- **Virtual:** Many new media experiences create virtual environments or representations of reality, such as in video games or virtual reality applications.
- **Simulated:** Some new media goes beyond virtual representation to create immersive, artificial experiences, like flight simulators or online role-playing games.
- **Convergent:** New media often blends different forms of media together. A website might include text, images, audio, and video. Smartphones converge many media technologies into one device.
- **Asynchronous:** Communication doesn't always happen in real-time. You can send an email and the recipient can read and respond later.
- **Accessible:** Creating and distributing content can be more accessible to individuals than with traditional media. Anyone can start a blog or a social media profile.
- **Storage:** Vast amounts of digital information can be stored relatively easily and inexpensively.

Forms of New Media

- **Social media:** Platforms like Facebook, Instagram, X (formerly Twitter), TikTok, LinkedIn, and Reddit, enabling users to create, share, and interact with content and connect with others.

- **Websites and Blogs:** Online platforms for sharing information, opinions, news, and e-commerce. Examples include WordPress and Blogger.
- **Streaming Services:** Platforms for on-demand access to audio and video content, such as Netflix, Spotify, YouTube, Amazon Prime Video, and Disney+. Taylor Swift was the most-streamed artist on Spotify in 2024 with over 26 billion streams.
- **Podcasts:** Digital audio programs available for download or streaming, covering a wide range of topics.
- **Online Video Games:** Interactive digital games, often played online with other users, fostering communities and collaboration.
- **Mobile Apps:** Software applications designed for smartphones and tablets, offering a vast array of functions from communication to entertainment to productivity.
- **Virtual Reality (VR) and Augmented Reality (AR):** Technologies that create immersive digital experiences or overlay digital information onto the real world.
- **Online Courses:** Educational content delivered via the internet, allowing for remote learning.
- **Email and Messaging Apps:** Digital tools for direct communication between individuals or groups.

INTERNET AS THE MEETING POINT FOR ALL MASS MEDIA

The internet has evolved into a central hub where all forms of traditional and new mass media converge. It acts as a unifying platform that brings together print, radio, television, cinema, and digital media in a single, interactive space accessible globally and instantly.

Traditional Media Before the Internet

Before the advent of the internet, traditional forms of media operated independently, each within its own framework of production, distribution, and audience engagement. Print media, such as newspapers and magazines, relied on physical printing and delivery systems to reach their readers, offering limited interactivity and a one-way flow of information. Broadcast media, including radio and television, delivered content through scheduled programming, requiring audiences to tune in at specific times with little to no opportunity for direct feedback or interaction. Cinema, too, functioned as a standalone medium, where films were produced for theatrical release and viewed in dedicated venues. Each of these media types had distinct characteristics, technologies, and audiences, with minimal overlap or integration among them.

Convergence of Media on the Internet

Traditional Medium	Converged Internet Format
Newspaper	Online news portals, blogs
Radio	Podcasts, live audio streams
Television	Video streaming platforms (YouTube, Netfix)
Cinema	Online movie platforms, short films on social media
Advertising	Social media ads, targeted online ads

The internet has revolutionized how media is produced, distributed, and consumed by enabling the convergence of various media formats into a single digital platform. This convergence allows text, audio, video, and graphics to coexist and complement each other within one space, creating rich multimedia experiences. One of the key features of the internet as a converging platform is ***multimedia integration***, where different forms of content—text, images, video, and sound—are seamlessly combined. It also offers a high level of ***interactivity***, enabling users to engage with content by commenting, sharing, liking, and even co-creating. The ***global accessibility*** of the internet allows users from anywhere in the world to access media instantly, breaking the limitations of geography. With ***on-demand consumption***, audiences are no longer bound by schedules and can choose what to watch, read, or listen to at their convenience. Furthermore, the ***searchability*** of online content, aided by keywords and algorithms, makes it easy to locate specific information quickly. Lastly, the internet provides ***personalization***, tailoring content recommendations based on individual user behaviour and preferences, thereby enhancing the overall media experience.

CHANGE IN BROADCASTING LANDSCAPE DUE TO NEW MEDIA

New media has fundamentally transformed the broadcasting landscape by enabling interactive engagement, diversifying content distribution, and democratizing content creation, moving beyond traditional one-way communication. Traditional broadcasting—whether radio or television—relied on centralized control, fixed programming schedules, and passive audiences. In contrast, new media platforms like YouTube, streaming services, podcasts, and social media allow users to access content anytime, anywhere, and on a variety of devices. Here are some key changes:

From Analog to Digital Transmission:

- **Improved Quality:** Digital signals offer superior audio and video quality compared to analog, leading to the prevalence of High Definition (HD) and Ultra-High Definition (UHD) broadcasting.
- **Increased Channel Capacity:** Digital technology allows broadcasters to transmit more channels within the same bandwidth.
- **Data Services:** Digital broadcasting enables the delivery of additional data services like electronic program guides, subtitles, and interactive features.

Shift from One-Way to Two-Way Communication:

- **Interactive Engagement:** Traditional broadcasting was a one-way communication model, where viewers passively consumed content. New media allows for real-time interaction and engagement with audiences through social media, comments sections, and live streaming.
- **Audience Participation:** New media platforms empower audiences to become active participants in the information dissemination process, sharing their own perspectives and experiences.

Rise of Internet-Based Platforms:

- **Streaming Services (OTT):** Platforms like Netflix, Amazon Prime Video, Disney+, and Spotify have disrupted traditional linear broadcasting by offering on-demand content accessible anytime, anywhere. This has led to "cord-cutting" as viewers shift away from cable and satellite subscriptions.
- **Online Radio and Podcasts:** The internet has enabled the proliferation of online radio stations and podcasts, offering niche content and greater choice for listeners. Traditional radio stations are also increasingly streaming their content online.
- **Social Media Integration:** Platforms like YouTube, Facebook, X (formerly Twitter), and Instagram have become significant channels for distributing video and audio content, often blurring the lines between traditional broadcasting and social media. Live streaming features on these platforms allow individuals and organizations to broadcast directly to audiences.

Diversification of Content Distribution:

- **Multiple Platforms:** Broadcasters now utilize various platforms, including traditional channels (TV, radio) and digital platforms (streaming services, social media) to reach diverse audiences.
- **On-Demand Content:** New media enables on-demand content consumption, allowing viewers to access shows and news at their convenience.
- **Global Reach:** New media facilitates instant global access to information and content, breaking down geographical barriers.

Shift in Consumption Habits:

- **Personalized Content:** Algorithms on streaming platforms and social media analyze user preferences to recommend tailored content, leading to more personalized viewing/listening experiences.
- **Multi-Screen Experiences:** Consumers often use multiple devices (smartphones, tablets, laptops, smart TVs) to access broadcast content. Broadcasters are adapting by creating content optimized for different screens and offering seamless transitions between devices.
- **Binge-Watching:** The availability of entire seasons of shows on streaming services has led to the phenomenon of binge-watching.

Democratization of Content Creation:

- **Citizen Journalism:** The rise of citizen journalism, where individuals report on events and share their experiences through social media, has diversified the media landscape.
- **Micro-Storytelling:** New media has given rise to micro-storytelling, or the use of small moments or creative content to champion a narrative or product.
- **Increased Content Variety:** The internet and social media have made it easier for people to access news and information from a wide range of sources, both local and global.

Data Analytics and Targeted Advertising:

- **Audience Measurement:** Digital platforms provide detailed data on audience behaviour, allowing broadcasters and advertisers to gain insights into viewing/listening patterns and demographics.
- **Targeted Advertising:** Online platforms enable more precise targeting of advertisements based on user data, potentially leading to more effective advertising campaigns compared to traditional broad-reach broadcasting.

New Revenue Models:

- **Subscription Services:** Streaming services primarily rely on subscription fees for revenue.
- **Advertising on Digital Platforms:** While traditional broadcast advertising still exists, online platforms offer new advertising formats and models.

- **Hybrid Models:** Many traditional broadcasters are adopting hybrid models, offering both linear broadcasts and on-demand streaming content, often with different monetization strategies.

Technological Innovations:

- **Artificial Intelligence (AI):** AI is being used for content recommendation, automated content creation (e.g., news summaries), audience analytics, and targeted advertising.
- **Augmented Reality (AR) and Virtual Reality (VR):** These technologies are beginning to be explored for immersive broadcasting experiences, particularly in areas like sports and live events.
- **5G Technology:** The rollout of 5G networks promises faster and more reliable mobile broadband, enabling seamless streaming of high-quality video and facilitating remote live broadcasts.
- **Cloud-Based Workflows:** Cloud computing is streamlining content production, storage, and distribution for broadcasters, offering scalability and cost-efficiency.

TRANSMISSION OF INFORMATION IN TIMES OF NEW MEDIA

New media has revolutionized technical infrastructure in transmission, shifting from linear, centralized models to decentralized, interactive ones, enabling instantaneous, global content distribution through digital platforms and devices.

Shift from Traditional to Digital:

- **Linear to Networked:** Traditional media transmission was a linear process, with content creators sending information to a limited number of distributors, who then delivered it to consumers. New media, however, is characterized by a networked approach, where content can be distributed directly to users through the internet and various digital platforms.
- **Centralized to Decentralized:** Traditional media often relied on a few large organizations controlling content creation and distribution. New media democratizes this process, allowing individuals and smaller groups to create and share content, bypassing traditional gatekeepers. Example: small news channels on YouTube.
- **Physical to Digital infrastructure:** The physical infrastructure of traditional media outlets (e.g., printing presses, broadcast towers) is being replaced by digital infrastructure (e.g., servers, internet networks, mobile devices). Bigger Production Control rooms have transformed into smaller production rooms with compact and multifunctional digital consoles working through internet.

Speed and Immediacy:

- **Real-time Updates:** News and information can now be transmitted and accessed virtually instantaneously across the globe. The rapidity of information transmission is unprecedented. Forget waiting for the morning paper or the evening news; events unfold and are reported live through social media, online news outlets, and citizen journalism.
- **Breaking News:** The speed at which information travels means breaking news reaches audiences far faster than traditional media could manage.

Accessibility and Reach:

- **Global Audience:** The internet has no geographical boundaries. Information can be transmitted and accessed by anyone with an internet connection, anywhere in the world. This has created a truly global information network. As of early 2024, over 5 billion people worldwide were active internet users.
- **Lower Barriers to Entry:** Individuals can now become information broadcasters themselves through blogs, social media, podcasts, and video platforms, bypassing traditional gatekeepers of media.

Interactivity and Engagement:

- **Two-Way Communication:** Unlike traditional one-way broadcasting, new media allows for interaction. Audiences can comment, share, debate, and contribute their own perspectives, creating a dynamic information ecosystem.
- **Citizen Journalism:** The ability for anyone with a smartphone to capture and share events has led to the rise of citizen journalism, providing firsthand accounts and diverse viewpoints often missing in mainstream media.

Multimedia Integration:

- **Convergent Platforms:** New media seamlessly blends text, audio, images, and video, creating richer and more engaging ways to convey information. A single online news article can include embedded videos, interactive graphics, and social media feeds.

Personalization and Customization:

- **Tailored Content:** Algorithms and user preferences allow individuals to curate their own information feeds, accessing news and content that aligns with their interests.
- **Niche Information:** The vastness of the internet allows for the dissemination and consumption of highly specific and niche information, catering to diverse interests and communities.

Decentralization of Information Sources:

- **Beyond Mainstream Media:** New media has diversified the sources of information. Individuals can access news and perspectives from a multitude of independent journalists, bloggers, experts, and organizations, reducing reliance on a few dominant media outlets.

Cost-Effectiveness:

- **Lower Distribution Costs:** Transmitting information digitally is often significantly cheaper than traditional printing, broadcasting, and physical distribution methods.

Data-Driven Insights:

- **Measurable Impact:** Digital platforms allow for the tracking and analysis of how information is consumed, shared, and received, providing valuable insights for content creators and distributors.

REVENUE MODELS IN NEW MEDIA

New media has significantly reshaped the way revenue is generated in the media and communication industries. New media has opened up innovative and flexible ways to generate revenue, allowing individuals and organizations to monetize creativity and content like never before. Unlike traditional media, which relied heavily on advertising, subscriptions, and ticket sales, new media offers a diverse range of monetization models driven by technology, user engagement, and data analytics.

Digital Advertising

- Pay-per-click (PPC), banner ads, sponsored posts, and video ads generate income based on impressions or user interactions.
- Platforms like Google, YouTube, Facebook, and Instagram earn billions from targeted advertising using user data and algorithms.
- Programmatic Advertising: Automated buying and selling of ad space.

Subscription Services

- Platforms like Netflix, Spotify, and news websites use monthly or yearly subscription models.

Freemium Models

- Basic content is free, but users pay for premium features, like ad-free access, extra tools, or exclusive content.
- Popular in apps, games, and platforms like LinkedIn or Spotify.
- Premium content is locked behind a paywall, encouraging regular income.

Pay-Per-View/Transactional Models

- Charging users for one-time access to specific content or events (e.g., online movie rentals viz. on Prime Videos and YouTube, live sports events viz. UFC).

Influencer & Content Creator Economy

- YouTubers, podcasters, and social media influencers earn from brand deals, sponsorships, affiliate marketing, and fan donations (e.g., Patreon, Buy Me a Coffee).
- Revenue is driven by audience size, engagement, and niche appeal.

Affiliate Marketing

- Earning commissions by promoting other companies' products or services through unique links.

Sponsored Content

- Creating content in partnership with brands that aligns with the publisher's audience (e.g., sponsored blog posts, videos).

E-commerce Integration

- Platforms allow direct selling of merchandise, digital products, or services.
- Social commerce is booming—users can buy products directly via Instagram, TikTok, or YouTube integrations.

Crowdfunding & Donations

- Platforms like Kickstarter or GoFundMe enable creators to fund projects through public contributions.
- Content creators also use donation-based models during live streams or through memberships.

MULTIPLE CHOICE QUESTIONS

1. The process of broadcasting involves sending and receiving the messages through ....
   A. Electromagnetic Spectrum
   B. Electromagnetic Waves
   C. Electromagnetic Radiation
   D. None of these

2. In media studies "converging" refers to the coming together of
   A. Two or more people, in public
   B. Different professional ideas about media
   C. Computer, telephone, and mass media technologies
   D. Mass media and mass communication

3. What defines New Media?
   A. Only print newspapers
   B. Digitally interactive platforms
   C. Old TV shows
   D. Film reels

4. Which of the following is NOT a feature of New Media?
   A. Interactivity
   B. On-demand content
   C. One-way flow of communication
   D. Multimedia content

5. A major change brought by the Internet in media is:
   A. Decrease in audience participation
   B. Linear communication
   C. Two-way interaction
   D. Higher cost of production

6. Which of the following is a characteristic of the Internet as a medium?
   A. Passive consumption
   B. High-cost access
   C. Interactivity and personalization
   D. Print-only content

7. Broadcasting is the most powerful medium of mass communication in India.
   A. True
   B. False

8. .... committee was formed to work on the media policies of the country.
   A. Air Committee of India
   B. Paswan Committee
   C. Joshi Committee
   D. Vardana Committee

9. The term "media convergence" refers to:
   A. Different media working independently
   B. Blending of various media on a single platform
   C. Use of old technology only
   D. Elimination of traditional media

10. Sharad Pawar Committee was set up in ....
    A. 1970 B. 1981
    C. 1997 D. 1985

11. What key aspect differentiates today's digital media from traditional media?
    A. Longevity B. Interactivity
    C. Portability D. None of these

12. In which year did television emerge in India?
    A. 1955 B. 1959
    C. 1957 D. 1940

13. SITE stands for ....
    A. Satellite Informational Television Expansion
    B. Satellite Informational Television Extension
    C. Satellite Instructional Television Experiment
    D. None of these

14. .... headed the National Satellite Communications Group in 1968.
    A. Prasanta Chandra Mahalanobis
    B. Dr. Vikram Sarabhai
    C. Satish Dhawan
    D. None of these

15. New Media Technology is also known as
    A. Offline Technology
    B. Digital Media Technology
    C. Section Media Technology
    D. None of these

16. INSAT stands for ....
    A. Indian National Satellite System
    B. Indian Nation Satellite System
    C. Indian National Satellite Structure
    D. Indian National Satellite Scheme

17. Which of these is an example of New Media?
    A. Cable TV B. Radio
    C. Podcast D. Cinema

18. Television was separated from AIR in 1976 and formed a new body named Doordarshan.
    A. True
    B. False

19. The concept of live coverage in India occurred in the year ....
A. 1992 B. 1972
C. 1982 D. 1980

20. .... was the first private channel in South India.
A. Zee TV B. Sun TV
C. MTV D. CNN

21. The application areas of multimedia are:
A. Industry
B. Education and textbook
C. CAD and entertainment
D. All of these

22. "On-demand consumption" in new media means:
A. Users watch only scheduled programs
B. Users wait for release times
C. Users choose what and when to consume
D. Only live streaming is allowed

23. Which among the following is ***not*** a Domestic channel?
A. Zee TV B. Star TV
C. Sun TV D. None of these

24. The Internet has made mass communication:
A. Exclusive to elites
B. Less efficient
C. More accessible and interactive
D. Limited to radio and TV

25. What role does "searchability" play in new media?
A. Limits information access
B. Makes content hard to find
C. Helps users find content easily
D. Blocks users from accessing data

26. Which is NOT a benefit of new media?
A. Global reach
B. Multimedia storytelling
C. One-way communication
D. User engagement

27. Which of the following traditional media formats has been transformed by the internet?
A. Newspapers
B. Radio
C. Television
D. All the above

28. In new media, "personalization" refers to:
A. Generic content for all
B. Same content for every user
C. Content tailored to user preferences
D. Censorship by governments

29. Augmented reality refers to:
A. Our increased ability to better understand our situations thanks to easy Internet search.
B. How we lose track of time when we are engrossed in video games.
C. Digital overlays of information onto a screen that is showing the real world.
D. Increased capacities for the disabled thanks to digital technologies.

30. Information overload arises when
A. Too much data is saved onto a disc or USB.
B. Media, particularly electronic media, repeatedly cites the same information.
C. Vast amounts of information are available to us from a variety of sources.
D. All the above

31. Digital Broadcasting first emerged in United States.
A. True
B. False

32. Match the following:

(*a*) Aryabhatta	1. 1981
(*b*) Bhaskara-I	2. 1975
(*c*) Apple	3. 1982
(*d*) INSAT–IA	4. 1979

A. (*a*)-3, (*b*)-1, (*c*)-4, (*d*)-2
B. (*a*)-2, (*b*)-4, (*c*)-1, (*d*)-3
C. (*a*)-4, (*b*)-2, (*c*)-1, (*d*)-3
D. (*a*)-2, (*b*)-4, (*c*)-3, (*d*)-1

33. Department of Space was established in ....
A. 1992 B. 1982
C. 1979 D. 1972

34. Internet arrived in India in ....
A. 1990 B. 1992
C. 2000 D. 1995

35. The Information Technology Act was passed in 2010.
A. True
B. False

36. When did IT Act 2000 come into effect?
A. 17 October, 2000
B. 11 November, 2000
C. 17 October, 2001
D. 11 November, 2001

37. Media Convergence is the merging of television and print medium.
A. True
B. False

38. Which among the following is a magnitude of convergence?
A. Industrial B. Social
C. Technological D. All the above

39. .... is known as the patron saint of the digital revolution.
A. Steve Jobs
B. Marshall McLuhan
C. Thomas Nashe
D. Tom Wolfe

40. VOIP stands for ....
A. Voice Over Internet Protocol
B. Visual Over Internet Protocol
C. Voice Over International Protocol
D. Visual Over International Protocol

41. .... signals from a satellite can be transmitted to any place on earth.
A. Analog signal
B. Electromagnetic signal
C. Microwave signal
D. None of these

42. Cellphones, Smart phones, Video games and Video texts are the examples of media convergence.
A. True
B. False

43. Internet has modified the complete process of communication.
A. True
B. False

44. Which among the following statements regarding the examples of media convergence is/are correct?
(a) Holography is a process which allows the three-dimensional images to be made.
(b) Storage, Price and Font size are some of the advantages of the e-books.
(c) Media streaming allows a person to play an audio or video from the internet without having a need to download the file to the system.
(d) Online game is a technology rather than a genre.
A. (a), (b) and (d)
B. Only (c)
C. Both (b) and (c)
D. (a), (b), (c) and (d)

45. Which of the following are the characteristics of New Media?
A. Digital B. Interactive
C. Virtual D. All of these

46. Which of the following is ***not*** the function of New Media?
A. Information B. Education
C. Entertainment D. Fragmentation

47. Media convergence can lead to media folly.
A. True
B. False

48. The post broadcast media' refers to
A. Folk media B. Social media
C. Print media D. Electronic media

49. Convergence is an end point rather than a process.
A. True
B. False

50. Which among the following changes are associated with the media convergence?
(a) Access to high-speed internet
(b) Increase in user-created content
(c) Globalisation
(d) Empowerment of media users
A. (a), (b) and (d)
B. Both (c) and (d)
C. (a), (c) and (d)
D. (a), (b), (c) and (d)

51. ICT stands for ....
A. Indian Communication Technology
B. International Communication Technology
C. Information and Communication Technology
D. None of these

52. Phishing is ....
A. Criminally deceitful process of trying to acquire the sensitive information
B. A computer software which is installed on the system without the user's knowledge to track the user's interaction with the system
C. A technique commonly used for Spam e-mails
D. A program that can copy itself and infect a computer without the permission of the owner

53. Modern communication technology like the Internet has resulted in:
A. Community media culture
B. National media culture
C. Personalized media culture
D. Rural media culture

54. E-Governance comes under Section 4 to 10 A of the IT Act, 2000.
A. True
B. False

55. Which among the following is/are an element of digital divide?
A. Gap in ability to use ICT
B. Gap in actual use of ICT
C. Gap in access to use ICT
D. All the above

56. Which institution catalyzes e-governance activities in India?
A. National Informatics Centre
B. National Governance Centre
C. National Information Centre
D. None of these

57. What is the purpose of sharing best practices among States/UTs and Autonomous bodies through the Shagun portal?
A. To comply with government regulations.
B. To learn from one another and accelerate collective evolution.
C. To reduce administrative workload.
D. To promote competition among educational institutions.

58. Which of the following statements accurately describe the application of ICT in catering to the needs of children with special needs?
A. Talking books provide visual aids and translate texts into multiple languages.
B. Mobile phones with talk back offer auditory feedback and GPS-inbuilt walking sticks help communicate.
C. Talking books offer audio texts, talk back provides auditory feedback, and GPS walking sticks aid mobility.
D. ICT interventions limit access to resources and segregate students.

59. The 'Second media age' is characterized by the rise of:
A. Print media
B. Radio
C. Television
D. Interactive media

60. How can ICT bridge the digital divide in education?
A. By providing the same digital content for all students.
B. By developing solutions and content for disadvantaged groups.
C. By reducing the use of ICT in marginalized communities.
D. By focusing only on urban areas.

61. Which systems are used to monitor the progress and IT infrastructure usage in schools?
A. PRABANDH is used to monitor the physical and financial progress of sanctioned schools, and UDISE+ is used to monitor the IT infrastructure and its usage in schools.
B. UDISE+ is used to monitor the physical and financial progress of sanctioned schools, and PRABANDH is used to monitor the IT infrastructure and its usage in schools.
C. PRABANDH is used to monitor both the physical and financial progress of sanctioned schools and the IT infrastructure usage.
D. UDISE+ is used to monitor both the physical and financial progress of sanctioned schools and the IT infrastructure usage.

62. Which of the following ICT tools aids visually impaired students?
A. Screen readers and audiobooks
B. Standard computer monitors
C. Printed textbooks
D. Traditional chalkboards

63. What is the purpose of integrating UDISE+ with ICT at schools?
A. To reduce the number of teaching staff.
B. To bring efficiency to school operations and free teachers from non-teaching tasks.
C. To eliminate the need for monitoring resources.
D. To standardize teaching methods across all schools.

64. Digital signature service that has been launched on Aadhar platform is called
A. DigiSignDesk
B. eSignDesk
C. OnlineSignDesk
D. GoogleSignIn

65. Which of the following services can be accessed through the "UMANG" app?
A. Booking train tickets
B. Filing income tax returns
C. Applying for a passport
D. All the above

66. The recently launched e-RaKAM portal is related to the welfare of –
A. Mining Industry
B. Students
C. Income–Tax payers
D. Farmers

67. Which of the following ICT initiatives of MHRD deals with E-governance for institutions/universities?
A. SAMARTH
B. VIDWAN
C. IRINS
D. SWAYAM

68. Which of the following mobile payment application is developed by the National Payments Corporation of India based on UPI?

A. MYGOV B. BHIM
C. UMANG D. PhonePe

69. Assertion (A): Digital India program has a strong potential of increasing the number of Internet users in India.

Reason (R): Initiatives like broadband connectivity, mobile coverage and Internet access will provide a fillip to the usage of Internet in India.

A. Both A and R are true and R is the correct explanation of A
B. A is true but R is false.
C. A is false but R is true.
D. Both A and R are false.

70. Internet.org is initiated by:

A. Satya Nadela
B. Tim Berners Lee
C. Bill Gates
D. Mark Zuckerberg

71. Which of the following terms are NOT related with OTT platform.

(a) Streaming (b) Bleed
(c) Pay Per View (d) Equalizer
(e) Decibel

A. (a), (b) and (d) only
B. (b), (c) and (d) only
C. (b), (d) and (e) only
D. (a), (c) and (d) only

72. Data Security Council of India was formed in ....

A. 2000 B. 2007
C. 2008 D. 2002

73. .... converts an optical image into an electrical image.

A. Sound recorder
B. Lights
C. Camera
D. None of these

74. Blogs and vlogs are forms of:

A. Print media
B. Traditional media
C. New media
D. Static media

75. In digital mass communication, the audience is

A. large B. passive
C. participatory D. uncultured

76. Citizen journalism is enabled primarily by:

A. Cinema halls
B. Traditional newsrooms
C. The Internet and smartphones
D. Typewriters

77. Color television transmission in India started with

A. Commonwealth Games 2010
B. SAARC Sports 1987
C. Asian Games 1982
D. World Cup Cricket 1987

78. The term used for the co-existence of private sector with public sector in broadcasting is

A. duopoly B. oligopoly
C. monopoly D. triopoly

79. New media has transformed audiences into:

A. Only consumers
B. Only viewers
C. Consumers and producers (prosumers)
D. Silent spectators

80. The addressability of mass communication is altered by

A. the digital media
B. the folk media
C. the personality-oriented media
D. the non-real time media

81. Assertion (A): The do-it-yourself digital tools offer an audience public control over media environment.

Reason (R): The dominant media models are resorting to unbridled supply of frivolous entertainment to survive.

A. Both (A) and (R) are true
B. Both (A) and (R) are true, but (R) is not the correct explanation of (A)
C. (A) is true, but (R) is false
D. (A) is false, but (R) is true

82. Transferring thoughts, ideas and messages into verbal and non-verbal signs is referred to as

A. channelization
B. meditation
C. encoding
D. decoding

83. The first Chairman of the Press Council of India was

A. Justice Rajagopala Ayyangar
B. Justice PB Sawant
C. Justice Jeevan Reddy
D. Justice JR Mudholkar

84. Assertion (A): The convergent technology is transforming the socio-cultural orders all over the world.

Reason (R): The new media have offered expanded options for the users to experiment with.

A. Both (A) and (R) are true
B. Both (A) and (R) are true, but (R) is not the correct explanation of (A)
C. (A) is true, but (R) is false
D. (A) is false, but (R) is true

85. Assertion (A): The distinctions among different media are getting erased fast.

Reason (R): The convergent digital technology has made the hybrid media possible.

A. Both (A) and (R) are true
B. Both (A) and (R) are true, but (R) is not the correct explanation of (A)
C. (A) is true, but (R) is false
D. (A) is false, but (R) is true

86. Assertion (A): Video podcasting and peer-to-peer networking represent a new architecture of aesthetics.

Reason (R): Technological evolution has hindered the public access to media.

A. Both (A) and (R) are true
B. Both (A) and (R) are true, but (R) is not the correct explanation of (A)
C. (A) is true, but (R) is false
D. (A) is false, but (R) is true

87. DigiLocker, recently in news, is a flagship initiative of which ministry?

A. Ministry of Commerce and Industry
B. Ministry of Communications
C. Ministry of Civil Aviation
D. Ministry of Electronics & Information Technology

88. The eShram-One Stop Solution initiative is primarily designed for which group of workers?

A. Organized workers
B. Unorganized workers
C. Migrant workers
D. None of the Above

[illegible] analog mass communication, contents are linear

A. [illegible]
B. static
C. [illegible]mic
D. sensational

90. Live telev[illegible] audience are [illegible]d radio that need the presence of [illegible]d as

A. transmission [illegible]
B. signal media
C. asynchronous media
D. synchronous media

91. In frequency modulation

A. frequency of carrier wave varies according to the frequency of the signal
B. frequency of carrier wave varies according to the amplitude of the signal
C. frequency of signal varies according to the amplitude of carrier wave
D. frequency of signal varies according to the frequency of carrier wave

92. In the questions given below are two statements labeled as Assertion (A) and Reason (R). In the context of the two statements, which one of the following is correct.

Assertion (A): Television and Internet have become a major source of news these days for daily newspaper.

Reason (R): Since news agency services have become less dependable due to global recession.

A. Both A and R are true
B. Both A and R are true, but R is not the correct explanation of A
C. A is true, but R is false
D. A is false, but R is true

93. The possible harmful effects of mediated communication always led to

A. production glut
B. ad attention
C. economic concerns
D. moral panics

94. A rate of decline in response to advertisements is called

A. response decay
B. staggered responses
C. response downturn
D. response entropy

95. A cut from one sound to another without breaking a continuity is

A. segue
B. harmonics
C. hiss
D. timbre

96. The process of working on sound after studio production is known as

A. audio fade
B. RCA
C. audio boost
D. audio sweetening

97. A canted shot is also referred to as

A. dangled angle
B. dutch angle
C. over shot
D. clear shot

98. In the questions given below are two statements labelled as Assertion (A) and Reason (R). In the context of the two statements, which one of the following is correct?

Assertion (A): Local content-dominated local editions of large newspapers have reduced them to be local newspapers in reality.

Reason (R): Modern technology and commercial considerations are responsible for such a trend in Indian Journalism.

A. Both A and R are true
B. Both A and R are true, but R is not the correct explanation of A
C. A is true, but R is false
D. A is false, but R is true

99. In the questions given below are two statements labelled as Assertion (A) and Reason (R). In the context of the two statements, which one of the following is correct?

Assertion (A): The digital divide in India is a serious national issue.

Reason (R): The concept of knowledge economy will become a reality when the civil society addresses the issue of digital divide.

A. Both A and R are true
B. Both A and R are true, but R is not the correct explanation of A
C. A is true, but R is false
D. A is false, but R is true

100. In the questions given below are two statements labelled as Assertion (A) and Reason (R). In the context of the two statements, which one of the following is correct?

Assertion (A): Folk media are now museum artefacts.

Reason (R): They are unable to survive against the power of technology propelled mass media.

A. Both A and R are true
B. Both A and R are true, but R is not the correct explanation of A
C. A is true, but R is false
D. A is false, but R is true

101. In the questions given below are two statements labelled as Assertion (A) and Reason (R). In the context of the two statements, which one of the following is correct?

Assertion (A): The concept of development communication has failed to take-off in India.

Reason (R): Lack of professional approach and the people's passion for entertainment, not development is responsible for the situation.

A. Both A and R are true
B. Both A and R are true, but R is not the correct explanation of A
C. A is true, but R is false
D. A is false, but R is true

102. Broadcasting subject falls under?

A. State list
B. Union list
C. Concurrent list
D. Changes from time to time

103. Who become the first Information and Broadcasting minister after Independence?

A. Sardar Patel
B. Radha Krishnan
C. B.R. Ambedkar
D. Jawahar Lal Nehru

104. Which of the following is not an advantage of DTH?

A. Signals are clear because they are digital
B. The initial installation costs as well as operational costs are quite high
C. Some TV channels can be blocked so that children may not have access to them
D. The viewer can select as many channels as he wishes

105. When the TV announcer explains the event even as the VTR rolls to broadcast the event, the action of the TV announcer is called:

A. Line Cover
B. Voice Over
C. Audio Back-up
D. Line Audio

106. The last stage in the process of digital ad insertion (on TV program) is the following.

A. Scheduling
B. Insertion
C. Verification
D. Distribution

107. **Statement 1:** The Interactive model includes both feedback and shared fields of experience.

Statement 2: The Linear model includes feedback and shared fields of experience.

A. Both statements are true.
B. Both statements are false.
C. Statement 1 is true, but Statement ... true.
D. Statement 1 is false, but State...

108. Forces affecting organizationa...onment

A. People
C. Technology
...ll the above

109. Which of the following statement is incorrect regarding Google Drive?
A. It is a cloud-based file storage service by Google.
B. Files stored on Google Drive cannot be shared.
C. It is integrated with Gmail.
D. It offers limited free storage.

110. The most influential part of the new web is ....
A. Social Networking Sites (SNSs)
B. World Wide Web (WWW)
C. Hyper Text Markup Language (HTML)
D. None of these

111. The different types of online communication tools are
A. Video Conferencing
B. Webcasting
C. Podcasting
D. All of these

112. VoIP is a term that is used in reference to a .... conversation.
A. audio B. video
C. text D. None of these

113. Which online communication tool is broadly utilized for public communication, particularly in mailing lists?
A. WhatsApp B. Email
C. Skype D. Line

114. Which of the following is an advantage of online communication?
A. Information Overload
B. Flexibility of time and Space
C. Only Text based
D. Documented

115. Who invented WWW?
A. Denis McQuail
B. George Tag
C. Tim Berners Lee
D. Phoebe Joseph

116. The first generation of the web1.0, also known as
A. informational web
C. communicative web
D. su web

117. A web serb to computer in software that supports computer- over the Internet
A. access B. axis
C. wire

118. What does URL stand for?
A. Universal Resource Locator
B. Uniform Resource Locator
C. Unified Resource Locator
D. United Resource Locator

119. Which of the following is not a way of communicating using the Internet?
A. Instant Messaging
B. Emailing
C. Chat Rooms
D. Phishing

120. Which of the following are the characteristics of Internet Communication?
A. Immediacy
B. Interactive
C. Community building
D. All of these

121. Which of the following includes digital audio files?
A. Webcasting B. Podcasting
C. Serie D. None of these

122. Webcasting is .... over the internet.
A. broadcasting B. narrowcasting
C. station casting D. hollow casting

123. Web 3.O is also called as ....
A. adhere web B. semantic web
C. sentence web D. tactic web

124. GPS stands for
A. Global Positioning System
B. Global Positioning Station
C. Global Posting Signal
D. Global Point Solution

125. WordPress is used to create
A. films B. blogs
C. virals D. aesthetics

126. Web archives are
A. Digital Library B. Websites
C. Blogs D. Templates

127. Cloud meeting is an example of
A. Browsing B. Webcasting
C. Podcasting D. Video Conferencing

128. What is the proposed punishment for Cyber Terrorism in IT Act?
A. 1 crore rupees penalty
B. Life Imprisonment
C. 10-year imprisonment
D. 6-year imprisonment

129. On what media there is large scope of using multimedia?
A. Digital B. Television
C. Radio D. Print

130. Which advertising is most expensive as company must pay for both airtime and production?
A. Radio B. Television
C. Digital D. Print

131. Online journalism refers to content created and distributed over
A. desk B. traditional media
C. offline D. internet

132. Online Journalism follows the .... similar to traditional journalism
A. professional code of conduct
B. free journalism
C. vibes
D. variations

133. Which journalism is not bound by any ethical and professional code of conduct in new media?
A. open-source reporting
B. citizen journalism
C. traditional reporting
D. distributive reporting

134. Which of the following will not protect you from spam?
A. Filters B. Popup blocker
C. E-mail rules D. Spam blockers

135. .... is a software program that filters all the data coming through the internet.
A. Antivirus B. Cookies
C. Malware D. Firewall

136. Which technology is commonly used for wireless communication in IoT devices?
A. Bluetooth B. Ethernet
C. Fiber Optic D. USB

137. Which of the following term is associated with Internet/e-Mail?
A. Plotter B. Slide presentation
C. Bookmark D. Pie chart

138. In Uttar Pradesh, where is the Cyber Crime Headquarters located?
A. Meerut B. Lucknow
C. Prayagraj D. Kanpur

139. A set of rules that govern all aspects of information communication are called –
A. Server B. Internet
C. Protocol D. OSI model

140. Knowing the password of a user for hacking is called?
A. Sneaking
B. Spoofing
C. Cyber stalking
D. Spamming

141. An email address consists of .... parts.
A. 3 B. 4
C. 2 D. 5

142. The 'digital divide' refers to:
A. The contrast between information rich and information poor audiences
B. Not everyone having the same access to technology and information
C. Both A and B
D. None of these

143. A digital native is a person who is born before the Internet, for whom the language, metaphors and online communication had to be learnt.
A. True
B. False

144. New media technologies can affect the quality of productions because:
A. Media producers are able to make exact copies of the product
B. Media distributors are able to make exact copies of the product
C. Media consumers are able to make exact copies of the product
D. All the above

145. New media technologies can affect the proliferation of media products because:
A. Media producers, distributors and audiences can interact with the product
B. Media forms and texts converge to create new forms and texts
C. New media texts and forms can be easily created and reproduced
D. All the above

146. New media technologies can affect the convergence of media products because:
A. Media texts and forms converge to create new texts and forms
B. Media producers, distributors and consumers are able to make exact copies of products
C. New media forms and texts can be easily created and reproduced
D. All the above

147. New media forms and texts can be controversial. People are afraid of what effects new technology might have on people—especially 'susceptible audiences' like children and teenagers. Which of the following new technologies have caused 'moral panic'?

A. The Internet B. Mobile phones
C. The Television D. All the above

148. In what year was digital music first demonstrated?

A. 1975 B. 1976
C. 1977 D. 1978

149. 'Napster' - an online music file-sharing program is an example of new media convergence. Which two forms of media were combined to create Napster?

A. Radio and Television
B. Internet and Music files
C. Print and Internet
D. Film and Music videos

150. YouTube is an example of new media convergence. Which media forms primarily combined to create YouTube?

A. Radio and print journalism
B. Television and the internet
C. Film and radio broadcasting
D. Newspapers and music streaming

151. New media technologies that make it easier to copy music, films and television programs, are challenging traditional ....

A. broadcasting methods
B. copyright laws
C. distribution models
D. All the above

152. In recent decades, the mass media has become far more participatory, putting greater power in the hands of:

A. Government regulators
B. Media conglomerates
C. Individual users and the public
D. Traditional journalists

153. Good media criticism should always

A. Reveal negative aspects of media
B. Offer analysis based on reason
C. Warn us that ads sell us things we don't need
D. Condemn our emotional reactions to media

154. According to the text, which level of the media industry is the key to understanding today's media business?

A. Global B. Regional
C. Local D. National

155. In terms of media/government relationships in the world today, the media in most countries area.

A. Government owned and operated
B. Privately owned and government controlled
C. Privately owned and free from government control
D. Mixed in terms of government and private ownership and control

156. What is Brand Consistency, and why is it crucial in social media marketing?

A. Posting random and unrelated content
B. Maintaining the same brand voice, visuals, and messaging across all platforms
C. Ignoring brand aesthetics
D. Focusing only on short videos

157. What is the main purpose of email marketing?

A. To increase website bounce rates
B. To create press releases
C. To build brand loyalty and communicate with customers
D. To promote blog traffic

158. What does the term "Open Rate" refer to in email marketing?

A. Bounce rate of email delivery
B. Number of sales generated
C. Percentage of recipients who opened the email
D. Number of new subscribers

159. What does the term "Open Rate" refer to in email marketing?

A. Bounce rate of email delivery
B. Number of sales generated
C. Percentage of recipients who opened the email
D. Number of new subscribers

160. What is an unsubscribe link's purpose in an email campaign?

A. To add images to emails
B. To encourage engagement
C. To allow recipients to opt-out of future communications
D. To increase click-through rates

161. What is the significance of "personalization" in email marketing?

A. Sending plain text only
B. Avoiding calls to action
C. Changing fonts for design purposes
D. Using recipient's name and specific content to improve engagement

162. What is mobile marketing?
A. Marketing through newspapers
B. Marketing through mobile devices like smartphones and tablets
C. Marketing solely through television
D. Marketing through desktop computers

163. What is Geo-Targeting in mobile marketing?
A. Delivering personalized messages based on users' geographical location
B. Sending bulk emails
C. Displaying long videos
D. Sending marketing messages based on time zones

164. What is In-App Advertising?
A. Broadcasting on radio
B. Placing ads within smartphone apps to engage users
C. Advertising on social media platforms
D. Sending newsletters via email

165. What is a major benefit of App-Based Marketing?
A. Higher engagement and personalized communication
B. Limited targeting
C. Less interaction with consumers
D. Reduced brand presence

166. Which metric measures the percentage of users who leave a website after viewing only one page?
A. Engagement Rate
B. Conversion Rate
C. Bounce Rate
D. CTR (Click-Through Rate)

167. What is the main benefit of Mobile Marketing for eCommerce brands?
A. Increased brand reach and quick conversion opportunities
B. Limited customer engagement
C. Reduced competition
D. Reduced need for social media presence

168. What is Digital Marketing?
A. Marketing using digital channels like search engines, social media, and email
B. Using only radio advertisements
C. Distributing flyers door-to-door
D. Marketing through print media

169. What is the primary goal of digital marketing?
A. To build brand awareness online
B. To increase offline sales
C. To reduce online customer support
D. To increase print advertising

170. Which of the following is NOT a type of digital marketing?
A. Content marketing
B. Print advertising
C. Email marketing
D. Social media marketing

171. What is a key difference between B2B and B2C marketing?
A. B2B marketing is cheaper than B2C marketing
B. B2C marketing focuses on personal communication; B2B relies on automation
C. B2B marketing involves TV ads; B2C does not
D. B2B marketing targets businesses; B2C targets individual consumers

172. What does SEO stand for in digital marketing?
A. Search Engine Optimization
B. Secure Email Operation
C. Sales Engagement Online
D. Social Engagement Operation

173. What is the primary difference between SEM and SEO?
A. SEM is free, and SEO is paid
B. SEM uses blogs, while SEO uses ads
C. SEO involves social media, while SEM involves email marketing
D. SEM focuses on paid traffic, while SEO focuses on organic traffic

174. What is the purpose of Google Ads?
A. Free social sharing
B. Paid search engine marketing
C. Unpaid press releases
D. Video editing

175. .... is a navigation link from one website page to another.
A. Hypertext B. Text
C. A homepage D. A button

176. What six elements can be combined to create multimedia?
A. Color, hypertext, images, music, voiceover and video
B. Audio, hypertext, images, color, music and animation
C. Text, links, animation, video, sound effects and music
D. Audio, images, animation, hypertext, text and video

177. What does PPC stand for in digital advertising?
A. Pay Per Content
B. Pay Per Promotion
C. Pay Per Click
D. Print Per Conversion

178. Which of the following is a key benefit of digital marketing?
A. Global reach and accessibility
B. Higher printing costs
C. Decreased brand visibility
D. Irrelevant content sharing

179. What is Google Analytics primarily used for?
A. Creating press releases
B. Monitoring website traffic and user behaviour
C. Printing brochures
D. Managing email lists

180. Why is Keyword Research important in SEO?
A. To ignore search engines
B. To understand what terms your audience is searching for
C. To create long URLs
D. To reduce web traffic

181. What is Retargeting in digital marketing?
A. Attracting new visitors only
B. Creating irrelevant content
C. Sending spam emails
D. Retargeting existing website visitors with ads

182. What are KPIs (Key Performance Indicators) in digital marketing?
A. Metrics that measure the success of marketing activities
B. Random guesses about user preferences
C. Irrelevant metrics for sales
D. Disregarding search trends

183. What is the primary purpose of a Landing Page in digital marketing?
A. Redirecting to other websites
B. Capturing email leads and driving conversions
C. Ignoring website navigation
D. Creating long URLs

184. Which platform is ideal for B2B digital marketing?
A. TikTok B. Facebook
C. LinkedIn D. Snapchat

185. What is meant by CTR (Click-Through Rate)?
A. Cost-to-Return
B. Click Time Ratio
C. Conversion Traffic Rate
D. Percentage of people clicking an ad link

186. What is Inbound Marketing?
A. Cold emailing
B. Attracting customers through content and engagement
C. Ignoring search engine algorithms
D. Creating banners only

187. What is a Marketing Funnel in digital marketing?
A. Ignoring website visitors
B. A multi-step process guiding users from awareness to conversion
C. Random social media posting
D. Only creating print flyers

188. What does Content Optimization mean in digital marketing?
A. Creating random content
B. Editing content to improve engagement and search engine rankings
C. Ignoring keywords
D. Distributing content across social media

189. What does "RGB" stand for in the context of digital graphics?
A. Red, Green, Blue
B. Realistic Graphics Builder
C. Rapid Graphic Browsing
D. Random Graphics Buffer

190. Which file format is commonly used for storing digital graphics with transparency and support for layers?
A. JPEG B. BMP
C. GIF D. PNG

191. What is the function of Google Search Console in digital marketing?
A. Only email communication
B. Monitoring website performance, indexing, and search rankings
C. Creating press releases
D. Printing brochures

192. What is the primary goal of Conversion Rate Optimization (CRO)?
A. Decreasing user interactions
B. Increasing the percentage of website visitors who complete a desired action
C. Distributing physical brochures
D. Ignoring search engine traffic

193. What is Social Proof in digital marketing?
A. Customer testimonials, reviews, and influencer endorsements
B. Posting random content
C. Ignoring website loading speed
D. Creating press-only communication

194. Why is Mobile Optimization important in digital marketing?
A. For paper brochures
B. Ignoring social interactions
C. To ensure websites work well on smartphones and tablets
D. Only for offline visitors

195. What does ROI stand for in digital marketing?
A. Return on Investment
B. Rate of Interaction
C. Redirecting Online Information
D. Real-time Online Interaction

196. What is Google Tag Manager (GTM)?
A. A paid social platform
B. A tool to manage website tags and analytics
C. A tool to manage website tags and analytics
D. A video-editing platform

197. What is a major concern regarding privacy in digital marketing?
A. Ignoring social interactions
B. Collecting and storing personal data without user consent
C. Avoiding website traffic
D. Deleting social media profiles

198. What is Ad Quality Score in Google Ads?
A. A Google metric evaluating ad relevance, landing page experience, and CTR
B. Number of email subscribers
C. Ignoring keyword strategy
D. Avoiding competitor analysis

199. Why is Link Building important in Search Engine Marketing?
A. Ignoring competitors
B. Avoiding social shares
C. Improving a website's authority and search engine rankings
D. Disregarding content creation

200. Which of the following is an example of organic traffic?
A. Visitors from Facebook ads
B. Visitors from Google Ads
C. Visitors from unpaid search engine results
D. Visitors from email campaigns

201. Which of the following is NOT a search engine?
A. Facebook B. Google
C. Bing D. Yahoo

202. What does SERP stand for?
A. Search Engine Redirect Page
B. Search Engine Results Page
C. Structured Engine Ranking Page
D. Secure Engine Routing Protocol

203. What is a featured snippet?
A. A paid ad at the top of search results
B. A tool for website auditing
C. A special box showing quick answers to queries
D. A list of images in search results

204. Why is SEO considered a long-term strategy?
A. Because it takes time to build authority and rankings organically
B. Because rankings cannot change
C. Because search engines do not update regularly
D. Because it involves only paid strategies

205. Which of the following factors directly affect SEO?
A. Keywords
B. Mobile-friendliness
C. Backlinks
D. All of the mentioned

206. What type of content performs best for SEO?
A. Keyword-stuffed content
B. Over-optimized content
C. Original and high-quality content
D. Duplicate content

207. What is a "seed keyword"?
A. A broad term used to generate more keyword ideas
B. A keyword planted for future growth
C. A keyword with zero competition
D. None of the mentioned

208. Which tool is commonly used for keyword research?
A. WordPress
B. Canva
C. Adobe Photoshop
D. Google Keyword Planner

209. What is keyword stuffing?
A. Creating a keyword list for your website
B. Using too many keywords unnaturally
C. Using high-ranking keywords only
D. Ignoring keyword research

210. What does the term "canonical tag" refer to in SEO?
A. A tag that blocks search engines from indexing
B. A tag for displaying ads on pages
C. A tag for styling the website
D. A tag that indicates the preferred version of a webpage

211. Why is mobile optimization important for On-Page SEO?
A. It adds more backlinks to the website
B. It decreases the page loading time
C. Because search engines give higher rankings to mobile-friendly websites
D. It prevents visitors from leaving the site

212. What is a backlink?
A. A link that loops back to the same page
B. A link from another website to your website
C. A link within your website
D. A link that points to an internal page

213. What are toxic backlinks?
A. Links that pass no value
B. Low-quality or spammy links that harm a website's rankings
C. Links that improve rankings quickly
D. Links that only come from social media

214. What is guest blogging?
A. Writing articles for other websites to gain backlinks and exposure
B. Blogging about technical issues
C. Allowing users to write blogs on your website
D. Writing blogs without using keywords

215. What is Technical SEO?
A. Optimizing a website's infrastructure for search engines
B. Creating backlinks for a website
C. Writing high-quality content
D. Posting on social media

216. What is a 404 error?
A. A status code indicating a page is not found
B. A type of backlink
C. A sign of a secure website
D. A keyword optimization technique

217. .... is selling and buying of goods and services through internet.
A. E-commerce B. Internet
C. E-mail D. Website

218. What is the primary goal of E-commerce SEO?
A. To improve website load speed
B. To write blog posts for product reviews
C. To create social media content
D. To increase website traffic and sales

219. Which of the following tools helps analyze website performance and page speed?
A. Google Search Console
B. Moz Pro
C. Ahrefs
D. Google PageSpeed Insights

220. Which SEO tool is ideal for tracking website rankings over time?
A. Google Search Console
B. RankTracker
C. Google Analytics
D. SEMrush

221. Empowering individuals to post data on the Internet is a characteristic of:
A. Traditional Media
B. Broadcast Media
C. New Media
D. Print Media

222. What term refers to the ability of users to publish their own content online?
A. Gatekeeping B. User Empowerment
C. Broadcasting D. Censorship

223. Which of these allows many sources to provide the same information?
A. Convergence B. Monopoly
C. Single sourcing D. Exclusivity

224. Triggering activity in different media platforms from one message is known as:
A. Media confusion
B. Cross-platform synergy
C. Data redundancy
D. Static content sharing

225. The concept of "digital natives" refers to individuals who:
A. Avoid using the internet
B. Have grown up with digital technologies and the internet
C. Primarily consume traditional media
D. Lack the skills to post online

226. Which of the following is a barrier that new media has largely overcome for individual content creators?
A. Production costs
B. Audience reach
C. Distribution channels
D. All the above

227. The empowerment of individuals to post data online has impacted which aspect of traditional media?
A. Revenue models B. Audience size
C. Gatekeeping roles D. All the above

228. Which of the following best describes traditional media?
A. Interactive B. User-generated
C. One-to-many D. Collaborative

229. The concept of "Many to Many" communication is associated with:
A. Print B. Broadcast
C. Internet D. Radio

230. Which of these is an example of user-generated content?
A. TV serials B. YouTube vlog
C. Newspapers D. Radio news

231. Content going viral across platforms shows:
A. User isolation
B. Single media domination
C. Media integration
D. Passive engagement

232. What allows data to be shared instantly across platforms?
A. Firewalls B. Algorithms
C. Internet Protocols D. Paper distribution

233. Podcasting represents convergence of:
A. Audio and print
B. Audio and Internet
C. Print and video
D. Television and film

234. Which of the following is not a new media platform?
A. Newspaper B. Podcast
C. Twitter D. Blog

235. When a social media influencer promotes a product on multiple platforms (Instagram, YouTube, Twitter), this demonstrates:
A. Media fragmentation
B. Consistent messaging across different media
C. Limited audience overlap
D. The separation of online and offline experiences

236. The ability to seamlessly move between different media platforms to access related content enhances:
A. Media consumption barriers
B. User convenience and engagement
C. Information scarcity
D. Limited content accessibility

237. The proliferation of news websites, social media, and blogs has led to:
A. A decrease in the amount of available information
B. Multiple sources reporting on the same events
C. Greater control over information by a few entities
D. A decline in information verification

238. Cross-referencing information from multiple sources is crucial for:
A. Limiting one's perspective
B. Verifying the accuracy and reliability of information
C. Relying solely on the first source encountered
D. Avoiding diverse viewpoints

239. The abundance of information sources makes it important for individuals to develop:
A. A reliance on single sources
B. Critical media literacy skills
C. An avoidance of online information
D. A preference for traditional media only

240. RSS feeds distribute content by:
A. Email only
B. Newspaper circulation
C. Syndicating across platforms
D. Ignoring web traffic

241. Fact-checking organizations play a vital role in:
A. Limiting the number of information sources
B. Verifying the accuracy of information shared across multiple platforms
C. Promoting biased information
D. Discouraging the sharing of news

242. The shift from analog to digital content has led to:
A. Media silos
B. Greater audience reach
C. Fewer platforms
D. Slower content delivery

243. The ease of publishing information online has led to:
A. A decrease in the need for source evaluation
B. The challenge of distinguishing credible from non-credible sources
C. Greater uniformity in information
D. A reduction in the volume of available data

244. Traditional media becoming available online is known as:
A. Digital shift
B. Print convergence
C. Static programming
D. Retro media

245. Access to many sources of the same information can empower individuals to:
A. Form opinions based on limited perspectives
B. Conduct their own research and compare different accounts
C. Rely solely on mainstream media narratives
D. Avoid engaging with diverse viewpoints

246. YouTubers creating their own channels demonstrate:
A. Mass censorship
B. Decentralized content creation
C. Media monopoly
D. Broadcast control

247. Online forums where anyone can share opinions show:
A. Controlled communication
B. Open participation
C. Restricted media
D. One-way flow

248. YouTube + Live Chat feature demonstrates:
A. Passive watching
B. Interactive broadcasting
C. Monologue format
D. Audio only

249. Citizen journalism, facilitated by individual posting online, can contribute to:
A. A decrease in the number of news sources
B. A wider range of perspectives on events
C. Greater control by established media outlets
D. Less engagement with local news

250. The challenge of verifying information from many online sources underscores the need for:
A. Less access to diverse viewpoints
B. Stronger media literacy education
C. Greater reliance on single, authoritative sources
D. Discouraging individual content creation

251. Cross-media storytelling, where a narrative unfolds across different platforms, leverages:
A. The separation of media audiences
B. The ability of one medium to trigger engagement in others
C. Limited audience attention spans
D. The decline of immersive experiences

252. The challenge for individuals in a media environment with many sources and cross-platform information flow is:
A. Lack of access to information
[illegible]ly filtering, evaluating, and synthesizing information
C. Limited opportunities for participation
D. The dominance of a few media outlets

253. Media convergence benefits users by:
A. Limiting choices
B. Increasing accessibility
C. Reducing content variety
D. Fixing time slots

254. Cross-media synergy occurs when:
A. One message works independently
B. Different platforms enhance each other's reach
C. Content remains siloed
D. Platforms compete exclusively

255. The Internet has created:
A. A decline in media
B. Isolated content systems
C. A unified space for all media formats
D. Print-only access

256. Dog pile is an example of
A. Directory B. Program
C. Meta search engine D. All the above

257. Web analytics services may also use .... to track individual sessions.
A. Cookies B. Browser
C. History D. Database

258. HTTP stands for
A. Hypertext testing protocol
B. Hypertext transfer protocol
C. Hyper test transfer permit
D. Hypertext Transmission Protocol

259. A type of website which doesn't have interactivity with the users is ....
A. Dynamic B. Social
C. Business D. Static

260. Which one of the below is not a blogging platform?
A. Blogger B. LiveJournal
C. WordPress D. Go daddy

261. Copyright is a form of .... property.
A. Business B. Intellectual
C. Private D. Personal

262. Copyright is the exclusive legal right to use, copy, publish, sell or distribute someone else's creative work such as a photograph, music or artwork.
A. True
B. False

263. Which of the following describes e-commerce?
A. Doing business electronically
B. Doing business
C. Sale of goods
D. All the above

264. Under which section of IT Act, stealing any digital asset or information is written a cyber-crime.
A. 65 B. 66
C. 67 D. 70

265. A tweet going viral across countries demonstrates:
A. Regional isolation
B. Global distribution of information
C. Controlled messaging
D. Time zone limitations

266. The global distribution of information is characterized by:
A. Limited reach B. Unprecedented scale
C. Centralized control D. Slow dissemination

267. Global trends and hashtags originate and spread due to:
A. Manual news delivery
B. Central control
C. Real-time online interaction
D. Slow broadcasting

268. Hashtags help opinions to:
A. Remain hidden B. Go global rapidly
C. Stay in print D. Disappear offline

269. New media allows people to react to news:
A. After days
B. Instantly
C. Only after official reporting
D. Through newspapers

270. New media contributes to democracy by:
A. Restricting views
B. Enabling only elite voices
C. Providing platforms for all citizens
D. Filtering public opinion

271. Digital activism means:
A. Street protests only
B. Silent movements
C. Using online tools for social change
D. TV debates

272. Political campaigns today use:
A. Print-only flyers
B. Podcasts and social media
C. Loudspeakers only
D. Morse code

273. Which movement used new media for global political awareness?
A. Civil Rights (1960s)
B. Greta Thunberg's climate protests
C. World War I
D. Indian Mutiny

274. Fake news is a risk due to:
A. Professional journalism
B. Lack of digital access
C. Speed and ease of publishing without verification
D. Editorial boards

275. What challenge does new media pose to governments?
A. Faster taxes
B. Controlled news cycles
C. Spread of unregulated content
D. Reduced screen time

276. Has new media increased civic engagement?
A. No
B. Only for celebrities
C. Yes, via open discussions and petitions
D. Only for journalists

277. Which of the following reflects the socio-political power of new media?
A. Watching old shows
B. Passive viewership
C. Organizing protests through Facebook events
D. Waiting for daily newspapers

278. Online petitions and campaigns are examples of:
A. Traditional politics
B. Grassroots digital activism
C. Censorship
D. Corporate lobbying

279. What is one key way new media strengthens democracy?
A. Promotes censorship
B. Increases government control
C. Enables citizen participation
D. Eliminates elections

280. Which of the following allows the public to directly interact with policymakers?
A. News bulletins
B. Radio shows
C. Social media platforms
D. Classified ads

281. Online petitions are an example of:
A. Political propaganda
B. Civic engagement
C. Traditional media
D. Commercial advertising

282. What role does new media play in elections?
A. Limits debate
B. Prevents polling
C. Disseminates information and encourages debate
D. Stops campaigning

283. Which feature of new media fosters transparency?
A. Paywalls
B. Live-streaming and public commentary
C. Censorship
D. Subscription-only content

284. Hashtags like #BlackLivesMatter show how new media can:
A. Hide issues
B. Delay action
C. Mobilize social movements
D. Prevent democracy

285. What is citizen journalism?
A. Journalism by only professionals
B. News shared by common people using digital tools
C. State-run media
D. Academic publications

286. Digital platforms allow voters to:
A. Ignore politics
B. Participate in democratic discourse
C. Avoid debates
D. Vote anonymously online

287. What does "media literacy" help citizens do?
A. Accept all information
B. Spread fake news
C. Critically evaluate digital content
D. Stop reading news

288. New media can make government policies more accessible through:
A. Verbal instruction
B. Printed pamphlets
C. Official websites and social posts
D. Private meetings

289. What is a "meme" in the context of new media?
A. A government document
B. An encrypted message
C. A humorous image or video shared rapidly online
D. A type of press release

290. OTT platforms like Netflix and Hotstar are examples of:
A. Print publishers
B. Traditional broadcasters
C. On-demand streaming services
D. Telemarketing platforms

291. Influencers represent a shift toward:
A. State media
B. Decentralized communication
C. Editorial control
D. Censorship

292. AI-generated content is becoming more common in:
A. Print-only media B. Digital newsrooms
C. Postal letters D. Stage performances

293. Which technology has transformed real-time news broadcasting?
A. Landlines
B. Satellite TV
C. Live social media streaming
D. Fax machines

294. What is "personalized content"?
A. News chosen by the editor
B. Generic content for all
C. Algorithms recommending news based on user behaviour
D. Manual selection of headlines

295. Which trend has changed how people consume news?
A. Morning newspaper delivery
B. Scheduled radio shows
C. 24/7 mobile access and notifications
D. Weekly bulletins

296. What trend involves using multiple media platforms to deliver a single story?
A. Monomedia storytelling
B. Static journalism
C. Transmedia storytelling
D. Print publishing

297. Which of the following is/are types of interaction in e-Governance?
(i) G2G
(ii) G2C
(iii) G2B
A. (i) and (ii) B. (ii) and (iii)
C. (i), (ii), and (iii) D. Only (iii)

298. Which of the following is an advantage of using direct mail as a media vehicle?
A. Combines sight, sound and movement
B. Larger than life
C. Social Dominance
D. Highly Personal

299. Strategic media planning is a complex challenge because advertises must use their knowledge of
A. Demographics
B. Psychographics
C. Behavioral Characteristics
D. All the above

300. .... is a scheduling strategy in which planned messages run in intermittent periods.
A. Media run B. Continuous scheduling
C. Pulsing D. Flighting

301. .... have different expectations and different relationships with companies from which they purchase products and services.
A. Heterogenous Consumers
B. Homogenous Consumers
C. Cyber Consumers
D. Diverse Consumers

302. .... are filled with videos, podcasts, Really Simple Syndication (RSS) feeds for targeted news and information, downloadable images, and presentations.
A. Online newsrooms
B. Websites
C. Mobile advertising
D. Interactive newsrooms

303. The pricing of .... advertising could vary across devices and access formats.
A. print B. broadcast
C. digital D. out of home

304. Digital branding, in general need to have the consumer- specific orientation addressed to consumers in a .... context.
A. geographic B. natural
C. confined D. cultural

305. .... advertising affords the marketer the ability to engage the consumer in a direct and personal way.
A. Interactive B. Contextual
C. Traditional D. Website

306. New media is very cost-effective when compared to the traditional media and is highly ....
A. reliable B. reputed
C. resourceful D. result-oriented

307. Companies are exploring the .... for communicating their advertising message because of its several attractive features and advantages.
A. television B. newspaper
C. radio D. new media

308. Reach is defined as?
A. Insufficient exposure to the target audience
B. The Number of times a reader is exposed to a message
C. The total number of duplicated exposures
D. The total number of unduplicated exposures

309. Which of the following is the flagship program of the Government of India to transform India into a digitally empowered society and knowledge economy?
A. Digital India B. Make in India
C. Skill India D. Startup India

310. Which platform facilitates online trading of agricultural commodities across India?
A. UMANG B. DigiLocker
C. e-NAM D. MyGov

311. Which of the following initiatives focuses on providing broadband connectivity to rural areas in India?
A. BharatNet
B. Startup India
C. Atal Innovation Mission
D. Swachh Bharat Abhiyan

312. Which ICT initiative aims to modernize land records and make them accessible online?
A. e-NAM
B. Digital India Land Records Modernization Program (DILRMP)
C. UMANG
D. DigiLocker

313. What is the objective of the National Digital Health Mission (NDHM)?
A. To promote digital payments for healthcare services
B. To create an integrated digital health infrastructure for the country
C. To provide online yoga and wellness programs
D. To regulate the pricing of pharmaceutical products

314. What is the purpose of the Aadhaar Enabled Payment System (AePS)?
A. To provide digital literacy to citizens
B. To facilitate financial inclusion through Aadhaar-based authentication
C. To track the attendance of government employees
D. To manage land records online

315. Which initiative provides citizens with a platform to access various government services through a single mobile app?
A. ePathshala B. UMANG
C. SWAYAM D. e-District

316. What is the focus of the SWAYAM platform?
A. Providing financial assistance to startups
B. Offering online educational courses
C. Promoting cleanliness and sanitation
D. Facilitating online registration for government jobs

317. Which of the following initiatives is related to the digitization of court records?
A. e-NAM B. eCourts
C. DigiLocker D. MyGov

318. What is the primary aim of the e-District project?
A. To provide online voting facilities
B. To deliver citizen-centric services at the district level electronically
C. To monitor the implementation of central government schemes
D. To promote tourism in different districts

319. Which e-governance initiative is used for online passport applications?
A. mPassport B. Passport Seva
C. ePass D. DigiVisa

320. Which portal is launched for job seekers and employers?
A. JobSeva
B. Kaushal Portal
C. National Career Service (NCS)
D. Rozgar India

321. e-NAM platform is used for:
A. National Agriculture Market
B. E-learning portal
C. Employment tracking
D. Law enforcement

322. Which service is used for online filing of income tax in India?
A. eFile India B. IT Portal
C. TRACES D. e-Filing Portal

323. What is the aim of the eKranti initiative?
A. Online payment system
B. Electronic delivery of services
C. Internet connectivity in metros
D. Media regulation

324. Digital India initiative was launched in which year?
A. 2005 B. 2010
C. 2015 D. 2018

325. With reference to the Information Technology (Intermediary Guidelines and Digital Media Ethics Code) Rules 2021, consider the following statements:
1. A significant social media intermediary is a social media platform with more than 50 Lakh registered users in India
2. The rules make compulsory for social media intermediaries to appoint Grievance Redressal Officer (GRO) who should be a resident in India

Which of the above is / are correct statements?
A. Only 1 is correct
B. Only 2 is correct
C. Both 1 & 2 are correct
D. Neither 1 nor 2 is correct

326. Which Union Ministry has announced to set up 'Grievance Appellate Committees' to resolve social media users' grievances?
A. Ministry of Electronics and Information Technology
B. Ministry of Science and Technology
C. Ministry of Communication
D. Ministry of Home Affairs

327. Which social media network collaborated with India Post Payments Bank in September 2022 to promote financial inclusion in remote cities?
A. Koo B. YouTube
C. WhatsApp D. Twitter

328. With respect to the draft amendments to the Information Technology Rules, 2021, consider the following statements:
1. Social media firms have to appoint a chief compliance officer.
2. If there are complaints against the dignity of users, social media platforms will be required to remove that within 24 hours after a complaint is made.
3. They also will have to publish a weekly report about the number of complaints received and the status of redressal.

Which of the statements given above is/are correct?
A. Only 1 B. Only 2 & 3
C. Only 1 & 2 D. 1, 2 & 3

329. eBay is an example of a/an ……….. e-commerce site.
A. B2C B. EDI
C. C2C D. B2B

330. Amazon.com comes under the model
A. B2B B. B2C
C. C2C D. C2B

331. The primary e-book revenue model is
A. advertising B. subscription
C. pay-per-download D. marketing

332. Digital signature provides
A. security B. privacy
C. authentication D. all of these

333. Government-to-Government (G2G) transaction is also known as
A. e-Governance B. e-Commerce
C. e-Administration D. e-Payment

334. Which is a function of E-commerce?
A. Marketing B. Advertising
C. Warehousing D. All the above

335. A combination of software and information designed to provide security and information for payment is called a what?
A. digital wallet B. pop up ad
C. shopping cart D. encryption

336. Digital marketing revolves around these 5Ds:
A. digital devices, digital platforms, digital media, digital data, and digital technology.

B. digital interaction, digital platforms, digital media, digital data, and digital technology.
C. digital devices, digital platforms, digital media, digital data, and digital storage.
D. All the above

337. A content provider:
A. Provides product, pricing, and availability information to individuals and businesses.
B. Provides a digital environment where buyers and sellers can meet, search for products, display products, and establish prices for those products.
C. Creates revenue by providing digital content, such as digital news, music, photos, or video, over the Web.
D. None of these

338. A method of publishing audio broadcasts via the Internet, which can later be downloaded to portable music players, is called:
A. Podcasting B. Streaming
C. Uploading D. Blogging

339. What are plastic cards the size of a credit card that contains an embedded chip on which digital information can be stored?
A. Customer relationship management systems cards
B. E-government identity cards
C. FEDI cards
D. Smart cards

340. If you need to transfer money to another person via the internet, which of the following methods could you use?
A. financial cybermediary
B. electronic check
C. electronic bill presentment and payment
D. All the above

341. Digital marketing is often referred to as ....
A. online marketing B. internet marketing
C. web marketing D. All the above

342. Which of the following is a type of digital marketing activity?
A. Email marketing B. Social web marketing
C. Viral marketing D. All the above

343. What is the term for the process of combining multiple video clips into a single video in digital video editing?
A. Trimming B. Splicing
C. Rendering D. Compositing

344. What is copyright protection primarily designed to protect?
A. Ideas and concepts
B. Inventions and patents
C. Original creative works
D. Trade secrets

345. Which of the following would be leveraging both social network and traditional marketing?
A. Handing out print with a coupon for a store
B. A print advertisement in a magazine which drives people to a website where there is a free trial offer
C. Posting an advertisement on a message board
D. Hosting a video ad on YouTube not otherwise seen elsewhere

346. PSB stands for ....
A. Private Service Broadcasting
B. Public Service Broadcasting
C. Public Sector Broadcasting
D. Public Service Broadcasters

347. Prasar Bharati through AIR and Doordarshan are one of the largest terrestrial networks in the world.
A. True B. False

348. Match the following:

(a) Kuldip Nayyar Committee	1. 1991
(b) Sakaria Commission	2. 1977
(c) Varadan Committee	3. 1995
(d) Sengupta Committee	4. 1983

A. (a)-2, (b)-3, (c)-1, (d)-4
B. (a)-3, (b)-1, (c)-4, (d)-2
C. (a)-2, (b)-4, (c)-1, (d)-3
D. (a)-1, (b)-4, (c)-2, (d)-3

349. Kuldip Nayyar Committee was formed in .... after the emergence of .... news agency.
A. 1978, Samachar B. 1977, UNI
C. 1985, PTI D. 1977, Samachar

350. Match the following:

(a) Vardana Committee	1. The priority of broadcasting should be changed from urban to rural areas.
(b) Chandra Committee	2. Does not recommend leasing out time from an existing radio or television channel.
(c) Verghese Committee	3. Recommended to establish an inter-governmental council under Article 263.
(d) Sarkaria Commission	4. Improvement of quality of the government information

A. (a)-3, (b)-2, (c)-1, (d)-4
B. (a)-4, (b)-2, (c)-3, (d)-1
C. (a)-2, (b)-4, (c)-1, (d)-3
D. (a)-2, (b)-1, (c)-4, (d)-3

ANSWERS

1	2	3	4	5	6	7	8	9	10
B	C	B	C	C	C	A	B	B	C
11	**12**	**13**	**14**	**15**	**16**	**17**	**18**	**19**	**20**
B	B	C	B	B	A	C	A	C	B
21	**22**	**23**	**24**	**25**	**26**	**27**	**28**	**29**	**30**
D	C	B	C	C	C	D	C	C	C
31	**32**	**33**	**34**	**35**	**36**	**37**	**38**	**39**	**40**
B	B	D	D	B	A	B	D	B	A
41	**42**	**43**	**44**	**45**	**46**	**47**	**48**	**49**	**50**
C	A	A	D	D	D	A	B	B	D
51	**52**	**53**	**54**	**55**	**56**	**57**	**58**	**59**	**60**
C	A	C	A	D	A	B	C	D	B
61	**62**	**63**	**64**	**65**	**66**	**67**	**68**	**69**	**70**
A	A	B	B	D	D	A	B	A	D
71	**72**	**73**	**74**	**75**	**76**	**77**	**78**	**79**	**80**
C	C	C	C	C	C	C	A	C	A
81	**82**	**83**	**84**	**85**	**86**	**87**	**88**	**89**	**90**
A	C	D	A	A	C	D	B	B	D
91	**92**	**93**	**94**	**95**	**96**	**97**	**98**	**99**	**100**
B	A	D	A	A	D	B	A	C	A
101	**102**	**103**	**104**	**105**	**106**	**107**	**108**	**109**	**110**
B	B	A	B	B	C	C	D	B	A
111	**112**	**113**	**114**	**115**	**116**	**117**	**118**	**119**	**120**
D	A	B	B	C	A	D	B	D	D
121	**122**	**123**	**124**	**125**	**126**	**127**	**128**	**129**	**130**
B	A	B	B	B	A	D	B	A	B
131	**132**	**133**	**134**	**135**	**136**	**137**	**138**	**139**	**140**
D	A	B	B	D	A	C	B	C	B
141	**142**	**143**	**144**	**145**	**146**	**147**	**148**	**149**	**150**
C	C	B	D	C	A	D	B	C	B
151	**152**	**153**	**154**	**155**	**156**	**157**	**158**	**159**	**160**
D	C	B	A	D	B	C	C	C	C
161	**162**	**163**	**164**	**165**	**166**	**167**	**168**	**169**	**170**
D	B	A	A	A	C	A	A	A	B
171	**172**	**173**	**174**	**175**	**176**	**177**	**178**	**189**	**190**
D	A	D	B	A	D	C	A	B	B
181	**182**	**183**	**184**	**185**	**186**	**187**	**188**	**189**	**190**
D	A	B	C	D	B	B	B	A	D
191	**192**	**193**	**194**	**195**	**196**	**197**	**198**	**199**	**200**
B	B	A	C	A	C	B	A	B	C
201	**202**	**203**	**204**	**205**	**206**	**207**	**208**	**209**	**210**
A	B	C	A	D	C	A	D	B	D
211	**212**	**213**	**214**	**215**	**216**	**217**	**218**	**219**	**220**
C	B	B	A	A	A	A	D	D	B
221	**222**	**223**	**224**	**225**	**226**	**227**	**228**	**229**	**230**
C	B	A	B	B	D	D	C	C	B
231	**232**	**233**	**234**	**235**	**236**	**237**	**238**	**239**	**240**
C	C	B	A	B	B	B	B	B	C
241	**242**	**243**	**244**	**245**	**246**	**247**	**248**	**249**	**250**
B	B	B	A	B	B	B	B	B	B
251	**252**	**253**	**254**	**255**	**256**	**257**	**258**	**259**	**260**
B	B	B	B	C	C	A	B	D	D
261	**262**	**263**	**264**	**265**	**266**	**267**	**268**	**269**	**270**
B	A	A	A		B	C	B	B	C

271	272	273	274	275	276	277	278	279	280
C	B	B	C	C	C	C	B	C	C
281	282	283	284	285	286	287	288	289	290
B	C	B	C	B	B	C	C	C	C
291	292	293	294	295	296	297	298	299	300
B	B	C	C	C	C	C	D	D	D
301	302	303	304	305	306	307	308	309	310
C	D	C	D	A	D	D	D	A	C
311	312	313	314	315	316	317	318	319	320
A	B	B	B	B	B	B	B	B	C
321	322	323	324	325	326	327	328	329	330
A	D	B	C	C	A	A	C	C	B
331	332	333	334	335	336	337	338	339	340
C	D	A	D	A	A	C	A	D	D
341	342	343	344	345	346	347	348	349	350
D	D	D	C	B	B	A	C	D	C

EXPLANATORY ANSWERS

7. (A): Due to its reach and impact, broadcasting has emerged as a powerful means of communication. It has a great importance as it acts as a medium of education and information in developing countries like India. India has approximately 220 million television households, and approximately 954 million internet users as of 2024.

8. (B): The Paswan Committee was formed to work on the media policies of India in the year 1996. The Committee was headed by Ram Vilas Paswan. The committee stated that a regulatory body is necessary to look after the private and public broadcasting in India.

10. (C): Broadcasting bill was passed in 1998 as a Prasar Bharati bill. Before this Pawar committee in 1997 did the review of that bill.

12. (B): Television emerged in India on 15 September, 1959. The first experiment related to transmission was started at Delhi with a small transmitter. The television service was extended up to Amritsar and Bombay by 1972.

13. (C): It was a satellite communication project experiment which was launched in 1975. With the help of this project, the television programs were made available to the rural India. The experiment covered nearly 2400 villages in 20 districts of six Indian states and Union territories. SITE was an important advancement in the field of Television education.

14. (B): Dr. Vikram Sarabhai is considered as the father of the Indian space program. He established ISRO (Indian Space Research Organization). Sarabhai's interaction with the NASA in 1966 led to the formation of SITE. He started a project for the launch of an Indian satellite.

18. (A): Doordarshan was formed after the separation of television from AIR in 1976. It caters to the public service broadcasting and the main aim of Doordarshan includes informing, educating and entertaining people. It has a three-tier program – local, regional and national.

19. (C): The success and the live coverage of the 9th Asian Games by Doordarshan through satellite INSAT IA led to the birth of the concept of live coverage. The emergence of this concept took place in the year 1982.

31. (B): Digital Broadcasting first emerged in Europe (United Kingdom – 1995 and Germany – 1999).

34. (D): The Internet arrived in India in the year 1995 through the Videsh Sanchar Nigam Limited (VSNL).

35. (B): The Information Technology Act was enacted on 9 June, 2000 by the Parliament of India.

37. (B): Media convergence is defined as the merging of various mediums of mass communication such as the print, television, radio, internet etc. Media convergence gives an opportunity to the professionals to present the story and the information in various ways.

42. (A): Smart phones have various kinds of applications such as internet access, email etc. These phones allow people to stay connected to the internet, wherever they go. Today, video games have also become a main source of entertainment. The entire entertainment package is installed on one device such as mobile or computers etc. Video texts are also a best example of the media convergence.

51. (C): ICT refers to the technologies which provide a wide access to the information though telecommunications. It is almost similar to IT and includes internet, wireless networks etc. In the past few years, ICT has provided its customers with a wide range of communication facilities. ICT has led India into a significant growth in the field of technology.

54. (A): The concept of e-governance or electronic governance is dealt under the Section 4 to 10A of the IT Act of 2000. It provides a legal identity for the electronic records or signature.

56. (A): The National Informatics Centre (NIC) was set up by the Government of India to drive and facilitate the adoption of e-governance across the country. NIC offers robust ICT infrastructure solutions, develops digital platforms for service delivery, and enables efficient delivery of government services to citizens and businesses.

63. (B): Unified District Information System for Education Plus (UDISE Plus) is one of the largest Management Information Systems initiated by Department of School Education and Literacy, Ministry of Education, on school education and was launched in 2018-2019 to speed up data entry, reduce errors, improve data quality and ease its verification.

80. (A): Addressability of mass communication is the ability of the digital device that responds individually to messages sent to many similar devices. Every digital device whether a computer or mobile have their own address in the form of IMEI and IP address.

90. (D): Synchronous Media involves the communication process with all the communicants present at the same time. It is a type of communication that takes place between two or more individuals simultaneously. Like television and radio are examples of synchronous electronic communication.

95. (A): In broadcasting when we jump from one sound effect to another without breaking continuity it is known as transition and using that transition, we move from one sound to another known as segue.

97. (B): The Dutch angle is also known as canted angle which is a type of camera shot. To obtain vertical lines at an angle to the side of the frame, here the camera is set at an angle on its roll axis.

136. (A): Here are some of the other commonly used wireless communication technologies for IoT devices: Zigbee Wi-Fi, LoRa, NB-IoT, LTE-M. The choice of wireless communication technology for an IoT device depends on factors such as the range, data rate, power consumption, and cost requirements of the application.

141. (C): A valid email address is an address composed of two parts, a username, and a domain name. The prefix appears to the left of the @ symbol. The domain appears to the right of the @ symbol.

143. (B): The statement is false because a digital native is actually a person who is born after the advent of the Internet and has grown up using digital technology from a young age. They are considered to be more comfortable and familiar with technology and online communication compared to those who were born before the Internet era.

148. (B): In 1976, digital music was first demonstrated. This means that someone showcased or presented digital music for the first time during that year. It implies that prior to 1976, digital music was not yet publicly demonstrated or made widely known.

173. (D): SEM is a paid strategy to drive traffic through search engine ads, while SEO focuses on organic traffic using optimization techniques.

181. (D): Retargeting focuses on displaying ads to website visitors, encouraging them to complete purchases or engage further.

185. (D): CTR stands for Click-Through Rate, measuring how often users click on an ad link or content.

187. (B): A marketing funnel guides users through a multi-step process, from awareness and interest to consideration and conversion, ensuring seamless interactions.

191. (B): Google Search Console provides insights into website indexing, search rankings, and performance metrics, helping improve visibility and SEO rankings.

195. (A): ROI (Return on Investment) measures the profitability of digital marketing campaigns, helping businesses understand the value of their spending.

210. (D): A canonical tag informs search engines about the preferred version of a webpage when duplicate or similar content exists. This prevents duplicate content issues and consolidates ranking signals.

211. (C): Mobile optimization is crucial for On-Page SEO because search engines like Google prioritize mobile-friendly websites in their rankings. With the increasing use of mobile devices, search engines aim to provide users with the best experience, which includes responsive and mobile-optimized websites.

215. (A): Technical SEO involves optimizing a website's infrastructure, such as improving site speed, mobile-friendliness, secure connections, and crawlability, to ensure it ranks well on search engines.

256. (C): A meta-search engine is a search tool that sends user queries to several other search engines and aggregates the results into a single list. Dogpile fits this description as it retrieves results from various search engines.

349. (D): Four news agencies named PTI, UNI, Hindustan Samachar and Samachar Bharati were merged on 1 February, 1976 and thus, Samachar news agency was born. After the formation of Samachar news agency, the Kuldip Nayyar committee was set up in March, 1977. Kuldip Nayyar was a well-known columnist and a journalist.